ISRAEL:
SOCIAL STRUCTURE
AND
CHANGE

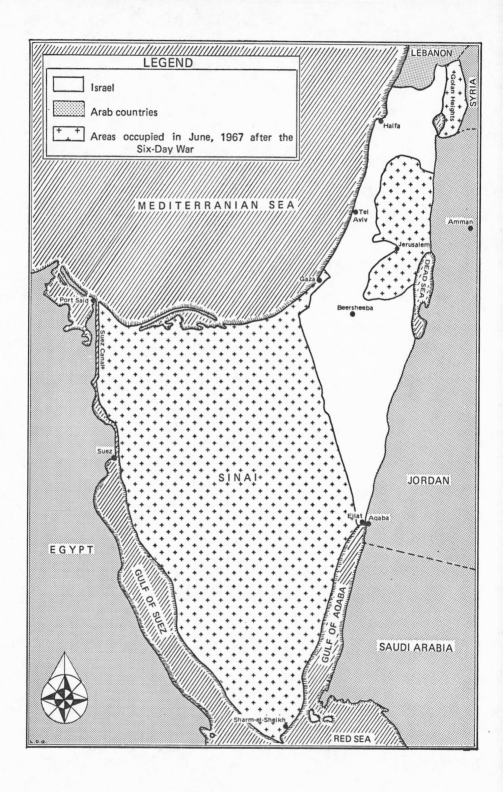

LEGEND

Israel

Arab countries

Areas occupied in June, 1967 after the Six-Day War

MEDITERRANIAN SEA

LEBANON

SYRIA

Golan Heights

Haifa

Tel Aviv

Amman

Jerusalem

Gaza

DEAD SEA

Beersheeba

Port Said

Suez Canal

Suez

SINAI

JORDAN

EGYPT

GULF OF SUEZ

Ejlat Aqaba

GULF OF AQABA

SAUDI ARABIA

Sharm-el-Sheikh

RED SEA

edited by
Michael Curtis
Mordecai S. Chertoff

ISRAEL:
SOCIAL STRUCTURE
AND
CHANGE

TRANSACTION BOOKS
New Brunswick, New Jersey
Distributed by E. P. Dutton and Co.

Transaction Books
Rutgers University
New Brunswick, New Jersey 08903

Library of Congress Catalog Card Number: 73-78696
ISBN: 0-87855-080-1 (cloth); 0-87855-575-1 (paper)

Printed in the United States of America

*This book is based in part on the proceedings of the 1971-72 con-
ferences of the American Academic Association for Peace in the
Middle East.*

CONTENTS

ECONOMIC AND LABOR DEVELOPMENT

ETHNIC RELATIONS AND PROBLEMS

SOCIAL AND EDUCATIONAL CHANGE

PREFACE

This book is made up largely of papers presented during a number of conferences held in Washington, Los Angeles, Chicago and Philadelphia during the 1971-1972 academic year and sponsored by the American Academic Association for Peace in the Middle East. In addition to the papers and remarks from these conferences are papers from other meetings held by the American Histadrut Cultural Exchange Institute at Pittsburgh and Arden House, Harriman, New York in 1972, and some essays commissioned especially for this volume.

These conferences and meetings were devoted to the question of social change and experimentation in Israel. They were concerned with the economic modernization, political development and social progress made by that state. The focus of attention was on social issues and tensions, not on security problems or relations with neighbors or with the outside world. The papers and the ensuing discussions were critical attempts to evaluate the progress and achievements made by the state, which is now celebrating its 25th year of existence. They examined some of the problems that have emerged in recent years and to which attention must now be paid: consciousness of ethnic differences, housing needs, class relationships, urban difficulties, occupational differentials and educational needs. In this they reflected the great priority given by Israel itself to urgent social issues.

We wish to thank Judith Diesendruck and the national and local staffs of the American Academic Association for Peace in the Middle East and Allen Pollack, national president of the American Histadrut Cultural Exchange Institute, for invaluable aid in arranging the different conferences and facilitating the publication of this book. We would also like to thank Anne Sinai for her assistance in preparing the index.

Michael Curtis
Mordecai S. Chertoff

ISRAEL:
SOCIAL STRUCTURE
AND
CHANGE

URBAN AND
INSTITUTIONAL
DEVELOPMENT

I

Judah Matras

ISRAEL'S NEW FRONTIER:

THE URBAN PERIPHERY

The Jewish population in Israel is now and has always been very highly concentrated in or around the three large cities—Tel Aviv, Haifa and Jerusalem. But Jewish settlement outward toward the frontiers and away from the urbanized center of the country has always been encouraged. This was the policy of the Zionist bodies and institutions before 1948, and it has remained the policy of the Zionist movements and bodies and of the government of Israel since 1948.

This is not as unique a situation as it might appear at first glance. Other countries have had and still have programs and policies intended to promote settlement and development of frontier areas. Examples that come to mind include Australia, Brazil, the United States and the Soviet Union. What is somewhat unusual about Israel is that there has been practically no significant settlement of peripheral areas independent of deliberate, policy-originated and policy-supported settlement: there has been no "gold rush" in Israel, no really impressive discovery of oil fields or mineral deposits, no important development of inherently attractive tourist or retirement areas. Very little has been done to stimulate and attract movement to and settlement in peripheral areas akin to the booms and bonanzas that have occurred in the settlement histories of other countries.

There are essentially two problems in promoting settlement of peripheral areas, in Israel and elsewhere: getting people to go to

3

them, to move and settle in such areas; and getting people who have moved there to stay there. The latter of these, in turn, involves development of an economic base to provide employment and income for the settlers; and community and social development to provide an acceptable level of social services and of individual social options and amenities.

In the pre-state or pre-independence period in Israel geographical expansion of Jewish settlement and settlement of the frontier areas were primarily rural and agricultural; in the period since independence expansion has been primarily nonagricultural and largely urban. The contrasts between these two different national "strategies" of settling the periphery and the problems associated with the shift from a rural to an urban policy and program for settlement of the frontier areas are the subjects of this chapter. Individual instances of success or failure in the establishment of viable communities in the frontier areas will largely be ignored.

Prior to independence, toward the end of the period often referred to as the "pioneering era," roughly 85 percent of the Jewish population of Palestine was concentrated in or around the three large cities—Jerusalem, Tel Aviv and Haifa. Adding the population of the Rehovot and Ramat Gan/Petah Tikva areas we have accounted for the place of residence of almost 93 percent of the entire Jewish population at the end of 1945. The total Jewish population then was estimated at 592,000, of which some 85 percent were urban. About 41,000 lived in the northern periphery or outlying areas and about 3,500 in the southern periphery. About one fourth of the northern outlying-area population lived in urban places— mostly Safed, Tiberias, Afula and Nahariya—and the rest in rural settlements. Virtually all of the Jewish population in the southern outlying areas before independence lived in rural settlements.

Table 1. ESTIMATED JEWISH POPULATION
OF URBAN AND RURAL PERIPHERIES*

	Northern District	Southern District	Total
Urban	157,400	221,100	378,500
Rural	83,500	58,700	142,200
Total	240,900	279,800	520,700

*As of December 31, 1968.

By the end of 1968 the total Jewish population reached just over 2.4 million—including some 241,000 in the northern outlying areas and about 280,000 in the southern outlying areas. Together, these now comprise about 12 percent of the total.

Of the total population in the outlying areas, about two thirds of those living in the northern district and four fifths of those living in the southern district live in cities and towns, most of which either did not exist at all prior to 1948 or else had no Jewish population at that time. If we exclude the cities of Beersheba (72,000), Ashkelon (38,000) and Ashdod (32,000), which are really quite sizeable towns now, and Tiberias (24,000)—not so large, but special because it is not really a "new" town—and Nahariya (21,000) and Acre (33,000), which are really part of the Haifa Bay metropolitan area, then the rest of the urban population of the northern and southern districts—roughly 158,000 persons—inhabits the urban periphery, or urban frontier, of Israel.

NEW URBAN SETTLEMENT POLICIES

It is important to note that there has been very little spontaneous, undirected founding of new Jewish settlements, either recently in Israel or previously in Palestine. There has been no Homestead Act, no explorers or missionaries setting up trading posts, or crossroads service and storage points that eventually become metropolises. In the pre-independence period the great majority of immigrants settled more or less spontaneously in the urban center of the coastal plain. Typically, a new peripheral settlement was set up by decision of the Zionist institutions: the Jewish National Fund would provide land; Keren Hayesod would finance; and the Jewish Agency immigration and settlement departments, one or another of the political parties or pioneering-settlement-youth movements and the Jewish Agency political and defense arms all may have been involved in a decision to establish a new settlement at a given location.

The process by which groups and institutions consider and decide to set up a frontier or peripheral Jewish settlement continues in Israel as it did under the British Mandate, sometimes with the very same persons involved, even if under nominally different organizational rubrics. But there has been one important change: the reasons for setting up rural agricultural settlements in the pre-state era were both ideological and pragmatic, while the reasons for initiating new urban settlement in Israel have been largely pragmatic.

In the Labor Zionist movement, and perhaps among Zionists generally, physical labor, especially agricultural labor, was idealized, as were collective and cooperative life and institutions. These were neatly combined, especially in the agricultural settlement innovations in Palestine, in the *kibbutz* and the *moshav ovdim*. But, as Dov Weintraub has shown, the founding of agricultural settlements of different forms was never undertaken independent of practical economic and political conditions: the employment and unemployment situation in the cities, the availability of private or public or institutional capital, and the political and military defense situation were always factors in the establishment and timing of new settlement enterprises. All told, there are now about 260 rural settlements which date from the pre-independence period, including about 135 *kibbutzim*, 85 *moshavim* and 30 private villages. The ideological and pragmatic reasons for setting up more agricultural settlements carried over into the post-independence period, and about 450 additional rural settlements have been founded after 1948—including about 285 new moshavim, 100 new kibbutzim and 65 private villages, "rural centers" and rural educational institutions.

But the founding of new urban settlements has no precedent in the pre-state period and, in the post-independence period, took place strictly on pragmatic grounds—indeed, in the face of a certain amount of ideologically grounded opposition. Despite their commitment to promoting, favoring and steering resources toward agricultural settlement, the Zionist and new government elites were forced into supporting, subsidizing and providing employment and social services for new urban communities for two overwhelming reasons: first, the flood of new immigrants in the aftermath of the 1948 War of Liberation was initially housed in abandoned Arab housing—in Jaffa, in Ramleh, in Lod, in Acre, in Safad and elsewhere; and second, when all available housing was exhausted new immigrants were placed in temporary tent cities—and these, in turn, were located near existing cities and towns, so that it would be possible to provide employment and basic health and educational services.

Some of the new immigrants were subsequently settled in new agricultural settlements—almost always in moshavim, rarely in kibbutzim. But it soon became clear both that only limited numbers of the immigrants were willing to settle in agricultural communities (and a considerable proportion of those who did eventually abandoned them) and that, in any case, the absorption of immigrants and the creation of employment in agriculture were becoming progressively more costly and less practical as land was fully utilized and water resources were drawn close to the limits.

In these circumstances the establishment of urban settlements on the peripheries appeared to be an alternative to the continued rapid growth, increased density and increasing pressure to supply labor markets in the urban center of the country. A variety of schemes for establishing and developing distant urban centers were initiated under the auspices of the Jewish Agency and various government ministries, and the urban frontier was born in the 1950s as Beersheba and Ashkelon grew spectacularly in the south, and as Kiryat Shmona in the north and Beit Sha'an in the Beisan Valley were established and grew. The urban frontier flourished later in the 1960s with the development of Dimona, Mizpeh Ramon, Elath, Kiryat Gat and Yeruham in the south, and Migdal Haemek and Hazor in the north. The 1960s saw the growth of towns like Kiryat Malahi, Sederot, Ofakim, Netivot and Arad, as well as the booming new port of Ashdod in the south, and Shlomi, Maalot and Carmiel in the north. During these two decades, new life and new population was also channeled to the old northern towns of Tiberias and Safad and to the development of an entirely new Jewish section of the large, previously all-Arab town of Nazareth.

RECRUITMENT OF SETTLERS

How are people persuaded to go to the urban periphery? Basically, potential settlers of the urban frontier are offered subsidized housing and/or employment. For the most part, new immigrants have been attracted to and have availed themselves of such opportunities. New immigrants with no personal or social resources of their own have been most eager to obtain the housing and services offered in the development towns and new settlements on the urban periphery. Obviously the new immigrant with money in hand, with a profession or with relatives or other contacts offering him favored access to opportunities in the established urban center was much less likely to rely on the benefits of subsidized settlement on the frontier. Similarly, the veteran resident of Israel has often been excluded from eligibility for such subsidies and typically has less need for them, presumably because he is already established in home and employment.

It has been argued that recruitment of "pioneers" to the pre-state agricultural settlement enterprises was based essentially on the same formula: subsidized or guaranteed housing, employment and services; and that individuals with sufficient personal and social resources either were never recruited or did not long remain in the rural settlements. However, there can be no doubt that strong, elaborate, and articulate ideologies plus firm institutions and frameworks associated with pre-state agricultural settlement reinforced social, economic and political adaptations throughout the development of this type of settlement.

In concrete terms, settlement on the new urban periphery has been dominated numerically by relatively recent immigrants from Mediterranean or Islamic countries—i.e., by Oriental immigrants. Such settlers have been characterized by relatively low levels of educational achievement and occupational skills, lack of experience in extrakinship community or political affairs, and subordination of women. They have, generally, large families and high rates of dependency, high frequencies of family predicaments and low levels of resources for coping with such predicaments.

ECONOMIC ACTIVITY AND EMPLOYMENT

How do people make a living on the urban periphery? What is the economic base? What supports the population? Two basic economic strategies have been employed in these developing areas: services to the surrounding agricultural communities, and industry. The first strategy, the idea of urban centers "serving rural hinterland communities" with transport, storage, processing, wholesale and retail and professional services was relatively more palatable to the heirs of the "back-to-the-soil" tradition in Israel and more consistent with the image of a revived Jewish agricultural society. However, with the notable exception of Beersheba, the new towns have not been able to compete effectively with the suppliers of similar services in the larger cities—Tel Aviv and Haifa—which, after all, are not that far away. The idea of a size-hierarchy of settlements—with a dominant regional capital and small satellite cities—which influenced the planning of this type of economic base was applicable, perhaps, to larger countries and to regions much larger than those of Israel, and to horse-and-buggy or rail types of transportation. However once a heavy truck is loaded, no matter what its starting point, it can get to Tel Aviv just about as quickly and conveniently as it can get to Kiryat Malahi or Kiryat Gat, or to Haifa just about as quickly and conveniently as to Maalot or Migdal Haemek. Thus local enterprises intended to serve rural communities had, in general, no particular advantage over their more distant but larger-city counterparts. As a matter of fact, local service enterprises labored under several disadvantages, which included size and composition of the labor market, personnel recruitment at various levels of skill and responsibility, costs of transport and, sometimes, communication to peripheral areas.

The idea of industrial development in the urban periphery has two guiding principles: exploitation of locally available natural resources—like the potash and chemical works, ceramics industry, or oil storage and copper mining—and establishment of light industry which can be operated with less-than-top-skill workers and does not require very elaborate supporting industries and services—like the textile and food-processing industries. These enterprises have had only limited success, with periodic failures or crises caused by inexperience or by difficulties in management, marketing and finance no less than in recruitment and training of appropriate personnel at various levels of skill and responsibility. As a result, industrial employment on the urban periphery has tended to be unstable; and many of these communities have been subject to almost chronic underemployment or unemployment.

An important feature of industrial development on the urban periphery has been the steady need for government protection, subsidies, financial concessions or financial incentives for their establishment and continued operation. This characteristic of the urban periphery is probably typical of the nonurban frontier as well. Both before and since independence subsidy of agriculture and of settlement or village industrial enterprises by the state or by the Zionist institutions has been and remains very common. However, as Eric Cohen has pointed out, government subsidization of rural settlement and agricultural (and kibbutz and other industrial) enterprises has been very highly organized and centralized, has been administered through a number of clearly defined organizations and institutions, and has carried a clear set of priorities. By contrast, there are many different ways to subsidize industrial and other enterprises on the urban periphery—from large low-interest loans to government or Jewish Agency partnership to outright grants, tax concessions, protection against import competition, guaranteed markets, free services and other kinds of subsidy to individuals, cooperatives, private entrepreneurs, local civil authorities and others. Not only have the measures to promote and subsidize industry on the urban frontier been quite disorganized—indeed, chaotic, in Cohen's opinion—they have not been guided by any coherent policy, ideology or set of priorities. One outcome of this disorganization has been that various industrial enterprises have been located in a single or in several neighboring frontier towns and eventually end up in sharp competition with one another for the subsidies and funds allocated by the government. Perhaps even more serious is the on-going competition between local officials of the various settlements and towns for funds and resources.

SOCIAL, CULTURAL, HEALTH AND WELFARE SERVICES

The people who have been recruited as permanent settlers on the urban frontier often come to their new home lacking specialized knowledge and skill. Accordingly, many of the technical and ad-ministrative tasks of the peripheral urban settlement have been per-formed initially by outsiders who have been hired to do such jobs and who live only temporarily in—or commute daily to and from—the settlements. The types of services provided—educational, medi-cal, labor exchange, utilities, sanitation, recreation and welfare—are set according to standards prevalent in the country, and one of the government ministries or some department of the Jewish Agency typically has taken initial responsibility for providing such services and the personnel to operate them.

Of course this process generates a cadre of outside bureaucrats, technicians and professionals—typically veteran residents of Israel—serving a clientele of local settlers. The nature of these services and relationships—the constituency, orientation, values, commitments and behavior of the outsiders in relation to those of the locals has been studied and discussed fairly extensively in Israel. The general conclusion is that success in providing services and personnel is greatly affected by the social, cultural, material and ideological gaps between the permanent settlers and the service-delivering cadre.

The services and resources are provided, basically, from the out-side, with the cadre serving as go-between. The very dependence of the new communities on the relatively powerful, privileged bu-reaucracy-technocracy for access to these resources and services typically generates a certain instability in community organization. This is particularly the case insofar as settlers feel that they are being provided with fewer or lower-level services than more privi-leged classes.

In the pre-state and in the post-independence periods services and material assistance to the rural frontier were initially provided from outside and were available to settlers in accordance with some image of standards appropriate to such settlements rather than as a func-tion of the ability of the settler communities to provide or buy their own services. In the pre-independence period—for both kib-butzim and moshavim and in the post-independence period for the kibbutzim—such services were channeled through the institutions of the settlement movements, in which settlers themselves were in-dividually and collectively intimately involved in contrast to most urban periphery settlers. And if the services were administered or performed by outsiders, the outsiders were persons of similar back-ground, social and cultural characteristics. The settlers themselves claimed for themselves—and were accorded by the outside commu-nity—the great prestige due to pioneers and the Zionist vanguard. The total scale of operations and the volume of aid and services were small. And though there may well have been competition for the limited resources or for access to services, the competition itself was much more highly organized; and it took place within recog-nized movement institutions and in acceptable forms. Finally, com-petition generally occurred between different settlements and was not visible within settlements. Thus it was neither very threatening nor disruptive of community life.

RETURN MIGRATION

A trend that is commonly ascribed to the difficulties, instability, absence of social integration and community crises on the urban periphery is the return migration to the urban center of Israel. Large numbers of persons leave the settlements on the urban periphery, but such people belong to a special group, which in-cludes those individuals and families with the most personal and social resources—those who least need, or no longer need the subsidized housing and employment of the urban periphery and can make it on their own in the unsubsidized center. Thus, those remaining in the urban frontier are the least able to get on unaided, the least able to do without subsidized housing and employment. The difficulties and instabilities, the shortage of an able, qualified, economically self-sufficient population in the urban periphery are thus both cause and effect of the selective pattern of in- and out-migration.

The rural frontier has also had a high rate of population turn-over. And it has been argued that this turnover resembled that of the urban periphery. But again, regardless of the extent and direc-tion of the selection process in the old rural frontier turnover, it is clear that in the pre-state period those remaining in the frontier

11

rural settlements were reinforced by ideologies, prestige and opportunities for active participation in national affairs, either directly or
through their movements. Settlers' dedication was also reinforced
by the image of the special social and community forms that their
movements were committed to promoting.

A summary of the argument up to this point gives a fairly discouraging picture of Israel's urban periphery:
1. The inducement for moving to and settling on the urban
   frontier (subsidized housing and employment) draws those
   immigrants who have low levels of personal and socioeconomic resources and qualifications.
2. Commercial and industrial development has been spotty,
   despite massive government investment and subsidy; and
   employment has been unstable, with average family income
   somewhat lower than in the rest of the country.
3. The social, health, employment, school, government and welfare services have been managed by bureaucratic-technocratic
   cadres, who typically are not socially or culturally integrated
   into the communities. This lack of integration has resulted
   in constant instabilities and crises in community relations.
4. Return migration to the urban center of the country has
   been extensive—and, because it selects out the most successful, weakens the urban frontier communities.

Eric Cohen has attributed the weakness of such urban frontier
settlements to two factors. First, is the absence of any ideological
support of such settlement—the lack of a vision or an image of a
community that is in some way new, different from or better than
the urban communities which settlers were familiar with in the past.
Second, there is no coherent government policy concerning priorities for investment, development or subsidy on the urban frontier.

Cohen finds that the resultant disorganized, chaotic, individualistic
competition for power, influence and access to resources and subsidies disrupts both social relations and the building of community
institutions. What is more, the return migration from the urban
frontier to the cities in the center of the country—in which there
is little or no subsidized housing or employment—contributes
greatly to slum and poverty problems in the cities.

Although much of Cohen's argument bears careful attention, this
kind of summary is premature. As human communities are reck-
oned, the settlements and communities of Israel's urban periphery

12

are still very young. Many of the problems of the frontier communities derive from their relative youth, from their being in the earliest stages of the community development process, and are not a direct result of the way settlement and resource channeling are organized or left unorganized.

By almost any criteria Beersheba, Dimona and Kiryat Gat are examples of successful urban frontier towns. All three are really quite new, as cities go. Until very recently none of them existed. All now have some going concern, industries and businesses, some population that has lived and worked there for a number of years, some adults who were actually brought up, or spent parts of their childhood and adolescence in these towns, some community institutions, voluntary organizations and local political activity and participation.

The subsidized-housing-and-employment formula is no longer a sufficient explanation of why people go to live in Beersheba, in Dimona or in Kiryat Gat. Not only new immigrants settle there. Others may be attracted by kinship, employment, climate or opportunities to improve their housing, style of life, etc. Just as in Tel Aviv and Haifa, a considerable part of the economic activity in these successful urban periphery towns still depends upon government policies, controls, subsidies, loans and so forth. However, none of them is any longer a single-industry town, and all now have industries and services with stable production, markets and employment in addition to resident employees at all levels of skill and responsibility.

Teachers, social workers, doctors, public officials, technicians and professionals of every type were brought up and had their elementary and secondary education in Beersheba and are now the backbone of the network of community services in that town; they are *not* outsiders, and the gaps so characteristic of outsider bureaucratic-technocratic cadres and local clientele have given way to other gaps ("generation gaps" perhaps), but not gaps like those typical of outsider-local relationships. The work and relationships of these local professionals are basically integrative rather than disruptive or threatening. Finally, in Beersheba, Dimona and Kiryat Gat both new and old residents are beginning to expand their political participation in both local and national affairs. Political involvement has given the communities direct access to the national political elites and influence upon and direct participation in national and local decision-making and the allocation of resources.

Thus, a cross-sectional view of urban frontier communities in the urban periphery shows that most such communities consist largely of recent immigrants who still depend upon subsidies and outside initiative and organization to assure employment and minimum economic activity, and upon outside bureaucratic and technocratic cadres to provide elementary health, educational, and community and welfare services. But a longitudinal view of the urban periphery may, in time, disclose a cycle or process in which such communities emerge from their state of dependence and disorganization to develop their own networks of stable social, economic and political participation and institutions.

2

Daniel J. Elazar

LOCAL GOVERNMENT AS AN INTEGRATING FACTOR IN ISRAELI SOCIETY

Political power in Israel is generally taken to be concentrated in the country's central institutions, its government and party.[1] The small size of the country, the ideologically motivated effort required for its development, and the political tradition it has inherited from both Jewish and non-Jewish sources are interrelated factors in this power concentration.[2] At the same time, it is a mistake to think of the Israeli government as "centralized" in the usual sense of the word. Elsewhere, continuing Max Ascoli's argument, I have suggested that Israel is best understood as a federation of ideologically based political parties that share power among themselves in a form that is almost as uncentralized as in a federal system.[3] In addition, the various religious communities in the state—presently defined as including separate Jewish, Muslim, Druze and Christian communities—are also treated as essentially autonomous in religious and cultural matters; this religious separation is a survival of the *millet* system long traditional in the Middle East.

Power is thus divided among several centers within the Israeli polity, but the centers are organized along cultural-ideological rather than territorial lines. This means that local government in

15

Israel, which is necessarily territorially based, operates at a handicap. It is often correctly seen as the weakest link in the state's political system. From a power perspective, local governments are subordinate not only to governmental and party centers, but also to the religious communities.

At the same time, local government plays an important role in Israeli society, particularly in connection with: providing and administering governmental services; recruiting and advancing political leadership; fostering channels of political communication between the governors and the governed; and maintaining necessary or desired diversity within a small country where there are heavy pressures towards homogeneity. All four of these tasks are extremely important in the integration of what is still a very new society of immigrants or the children of immigrants. The role played by local government in meeting the challenges they pose makes it a far more vital factor on the Israeli scene than is generally recognized.

Local government in Israel has honorable and almost ancient origins. Local self-government was the first vehicle for asserting the national goals of the Zionist movement. The first Zionist colonies were created as self-governing covenant communities similar in the fundamentals of their political organization to the early Puritan settlements of New England. Somewhat later, under the laws of the British Mandate, governments in their present forms were organized by the Jewish pioneers. They were designed to give the pioneers as much autonomy as possible while the country was still under British rule.[4]

Thus the first local governments were fostered as alternatives to foreign government and were treated by the organized Jewish community in Palestine as important elements in the drive for a Jewish state. Jewish municipalities such as Tel Aviv, local councils such as Petah Tikva, regional councils (which were federations of Jewish agricultural settlements) such as Emek Hayarden and Hagalil Haelyon, as well as the governing committees of the kibbutzim and moshavim, were all encouraged by the Zionist authorities as a means of advancing the cause of Jewish self-government. In those pre-statehood days, the Jewish local governments took on many of the responsibilities that were later to become the province of the state, and they initiated, organized and provided a wide range of services. In this they were specifically encouraged by the Mandatory government which, for political reasons, maintained only a minimum level of governmental services; instead the Jews and Arabs of what was then Palestine determined for themselves the level of services to be provided in their own sectors.[5] It should be noted that the Arabs resisted any British efforts to establish local government in their communities on the grounds that such institutions would interfere with traditional patterns of local rule in which the leading family or families maintained well-nigh absolute control over their fellow villagers.[6]

Even in the Mandatory period, local governments also helped to maintain diversity within the framework of the Zionist movement. The General Zionist and other right and center parties that were excluded from positions of power in Histadrut-dominated country-wide organs of the Jewish "state within a state" were able to establish power bases of their own in a number of the Jewish municipalities, and in this way acquired a share and a stake in the building of the land. Moreover, many of the future leaders of the state took their first steps on the road to political careers in the local polities, urban or rural, especially in the kibbutzim.[7] Finally, the very nature of the *yishuv* (the Jewish community in Palestine) meant that the Jewish local governments would be central factors in enhancing political communication among the members of the new society. When the history of local government in pre-state Israel is written, the record will no doubt show that it played an important role as a training ground for the embryo state. With the establishment of the state in 1948, local government passed from the center of the political stage. Not unexpectedly, the new state began to assume responsibility for many public functions which had rested in local governmental hands when central institutions were absent. Political leadership gravitated toward the offices of the new state and left in local government only those members of the opposition parties for whom the limited responsibilities of service in the Knesset were not sufficient and those *kibbutzniks* who wished to stay home to actively seek local office. In the process of sorting out state and local functions, the party organizations and Histadrut interposed themselves between the fledgling state and the local governments, further weakening the autonomy of the local leadership.

At the same time, mass immigration to Israel in the five years following 1948 shifted the patterns of settlement in the country in such a way that the kibbutzim and veteran moshavim, the local communities possessing the best access to the state and the most power to maintain their local autonomy, declined in importance relative to other local communities. On the other hand, the development towns and the immigrant settlements, potentially the least powerful local communities, became significant elements in the constellation of local governments. Even though new kibbutzim were established in this period, such settlements failed to attract many of the new immigrants, so that, although existing kibbutzim preserved their own relatively autonomous position within Israeli civil society, they were unable to extend the benefits of their influential role to many of the new arrivals.

The reduction in the power of local government was not necessarily the result of calculated policy; but the transfer of powers described above could have only that effect. Indeed, the new state fostered local governmental institutions from the beginning. Reversing the pattern established in Mandatory days, the central authorities themselves moved to establish new local authorities. The number of Jewish settlements enjoying municipal status rose from 36 in 1948 to 102 by 1968. The number of regional councils (federations of rural settlements) rose from four to 50. (Consolidation has since reduced the number to 47.) Moreover, new rural settlements (of which there were 666 in 1968) were all encouraged to develop local committees for their internal self-government.[8] Finally, and perhaps most significantly, the Arab and Druze villages were also encouraged to establish modern municipal governments of their own and did so in substantial numbers, thereby opening the door to political participation for thousands of non-Jews who had previously been caught in the embrace of a traditional society that confined political power to the hands of a tiny elite.[9] In addition to the establishment of new local governments, established local governments were upgraded and their structures and functions more or less regularized according to standard statewide patterns.

The same standardization that was brought to governmental activities was extended to politics as well. Regularization brought with it patterns of voting at the local level that were becoming fixed statewide. The opposition parties lost control of most of the local governments which had been in their hands in the pre-state period and were replaced by new coalitions dominated by Mapai, the Israeli labor party that was dominant in the country as a whole. If the establishment of the state strengthened the hands of central government institutions, the mass immigration strengthened the hands of the political party organizations. Whereas in the small yishuv before statehood the party members could play significant roles in party decision-making, as the population grew and the elements who came in were for the most part politically unsophisticated, the professional party leaders took over direction of party affairs, relying upon the new voting masses who turned out regularly for them at the polls but who were not prepared to participate actively in party government. This had the effect of increasing the role of the central organs of the political parties, enabling them to mediate between state and local governing bodies with their respective versions of coalition politics.

In keeping with the party federalism that is a major feature of Israel's political system, the new immigrants were divided among the parties according to each party's strength in the general elections, as soon as they arrived in the country. Each party was made responsible for providing the new immigrants with jobs, assisting them in settling in, and providing for their basic social and religious needs, thereby creating bonds of dependence between them. This pattern of division, which is known in Israel as the "party key," was institutionalized at all points in the political system and through much of the economic system, across all levels of governmental society. Use of the party key system meant that each party would retain the same relative strength from election to election while assuring that all new immigrants would fit into the political system through some lasting tie with "their" political party. So it has been since 1948.[10]

Local government reached its lowest point in the political system sometime in the mid 1950s. At that point, the older local governments had lost many of their original functions and had been absorbed in the statewide party system along lines that harmonized with the patterns of rule established in Jerusalem. The most powerful local governments, those of the kibbutzim and, secondarily, the older moshavim, were attracting a proportionately smaller share of the new immigrants and losing their importance in the local government constellation as a result. The new immigrant settlements that had been established after statehood were still too raw and immature to be self-governing. Even where they were given municipal status, their government offices were occupied or dominated by outsiders sent in by their respective political parties to manage local affairs until such time as "proper" local leadership should emerge.

In the late 1950s, the tide began to turn as the local governments began to find their place in the framework of a state in which power was divided on other than territorial bases, first and foremost, but which also wished to encourage local governmental activity across most if not all of the four tasks or roles listed at the beginning of this chapter. The process of adjustment begun then is not yet completed, for it has been going on for barely half a generation, the minimum amount of time that must pass before a reasonable assessment can be made.

The case of government services provides a good example of this adjustment. After the period when most functions were transferred from local government (and Histadrut) to the state, the country entered into a period in which shared or cooperative activity began to be stressed. While the state took primary responsibility for program-initiation, policy-making and finance, program administration—the actual delivery of services—was increasingly transferred to local government or, in cases where the division was not so clear-cut, responsibility for the delivery of services was somehow divided between the state and the localities. This became true over a wide range of functions from welfare to education to civil defense to sewage disposal.[11]

The nature of these sharing arrangements should be made clear. They did not involve a sharing among equal partners but rather a sharing by superior and subordinate. But sharing has become the norm, which means that at the very least the local governments are forced to develop cadres of civil servants with sufficient administrative skill to provide the services that the state promises all its citizens. This has opened the doors to the recruitment and development of a new class of participants in the governmental process that out of necessity has drawn people from all segments of Israeli society.

So, too, local government plays a crucial role in dealing with diversity within the homogeneous society which is forming in the country. The goal of the Israeli government is to foster maximum integration among the "communities" (that is to say, the country-of-origin groups) that divide the Jewish population. This goal is essentially shared by the Israeli population as a whole, though some individuals are more ambivalent about it than the country's political leadership. At the same time, after an initial period of overoptimism, when it was believed that all differences would disappear upon contact with the soil of the land, there has been growing recognition that there are diverse strands, even within Jewish Israel, that will at the very least persist for several generations and may indeed have some value if they are properly integrated into the common Israeli society that is being developed.[12] Israel's local polities embrace populations that, as a result of the patterns of migration and settlement, are frequently homogeneous in and of themselves, because residents come from the same countries or regions of origin.

Consequently, such local polities offer their citizens opportunities to adapt themselves to the Israeli scene without surrendering all of the cultural baggage which they have brought with them. This is most true in the development towns and the immigrant villages. It is less true in the big cities, where neighborhoods or nongovernmental subdivisions are the only real custodians of that kind of diversity. As might be expected this is equally true of the native Israeli-populated kibbutzim and development towns which provide their residents with havens for their own life-styles no less important than the havens provided by the immigrant towns for those from non-Western backgrounds. Here the first signs of territorial democracy have begun to emerge, with local governments providing residents both political opportunity that is linked to their cultural background and political space to separate them from their neighbors.[13]

Whatever advantages for political and social integration have been gained through local government responsibility for the delivery of services or local government assistance in the perpetuation of legitimate diversity, it is the role of local government in enlarging the arena of political recruitment and fostering channels of political communication that is having the most impact towards bridging the cleavages within Israeli society. The former is the key to the latter. It has been noted that the central organs of the Israeli state are dominated by pre-state immigrants or native Israelis, overwhelmingly of Ashkenazi stock. Indeed, that is one of the factors pointed to by critics of Israeli society as reflecting discrimination against Sephardic and Oriental Jews.[14]

The situation in local government is quite the reverse; there the Sephardic and Oriental groups are represented by local officeholders to a degree that is roughly proportionate to their share of the total population. Between 1955 and 1965, the percentage of Sephardim and Orientals holding local elective or appointive office rose from 23 percent to 43 percent at the same time as these groups grew to comprise 47 percent of the total population. It is now estimated that the former figure has risen to 47 percent and the latter to over 50 percent.[15] Moreover, in the development towns where Sephardim and Orientals are the dominant elements in the population, they are overwhelmingly in control of the elective and administrative offices of local government. In other places they are unevenly distributed, with only 20 percent of the members of local councils in the large and medium-sized cities (the older settlements) drawn from among Sephardim and Orientals in 1965 despite the fact that they comprise 60 percent of the population in those polities. Even so, 37 percent of the deputy mayors of those cities came from Sephardic and Oriental groups in 1965, an increase from 11 percent in 1955.[16] Considering the fact that these officeholders or their parents were not even located in societies which permitted citizen participation or participation outside of selected elites 20 years ago, their rise has been phenomenal even if it is still confined to local government.

Because of this opportunity at the local level talented Sephardim and Orientals have been encouraged to pursue satisfying political careers within the system rather than agitate against it. The outside observer may well note that they receive proportionately less for their efforts than those of Ashkenazi background. However, with few exceptions, their expectations are lower to begin with, and therefore they can be satisfied with less. This fact is not surprising. Comparisons between them and the present generation of American "ethnics" are misleading; rather, Sephardim and Orientals are more appropriately compared to the new immigrants to the United States of 40 to 60 years ago. For them, any recognition in the political sphere was considered a great sign of acceptance and advancement, while equality or parity at the highest level was not even within their range of expectations. There is every likelihood that within another generation what is happening on the local scene will extend itself to the state level as well, as political socialization, general acculturation and expectation levels rise and new opportunities for advancement open up.

The rapid infiltration of members of the disadvantaged immigrant groups into political life at the local level is due to the efforts of the political parties. Their leaders were among the first to recognize the persistence of ethnicity among Israelis of all kinds, even while the more "statesmanlike" leaders of the country and its more idealistic elements were still hoping for rapid and complete amalgamation of populations. They recognized that ethnic patterns would influence voting and that they would either assimilate those patterns into their own party organizations, or ethnic tickets would develop at the local level and perhaps siphon votes away from their tickets, statewide as well as local. They moved in to align themselves with specific ethnic groups locally and to recruit the more talented individuals for political office.[17] By doing this they not only succeeded in binding the new immigrants to the existing parties, but also bound them to the political system itself. As a result of these efforts, combined with the widely shared ideology of the integration of the exile communities, ethnic tickets have had a dismal record on the Israeli political scene, even though ethnic voting patterns are very noticeable in the party alignments in locality after locality.[18]

The parties' efforts to bind the new immigrants to them has led to the growth of opportunities for political communication between the governors and the governed. Given the Eastern European background of so much of Israeli politics, such political communication was not a dominant feature of the political system in its original form. Indeed, most communication between governors and governed takes place outside of the political arena in essentially or obstensibly nonpolitical categories. The country survives as a democracy because it is small and Jewish and such communication can take place easily without formal political channels being perfected.

At the same time, the need to satisfy the new immigrants sufficiently so that they would be bound to the party system made the party professionals far more open to communication in both directions than they might otherwise have been. Here, too, the existence of local government has made a big difference. Since the first line of political communication was invariably within the locality, communication with political influentials outside of the locality was effected through local officials who could serve as communicators by virtue of their formal positions on one hand and their reference group ties on the other.

In sum, by fostering a certain amount of protective localism, local government in Israel has done much to nourish among the new immigrants a sense that they have a stake in society, and a sense among the oldtimers or their children that they can survive in a society that is changing in ways not always pleasing to them. While these factors may be contradictory in a sense, they are typical of so many political contradictions in that they seem to work until a confrontation occurs. To date, that confrontation has not occurred. Indeed, it has been prevented precisely because local governments create political distance between groups where physical distance is lacking. Local government plays its role not in isolation but because it is so intimately connected with the state and the party system. It is not isolation that is necessary here but the ability to capitalize on the forces of integration by adapting them to local situations and needs.

There is an additional factor in the relationship between local

23

government and non-Jewish minorities. If the task of local government among the Jewish majority is fundamentally to foster across-the-board integration of diverse groups, the function of local governments toward the non-Jewish minorities is to foster political integration while encouraging cultural autonomy.

In 1948, there was only one non-Jewish local council within the borders of the new state, a clear result of the British policy of not encouraging the development of municipal institutions among the Arab population. By 1968, following a period of encouragement by the Israeli authorities, there were 42 Arab and Druze local councils, 18 self-governing villages within mixed regional councils, and 42 self-governing Bedouin tribes. Three quarters of the non-Jewish population lived under its own local government as compared with 27 percent for the whole of pre-1948 Palestine.

Local governments based on the uniform practices of the state, serving the same functions as all other local governments, have given the non-Jewish minorities a political stake in Israeli society that they could not have obtained in any other way. At the same time, these local governments offer their constituents an opportunity to mobilize political and governmental support for the preservation of their own religious and cultural heritage insofar as they choose to do so. There is no pressure on the part of the Israeli government for the non-Jewish minorities to assimilate into some new Israeli nationality. Quite the contrary, the Israeli government is more than content to encourage cultural diversity in recognition of the realities of the Middle East and the values for cultural separatism shared by Jew and non-Jew alike in that part of the world. There, too, local government has become a very useful tool in achieving what seem to be contradictory goals but which are actually most compatible in the real, paradox-ridden world.[19]

Ignazio Silone, in his excellent work, *School for Dictators* (1938), provided a lasting rationale for the strengthening of local government in democracies:

> The school of democracy is in local self-government. For a worker to take a serious part in the life of his trade union, or for a peasant to take part in the life of his village, there is no need for higher education. The first test to be applied in judging an alleged democracy is the degree of self-governing attained by its local institutions. . . . Only local government can accustom men to responsibility and independence, and enable them to take part in the wider life of the state.

According to Silone's standards, Israel is not doing badly and may well be moving along the right path.

NOTES

1. For exemplary studies of Israeli society and politics, see S. N. Eisenstadt, *Israel: Society* (New York: Basic Books, 1967) and Leonard J. Fein, *Politics in Israel* (Boston: Little, Brown, 1967).

2. In addition to the two works cited above, Emil Marmorstein discusses these phenomena in *Heaven at Bay* (New York: Oxford University Press, 1969).

3. Daniel J. Elazar, *Israel: From Ideological to Territorial Democracy* (New York: General Learning Press, 1971). See also Max Ascoli, "Notes on Israel," *The Reporter* 17 (July 11, 1957) 1: 6-17.

4. The study of local government in Israel is still in its infancy. No comprehensive study of the subject has been published. Eisenstadt, *Israel,* and Fein, *Politics in Israel,* have sections on local government, and Eisenstadt provides a selective bibliography. The most comprehensive work is that of Szewach Weiss, "Local Government in Israel: A Study of Its Leadership," (Ph.D. diss. Hebrew University, 1968), which examines the situation until 1965. Emanuel Gutmann provides a standard description in *The Politics of Israel Local Government* (Milan: Edizioni di Communita, 1963). The structure and formal powers of local government are described in Yehoshua Freudenheim, *Government in Israel* (Dobbs Ferry, New York: Oceana Publications, 1967), Chapter 9. The Center for the Study of Federalism, Temple University, maintains extensive files on local government and intergovernmental relations in Israel, including bibliographies, several dozen research papers and raw materials for further research, all part of its continuing study of the subject. Other prime sources include *Dvar Hashilton Hamekomi,* the journal of the Israel Union of Local Authorities, and the reports of the State Comptroller of Israel, which include individual reports on virtually every local authority in the country at intervals going back nearly two decades, as well as annual reports that deal with general problems of local government and state-local relations. See also Eliezer Brutzkus, *Physical Planning in Israel* (Jerusalem: n.p. 1964); Zeev Meljon, ed., *Towns and Villages in Israel* (Tel Aviv: Union of Local Authorities in Israel, 1966); Dov Rosen, ed., *Municipal Survey: Jewish Cities and Local Councils* (Jerusalem: Ministry of the Interior, 1968), an electoral survey in Hebrew; and the annual statistical reports of the Israel Central Bureau of Statistics for local authorities, issued since 1964-1965. The studies of the Center for the Study of Rural Settlement (Rehovot) include some empirical material on regional councils.

5. Y. Gevirtz, *Rural Local Government in Israel* (Jerusalem: International Seminar for Local Government Administration, 1962). Yehoshua Ben-Aryeh describes one of these "small republics" in *Emek Hayarden Hatichon* (Merhavia: Hakibbutz Hameuchad, 1965).

6. A good summary of the development of local self-government in the Arab towns is available in Ori Stendel, *Arab Villages in Israel and Judea-*

Samaria (Jerusalem: The Israel Economist, 1967). The best sources of specific data are the reports of the State Comptroller for specific towns. See also Ernest Stock, *From Conflict to Understanding: Relations Between Jews and Arabs in Israel Since 1948* (New York: Institute of Human Relations Press, 1968).

7. Eisenstadt, *Israel.*

8. See, among other sources, Freudenheim, *Government.*

9. Stendel, *Arab Villages.*

10. Eisenstadt, *Israel,* and Fein, *Politics in Israel* discuss this.

11. See Rosen, *Municipal Survey,* and the reports of the Comptroller General.

12. This new trend is reflected in the press, media, and periodicals of Israel since the mid-1960s. The author has material in his files documenting the change in Israeli thinking from a strict "melting pot" approach to one which at least recognizes the value of cultural synthesis, if not pluralism.

13. See Elazar, *Israel,* and the studies of the Israel Local Government Seminar which the author directed in 1968-1969, on file in the Center for the Study of Federalism, Temple University.

14. Eisenstadt, *Israel,* and Fein, *Politics in Israel.*

15. Weiss, "Local Government."

16. Ibid.

17. Weiss discusses this in his dissertation. See also *Statistical Abstract of Israel, 1968* (Jerusalem: Central Bureau of Statistics, 1968). In a significant number of cities and towns, territorial neutrality has led to the development of ethnic neighborhoods, which, however, under the present electoral system, are unable to obtain direct local representation. Perhaps as a result, ethnic ticket-balancing is even more pronounced on the local level than in Knesset elections.

18. Rosen, *Municipal Survey,* presents a complete picture of electoral activity at the local level from the first post-independence elections through 1965. The 1969 data are readily available in the Israeli press, see, particularly, *Maariv* for summer and fall, 1969.

The extent of this new independence from party discipline is reflected in the rise of "kalanterism," perhaps one of its worst manifestations, whereby members of the council who have supported the coalition holding power locally are persuaded or seduced into joining with one of the opposition factions to vote the sitting coalition out of office. The original "kalanterist," a Jerusalem city councilman named Kalanter, made his move in 1959. Since then the number of instances has grown considerably. In several cases serious differences in approach to government were involved, though in most cases personal ambition has been the motivating force. The Knesset regularly debates this "problem," to them particularly serious because it weakens party control over local officials, but has not yet been able to devise an acceptable way to prevent it. By the same token, inter-party agreements to avoid "kalanterism," made at the headquarters level, have proved unenforceable in the localities.

19. Stendel, *Arab Villages,* and Stock, *From Conflict to Understanding.*

3

Myron J. Aronoff

DEVELOPMENT TOWNS
IN ISRAEL

In examining the background and context in which new towns have been developed in Israel it is important to note the almost total disregard of the role of the city in Zionist pioneering ideology.[1] Rather, a return to manual labor, and in particular a return to the soil, characterized the ideological emphasis that was given to the rejuvenation and restructuring of Jewish Diaspora society. These ideological concerns were given organizational expression in the development of the communal farming system known as kibbutzim. The unification of the kibbutzim into institutionally and ideologically cohesive kibbutz movements gained them strong representation and pivotal positions in the institutions of the labor movement, such as the political parties and Histadrut, which were developing at the same time. This simultaneous development of the kibbutz movement, the labor patries and Histadrut allowed kibbutz spokesmen to get in on the ground floor and to consolidate strong positions in these major institutions, positions which they were able to exploit

This research was done under the SSRC grant HR779/1, Socio-Cultural Patterns of Adjustment and Conflict Among Israel's Veterans and Immigrants. I am grateful to the Social Science Research Council of the United Kingdom for this generous support. The previous research on Frontiertown, part of which is used in this essay, was generously financed by the Bernstein Israeli Research Trust to which I express my thanks. I am also grateful to Professor Max Gluckman for his helpful comments on an earlier draft.

27

in gaining major concessions over economic and political resources for the agricultural settlements.[2] The strong political position of the agricultural movements contrasts sharply with the very weak political position of the new towns.[3]

The mass immigration to Israel which followed independence forced the authorities to consider and devise various ways of settling the newcomers. One of the alternatives was within the framework of agricultural settlement. The settlement department of the Jewish Agency, in cooperation with the Ministry of Agriculture, was given the task of settling tens of thousands of new immigrants on cooperative farms (moshavim).[4] In addition, 30 new towns (since independence) were created, both to absorb new immigrants and to achieve controlled dispersal throughout various areas, particularly the less developed ones.[5]

The fact that most of the new towns were established in outlying development areas has led also to their being identified as "development" towns. There is no commonly agreed-upon definition of new towns or development towns among the various government ministries and public agencies involved in their establishment, nor is there consensus among the professionals who have concerned themselves with their problems. Eric Cohen, for example, stresses the following characteristics of development towns: they are in underdeveloped areas; they have been planned more or less comprehensively; they have predominantly immigrant populations; and they are small in size (3,500 to 15,000).[6] The variables which the Lichfield group's stage I study used differed slightly. They included: establishment of the town after 1948; significant change in its physical size since 1948; receipt of significant amount of directed immigration; and planned size of town defined as "urban" settlement by the Central Bureau of Statistics. The terms "new" and "development towns" will be used interchangeably in this chapter. The lack of consensus over the definition of the terms "new towns" and "development towns" reflects a very significant lack of agreement on what these towns actually were meant to be and what role they were to fill in Israeli society. This stands in sharp contrast to the well-crystallized conception of the role of the agricultural settlements mentioned earlier.

THE LEGAL AND INSTITUTIONAL BACKGROUND OF PLANNING

The process by which new towns were planned, established and developed in Israel demonstrates several unique features that differentiate it from processes of establishment of new towns in other parts of the world.[8] No single consolidated body of Israeli law covers legal aspects of the establishment and development of new towns.[9] Until the passage of the new Planning and Building Law in July 1965, the planning and construction of new towns was carried out under the general legislation of the Town Planning Ordinance (1936) of the British Mandatory government, with minor modifications. There was no provision for a central authority to which the various local and district planning commissions would be responsible, nor was there provision for any form of centralized coordination of the various commissions and government ministries and public agencies involved in the establishment of the towns. No single ministry or agency has primary jurisdiction in the planning, establishment and development of the new towns. In fact there seems to have been a marked lack of consensus about the appropriate apportioning of jurisdiction among the various government ministries and public agencies which have been involved in the creation of the Israeli new towns.

The lack of centralized planning authority, special legislation for new towns and clear lines of authority for responsibility in developing the new towns all led to a situation in which any one of a number of ministries or agencies could and did take the initiative in the establishment of individual new towns. Since the cooperation of various other ministries had to be mobilized to achieve various goals in planning and development, their efforts had to be coordinated, and therefore a number of interministerial committees and ad hoc authorities were created. But none of these bodies had legal power to act on its own: it could only try to coordinate the activities of the ministries and agencies. When ministries disagreed, as they often did, since jurisdictional lines of authority were far from clear, such ad hoc committees and authorities could not enforce their decisions.

A National Planning Office was transferred from the Prime Minister's office and made the Planning Department of the Ministry of Interior in 1953. Population distribution ideas have been the only plans of this department which have been explicitly declared official policy of the government, and consequently the only ones which have had much influence. The Ministry of Housing, which was responsible for the construction of practically all housing in the new towns, while operating under a gentlemen's agreement to coordinate its activities with the national plans of the Ministry of Interior, in fact had the independence, and the staff and resources, to follow its own designs and plans. The Ministry of Housing was formerly a department in the Ministry of Labor, and its former parent ministry continued to have considerable interest in the new towns. The Ministry of Labor was responsible for public works and employment in the new towns. The Ministry of Development was responsible for the development of the mineral wealth concentrated in the southern Negev region, and consequently it considered the development towns in this region within its sphere of interest.

The Ministry of Commerce and Industry was one of the most important institutions in the development of the new towns, for it was the official provider of industry. One of the greatest problems in the development towns has been the lack of proper types of industry. I stress the word proper, since there have been several sad cases where an industry has been established in a town where the proper work force was not available. The categorization of the various types of development towns by the Ministry of Commerce and Industry determined the types of incentives which were offered to industry to locate in the town; and the ministry's recommendation could frequently be the determining factor in an industry's location.

Part of the functions of the Ministry of Commerce and Industry were being performed, at least unofficially, by the former Minister of Commerce and Industry, the present Minister of Finance. The single most important ministry for the new towns was unquestionably Finance, since budgets were almost entirely derived from the national development budget determined by this ministry and because its leader had an exceptionally strong political position.

There were other agencies and ministries which had traditionally been involved in the creation of the new towns. The settlement department of the Jewish Agency not only had been responsible for agricultural settlement, but through its regional planning was the prime authority, in collaboration with the Ministry of Agriculture, in the establishment of Kiryat Gat, the urban center of the Lachish region. The absorption department of the Jewish Agency, some of the functions of which have recently been taken over by the Ministry of Immigration Absorption, was responsible for send-ing the new immigrants to the towns. In fact, they provided a majority of the residents for all but one of the new towns.

The Ministry of Defense played an important role in establishing and developing three towns: Acre, Nazareth Elite and Mizpe Ramon. The Land Authority, which was responsible for public land, and the Water Authority, which allocated the vital water resources, were involved in various stages of the development of all the towns. Spiegel has said of this situation: "The picture is rich and colourful, not always without contrast and contradictions, but distinguished by flexibility and improvisation, allowing legal and institutional handicaps to be overcome, and missing legal and insti-tutional supports to be substituted." [10]

AREAS OF POLITICAL PROBLEMS

Interministerial Conflicts

One of the most critical "political" problems in the establishment of the new towns has concerned disputes over jurisdiction and authority in various aspects of their development. Although Fron-tiertown was in many respects atypical, it was one of the newest and best planned towns and, in many ways, one of the most success-ful, and therefore offers a particularly appropriate example to illus-trate this point.

Frontiertown was originally planned by the late Giora Josephthal when he was Minister of Labor. At the inception of the planning of Frontiertown, the housing department was still under the Min-istry of Labor. A special planning team, which worked on the site where the town was to be located, drew up the master plan and acted as a development authority. However, this planning team was responsible to an interministerial committee composed of the repre-sentatives of those previously mentioned ministeries which have primary interest and authority in the new towns.

There is no question that at least one of the causes of the failure of Frontiertown to achieve the targets set in its original master plan was that conflicts between the members of the interministerial com-mittee helped stunt its growth in its first (and most impressionable) years. Frontiertown was deprived of its original champion when Josephthal died unexpectedly. Matters were complicated consid-

31

erably when the housing department was split off from the Ministry of Labor to form the Ministry of Housing. This was done largely in consideration of political party interests. The split left at least two claimants for the primary responsibility for the development of the town—the new Ministers of Labor and of Housing. Matters were further complicated by the fact that these two ministers represented two different political parties (Mapai and Achdut Haavoda). The Prime Minister, trying to keep peace in the coalition, decided in favor of the Minister of Labor, and the Minister of Housing was later given, as a consolation prize, primary responsibility for the development of another new town. Unforfortunately, some people in each of the ministries viewed the development of the towns as a competition, and there were mutual charges of favoritism and discrimination between the rival ministries. In the end it was the towns and their residents who suffered.

There were other conflicts within the interministerial committee, the most serious of which led to the arrest of the director of the Frontiertown planning team for planning the development of natural resources without the permission of one of the ministries. His general lack of autonomy frustrated the director so much that he resigned.[11]

Significantly (and not surprisingly), the large and cumbersome interministerial committee was destroyed by internal conflicts and was replaced by a committee of three, representing the Ministry of Housing, the Ministry of Labor and the new director of the Frontiertown planning team (a deputy director-general in the Ministry of Labor). The situation improved, but damage had already been done.

Unfortunately, this case of rivalry and competition between ministries is not unique to Frontiertown. Similar examples, often involving different antagonists (for example, the Ministry of Housing versus the Ministry of Commerce and Industry in the establishment of Frontiertown's new "rival" town) could be cited for most of the other new towns in Israel. Given the nature of the Israeli political system, with its coalition government, the influence of political parties in government ministries, the lack of special laws and of a central planning authority for new towns, the lack of clear lines of jurisdictional authority between ministries with regard to new towns and so forth, this type of competition and rivalry is quite understandable.

Representation: Relationships between Local Residents
and Administration

A second political problem raised in the establishment of new
towns was that of representation. Since new towns were created by
ministries and agencies of the national government and financed
from the national development budget, they tended to be controlled
at first directly—and later indirectly—by agents of these national
ministries. In a very real sense the new towns were "remote-controlled communities." The overwhelming dependence of the new
towns on "outside" agencies posed some very real problems about
responsible elected local government in a democratic society. This
chapter examines the problem at two stages: first, when the town
was still under the administration of the planning or development
authority, and second, after it had achieved representative local
government.

In his excellent article on the social dynamics of development
towns, Cohen calls them

> "planted" communities, established "by decree" for overall
> social purposes . . . which have not evolved in accordance
> with the pressures and demands of local conditions. This
> means that these communities and their inhabitants are, or at
> least are considered to be, passive objects of manipulation by
> central agencies. The local population has no clearly defined
> place in the planning and development set-up.[12]

In the early stages of the development of a new town, the
planning and development agency had complete local governmental
authority, and there was generally no officially elected body representing the interests of the local residents. This situation is not
unique to Israel, but has also occurred when new towns have been
established in the United States, Britain and the Netherlands. Although very little research has focused on sociopolitical problems
resulting from the unrepresentative nature of the agencies which
plan and develop new towns, this does not mean that there are
no such problems.

In fact, the unrepresentative nature of the local administration
is one of a number of factors which generally lead to the development of local political strife and demands for representative local

government. Another important variable is the interhierarchical position of the administrator who, because of the nature of his position, is almost inevitably caught between cross-pressures and conflicting demands. In many ways he is like the tribal African chieftains and district commissioners in colonial regimes as analyzed by Gluckman,[13] who are caught between the conflicting interests and demands of the government ministries, whose interests they must serve, and those of the local residents, whose interests and demands they must articulate to their superiors. Like the African chief, the Israeli administrator of a new town derives his legal authority from his position in the government ministry or agency for whom he works, but in order to be effective he must also gain and maintain the support of local residents.

In Israel there was no clear timetable for the transfer of the functions of local government from administration by the representatives of the national agencies to the elected representatives of the local residents; and this also contributed to the development of political strife. In fact, the devolution of local governmental authority generally proceeded in several stages from absolute rule by the representatives of national agencies, to an "appointed" local council, to an "elected" local council. Nominations to the "appointed" council were made by the Minister of Interior, who generally chose the incumbent representatives of the national agencies. These persons usually continued to constitute a majority on the council; the remaining members represented the local residents, and were typically selected by the minister from candidates nominated by the major national political parties. These stages in the devolution of local governmental authority were generally preceded by pressure from the local residents for greater representation in local government, and the move to the next stage was generally not taken until sufficient local pressure had been built up to force the decision.

The course which the development of local strife takes varies a great deal from town to town. One very important factor which influences the character of the local strife is the socioeconomic and ethnic composition of the local residents and the administrative personnel. I have already alluded to the parallel between the administration of the new towns and colonial administration. The parallel holds true for other aspects of the Israeli new towns.

Most of the residents of the new towns were sent there soon after their arrival in Israel. Few of these new immigrants were familiar with the language, laws and customs of Israeli society. The majority of the residents of the new towns came from countries of North Africa and the Middle East, where they had had little or no experience of participation in democratic forms of government. Most of the better educated and economically better off from those communities did not immigrate to Israel; but most members of those classes who did go to Israel either did not go to or did not remain in the new towns. Thus deprived of their natural potential leadership, and without formal means of representation in local government, the residents of the new towns were for a while generally the passive objects of manipulation. Under such conditions individuals and family groups competed with one another for the attention of the representatives of the government agencies and political parties, and for the limited resources which these individuals distributed. Given the fact that almost all of the representatives of the national institutions were European veterans with many years of residence in Israel, there was the additional possibility that strife might be provoked by the ethnic differences between the rulers and the ruled. In fact, this became an issue on which local strife focused in many development towns. Generally, the overall effects of this kind of strife had a negative effect on the development of responsible local leadership and tended to inhibit the resident from developing a sense of identification with the community as a whole. The fact that the external agencies exploited internal divisions within the town only intensified a tendency toward identification with the particularistic interests of various groups without a concomitant development of a "community spirit."

"FRONTIERTOWN": A CASE STUDY

Frontiertown's development stands in sharp contrast to the model of community development described above. The example of Frontiertown is offered to illustrate the positive effects of social strife under entirely different conditions. Unlike the other new towns which preceded it, Frontiertown was planned when the government was not hard pressed by mass immigration and could afford the "luxury" of considering the many aspects involved in planning a new town. The results of this very careful planning are immediately apparent when contrasting, for example, the physical appearance of the town with its earlier predecessors. However, there are other dramatic differences between Frontiertown and most of the other new towns which, although they may not be as easily observable as the physical appearance, are very important. Sociologically, Frontiertown offers some striking contrasts to the other towns.

Unlike the other towns Frontiertown was not populated with new immigrants, but by native-born Israeli sabras and *vatikim*, veterans who had come to Israel before the War of Independence in 1948. It is important to emphasize that the planning of Frontiertown was conceived and executed within the frame of reference of the ideological role of the pre-state idealistically oriented voluntary pioneer. Great publicity was given to the pioneering role of this new town, and when appeals were made for young Israeli couples to be among the pioneering vanguard of settlers, the Frontiertown planners were able to select from a great many applicants those who they felt would be the most successful pioneers for the new town. Although some criticism has been leveled against this selection process as undemocratic and conducive to snobbery both among those who were selected, and eventually among the townsmen in general (in regard to other towns), the positive benefits of this experiment far outweigh the criticisms which have been leveled against it.

The "benevolently" paternalistic bureaucratic authority appointed by the responsible ministries and agencies to administer the relatively passive new immigrants of other new towns initially was particularly inappropriate for the pioneering settlers of Frontiertown. Unlike their counterparts in the other development towns, the settlers of Frontiertown had either been born in Israel or spent most of their adult lives in the country. They were all fluent in Hebrew and were also intimately familiar with Israeli customs. Most had served in the Israeli army, many had been members of kibbutzim, youth movements and political parties. In addition they had been chosen partially because of their desire to participate in a pioneering venture, and most of the residents felt a personal commitment to the task of building a new community. Therefore, when the residents discovered that they had no institutional means of participating in the governing of their town, and therefore had no means of influencing the course of its development, their discontent and frustration eventually became channeled into agitation for some form of public representation.

The leadership and form which this agitation took was influenced by the nature of the internal strife within the administrative authority itself. While the particulars of the situation are not relevant to the present discussion, it is important to stress that members of the planning team lived in the town and that many of the members of the team remained in town even when the group's function became that of administering the development of the town after the residents arrived. It is also significant that many of the team remained in town after municipal status was granted. This is in sharp contrast with most of the other development towns, where most of the representatives of the government agencies did not reside locally, but commuted from other cities and kibbutzim. Even in those cases where they were local residents, because of socioeconomic and ethnic differences, and particularly the difference in length of stay in the country between the veteran administrators and the new immigrant settlers, the former tended to form a separate elite group. In Frontiertown there were no major socioeconomic or ethnic differences between the administrators and the majority of the settlers. While the administrators tended to have a higher education than the average settler, they had equal familiarity with the language and customs of the country and generally interacted in social relationships on a more or less equal basis.

Because the administrative personnel lived in the area and interacted with the local residents on equal terms socially, strife within the administration was carried over into the community as a whole. Within a short time almost all of the residents of the town were mobilized into two local factions led by members or former members of the administration. The two main leaders of the opposing factions each controlled local resources and enjoyed local prestige. In addition, they both had access to high levels of government, which is a very important resource in furthering the interests of the town. In fact the major area of local political dispute was over who could best execute the master plan and get the necessary funds for the development of the town. The level of the dispute was expressed in the general interest of developing the town, a goal upon which all were agreed. This was significantly different from many towns in which the particularistic interests of various groups were asserted without a concomitant emphasis on the general public good. This was largely a tribute to the quality of the local leadership in Frontiertown, and also a consequence of the selection process by which the first residents were chosen.

A striking feature of the factional struggle in Frontiertown was the strong "local ideology" which expressed the feeling that Frontiertown was a unique and special kind of town. Idealism and voluntarism played an important role in local ideology. Another important theme was the primacy of local interests over those of national political party affiliation. All local elections were at first carried out on a personal basis and by local factional lists, not on a basis of national political party affiliation. This was considered an essential element in maintaining the town's unique character.

Factional strife pervaded almost every aspect of social and communal life in the early stages of the town's development. The fact that there was hardly any difference between social and political leaders and activities was closely related to the high degree of public involvement in communal affairs. Political mobilization was very effectively implemented through the intermeshing of social and political leadership. The discussion of political issues in non-political recreational and social associations reinforced political involvement and recruited those who had been politically apathetic. Participation in factions actively involved people in the community, and a strong community spirit thus developed. The sense of community and feeling of personal identification with the community and fellow townsmen was due in large part to the involvement of such large numbers of residents in active participation in communal affairs.

I emphasize the importance of the common goal of furthering the development of the town, which was articulated constantly by both competing leaders and their followers. Such factors as ethnicity were forbidden as a basis for mobilizing political support. Because the leadership and followers obeyed these local rules of the game, the conflict was able to contribute to greater communal unity. This is dramatically different from other communities where divisive ethnic factors were exploited as a basis for the mobilization of political support. Undoubtedly the quality of the local leadership, the type of people who first settled the town, and the fact that they managed at least in the early stages to maintain priority of local, as opposed to national party interests, were all important factors contributing to the positive effects of the local political strife in Frontiertown. As Coleman has pointed out, the reaction of a community to disputes in its early formative stages "loads the dice" and helps determine the resolution of future disputes for many years to come. This was unquestionably the case in Frontiertown, and no doubt is true for many other towns. Where Frontiertown was fortunate both in the quality of its local leadership and in the type of people who first settled there, most of the other new towns were less fortunate, and the development of local political strife in response to paternalistic administration frequently resulted in serious divisions within the community, divisions which did not contribute to the development of a sense of communitywide identification and responsibility.

SOCIAL, ECONOMIC AND POLITICAL DEPENDENCE

The dependence of the new towns on the agencies of the central government did not end with the granting of representative local government. Many of the government ministries and public agencies established branches in the new towns during the earliest stages of their development. For example, the Ministry of Housing, which was responsible for all construction in the new towns, usually established a local office in addition to its regional centers. Amidar, th public housinga uthority, set up a local office through which all of the housing in town (which is almost all public) was rented and sold. The labor exchange (employment office) of the Ministry of Labor allocated jobs, and other appropriate agencies allocated social welfare, provided educational facilities and so forth. Two very important public agencies established branches in the new towns, the Jewish Agency and Histadrut. The Jewish Agency sent the new immigrants to the town and provided their housing and initial absorption needs. The immigrants were particularly dependent upon this agency in most of the new towns. Subsequently, some of these functions were taken over by the Ministry of Absorption. Histadrut, the Israeli Federation of Labor, in addition to being a giant and powerful federation of labor unions, was the owner of most of the industry in the new towns, and provided important social, educational, sports and health facilities and provisions to help absorb new immigrants. In many cases these duplicated similar services provided by local government.

The major characteristics of this institutional setup were in many ways similar to those of the early planning administration. A few of the major characteristics were: their "planted" nature (i.e., the institutions did not arise from the demands of the local situation, but were set up by outside national agencies replicating the institutional pattern already existing throughout the rest of the country); they were "remote-controlled" institutions in that they were very much controlled by their parent agencies, which restricted the authority of the local representatives and severely limited their ability to make independent decisions; the key people were brought in from outside the community to head these institutional branches, and most did not settle in the community; even when they did so, they tended to form a separate socioeconomic, cultural, ethnic and political elite. Their institutional positions tended to give them considerable local influence, even though their authority to make decisions within their national institutions tended to be restricted.

Among those national institutions which set up branches in the new towns and were generally managed by outsiders or resident veteran elites were the major political parties. These branches were particularly important in the new towns, because it is through the party institutions that candidates were nominated for the local council (municipality) and the local workers' council of Histadrut. These offices have provided one of the most important avenues of socioeconomic mobility for the new immigrants in the new towns. The parties have provided access to many of the most important local resources and have performed many important social functions for the residents.

LOCAL POLITICAL OFFICES AND INSTITUTIONS: COMPETING CENTERS OF POWER

The major centers of political power, resources and interests in most localities in Israel center around the municipality, the Histadrut branch and the branches of the major political parties (particularly of the Israeli Labor Party). In many of the development towns the local religious council is an additional center of political power and resources.

The mayor controls valuable resources of political patronage through the awarding of jobs, public contracts, licenses and franchises. He generally enjoys the highest status among local leaders and represents the community in dealings with higher national authorities. His position varies according to the size and resources of the community, his personal competence and control of these resources, his popularity in the community, his control of the local political machinery and his personal connections with national political leaders. One major problem that the mayors of most development towns face is that they generally must spend at least half of their time outside of their towns running around the various government ministries and public agencies in Jerusalem and Tel Aviv trying to promote the development of their towns, so that they frequently neglect their political home base and can lose out to a local challenger. There have been a number of cases where highly popular mayors who had succeeded in bringing developmental resources to their towns failed to gain renomination because they had lost their dominant position in their local party branch.

The secretary of the local workers' council of Histadrut is the second important local leader with control of major resources, and he is the one most likely to challenge the mayor's position. He is the leader of a powerful trade union, supervises enterprises and industries affiliated with Histadrut in his area and directs the health, social, educational, cultural, sports and immigrant activities of Histadrut in town. He has a personal staff which varies in size according to the number of Histadrut members in the community. This staff is frequently the base of his political backing in the local branch of the Israeli Labor Party. The institutional interests of the organization which he heads and his personal ambitions frequently bring him into conflict and competition with the mayor.

The secretary of the local branch of the Labor Party must balance the various internal factions (based on the three former parties which merged to form the Labor Party), alignments based on patron-client relationships, personal ambitions, personal likes and animosities, ethnic affiliations and other group pressures, and differing institutional interests (especially among municipality, party and Histadrut). He is frequently the political client of the mayor and performs the important service of maintaining a disciplined following to support the mayor's policies. Sometimes he is the client of the secretary of the workers' council and performs a similar function for him. When the branch secretary is in a stronger position he may form a coalition with the mayor or the secretary of Histadrut against the other or balance the two by playing one off against the other on different issues. The configuration of relationships among these three office holders to a large degree controls the outcomes of local politics.

The local religious councils are particularly important institutions in development towns where there are large concentrations of immigrants from North Africa and the Middle East with a significant percentage of traditionally observant Jews.[14] The religious council supervises and pays (from the joint subsidies of the Ministry of Religious Affairs and the local council) the salaries of local rabbis, ritual slaughterers, circumcisers and functionaries who supervise the enforcement of dietary laws (*kashrut*) in butcher shops, restaurants and hotels. They also issue marriage licenses, rule on divorce and run burial societies. The control of resources and patronage through these councils is a major source of local power for the National Religious Party (Mafdal) which, by a "secret" coalition agreement, has a majority on every religious council in the country. The control of the Ministry of Interior by Mafdal is another channel of influence on local councils, particularly in those cases where Labor and Mafdal are in close competition for dominance in a community.

FUNCTIONS OF LOCAL POLITICS
IN ISRAELI NEW TOWNS

As mentioned previously, most of the local branches of the national political parties in the development towns were established by outsiders or local veteran elites. Yet these branches and the other local political offices (of Histadrut and the local council) provide one of the most important avenues for socioeconomic mobility for the new immigrant residents of the towns. The new immigrants learned that they could manipulate the bureaucratic institutions as well as be manipulated by them. They discovered that by organizing they could apply pressures and bargain for jobs and other resources. They found that their organized votes brought material rewards, honor and privileges.[15] Some of them who began in minor local political jobs ten years later had worked their way up the local political hierarchy to attain positions of party branch secretary, secretary of the local Histadrut or chairman of the local council (or mayor) of their towns. Throughout the new towns members of the old political elite have been and are being supplanted by representatives of the dominant local ethnic groups and leaders representing various other diverse local interests.

Israeli political parties at the local level have performed many roles similar to the old political machines in an earlier stage of American political history. The social welfare function, intervention with officials and bureaucrats on behalf of the poor and ignorant (ignorant, that is, of the ways of the "foreign" bureaucracy), the provision of jobs and other forms of patronage, are vital functions provided by the parties. They were instrumental in helping educate those unfamiliar with the democratic process. Even though vote-buying directly or indirectly through the rendering of goods or services would hardly fit the middle-class image of democratic procedure, this was nevertheless a beginning for the

42

immigrant's involvement in and integration into the national political process. The avenue of social mobility provided by local politics was extremely important in recruiting the present generation of local political leaders who are more solidly rooted in their local constituencies than were many of their predecessors.

These more recent developments present new problems in the relationship between the local and national institutions. Whereas the old local political elites in the development towns had weaker ties with their constituencies, since they usually were from different ethnic groups and were veterans, they generally had close ties with the national parties and institutions. The newer leaders, while more representative of their constituents, tend to have less intimate ties with the national leaders. Cultural differences often reinforce differences of political interests between local and national leaders. In those cases where the national party headquarters has been slow to recognize the changes which have occurred in local power constellations, they have sometimes continued to back the old elite which had already lost control of the local political machinery. There is evidence which indicates that internal party strife within local branches (of the nature just mentioned) has been a major contributing factor to the loss of control of several municipalities by the Labor Party.

Local political positions, particularly in the new towns, have not been an important source of recruitment to positions of national political leadership. That mobility which has taken place into higher party positions has been primarily through cases of patron-client relationships. Therefore those new local leaders who have risen to local positions through "grass-roots" support are tending to assert more autonomy for themselves in local affairs. They have, in several cases, resisted the intervention in local affairs which the national party headquarters have traditionally taken as their prerogative.[16] The recent increase in "split-ticket" voting, that is, voting for a different party locally than nationally, may also be related to this trend towards an assertion of greater local autonomy from the national centers of power.[17] Several recent attempts by regional groupings of new towns, and the association of local councils to form pressure groups through which they can bargain with central party headquarters and the institutions of the central government, indicate another avenue through which local leaders are attempting to assert greater autonomy. However, these trends must be seen in the perspective of enormous economic dependence on the ministries of the government and political dependence on the central party headquarters which has been characteristic of the new towns in Israel.

Given all of the many problems and restrictions it is particularly remarkable to note that the development towns in Israel have made a major contribution toward the integration of new immigrants into Israeli society. The local political system in these new towns has provided one of the most effective and rapid avenues of social mobility, and has proven to be more responsive to social change than has the national system. In the long run the strength of Israeli democracy may be tested by the ability of the national political parties to respond to the innovations, pressures and demands which are being articulated from the grass roots, particularly in the development towns. Credit for the outstanding achievements of the development towns should go to a large extent to the unsung heroes, the "reluctant pioneers," who settled and developed them. In their struggle for resources, recognition and political representation, they have learned the game of democratic party politics, contributed toward their own integration in their new country and instigated innovations and changes in the society and political system which may possibly have long-range repercussions.

NOTES

1. E. Cohen, *The City in Zionist Ideology* (Jerusalem: The Institute of Urban and Regional Studies, Hebrew University, 1970).

2. D. Weintraub, M. Lissak, and Y. Azmon, *Moshava, Kibbutz and Moshav* (Ithaca: Cornell University Press, 1969).

3. M. Aronoff, "Party Center and Local Branch Relations: The Israel Labour Party," in *The Elections in Israel—1969*, ed. A. Arian (Jerusalem: Jerusalem Academic Press, 1972).

4. E. Baldwin, *Differentiation and Cooperation in an Israeli Veteran Moshav* (Manchester: Manchester University Press, 1971); M. Shokeid, *The Dual Heritage* (Manchester: Manchester University Press, 1971); A Weingrad, *The Reluctant Pioneers* (Ithaca: Cornell University Press, 1966).

5. E. Spiegel, *New Towns in Israel* (Stuttgart/Bern: Karl Kramer Verlag, 1966).

6. E. Cohen, "Development Towns—The Social Dynamics of 'Planted' Urban Communities in Israel" in *Integration and Development in Israel*, ed. S. Eisenstadt, R. Bar Yosef, and C. Adler (Jerusalem: Israel University Press, 1970). E. Marx, "Some Social Contexts of Personal Violence," in *The Allocation of Responsibility*, ed. Max Gluckman (Manchester: Manchester University Press, 1972).

7. N. Lichfield, *Israel's New Towns: A Strategy for their Future* (Tel Aviv: Israel Ministry of Housing, 1970), p. 3.

8. Cf. Viet-Jean, "Les Villes Nouvelles (New Towns): A Selected Annotated Bibliography" (UNESCO, 1960).

9. Central Office of Information, *The New Towns of Britain* (London: British Information Services, 1969); F. Schaffer, *The New Town Story* (London: McGibbon & Kee Ltd., 1970).

10. E. Spiegel, *New Towns in Israel*, p. 95.

11. From a personal interview with the former director of the Frontier-town planning team.

12. E. Cohen, "Development Towns," p. 589.

13. M. Gluckman, "Inter-Hierarchal Roles: Professional and Party Ethics in Tribal Areas in South and Central Africa: in *Local-level Politics*, ed., M. Swartz (London: University of London Press, 1969).

14. M. Aronoff, *Frontiertown: The Politics of Community Building in Israel* (Manchester: Manchester University Press, 1973).

15. S. Deshen, *Immigrant Voters in Israel* (Manchester: Manchester University Press, 1970).

16. M. Aronoff, "Party Center."

17. A. Arian and S. Weiss, "The Changing Pattern of Split-Ticket Voting," in *The Elections in Israel—1969*, ed. A Arian (Jerusalem: Jerusalem Academic Press, 1972).

4

Ralph M. Kramer

URBAN COMMUNITY
DEVELOPMENT IN ISRAEL

Israel is not usually perceived as an urbanized society, yet 80 percent of its population now live in cities and towns, and even before
1948 only about a quarter of its inhabitants resided in rural areas.[1]
One reason that the highly urbanized character of Israel has been
obscured is the anti-city, Zionist ideology of *halutziut*. With its
emphasis on the values of rural society and agricultural labor, this
ideology was and still is a powerful obstacle to a *comprehensive*
national urban policy.[2] However, shortly after the establishment
of the state, out of the dire necessity of coping with an unprece-
dented mass immigration from Afro-Asian countries, a national
urbanization policy was adopted. Its two major goals were population dispersal and immigrant absorption. Dispersal was obviously
important for purposes of defense and assertion of political sovereignty, as well as for several demographic reasons: to limit the
growth of the Tel Aviv area, in which over 40 percent of the
country's population resided, and to fill in the urban hierarchy by
creating intermediate-sized towns.[3]

Portions of this chapter are summarized from the author's *Urban Community
Development in Israel and the Netherlands* (Berkeley, Calif.: University of
California, Institute of International Studies, 1970). Different versions have
appeared in the *Journal of Jewish Communal Service, Public Administration
in Israel and Abroad,* and as a research publication (in Hebrew) by the Paul
Baerwald School of Social Work, Hebrew University, Jerusalem.

The dispersion-of-population policy utilized not only the development towns as a means of providing housing and employment for the new immigrants, but also rural settlements, particularly the more than 150 moshavim which have absorbed about 10 percent of the total increased population in the last 20 years.

The development towns have been described as "planted" or "administered communities" because of the highly centralized, externally imposed and paternalistic style of planning and administration. Conceived as regional, urban service centers in their respective rural areas, the primary emphasis was on settlement, with basic economic goals and social planning secondary.

The policy of induced urbanization resulted in a very rapid filling up of the country, most of it within the first ten years. From a geographic and to a certain extent demographic point of view, the dispersion policy was a success. Thirty new towns were established which contain 18 percent of the 1970 population; the growth of the Tel Aviv area was limited and reduced from 43 to 34 percent of the country's population; the population residing in the three main cities declined from 80 to 55 percent, although this seems to be changing within the last few years. The urban hierarchy was filled in with more intermediate-sized towns and in general, the policy represents a significant accomplishment compared with most other countries.[4]

Yet, many if not most of the towns are neither economically nor socially viable. There is general agreement that there are too many that are too small, and few acquired urban characteristics. or became the regional centers they were meant to be. In part, this resulted because the population dispersal policy conflicted with the socioeconomic requirements of immigrant absorption. Economic development lagged, despite tax benefits, loans and grants, and other financial incentives. The emphasis on spatial and physical development, on moving people as quickly as possible without providing for the economic and social infrastructure, resulted in the exodus of the younger, more upwardly mobile, able and energetic residents, leaving behind those who were much less able to cope with the difficulties in these towns. The overwhelming proportion of the immigrants left their assigned towns despite the fact that they were not eligible for housing or employment assistance in their next community. The record of their exodus is testimony to the fact that people will leave under circumstances which they perceive as unsuitable. For example, 80,000 persons are estimated to have passed through Kiryat Shemona; 50,000 through Beersheba and 100,000 through Eilat. In this way, many of the development towns came to be residual communities. There is relatively little civic identification or citizen participation in most of these towns. Rather, there are extremely high rates of unemployment and public assistance, and few economic and social opportunities for the youth and returning soldiers. The pattern of commuting bureaucrats persists; there are few local leaders and institutions, and this situation has resulted in a low level of social development and integration.[5] Containing mainly poor, Afro-Asian immigrants with large families living in homogeneous ethnic blocs, many development towns have disconcertingly similar characteristics to U.S. black ghettos.

As one of a number of attempts to cope with the staggering array of problems stemming from this process of rapid urbanization without sufficient industrialization and socialization, a form of social aid involving citizen participation and known as *avodah kehilatit* (community work) was established in Israel around 1953. Social welfare and other officials believed that most of the Afro-Asian immigrants who arrived in the 1950s had little commitment to Zionism and that the manner of their resettlement, marked by rapid imposition of European cultural standards, encouraged dependency. Community work was thus intended to provide a means of overcoming dependency, and stimulating a sense of belonging, self-help and group initiative among the new immigrants in 21 of the development towns.

The program has had a modest growth since 1950, slowed by the paucity and turnover of personnel; in 1968 it involved approximately 50 staff persons working in 35 different localities under the auspices of the Ministry of Social Welfare (Saad) and Amidar, the national housing corporation.

In Saad, community work is one of five divisions in the family and community service department. A staff of five social workers set minimum standards for the subsidization of community work in 31 municipalities and provide rather close supervision of the community workers, all but six of whom are employed by local welfare departments. The professional role of the community work division does not extend to Jerusalem, Haifa and Tel Aviv, which have a much more tenuous and autonomous relationship with Saad. Within Saad, however, community work has not been regarded as a major function, since it is one of many welfare services subsidized by the government through 180 local offices. In addition, there are differences within the ministry regarding the appropriate function of community work and whether its coordinative, social planning or direct service aspects should be emphasized. In general, because of its relative newness, ancillary function and somewhat ambiguous character, community work seems to have a rather low status and priority in the organizational hierarchy of Saad.

In Amidar, community work was initiated in the late 1950s largely as a response to the rising tension between Amidar and its tenants, growing out of the restlessness of some of the North African immigrants and dissatisfactions which found violent expression in the Wadi Salib riot in Haifa in 1959. After ten years, the community work staff consisted of 26 workers deployed in 40 neighborhoods in 18 regional districts. A community worker is assigned to the district director along with a neighborhood superintendent who is responsible for building maintenance tasks. There is the same division between professional and administrative supervision as in Saad, but in Amidar, as will shortly be seen, this intraorganizational strain is of greater significance. Just as most of the Saad-subsidized community workers constitute an arm of the local public assistance system and its service programs, so the Amidar workers can also be conceived as "functional bureaucrats," [6] serving as agents of a paragovernmental corporation concerned with property management and whose professional task is regarded by their sponsor as educating tenants. These generalizations and the others that follow are derived from a case study of community work practice in Israel in 1968. Our primary sources were extended interviews with virtually all (44) of the community workers employed by Saad and Amidar in the cities and towns; nine mayors and four local welfare directors; 11 members of Histadrut neighborhood staff and over 60 key informants, including community and social workers, government officials and social scientists. Rural community development was not within the scope of this survey.

The 44 community workers interviewed in 1968 had a median age of 30. Two thirds of them had lived in Israel for 18 years or more. All but nine were married and had at least one child; 18 of the community workers, or 43 percent, were women. Almost half had some college education, and one third had graduated from college. About one fourth, mainly Saad staff, had completed some form of professional education for social work, and approximately 20 percent had some other form of professional education, usually teaching. Apart from some in-service training, only seven of the staff members had any professional education for group or community work, since this had not been available in Israel until recently.

Most of the community workers (18) were of European origin, with the remainder divided equally between those born in Israel or in an Afro-Asian country. The Saad staff tended to be slightly younger with proportionately more women (11 out of 24), Middle Easterners and sabras, while over half of the Amidar staff were of European descent, and most had some college education. There were twice as many men as women on the Amidar staff. Community workers born in the Middle East were more likely to be found in development towns; European and Israeli-born workers in the cities. Women were also more frequently found in the development towns rather than in the cities.[7]

The character of urban community work in Israel can be viewed in terms of its goals, issues and methods, outcomes and constraints. Within its institutional context in Israel, community work may appear somewhat out of place because its values, goals and methods do not seem to be congruent with the larger power structure within which it functions. For example, arrayed against the highly centralized nature of the government, the political parties and Histadrut, is the localism of community work which takes place in the neighborhoods where people live, but not where power is located. The professionalism of the community worker clashes with the widespread use of political criteria in decision-making; and the highly bureaucratized and paternalistic character of the dominant Israeli institutions contrast with the ideology of community development with its emphasis on self-help and group initiative. Questions can be raised regarding the possibilities for community development under these conditions, that is, the extent to which new, independent, locality-based interest groups can be developed under governmental sponsorship in a stratified society which has centralized decision-making structures but lacks a tradition of grass-roots citizen participation.

GOALS

Four community work goals were identified, two of which were directed at its clientele and two at the bureaucratic organizations which serve them:

1. To stimulate more effective social service delivery and the development of needed programs by prodding the bureaucracies on behalf of neglected groups such as the aged, children and youth.[8]

2. To bring different ethnic and religious groups together to improve their social relationships and to develop citizen participation.
3. To educate immigrants to modify socially undesirable living habits and to accept such values as cleanliness, respect for and maintenance of property, and volunteer participation.
4. To convene local agencies to encourage better communication and coordination.

In addition, there was a fifth goal found only in Jerusalem, in which community work sought to become more of a nonpartisan political force through various forms of social action.

These objectives are concerned with acculturation, involving processes of adult socialization, social brokerage and social planning, each of which is stressed differently by the Amidar and the Saad community workers. They express the mandate of community work, which includes the development of better citizens, clients or tenants, and improved social services. This involves getting other bureaucracies to function more efficiently and effectively by getting them to do what they are supposed to do, although not necessarily anything different. As expressed by one community worker: "Because I represent an agency I can't oppose another agency. The political structure here does not allow the community worker to be aggressive toward agencies." Reinforced by the diverse cultural backgrounds and relatively disadvantaged conditions of its clientele, the objective and style of community work tends to be more in the direction of social control and system maintenance rather than social change. Some evidence for this focus is found in the belief of many community workers that one of their underlying purposes is to "cool out" possibly troublesome population groups, discouraging protest by blunting the edges of controversy and minimizing the possibility of conflict.[9] Some support for this point of view can be found in the early history of community work, in which priority was given to the development towns by the Ministry of Social Welfare in its concern for helping the immigrant-settlers express themselves in more "constructive" ways than in the increasingly disruptive forms of protest which occurred toward the end of the 1950s. This was similar to the decision of Amidar to inaugurate community work following a growing deterioration in tenant relations at about the same time.

While the official goals of community work in Israel are compatible with the professional ideology of community development, with its emphasis on citizen participation, almost half of the

Amidar workers experience some conflict between professional and bureaucratic goals. Most of the Amidar staff believe that they have been quite successful in getting goals accepted which are much broader than the narrow problems of *shikun* (housing development) maintenance which are usually of such importance to the district managers. As one of them put it: "I don't think people understand the complete meaning of community work when they try to narrow it down to the problems of Amidar alone." A similar point of view is expressed by another worker: "I wanted to see immediate results in my work concerning the housing situation. I worked for a year and realized that it was impossible to be concerned just with housing because it included many problems. I finally achieved success in establishing some youth clubs." The staff prefers to take cues from client-expressed needs and "work with people where they are." Because most of the Amidar community workers do not want merely to be agents of the landlord, they may find themselves in conflict with their sponsor, which promotes buying rather than renting flats, encourages people to remain in development towns rather than move to the cities, and urges Afro-Asian immigrants to "westernize." In these situations, the community worker sometimes experiences role conflict as to whether his primary loyalty is to Amidar or the family he works with.

Yet, the overall impression that emerges from this study of community workers is that they are good "organization men," most of whom identify strongly with the goals of their sponsor, who regard their mandate as broad, ambiguous but functional, and who perceive their agency as a good or better than average place to work. Since organization theory might lead us to expect more conflict between professionals and the bureaucracies for whom they work,[10] how might one account for the evidence of the relatively little strain between community workers and their sponsors? Some community workers explain this in terms of the mutual interest and shared national values in Israel: "In general, I think that we in Israel tend more than in other countries to identify strongly with the values, goals and policies of the sponsor because we see in them the expression of national values and goals. These are very important and unifying factors in the light of our situation and our steady on-going war for survival." Other explanations might be the following:

1. While the community workers may regard themselves as professionals, almost all of them are untrained and subject

to rather close supervision by their agency. The diversity of their backgrounds, the lack of opportunities for professional education and their very recent, somewhat precarious legitimation could account for a low order of professionalism which would not clash with bureaucratic claims.

2. Another possibility is that apart from political involvement, there are few actual restrictions on their activities. Conflict does not arise because the community workers have considerable autonomy, so there is little reason to chafe under organizational constraints.

3. There is also considerable congruence between the professional ideology of community development and the values and interests of the sponsors. Both sanction only consensual educational methods and the avoidance of conflict. As a result of the issues selected and strategies employed, there is a strong predisposition to minimize any possible strain between the bureaucracy and the professionals it employs.

ISSUES AND METHODS

The goals of community work generate the issues around which people are organized. Analysis of "a recent characteristic project" described by the community workers reveals a wide range of activities with considerable differences between those sponsored by Saad and by Amidar. Substantively, the most frequently reported project of the Amidar staff was the organization of a house committee with primary concern for maintenance problems in the shikun such as cleanliness, garbage collection and payment of utilities. These committees, whether organized on a block or a neighborhood basis, were also regarded by the staff as a potential means of obtaining other benefits such as community centers, playgrounds, language classes, and a means of dealing with the special problems of children and youth.

While the Amidar community workers were typically involved with the creation of a new neighborhood-based tenant association, i.e., an organizational structure, the most frequently reported activities of Saad's staff were the establishment of a new facility or program such as a community center or a new social service such as meals-on-wheels for the elderly. Other typical projects carried out by *ad hoc* citizen groups were those concerned with preventing school dropouts or delinquency, or establishing recreational or cultural programs. Almost all of the projects involved tangible amenities and housekeeping matters which were usually noncontroversial, and constituted small-scale improvements within a narrowly circumscribed geographic area.

Where did these issues come from? Who defined them as the problem to be worked on or the condition to be changed? Most of the issues seem to be based on, or at least are congruent with needs as defined by Amidar or Saad, who have special interests in property management and social service program development.[11] At the very least, it is not coincidental that the community "needs" discovered and the issues selected by the community workers are congruent with their sponsor's definition of need. At the same time, this does not mean that some of these needs were not felt by some of the residents or that these issues were imposed by external agents. Because the range of "felt needs" is very great in these relatively deprived population groups which lack many amenities, practically any tangible improvement can be regarded as meeting a need.[12] One could safely say, however, that contrary to the expectations of community development theory, many of the needs identified by the community workers may not have been very clearly articulated or at least not given the same priority by their clientele. The difference in priorities is suggested by the fact that community workers frequently complained about the difficulties of sustaining participation after the house committee has been elected or the community center established. It is possible that if these projects were more firmly rooted in the wishes of the residents, there might be stronger incentives for them to participate. The dominant role of the bureaucratic sponsor in affecting the perceptions of community needs and priorities is further suggested by the propensity of the staff to define as "community problems" those on which they are working rather than the grave economic and housing conditions which prevail in these communities. The content of the issues selected is also explained by the localism of the community workers, a factor to be noted later.

The sponsors of community work, more than the clientele, influence not only the issues but also the locus of the subcommunity to be organized. This is particularly evident in Amidar, where the district superintendent usually decides which neighborhood and *shikunim* should be singled out for attention, and where the primary determinant seems to be the type of complaint or desired changes in tenant behavior. As one district superintendent expressed his expectations of community work: "more cleanliness and fewer problems." Similarly for the Saad workers, the selection of their functional community and the identification of which community conditions will be defined as problematic is shaped by the social service interests of their sponsor in specific groups, such as the aged or youth. Thus, in carrying out its mission, community work, despite its ideology of citizen participation, serves more as a means by which bureaucratic goals can be achieved than as a process for the development of collaborative competence as prescribed by community development theory. The confusion between agency-community relations and community development—between administrative involvement and substantive participation—is not unique to Israel.[13] Rather, the role of the sponsor in shaping the character of community work has generally been overlooked and obscured by an idealized model which presupposes congruence between the interests and perceptions of sponsor, professionals and their clientele.

In addition to the sponsor, another major determinant of community work is the professionals and their style of intervention. Although they say they want to work with client-expressed needs, they seem to function much more in an assertive, unilateral manner as they deliberately pursue predetermined goals and select appropriate issues and committee members. In actual practice staff members, particularly those working for Saad, do not always rely on committees to identify problems and to plan solutions. Instead, the community worker usually takes the initiative in introducing the need for a project and then tries to secure the consent of the residents. Many work alone in the early stages and do not seem encumbered by organizational structure. As one worker put it: "Afterwards I invite the committee, involve them and they do the rest." One gets the impression that the community worker, like his sponsor, knows what is good for his clientele and uses his efforts to mobilize support for these short-term projects. It may well be, however, that the failures to develop indigenous leadership, and the lack of continuing participation of which the workers complain, may be related to this somewhat paternalistic and episodic mode of operation, which is also characteristic of many community development programs in other countries.

CONSTRAINTS ON COMMUNITY WORK

From the staff point of view, however, there were two major sets of constraints which affect the character and outcome of community work, and which can be summed up in the concepts of "civic culture" [14] and "bureau pathology." The first refers to certain sociocultural attributes of the clientele in the political context of public decision-making. Among the chief obstacles consistently cited by the staff was the apathetic and dependent character of the people they try to organize, a reflection, in part, of the traditionalist orientation particularly prevalent among the immigrants from Arab countries. As a matter of fact, one of the important educational functions which community workers perform is helping their clientele learn how to organize and request services.

It is not only the clientele's lack of familiarity with citizen participation that impedes community work; there also is a basic conflict between the norms of the Israeli form of democratic centralism and the grass-roots values of participatory democracy assumed in the professional ideology of community development. The latter seeks to maximize consensus, harmony, unity of interests, collaboration of diverse groups for the common good, the denigration of conflict, factionalism and power struggles—in short, politics is viewed as "dirty business." [15] For example, the survey found, among virtually all respondents, invidious attitudes toward politics, a lack of acquaintance and an extremely low degree of interaction with the local political system and its leadership structure. Almost half of the community workers did not even know who the political leaders in the community were, and most of them regarded political parties as "not constructive" and not particularly relevant for their work.[16] Accordingly, it is not surprising to see how the community workers tend to avoid political issues; about one out of four asserted that they try to stifle discussion of any political issues at their meetings. In view of the highly politicized nature of Israeli society, this removal from political issues and the party system means that community work removes itself from most of the forces that directly affect the life of its clientele. An important exception, however, was found in Jerusalem where, in a most inhospitable organizational environment, community workers have had some success in handling controversial issues affecting schools, medical care and delinquents. At the same time, it should be noted that political questions in Israel are not usually defined in terms appropriate for independent local citizen action, since the Israeli party system relies on national party responsibility with little accountability or even responsiveness to local constituencies.[17] Thus, structurally and functionally there are sharp contrasts between the Israeli civic culture and the apolitical nature of community work. The latter may reflect an idealized version of distinctive American patterns of political socialization and volunteer participation which may not be applicable in Israel.

The factor mentioned most frequently as militating against community work was "bureau pathology," the unresponsiveness, disinterest and often negative attitudes of the bureaucracy towards people, as well as lack of staff and funds. In general, the Amidar workers were more critical of the governmental agencies and complained of red tape, inflexibility, lack of communication, coordination, poor judgment, mistakes and failures to keep promises.[18] As one worker described it: "The agencies just don't see the problems of the community. There is no consideration given to the desires of the residents. The agency knows better—it decides. It built the town, therefore it has first rights." The dominant methods for coping with bureaucratic recalcitrance are essentially educational, whereby the workers try to persuade, inform and interpret on behalf of their clientele. The community workers are aware that they have little leverage with the staff members of the other bureaucracies, but they persist, nevertheless, Amidar staff more than Saad, in trying to perform social broker roles between their clientele and the institutional systems.

Other methods used by the community workers to deal with the bureaucracies occasionally include the organization of a client group to bring pressure on an agency, and sporadic, usually unsuccessful attempts to establish an interagency committee.[19] The lack of communication and coordination among agencies is a perennial complaint in all countries, but in Israel the conventional obstacles to collaboration are complicated by the politicization of interorganizational relationships in a highly centralized structure. As local community workers, the Saad and Amidar staffs have very weak linkages to the decision-making structures in housing, education, social welfare, health, medical care and employment. With few channels of communication upward to the central offices of these bureaucracies, community workers must rely on the very limited influence they may have on the local staff functionaries who generally view them as representatives of just another agency. The localism of the community worker is also significant since most of the serious problems such as inequalities in income, housing and education, in addition to the overriding problems of defense and the economy, are not defined in terms amenable to community work. These major social conditions are regarded as national problems reserved for action by the central government and the other politicized bureaucracies such as Histadrut and the Jewish Agency, and not by means of local citizen participation. The lack of sanction for the type of nonpartisan interest groups that some community workers try to promote, along with conflict-avoidance, suggests that community work cannot and is not expected to have much of an impact on major community problems. As a result, while community work may be useful in getting a play lot or bus stop and in helping tenants deal with problems such as garbage collection (or even establishing a community center if funds are available), it will probably be much less effective in dealing with more substantial needs and controversial issues which would inevitably involve the government or Histadrut. As one worker put it: "Instead of doing something about the real needs for better bus transportation and fighting *Egged* [the bus corporation], we try to promote language classes."

Understandably, community workers are quite sensitive to the charge that they are concerned with marginal issues, and they justify their choice of problem area on several contradictory grounds. It is either argued that the type of issue chosen is unimportant because the main purpose of community work is to initiate a sociotherapeutic process which has intrinsic value; or that the issue is just a starting point, a means to an end. Sometimes it is claimed that the community worker performs an important educational function by heightening awareness and raising questions as a first step toward change. In this sense, it represents a constructive alternative to apathy and dependence, as well as to hostility and conflict. Others assert that the cultural barriers to participation, the professional ideology, the locus and status of community work within centralized, politicized bureaucracies and the specialized interests of its two governmental sponsors all serve to limit significantly the effort to develop autonomous self-help groups that can change the living conditions and increase the social competence of clients. Each of these beliefs deserves testing and careful evaluation since they are related to various judgments which have been made regarding the future role of community work.

THE FUTURE OF COMMUNITY WORK

Five alternatives views were found:

1. There are those who say that it is either too late or too soon for community work to be any different. Perhaps community work might have had a more substantial impact in the early sixties, but now the number of workers is small and most of them lack professional training.
2. Others, particularly some of the social scientists, argue against continuing support of community work on the grounds that it is hopelessly "foreign" to Israeli society because of its belief in local participation outside the political party structure as a means of change.
3. Still others see it as a useful instrument for all governmental bureaucracies who might employ community workers as agents between themselves and their clientele.
4. Another perspective sees community work as a social planning function on a local, regional and national level sponsored by the government, but involving other institutions. A small-scale demonstration of this view is currently being planned in Or-Yehuda.[20]
5. Finally, there is a more politicized version of community work advocated, whereby it would enter the public decision-making arena and establish formal and informal relationships with political parties by developing independent citizen associations.

Any predictions regarding the future of community work are influenced by an assessment of political and social trends in Israel, as well as a conception of the capabilities of community work. One of the critical elements determining the degree to which locality-based interest groups are feasible is the likelihood of more power devolving to the local community which would give residents more of a sense of local identification. This might result from the evolution of a more open, responsive political system, a lessening of the emphasis on ideology and an increase in the actual authority of local communities. Also, as more Israeli citizens become middle class, educated and politically sophisticated, despite the relative absence of community service and pressure groups in the past, increased desires and opportunities for citizen participation can be anticipated. Another impetus will come from the continuing need for various forms of social brokerage, advocacy and community development, particularly in the development towns and low-income neighborhoods in the cities, if they are to avoid the fate of residual communities similar to the "trap ghettos" of the United States with their concentration of poor people excluded from the mainstream. Under the best of circumstances, however, the role of community development in helping narrow the gap between "the two Israels" is extremely limited, since it is no substitute for comprehensive, long-range programs aimed at eliminating relative deprivation and increasing social mobility. Community work as presently sanctioned, structured and supported, however, seems to have a low capability of either playing a more effective political role or becoming a more assertive social broker for a disadvantaged clientele. The Saad and Amidar staffs are small in number, their mandate and locus too limited for an enlarged scope of operation. As a relatively new program operating outside the dominant decision-making system with low status and power, and with no long-range plans for expansion, community work will probably maintain its present character, becoming more institutionalized and bureaucratized within Saad and Amidar, maintaining its resemblance to group work and agency-community relations rather than to community development.

Under somewhat different circumstances and with additional sponsors, it is possible to conceive of an enhanced program of community work which could help people move into more participation in the political and other established structures, as well as create some new local, regional and national organizations for citizen action. These nonpartisan citizen associations could be concerned with social service issues such as improved education, medical care, housing and recreation. Conceivably, they might bring pressures to bear on the bureaucracies and, in addition, on the political parties, who might even compete for their support. At the same time, it should be recognized that these forms of social action might pit haves against have-nots and immigrants against veteran settlers and be a highly divisive force, further straining the delicate social fabric. From this perspective, the nonpolitical role of community work may be quite appropriate in Israel. Yet, on the other hand, if there are grievances and inequities it might be more socially desirable to provide for some institutionalized expressions of collective action rather than to ignore or suppress these problems, even though there is always the possibility of increasing frustration because community work might be unable to influence sufficiently the resource and decision-making systems. In any case, if community work is to be-

come more influential and more of a force for both social integration and change, it will have to become more political and not limit
itself to noncontroversial issues and collaborative and educational
methods. It is highly questionable whether more versatile political
methods and conflict strategies can be promoted under governmental auspices; [21] consequently, different sponsors who could sanction and tolerate more diverse and assertive forms of community
work, as well as specially qualified staff would be required. Alternative nongovernmental sponsors of community work who would
permit the use of a wider range of issues and methods might come
from ethnic, fraternal and civic associations, voluntary social service
agencies, the universities and their four schools of social work, etc.
Other groups that might be organized for civic action and sponsorship are the slowly increasing number of voluntary community
service clubs and associations whose energies could be directed at
both local and national projects. Different types of sponsors could
promote different forms of community work; for example, social
planning might be promoted as part of a demonstration project or
by the Ministry of the Interior. The schools of social work have
rather wide latitude in developing educational programs and could
create a training center which could send its students to staff a
broad range of groups in the country. These forms of locality-based
citizen action constitute only one part of what should be a two-
pronged effort, the other consisting of the strengthening of the
social planning function. While it would be presumptuous to specify
the details of such a structure without additional study, it is evident that social planning is a neglected aspect of community work
and deserves considerably more attention.

The future potential for urban community work in Israel, then,
lies in the possibility of greater diversity in sponsors and modes of
practice so that it would not be confined primarily to governmen-
tally sponsored work with neighborhood groups; it would also
include some forms of social planning and community action under
a variety of auspices.

The future role of community work in Israel also raises questions
about the emphasis on citizen participation in social planning rather
than the design and implementation of policies of income redistribution and institutional change. While it could be argued that efforts
to promote citizen participation are diversionary, there is no dis-
agreement that community work is no substitute for national policies that might reduce relative deprivation and increase social
mobility. The role of community work in relation to such social

policies is a rather modest one expressed through the promotion of citizen education, widening the base of civic awareness, pressing for public discussion of social issues, proposing alternative policies, and encouraging participants to join political organizations. In addition, it can press for improved social service delivery and amenities in the local community, but it is clear that these citizen efforts cannot be effective without the parallel development of appropriate economic and urban development policies.

NOTES

1. Alexander Berler, *New Towns in Israel* (Jerusalem: Israel University Press, 1970) pp. 6-10. This is now the most complete source of data in English on the development towns.

2. Eric Cohen, *The City in the Zionist Ideology* (Jerusalem: Institute of Urban and Regional Studies, Hebrew University, 1970).

3. Arie S. Shachar, "Israel's Development Towns: Evaluation of National Urbanization Policy," *Journal of American Institute of Planners*, 37 (November 1971) 6: 362-72.

4. Ibid.

5. Berler, *New Towns in Israel*, pp. 140-51. See also Shimon Gottschalk, "Citizen Participation in the Development of New Towns; A Cross-National View," *Social Service Review*, 45 (June 1971) 2: 194-204.

6. The concept of "functional bureaucrat" is derived from Leonard Reissman, "A Study of Role Conceptions in Bureaucracy," *Social Forces*, 27 (March 1949) 3: 305-10, and refers to bureaucrats who are more oriented to a professional group outside their agency than to the agency itself.

7. Additional data regarding the community workers and some of the findings of the survey are in the Hebrew publication *Seker Ovdim Kehilatim B'Yissrael* (Jerusalem: Keren Giora Yoseftal, 1969). This monograph also contains the interview schedule and instructions.

8. As one community worker put it: "To try to educate them to understand the need for organization in order to change the looks of the *shikun* . . . to teach them that you can't receive without paying, and to explain how one must behave."

9. This use of community organization by bureaucracies as a means of exerting control over their clientele and producing "political desocialization" is perceptively analyzed by Richard A. Cloward and Frances Piven, "The Professional Bureaucracies: Benefit Systems as Influence Systems," in *Readings in Community Organization, Practice*, Ralph M. Kramer and Harry Specht, eds. (Englewood Cliffs, N.J.: Prentice-Hall, 1969) pp. 359-71. See also Eliot A. Krause, "Functions of a Bureaucratic Ideology: Citizen Participation," *Social Problems*, 16 (Fall 1968) 3: 129-43.

10. While there is a voluminous literature on this subject, there are rela-

tively few studies dealing with social or community workers, perhaps because their professional status is not always fully legitimated. A definitive paper is W. Richard Scott, "Professional in Bureaucracies—Areas of Conflict" in *Professionalization*, Howard M. Vollmer and Donald L. Mills, eds., (Englewood Cliffs, N.J.: Prentice-Hall, 1966) pp. 265-75. The relationship between social workers and the bureaucracies that employ them is analyzed in Peter M. Blau and W. Richard Scott, *Formal Organizations* (San Francisco: Chandler, 1962); Andrew Billingsley, "Bureaucratic and Professional Orientation Patterns in Social Casework," *Social Service Review*, 38 (December 1964) 4: 400-7; and R. Bar-Yosef and E. O. Schild, "Pressures and Defenses in Bureaucratic Roles," *The American Journal of Sociology* 61 (May 1966) 6: 665-73.

11. Community work goals can be conceptualized as the product of an interaction between the interests of the organization, the worker and the clientele. What is being asserted here is that the goals and needs of the sponsoring organization and the community workers seem to be more determining than those of the clientele. This finding contrasts with the usual neglect of the role of the sponsor in most of the literature on community development. For example, the sponsor's role as it may affect the personal image of the community development agent is regarded as "least significant" in Arthur H. Niehoff, ed., *A Case Book of Social Change* (Chicago: Aldine, 1966) p. 15. A more realistic evaluation is that of Lloyd Ohlin: "In organizing the unorganized, the interests of the sponsoring organization determine selection of participants, form of organization, specification of objectives and control of activities . . ." ("Urban Community Development" in Kramer and Specht, *Readings in Community Organization, Practice*, p. 246).

12. A typical survey of needs and proposed projects for a development town is contained in Joseph Hodara, "Patterns of Action for a Demonstration Program in Beth Shemesh and Netivot" (Jerusalem: Henrietta Szold Institute, National Institute for Research and Behavioral Sciences, 1967). The results of two years' work are summarized by Dov Ancona, "The Beth Shemesh and Netivot Demonstration Project as a Local Enterprise and as a Pilot Project" (Jerusalem, 1969).

13. The distinction between administrative involvement and substantive participation is found in Philip Selznick, *TVA and the Grass Roots: A Study in the Sociology of Formal Organization* (New York: Harper and Row, 1966) pp. 220-1. The latter concept involves an actual role in policy-making; the former refers to a process in which unorganized citizens are transformed into a reliable instrument for the achievement of administrative goals, under a halo of democracy.

14. The usage here is somewhat modified from the original concept found in Gabriel A. Almond and Sidney Verba, *The Civic Culture: Political Attitudes and Democracy in Five Nations* (Boston: Little, Brown, 1965) pp. 1-35.

15. These are among the implicit assumptions of the community development literature as evidenced in such works as Murray G. Ross (with B. W. Lappin), *Community Organization: Theory, Principles and Practice*, 2nd ed. (New York: Harper and Row, 1967); Ward Hunt Goodenough, *Cooperation in Change* (New York: John Wiley, 1966); William W. Biddle and Louride J. Biddle, *The Community Development Process* (New York:

Holt, Rinehart and Winston, 1965); T. R. Batten, *Communities and Their Development* (London: Oxford University Press, 1964); Peter de Sautoy, *The Organization of a Community Development Program* (London: Oxford University Press, 1962).

16. These attitudes are, however, not peculiar to community workers, since politics is often identified with the older generation of leaders, and community workers share the negative opinions of many persons under 50 about Israeli politics.

17. The relative unimportance of local politics and issues is perceptively analyzed in Alex Weingrod, *Israel: Group Relations in a New Society* (London: Pall Mall Press, 1965) pp. 62-5. A scholarly treatment of this subject is found in Szesach Weiss, "Local Government in Israel: A Study of its Leadership" (Ph.D. diss., Hebrew University of Jerusalem, 1968).

18. A perceptive analysis of bureaucracies in Israel is contained in Gerald E. Caiden, "Israeli Administration after Twenty Years," *Public Administration in Israel and Abroad, 1967*, No. 8, Jerusalem, 1968. Also see his monograph, *Israel's Administrative Culture* (Berkeley, Calif.: University of California Institute of Governmental Studies). Also useful is Yehezkel Dror, "Nine Main Characteristics of Governmental Administration in Israel," *Public Administration in Israel and Abroad, 1964*, No. 5, Jerusalem, 1965, pp. 6-17, and Benjamin Akzin and Yehezkel Dror, *Israel: High Pressure Planning* (Syracuse, N.Y.: Syracuse University Press, 1966). A useful historical and sociological analysis of Israeli political structure and institutions in English is found in S. N. Eisenstadt, *Israeli Society* (New York: Basic Books, 1967). A more formalized account is Oscar Kraines, *Government and Politics in Israel* (Boston: Houghton Mifflin, 1961). An earlier, but more comprehensive and definitive work is Marver H. Bernstein, *The Politics of Israel: The First Decade of Statehood* (Princeton, N.J.: Princeton University Press, 1957).

19. There are at least three types of local coordinating structures in Israel: (1) the *Vaadot Saad*, welfare advisory committees; (2) *Mercaz Kehilati*, a community council, primarily in the development towns; (3) *Vaadot Kehilati Yot*, coordinating committees similar to a council of social agencies. In addition, there are numerous ad hoc, functional coordinating committees concerned with the aged or the prevention of juvenile delinquency, but their effectiveness appears to be quite limited.

20. "Proposal for a Social Planning Service in Or-Yehuda," by Ephraim Eliezri and Meyer Schwartz, Jerusalem, August 7, 1969 (restricted communication). The project is sponsored by the United Nations Office of Technical Cooperation and the Directors-General of the Government of Israel.

21. Ralph M. Kramer, *Participation of the Poor: Comparative Community Case Studies in the War on Poverty* (Englewood Cliffs, N.J.: Prentice-Hall, 1969) pp. 262-65.

5

Zvi Gitelman

THE ABSORPTION

OF SOVIET IMMIGRANTS

Before the immigration into Israel assumed mass proportions, there does not seem to have been a consistent, centrally coordinated Soviet emigration policy. The belief was widespread among Soviet Jews that most emigration decisions were made by officials on the provincial and republic levels, rather than in Moscow, and that officials in the Baltic states were more receptive to the idea of Jewish emigration than those in other parts of the country. It was felt that these officials welcomed Jewish emigration, for the departure of Jews lessened the Russian influence in these republics—since most Jews in the Baltic areas preferred acculturation into the Russian rather than the native culture—and also desirable positions and apartments became available to people of the local nationality.

It is difficult to judge the validity of this belief, but it is clear that by 1970-1971 Soviet emigration policy was being formulated on an all-Union level. Judging from the numbers and types of people arriving in Israel—and such a judgment is impressionistic, since the Israeli government has classified the relevant data—it seems that Soviet emigration policy is a selective one.

Reprinted with the permission of the Institute for Jewish Policy Planning Research of the Synagogue Council of America.

Year	Number*
Up to 1964	4,667
1965	750
1966	1,613
1967	1,109
1968	–
1969	2,100
1970	1,000
1971	13,905

*Figures for 1970-1971 are drawn from press reports; previous years from Kosygin's Ottawa speech.

There is no doubt that the great majority of immigrants to Israel come from the peripheries of the Soviet Union—from Latvia, Lithuania, Moldavia and Georgia. The first three are areas which were incorporated into the Soviet Union as recently as 1940, and both the general and Jewish populations in these areas are not as well socialized into the Soviet political and economic systems as those populations living under Soviet rule since 1917. Moreover, the Jews in these "Western" areas lived in thriving Jewish communities until World War II and are therefore much closer to Jewish tradition and culture than Jews in the central areas of the Soviet Union. It is not surprising that the movement to reassert Jewish consciousness and to demand the right to emigrate began in the Baltic states and then spread to other Soviet territories.

The Georgian Jews, though living in an area which has been under Soviet rule since 1921, also differ from Jews in Byelorussia, the Ukraine or the Russian Republic, in that they have managed to preserve their national identity and, especially, their religious faith and practice, to a far greater extent than other Jews in the Soviet Union. Thus, both geographically as well as sociologically they can be considered peripheral.

There are several reasons why the Soviet government has made it easier for Jews from these peripheral areas to leave. First, a higher proportion of people in these areas are demanding permission to emigrate. Second, they are considered less reliable and desirable politically, and because they can also "infect" others with their Zionist ideas it is thought best to get rid of them. Third, there is a higher percentage of nonintelligentsia among Jews from these areas than there is among Jews from, say, Moscow or Leningrad, and so they make a less important contribution to the Soviet economy. Among Georgian Jews the percentage of sales personnel, small craftsmen, workers and petty officials seems especially high, which makes these residents more expendable than engineers, scientists and other members of the intelligentsia. It is estimated that in 1968 nearly the entire emigration to Israel came from the Baltic states, and that the Balts and those from Bessarabia-Bukovina continue to be overrepresented as a proportion of Soviet Jews leaving for Israel. It has also been estimated that Georgian Jews, who also rank among the most militant fighters for emigration, constituted 40 percent of the 1971 emigration.

ABSORBING THE IMMIGRANTS: INSTITUTIONAL SETTING

The Jewish population of the state of Israel was 650,000 in 1948, the first year of the state's existence. Since that time over 1,300,000 Jews have immigrated to Israel. About half of the first wave of post-1948 immigration consisted of displaced persons from the European camps, with the other half being refugees from Arab lands. Between 1952 and 1956 a second large wave arrived, the great majority being people from Asia and Africa. With the limited resources at the young state's disposal, and the pressures of defense and economics forcing a very tight economic policy, many of these immigrants were housed in large temporary tent camps or in shacks (ma'abarot) where conditions were, of course, rather primitive.

Immigration declined at the end of the 1950s and the beginning of the 1960s, and fell to new lows when an economic recession hit Israel in 1965-1966. After the 1967 Six Day War immigration once again began to reach 20,000 and 30,000 a year, and the character of the immigration changed as well. For the first time, a relatively large proportion of the immigrants was coming from Western Europe and North America, and was coming not as refugees who were "pushed" to leave their home countries but as immigrants who were "pulled" to Israel. Of the 100,000 immigrants who came between June 1967 and June 1970, 18,500 were from North America and 33,000 from Europe. In 1971 almost 10,000 more came from the United States.

The recent immigration differs from previous movements in its participants' age structure and educational and occupational distribution. By and large, the recent immigrants are younger, better educated and more concentrated in the professions than were the immigrants of the first two decades of the state. In 1970, for example, 34 percent of the immigrants were 19 years old or younger; 46 percent were between 20 and 49; and only 8 percent were over 65. Fully 43 percent of the 1970 immigrants were classified as professionals or people having higher education (*akademaiim*), whereas such people constituted only 15 percent of the Israeli population as a whole. Finally, in contrast to some of the earlier waves, these immigrants did not come organized in whole communities, but as individuals, and also tended to concentrate in the three main urban areas, though for the most part they did not cluster in ethnic ghettos.

From the 1920s on, the Jewish Agency, a nongovernmental institution, was in charge of organizing immigrants abroad, arranging their transportation and helping them settle. In 1968, after repeated criticism of the agency's inability to handle the new type of immigration, the government established a Ministry of Immigrant Absorption whose function was to coordinate employment, housing and other services for the immigrants. Organization of immigration from abroad and the transitional stage of immigration—the absorption centers, hostels and intensive Hebrew courses (*ulpanim*)—were left in the hands of the Immigration and Absorption Department of the Jewish Agency. Over 200 employees of the agency were transferred to the Absorption Ministry. The demarcation of function and jurisdiction between the Absorption Ministry and the Jewish Agency is sometimes unclear, and most immigrants are confused by the overlapping activity of these two bodies. There is an open rivalry between the two, with the agency, which has a far larger budget than the ministry, and which raises its own funds rather than being dependent on the government's budget, repeatedly calling for the abolition of the Absorption Ministry and the return of all absorption functions to the agency. The Absorption Ministry, whose 1972 proposed budget is lower than that of any other ministry except the Ministry of Development, has relatively little autonomous power of its own: it does not build housing for immigrants, but coordinates housing policy with the Housing Ministry and with private contractors; it does not provide jobs for the immigrants, but works with the Labor Ministry and private employers to direct immigrants to potential work places.

In order to encourage immigration from the developed countries in particular, the government decided a few years ago to grant certain privileges to all immigrants, no matter what their country of origin, so that their presumed decline in living standard would be eased and their assumption of the burdens borne by every Israeli citizen—which include the highest personal income tax rate in the world and a month or more of reserve duty in the army for almost every male between 21 and 55—would be more gradual, and presumably less painful. The most important of these privileges are: lower personal income tax rates for the first three years of residence; the opportunity to import appliances, including automobiles and work tools, as well as household goods, duty-free. (The significance of the right can be seen most dramatically in regard to automobiles: the same Volkswagen that costs $2,000 duty-free costs the Israeli citizen about $5,600); in addition the immigrant receives various types of assistance in finding housing, including rentals-with-option-to-buy on very favorable terms, or mortgages up to 50,000 Israeli pounds at interest at half the rate paid by Israeli citizens. Until recently, these privileges have been granted without regard to the immigrants' financial status. Over the years several instances of abuse of these privileges for the purpose of illegal gain have come to light. As a result of public pressure and resentment of immigrants' privileges, the government has tried to tighten up its administration to prevent abuses, and to see that the wealthy immigrant may not be granted privileges which he could afford to do without.

All immigrants classified as akademaiim are entitled to spend up to six months in an absorption center where they receive intensive daily instruction in Hebrew, so that they can work in their fields in Israel. The assumption is that the factory worker's need to learn the language is not crucial to his successful performance of his duties, and he can begin to work before he attains complete mastery of Hebrew and can then learn the langauge at an evening *ulpan* or by some other means. The professional, on the other hand, must have at least a rudimentary working knowledge of the language before he goes out to work, and so he may stay in an absorption center up to six months. (Many people stay longer, since the apartment they have purchased is not yet ready, or they have not found an apartment, or the low rental at the absorption center makes them less eager to find an apartment.)

There are 16 vocational retraining courses for akademaiim, and there are retraining courses for nonprofessionals as well. The Labor Ministry and Histadrut have representatives in the absorption centers and in all localities who try to place immigrants in jobs. At present there is a shortage of manpower in the Israeli economy, and it is not surprising that a survey commissioned by the Absorption Ministry found that within one year of their arrival, 90 percent of the 1970 immigrants had found employment. Naturally, there are many problems in this area, and those specific to Soviet immigrants will be discussed later, but in general the Israeli economy is capable of absorbing the immigration, though some professions—engineering and medicine, for example—are more in demand than others (law, teaching).

ABSORBING THE IMMIGRANTS: SOCIAL AND POLITICAL INTEGRATION

In the past, the political parties played a major role in the political socialization and social absorption of the immigrants. There seems to have been a general agreement among the parties that the new immigrants would be divided up according to relative party strengths and each party would thus receive a quota of immigrants and would try to provide these people with a job, a place to live, a social circle, information about the country, etc. Naturally, each party would also be getting a quota of potential members and voters. Partly because the state itself was not equipped to undertake all aspects of immigrant absorption, and partly because in pre-state days the parties had played an important role in immigration—the parties sent certificates of immigration to their partisans abroad— the parties assumed many functions which in other systems would be assumed by the civil service. Arriving immigrants were sent to settlements belonging to the various parties according to the general agreement among the parties. In fact, some veteran Israelis say that even the ships bringing in the immigrants, legally or illegally, were divided up according to the "party key." Meyer Weisgal, the veteran Zionist leader and confidant of Chaim Weizmann, recalls in his memoirs his shock when, toward the end of World War II, he witnessed a shipload of European orphans arriving in Palestine and representatives of the parties almost immediately grilling these frightened children about their parents' partisan affiliations, so that the children could be sent to settlements and institutions according to the party key. This feature of what Benjamin Akzin once called *l'etat partitaire* helps to explain the remarkable stability of the partisan distribution in Israel wherein since 1948 the distribution of party strength has remained very much the same in all the national elections, despite the great change in population.

Today the parties cannot play their previous role in relation to the immigrants. For one thing, as in many other spheres of Israeli social and economic life, the state itself has assumed functions previously performed by parties and other nongovernmental bodies. The creation of the Ministry of Absorption in 1968, and the earlier transfer of the labor exchanges to the state, mean that the state now provides services and performs functions previously performed by partisan organizations. Secondly, the immigrants of the 1960s and 1970s are far more sophisticated than those from earlier waves, and are not as easily swayed by partisan appeals. Third, this immigration does not usually come as an organized partisan or ideological group and has no specific ideological commitment regarding the desirable structure of Israeli society and political institutions. Fourth, this immigration, consisting as it does of unaffiliated individuals, cannot be sent en masse to particular settlements or areas where the influence of one or another party is strong. Finally, in a situation of full employment, and where housing is provided by the state itself, there is not much basic aid that the parties can give, in contrast to the emoluments they were able to offer in the 1950s.

Nevertheless, immigrants represent potential voters, and the parties by no means ignore them. Almost all the parties have an absorption department whose self-defined function is to aid in "social integration." Some parties are able to provide small loans, leads to jobs and housing, and aid in navigating the stormy seas of the Israeli bureaucracy. A few parties are more active and attempt to organize social circles into which the immigrants can be inducted, and, working through local party branches, attempt to give immigrants the kind of help any new neighbor might need.

None of the parties seems to have been able to capture the imaginations and loyalties of the Americans who have come, and most of the parties report that the Americans are "naive," uninterested in politics or simply a puzzling group which neither understands Israeli politicians nor is understood by them. Since the American immigration is rather heterogeneous, is scattered about many localities and is an unstable immigration which sometimes shuttles back and forth between the United States and Israel, it is impossible to know how the American immigrants will line up politically in Israel.

Israeli politicians see the Soviet immigration as a much more promising furrow to plow. While some parties—the Liberals, and, perhaps surprisingly, the Israeli Communist Party (MAKI)—have made no attempt at all to approach the Soviet immigrants, other parties have tried to win the allegiance either of the entire Soviet immigration or of certain segments of it. The Labor Party, the dominant party since 1948, has been somewhat slow to approach the immigrants, but has quietly gone about establishing its presence in key positions. For example, the head of the Labor Party's absorption department works full time with the Union of Soviet Immigrants "in order," in his own words, "to teach the new immigrants how to operate within a democratic system and within the Israeli system in particular." The most widely read Russian language newspaper is clearly sympathetic to the Labor Party and to Histadrut, which is closely identified with that party and is dominated by it. But the Labor Party can afford to adopt a low profile since the immigrant tends to identify it with the state in any case. The Soviet immigrants' personal heroes—Golda Meir, Moshe Dayan, Haim Bar-Lev—are members and leaders of the Labor Party, and in the mind of the immigrant the party and the state are closely connected, perhaps partially as a result of his previous political culture. Within the Labor Party a number of Soviet immigrants have established a formal group, claiming that the Labor Party is not doing enough to win the loyalties of the new immigrants. There are indications that as the national elections draw nearer, the Labor Party will launch a more concerted effort to insure the loyalty of the Soviet immigrants.

The efforts of the main opposition party, Gahal (a coalition of the right-wing Herut and the Liberals), have been more direct and even spectacular. There is a popular, and probably unfounded, assumption that most Soviet immigrants sympathize with the Gahal opposition since this party is anticommunist, nationalistic, antisocialist, and seems to be spearheading the efforts for Soviet Jewry and for its right to emigrate from the Soviet Union. While it is not possible at present to accurately assess the strength of Gahal among the Soviet immigrants, there are some well-known Soviet immigrants prominently identified with Gahal, and the party has placed several of them in its national leadership.

There are several reasons for Gahal's appeal. First, the spiritual father of Herut, Vladimir (Zeev) Zhabotinsky, wrote many brilliant essays in Russian, some of which became widely distributed in the underground Zionist literature (*samizdat*) in the Soviet Union. Some intellectuals among the Soviet immigrants report that they were deeply impressed by these writings, and in some cases it was these essays which first brought them to the Zionist idea. Second, in the Baltic republics of Latvia and Lithuania there was a strong Zionist revisionist (Herut) movement before the war, and there were quite a few survivors of this movement who became the leaders and activists among Soviet Jews demanding national rights and the right to emigrate. Since the movement for emigration began in the Baltic states and then spread to the interior of the Soviet Union, the revisionist stamp was placed on the movement early, though it cannot be said that the movement is homogeneous or has a distinct political coloration. Nevertheless, among the first Jews to arrive in Israel from the Soviet Union in 1969-1970 were some of the revisionist activists. They became active in Gahal and have made intensive efforts to socialize the later arrivals, particularly from the Baltic areas. Third, since in the USSR the Jews felt deprived of national rights and the opportunity for national expression, they are highly sensitive to these issues and see in Gahal a party which places proper emphasis on national rights and self-determination. Many agree with Gahal's contention that under no circumstances should the territories captured in the Six Day War be given up. Gahal also appears to be a more militant and uncompromising fighter for Soviet Jewry than other parties, and this meets with the approval of the immigrants. Fourth, some Soviet immigrants abhor anything that smacks of "socialism," "labor" or "leftism," and they see Gahal as a party strongly opposed to these concepts, which are vaguely identified with the dominant (non-Marxist) Labor Party. It soon becomes clear that the Labor Party's "socialism" has very little in common with the Soviet variety, but some Soviet immigrants have developed a natural aversion to anything which may remind them of the evils they associate with the Soviet system.

It may be that Gahal's appeals will be strongest to the newly arrived immigrant, but as he becomes more familiar with the country and its political system, he will begin to differentiate between the Labor Party's notion of socialism and the Soviet brand, and, more importantly, he will learn that it is the Labor Party, not Gahal, which is the dominant force in Israeli politics and economics, and that the Labor Party is the one with power and patronage to distribute. Gahal's chronic inability to gain power, or even to participate in the government for an extended period, may work to its detriment.

The religious parties have made no serious attempts to vie for the allegiance of the Soviet immigration as a whole, but have concentrated their efforts almost exclusively on the Georgian Jews. Since the Georgians are by and large religious and observant of the traditions, they are a natural audience for the religious parties. Moreover, they are more easily approached than the other Soviet immigrants because they are less sophisticated, live in compact groups in certain areas of the country, and, in contrast to the other immigrants, have a recognized leadership, mainly rabbinical, to which they are devoted. Since the Georgians' unique characteristics have also created special problems, which will be discussed later on, the religious parties have seized the opportunity to turn this to their political advantage.

There are four groups competing for the allegiance of the Georgians: the National Religious Party, a partner in the government coalition; the oppositionist and further right Agudat Yisrael; the smaller and more moderate Poalei Agudat Yisrael; and the Habad (Lubavitcher) Hassidic movement, which is not identified with any party. Since the Habad movement was active in Soviet Georgia and had a major impact on certain Jewish communities there, it has had a strong influence among the Georgian immigrants, establishing Habad housing projects for them and recruiting their children into the Habad educational network. The National Religious Party has attempted to persuade the Georgians to send their children to the state-religious schools, while the Agudat Yisrael tries to enroll them in the independent school network it maintains. On several occasions, the Agudat Yisrael has accused the government, and particularly the Absorption Ministry headed by Natan Peled (of Mapam), of trying to seduce the Georgians away from religious practice, and of failure to provide religious facilities and educational opportunities. When several Georgian porters at Lod airport found themselves obliged to work on the Sabbath, Agudat Yisrael submitted a motion of no confidence in the government, charging that the state of Israel was forcing Georgian immigrants to violate their religious beliefs, something they had managed to avoid doing in the Soviet Union. As a member of the government, the National Religious Party could not support the motion—which was defeated when only the Rakah Communist Party voted with Agudat Yisrael —but the National Religious Party has criticized the government's treatment of the Georgians on several occasions. The religious parties have strongly supported the demand of the Georgians that they be allowed to live in concentrated settlements, as they have done for centuries, and not be scattered across the land. In recent months the government has taken steps to insure that several large concentrations of Georgians be created, and it has also made efforts to provide them with synagogues and other religious needs.

Several other parties—Mapam and the Independent Liberals— have also attempted to reach the Soviet immigrants through personal contacts and through Russian-language publications, but both their efforts and their success have been limited.

Aside from the parties, there are public bodies which deal directly with the Soviet immigrants. Chief among them are Histadrut and the Union of Soviet Immigrants. Histadrut, in which all parties are represented with the Labor Party dominant, ran 42 seminars for immigrants in 1971, their purpose being to introduce the immigrants to Israeli society in general and to Histadrut in particular. Histadrut provides loans to enterprises willing to absorb new immigrants, or to enterprises established by immigrants themselves, and it aids in settling immigrants on kibbutzim and moshavim. It also provides loans for setting up home workshops and tries to prevent employers from firing immigrants just before they are about to get job tenure. It also tries to persuade employers to hire immigrants who are over 45 or 50, something most employers are reluctant to do. The labor councils of Histadrut have volunteer absorption committees to help in the social integration of the immigrants. Despite the power and influence of Histadrut, it has been relatively unsuccessful among the immigrants. Whereas 60 percent of the adult population of the country as a whole, and 90 percent of the workers, are members of Histadrut, only 37 percent of the immigrants joined it in 1969, only 43 percent in 1970 and 40 percent in 1971. While there are no separate figures available for Soviet immigrants, the impression of the director of Histadrut's absorption department is that "they are afraid of the red flag" and that it will be some time before they come to trust Histadrut. Histadrut's medical insurance fund (Kupat Holim) is the largest in the country and nearly all immigrants are signed up for it automatically for the first six months of their stay in Israel, but this does not seem to have immediate payoffs for Histadrut as a whole.

The Union of Soviet Immigrants, one of many immigrant associations in the country, was founded only in early 1971, building on three dormant regional organizations of Soviet immigrants. At present there are about 16,000 members, 9,000 of whom came to Israel after 1957. There is reason to believe that by next year the organization will have 20,000 to 30,000 members. The union is run by an administration responsible to a central committee, which is in turn elected by a congress of the union. There are at present about 60 local branches of the union. In January 1972, 12 immigrants who came in 1971 were coopted to the administration and 72 were added to the central committee, giving the 1971 immigration over half the votes in each body. In part this was done in order to answer the complaint made by many new arrivals that the union is dominated by veteran Israelis of Russian origin who are out of touch with the problems of today's immigration. The fact is that the chairman of the union is a veteran Mapai politician who has been in the country since the 1920s and to whom there has been much opposition, both by new immigrants and by elements in the Labor Party who claim that he has not been effective in recruiting Soviet immigrants to the party. The union is a nonparty organization, but all political parties are represented, though not officially, in the leadership. All immigrants from the Soviet Union are eligible for membership, and Georgians, for example, can be simultaneously affiliated with the union as well as with a Georgian immigrant association. The union actively recruits members, sending people to absorption centers to do so, and relying on local branches to enlist others. The union provides basic information on Israel and Judaism, as well as assistance in solving the many problems an immigrant faces, helping him in translation of documents, in the preparation of invitations to relatives in the Soviet Union who wish to immigrate, in social integration, and in discussing common problems of jobs, cultural activities and the like. The union seems to attract older people, though a wide variety of immigrants is represented.

In addition to the union, there are smaller immigrant associations for those from Latvia and Estonia, Lithuania, Georgia and other areas of the Soviet Union. There is also an organization of Asirei Zion, composed of those who served in Soviet labor camps or jails because of Zionist activity. This organization is active in the struggle for further immigration from the Soviet Union and is linked to the Gahal party.

In addition to these organizations specifically designed to serve the needs of Soviet immigrants, several Israeli social and cultural organizations, such as WIZO, the Organization of Working Mothers, and others, have been active in the social integration of the immigrants.

PROBLEMS OF INTEGRATION

Immigration is always a traumatic experience, and in the case of Soviet Jews, who come to a country they have never visited and about which they could only gain limited and biased information, the trauma is tenfold. Coming from a radically different political and economic system, from a different climate and culture, and from a country in which they had almost no opportunity to prepare themselves linguistically and culturally for their new home, immigrants from the Soviet Union in some ways come not to a new country but to another planet. Though they may find the behavioral patterns of the Israeli bureaucracy somewhat familiar, they encounter little else to which they can readily apply their experience. The most obvious, but perhaps least difficult problem, is language. Only a handful of Soviet immigrants come with a knowledge of Hebrew, which they learned either in pre-war schools in the Baltic states and other areas annexed by the Soviet Union after 1939 or which they acquired in one of the small ulpanim in Moscow and other cities. No figures are available yet on Soviet immigrants in particular, but an ongoing panel study conducted by the Absorption Ministry and the Central Bureau of Statistics found that one year after their arrival, 31 percent of a representative sample of all immigrants reported that they could converse freely in Hebrew in a simple conversation; 37 percent reported having difficulty doing so; and fully 32 percent could not yet speak Hebrew at all. About 47 percent of the immigrants claimed to use Hebrew as a primary or secondary language. Presumably, those who attend ulpanim are more knowledgeable than those who must learn Hebrew on their own initiative. Since some of the Soviet immigrants can speak Yiddish and other languages which are widely known in Israel, and since there are two Russian newspapers and daily broadcasts in Russian, the Soviet immigrant can get by without knowing more than rudimentary Hebrew, unless his job demands a better knowledge, or unles he wants to actively participate in the social and cultural life of the country. There is no reason to assume that Soviet immigrants will find it any more or any less difficult than immigrants from other countries to learn Hebrew. Soviet-born students who have gone through the one-year preparatory course in the universities seem to be quite proficient in Hebrew and, unlike other immigrant students, tend to try to speak Hebrew among themselves.

Housing is a problem both for the state and for the individual immigrant. Since the size and frequency of the Soviet immigration is unpredictable, the government finds it very difficult to plan housing on the basis of expected immigration. Furthermore, there is a great shortage of manpower in the building trades—probably more than half the construction workers today are Arabs from Gaza, East Jerusalem and the West Bank—and it takes on the average two years to complete an apartment building. Since housing and jobs must be matched to the individual immigrant, the problem is further complicated. At present housing is very expensive for the Israeli citizen and is available to immigrants on much easier terms, a major factor in the resentment expressed toward the immigrants. Nevertheless, Soviet immigrants, the great majority of whom do not have the means to buy apartments on the open market, have housing problems. Apartments are available today mainly in development areas in the south—Arad, Dimona, Kiryat Gat, Beersheba—and many immigrants are reluctant to go to the Negev, to a radically different climate, to small towns populated mainly by Oriental Jews, so different in culture and background from the Soviet Jews. Furthermore, suitable employment is not always available in these areas. It is very difficult for the nonprofessional immigrant to find an apartment in the greater Tel Aviv area, though many of the Soviet immigrants prefer this area, since it is a major cultural and commercial center, and because quite a few have relatives there. Nevertheless, the Soviet immigrants have been given relatively good living conditions—new apartments, usually quite large by local standards, on easy terms (rental, rental-with-option-to-buy, outright purchase with the help of a government or Jewish Agency mortgage). A survey of Soviet immigrants who came in 1969-1971 found that fully 80 percent are satisfied with their housing conditions. Since the government has placed a high priority on providing suitable housing for today's immigrants, who could not possibly be put in the ma'abarot of the 1950s type, there is reason to believe that housing will be a temporary problem, and one that will be overcome.

Employment is a more troublesome area. The survey cited above revealed that only 57 percent of the Soviet immigrants are satisfied with their present jobs, while another survey of a representative sample of immigrants from all countries showed that fully 72 percent were satisfied with their jobs.

The dissatisfactions expressed by Soviet immigrants arise mainly from the difficulties of adjusting to a new economic and, in some cases, technical system. For example, Soviet engineers and technicians are trained as narrow specialists for a large and complex economy, and the Israeli engineer or technician is given a broader training and is expected to be able to perform more kinds of tasks. Additionally, many professions acquired in the Soviet Union are irrelevant to the Israeli economy. These include teaching Lithuanian or even Russian, giving instruction in Marxism-Leninism, philology, locomotive engineering, mining engineering and others. Further-more, several major professions have to be relearned: lawyers must learn a new system and philosophy of law; economists must learn non-Marxian economics; accountants and teachers must learn not only a new language but also new systems. Third, Soviet citizens are not used to looking for a job on their own—in the USSR they are usually assigned to a place of employment after completing their education or training. Almost all Soviet immigrants expect the state to provide them with a job suitable to their skills, whereas the Israeli economy operates with a free job market. Finally, shop-keepers and artisans are not used to attracting customers on their own. In the noncompetitive system of the Soviet Union they did not have to seek out customers actively, and it takes them a while to learn the ways of a competitive system which requires more initiative and imagination.

In addition to these problems, Soviet immigrants encounter sus-picion on the part of Israeli employers who question the quality of Soviet training. Frequently, Soviet immigrants must accept a drop in rank: the head of a department in a Leningrad hospital may be given nothing more than an ordinary job in an outpatient clinic, and it may be some years before he acquires sufficient language skills, seniority and trust to rise to his former level.

A less tangible but perhaps even more serious difficulty in the integration of Soviet immigrants stems from some of their assump-tions about the norms of social and political life, norms which in themselves may be admirable but which clash with the realities of Israel. Soviet citizens are conditioned to expect the state to under-take the ordering of their lives, and are at something of a loss when they discover that many things have to be done on their own initiative. This is as true in regard to social problems and commu-nity affairs as it is regarding jobs and housing. Many feel that the Israeli government is weak or lax in its duties because it does not prescribe enough to its citizenry, and perhaps does not proscribe enough as well. Soviet citizens wait for the signal from above, and then they are ready to act. Characteristically, when one Soviet im-migrant, who contended that the greatest problem facing the Soviet Union today was the lack of democracy, was asked what could be done about it, he answered, "The Soviet government should issue a directive to all state institutions and Party organizations to introduce democratic procedures immediately." Many immigrants feel the government should force the population to adopt a more friendly attitude to the Soviet immigration, and others feel the government is overly tolerant of criticism and opposition, particularly on security and foreign affairs issues. One immigrant was upset to see a picture of Anwar Sadat, "our enemy," on the front page of a newspaper. "That would never happen in the USSR."

Related to these kinds of attitudes is the feeling that there is too much freedom and license in Israeli society and that more social discipline would be a good thing. Soviet Jews are shocked and disturbed to find the streets so dirty, and consider this a sign of a lack of culture. They do not understand why those who litter the streets are not reprimanded and punished. Some also complain that young people are too free in their ways, that they do not show enough respect for their elders and their teachers, and that far too many are hooligans who should be arrested and punished for unruly behavior in public places. In general, Soviet immigrants are upset by the free and easy treatment accorded to government officials and other "important" people, and consider this a sign of boorishness and lack of culture. Even in the university, Soviet-born students tend to be more deferential to their instructors than are their Israeli colleagues, and they are often deeply embarrassed by the *chutzpah* Israeli students display. In short, there is an obvious carryover in the mentality of Soviet immigrants from the behavior patterns which they learned in their native country. While every immigrant from every country brings with him a mental "baggage," that of the Soviet immigrants differs from Israeli norms more than do those of the American or West Europeans.

There is some tension between the Soviet arrivals and the Oriental Jews when they live in the same neighborhoods. Oriental Jews— that is, those of North African or Asian origin—constitute over half the population, but they are at the lower end of the social scale. While they constitute 60 percent of the elementary school children, they are only 10 percent of the university student population. They are highly conscious of their lower social status and lower incomes, and resent the fact that today's immigrants are being placed in apartments, rather than in the ma'abarot they lived in as immigrants, and that the new wave is benefiting from the kinds of immigrant privileges that did not exist in the 1950s. Some Oriental Jews see the Ashkenazi establishment which runs the country conspiring to maintain its power by encouraging Ashkenazi immigration and by treating such immigrants better than the Oriental immigrants were treated. Of course, the fact is that all of today's immigrants—whether from the Soviet Union or Turkey, the United

States or Persia—are given the same rights and privileges, and that today's immigrant privileges have more to do with the progress of the Israeli economy than with planned discrimination. Still, there is a tendency to blame the "Russians" for the difficulties in getting better housing and in moving up the socioeconomic ladder. On their side, some Soviet immigrants, particularly the less educated, are astonished to discover that these dark people, with their strange foods and peculiar behavior, are also Jews. They quickly learn that Orientals are low on the totem pole, and they resent having to live in the same neighborhood. In one area near Tel Aviv, Neve Sharett, Soviet immigrants were housed in new buildings which were constructed in the midst of older ones populated largely by North Africans. The resulting tensions and misunderstandings were eventually eased, but not before the area's problems received wide publicity and further buttressed the prejudices of all parties. There is no doubt that the cultures and mentalities of the Soviet and Oriental Jews are worlds apart, and prejudices are very quick to develop. Nevertheless, probably only a minority of the less educated Soviet Jews develops strong feelings in this area.

Finally, Soviet Jews have some difficulty in adjusting to Israeli cultural life. Soviet Jews pride themselves on their involvement with music, art and literature, and they constitute a high proportion of the artists and performers, as well as of the consumers of culture, in the Soviet Union. In Israel, they cannot immediately become involved in the theater or literature because of the language barrier, but they quickly learn that cultural values in Israel differ from those in the Soviet Union. Like many West European countries, Israel has been strongly influenced by American pop culture, and one hears far more American pop music on the radio than classical music. To the Soviets this is a sign of decadence and lack of cultural development. One immigrant complained, "In the Soviet Union we used to fight each other for tickets to the philharmonic and tickets were cheap, and here, after I paid a very high price for a ticket, I was shocked to discover that most of the audience seemed to be old ladies speaking German." In the Soviet Union private instruction in musical instruments is provided free by the state, and many Jewish parents avail themselves of this opportunity. They are upset when they discover that music lessons will cost them money in Israel, and they interpret this as a sign of Israel's low regard for high culture. Quite a few artists and musicians have come in the Soviet immigration, and perhaps in time they may have an impact on Israeli cultural tastes. But for the time being, Soviet arrivals are quietly embarrassed by the fact that they appear to have left a country which was more cultured than the Jewish country to which they have come.

THE GEORGIANS: A SPECIAL CASE

As mentioned previously, Jews from the Soviet republic of Georgia have been able through the centuries to preserve their ethnic identity and religious way of life. Even in the darkest days of Stalinism, Georgian Jews successfully resisted attempts by the authorities to close the synagogues, and Georgian Jews neither intermarried nor assimilated nearly as much as did the Jews in the European parts of the Soviet Union. When the movement for emigration to Israel began, Georgian Jews were among the very first to take an active part, and their militant activity spearheaded demands for the right to emigrate to Israel. In 1971 over 4,000 Jews came to Israel from Georgia, and so the Georgian immigration constituted from 30 to 40 percent of the total immigration from the Soviet Union. According to the 1970 census, there are 55,000 Jews in Soviet Georgia—Georgian Jews claim that in reality there are at least 70,000—and foreign correspondents have reported that there are many thousands in Georgia who have initiated procedures for emigration.

Though they share some of the characteristics of Soviet immigrants described earlier, the Georgian community has some unique and distinct traits of its own. First of all, in contrast to most other immigrations in recent years, the Georgian immigration can be seen as a mass communal immigration, and not the immigration of discrete individuals. Because of their very strong family ties, and the strict and patriarchal nature of the Georgian family, Georgians are immigrating as whole communities and bringing their community structure along with them. For example, almost the entire populations of at least two Georgian towns—and this means several thousand people—have immigrated en masse. Because of such close ties, there is a chain reaction effect wherein the more people emigrate, the more are likely to do so in the future. Since Georgian families have traditionally been extended ones, and communities have made great efforts to live in concentrated settlements, the Georgian Jews were very disturbed to find that because of the shortage in housing and because of an Israeli policy of long standing to scatter the population throughout the country, they were being assigned to dwellings all over the country, with the result that there would be no large concentrations of Georgians in any one area, and even individual extended families might be broken up. The Georgians, a militant and cohesive group, immediately protested this policy and demanded not luxury apartments or "desirable" areas, but concentration of the immigration. Despite the fact that the Georgians were demanding housing in such "undesirable" areas as Lod-Ramle and several development towns in the north and south, the authorities seemed unable to meet their requests in light of the housing shortage. When several families threatened to return to Georgia, and when it became apparent that arriving immigrants had been forewarned by their predecessors and were arriving with demands for specific areas, the authorities began to make efforts to create concentrations of at least 200 families in 12 areas of the country, including Lod-Ramle, Ashkelon, Ashdod, Kiryat Malachi, Pardess Katz, Dimona and others. While Golda Meir criticized the Georgian desire to "isolate themselves into ghettos," the Absorption Ministry bowed to the Georgians' insistence on living in concentrated communities.

The second characteristic distinguishing the Georgian immigrants from the others is their adherence to religion. Even some Georgians who consider themselves nonreligious maintain religious customs, such as wearing skullcaps, because they feel this is an integral part of Jewish identity which they wish to affirm. Georgian immigrants, to whom Israel always represented a religious-national ideal rather than a political system or independent state, are shocked to discover that the majority of Israelis are not observant. As one plaintively observed, "How can I be sure that these people are Jews when they look just like everyone else. In Georgia at least you could always tell who was one of us and who was not." It disturbs them even more to discover that most of the leading personalities in the state are nonobservant. For this reason they have become suspicious of official institutions, and with the prompting of certain religious elements, they have insisted, sometimes in a dramatic and militant fashion, that efforts be made to enable them to continue and further develop their religious way of life. They have asked that teachers in ulpanim in which they are enrolled be male, that their children not be enrolled in the general state schools but only in state-religious or independent-religious schools, and that the state provide religious articles and synagogues for them. These are not unreasonable demands, and the government has not denied them. The Georgians have also asked that if no synagogue structures are available, some apartments should be set aside for use as temporary synagogues. In answer to Golda Meir's suggestion that they pray in the Sephardic ritual synagogues, the Georgians correctly point out that their ritual differs from both the Sephardic and the Ashkenazic and that for centuries they have had their own style of worship. The religious parties, and Agudat Yisrael in particular, have tried to capitalize on these complaints and have charged repeatedly that the government is trying to seduce the immigrants away from religion, much as it did to the Oriental Jews in the 1950s. In turn, the Labor Party and the Absorption Ministry charge that Agudat Yisrael is making demagogic use of Georgian dissatisfaction in order to win the political allegiance of the immigration. Since the government has recently been meeting the Georgians' demands, the political storm around them has died down somewhat.

The Labor Party has not stood idly by while the religious parties compete for the Georgians' sympathies. The long dormant Union of Georgian Immigrants, whose membership consisted of those who had come to Israel 50 years ago and more, was revived. The chairman of the organization is Yitzhak Yedidiah, a Labor Party activist, and the secretary is a young Israeli of Georgian origin, affiliated with the Rafi faction of Labor who found it expedient to reassume his family's Georgian-sounding name, Balvashvili, long after he had shortened it to Balva and shortly after he had further Hebraicized it to Bar-Lavi. Not to be outdone, the religious parties supported the formation of a Union of Georgian Immigrants, headed by an acknowledged leader of the immigrants, Rabbi Yehuda Butrashvili. The involvement of non-Georgians in the organization is indicated by the fact that its secretary is a rabbi with the distinctly non-Georgian name of Lifschitz. The Absorption Ministry contributes funds to all immigrant associations, and while it is known that it allocated 6,000 Israeli pounds to the Labor-dominated organization, it is not clear whether the other organization also receives financial support.

Only 8 percent of the Georgian immigrants are classified as akademaiim and practically all the immigrants seem to have found jobs with little difficulty. Whereas in Georgia many Jews worked as artisans, in retail trade and in other nonindustrial jobs, in Israel they have been successfully employed in light industry, as dock workers, porters and, most recently, construction workers. In contrast to other immigrants, the Georgians do not seem to mind living far from the bright lights of Tel Aviv, and their main concern is to live and work in close proximity to their families and to other Georgians. They are a proud people and take umbrage when officials treat them summarily, brusquely or with contempt. In interviews with journalists, they have emphasized that they wish to be treated with dignity and respect, and not as the problem children of the Soviet immigration. If various groups will abstain from the temptation of exploiting the Georgian immigrants for their own ends, it is likely that the Georgians will adjust successfully, on their own terms, to Israeli life.

THE IMMIGRANTS AND THE ISRAELI PUBLIC

"We like *aliyah* (immigration) but we don't like *olim* (immigrants)." This has become a widely quoted phrase of late. Throughout Zionist history, emphasis has been placed on the necessity for the "ingathering of the exiles" to Israel, and the Israeli population has been taught to regard immigration of Jews as one of the most important national goals. After 1967, with the inclusion of large numbers of Arabs in the boundaries of the state, and with the realization that the birth rate of Israeli Arabs is much higher than that among Jews, the government launched a campaign to attract additional immigration in order that the relative weight of the Jewish population be preserved, and that the total Jewish population grow, partially in order to enhance Israel's military security. The population seemed to accept the necessity for encouraging immigration, but when the extent of privileges granted to immigrants became widely perceived, the veteran population, or at least certain strata, began to resent what they saw as "discrimination" against the oldtimers, particularly when major social problems remained to be solved. For a time it was considered impolite to express these sentiments openly, especially in regard to the Soviet immigrants whose arrival was so unexpected, dramatic and initially gratifying. By now resentments against the immigrants are expressed freely in conversations, letters to editors, interviews in newspapers, public opinion surveys, classrooms and other public places. Naturally, this atmosphere has seriously impeded the social integration of the immigrants. A survey commissioned by the Ministry of Absorption found that in 1971 half of the Israeli population had not spoken to any immigrant in the past year, and that another third had spoken to immigrants only three times during the year. Nearly 20 percent of immigrant schoolchildren reported they had no Israeli friends. In another survey, 55 percent of the population thought that the help given to immigrants comes at the expense of the poor strata of Israeli society, and 35 percent did not think so. It is significant that when respondents were divided according to ethnic origin and age, it was discovered that 60 percent of Oriental Jews thought the poor were suffering because of the Soviet immigration and more than 66 percent of young (18-29) native-born Israelis thought so. While the older generation of European origin seems genuinely enthusiastic about the Soviet immigration and tries to aid in its social integration, it appears that those lower down on the socioeconomic ladder, and those from North Africa and Asia—and these two categories are highly congruent—are opposed to giving privileges to the immigrants, and this opposition spills over to resentment of the immigrants themselves. Very often even well-educated people have exaggerated notions of the immigrants' privileges: it is widely believed that Soviet immigrants receive housing at no cost, that they pay no income tax at all for an indefinite period, that they have mysterious sources of funds which they use to buy luxury items on favorable terms. It is charged that the state "gives the immigrants everything" and gets no army service or taxes in return. It is believed by some university students and potential students that unqualified immigrant students gain admission to universities and thereby displace qualified sabras. There have been many articles in the newspapers trying to assess the trade-off between what the immigrant costs the state and what he contributes to it by bringing with him a professional education, investment money and talent. The fact that the recent immigration is so highly educated does not always sit well with Israelis, since some of them fear that they will lose out in the competition for jobs, and many immigrants report that their superior knowledge or experience is resented at their places of work. The Georgians have become objects of resentment, perhaps because of the publicity given their difficulties. When asked whether all the demands of Georgian Jews should be granted rather than have them return to the Soviet Union, 64 percent of the adult population said they should leave the country and their demands ought not be met. Perhaps the most extreme expressions of resentment toward immigrants have been the physical harassment of immigrant tenants in a building in Ramat Gan, where an atmosphere of terror was created by young Oriental Jews, and a letter sent by "Sabras in Need of Housing" to Georgian immigrants which said: "We, the Sabras, were disappointed to learn that Jews like you exist in our state. . . . You should know once and for all: you will not milk this state like a cow. . . . New immigrant, the ma'abarot will await you; please clean them and let us try out your apartments."

These attitudes are clearly marginal, but milder expressions of at least doubt as to the justice of the privileges or incentives are widespread. Immigrants become aware of such attitudes very quickly, and Soviet immigrants are very much disturbed by them, particularly because they feel a deep need to be warmly and enthusiastically received and accepted. In part, the Israeli government and media are to blame for having extravagantly dramatized the Soviet immigration in the first months of its appearance: Golda running to the airport to kiss Soviet immigrant children, long interviews in the weekend magazines with leaders of the movement for immigration, pictures in the newspapers of the immigrants and attendance at their family celebrations by people such as Moshe Dayan, Menachem Beigin and other leading lights. The public soon tired of these "festivals," as it called them, especially when it became apparent that the Soviet immigrants were human beings and not superhuman freedom fighters all cast in the heroic mold. On several occasions Golda Meir and Moshe Dayan, among others, have condemned resentment and criticism of the immigrants, and the government has cut back on some of the privileges, as well as taking steps to stop their abuse and exploitation for illegal gain. Nevertheless, there is a noticeable lack of enthusiasm for the Soviet immigration, and for the American one as well, among large strata of the population. This only widens the gap between the immigrants and the veterans and makes the integration of the immigrants that much more difficult. Since there are many people of good will who are working hard to make the immigrants feel at home and to help them over the hurdles, the situation has not reached crisis proportions and probably will not do so in the near future. Furthermore, as the Hebrew saying has it, "What reason will not do, time will do." As the immigrants begin to fuse into Israeli society and assume the burdens borne by every Israeli they will probably find wider acceptance. One wit put it this way: during his first year the immigrant hates his former country and loves Israel; during the second, he hates Israel and loves his former country; during his third year he begins to hate new immigrants—he is well adjusted.

CONCLUSION

The Soviet government will probably continue its present policy of limited and selective immigration in the near future. It will continue to be easier to leave from the Baltic states, the areas formerly under Polish and Romanian rule, and Georgia. It is likely that the Soviets will not permit an even flow of migration, but that there will be fluctuations in the number and types of people allowed to depart. The size of those fluctuations and the continuation of emigration will depend heavily, though not exclusively, on two factors: the continued militancy and activism of Jews within the Soviet Union, and vigorous support for them around the world. Because there is feedback from Soviet immigrants in Israel, Soviet Jews are more knowledgeable about actual conditions in Israel. This will not deter them from emigrating, since, by and large, Soviet immigrants seem to be decidedly pleased with their decision to come to Israel, but it will make their adjustment easier, as they will know better what to expect. Despite all the financial and social problems created by the unexpectedly large immigration wave, Israel is well on the way to successfully absorbing the immigrants. The government and many sectors of the population are keenly aware of the great significance of this immigration and are highly alert to the need to absorb it successfully. Some Soviet sources have hinted that the Soviet Union may try to undermine Israel's economy and social fabric by flooding the country with immigrants it will be unable to absorb, but the official Israeli reaction has been, "First flood us, and let us worry about the rest." Prominent industrialists have launched a campaign to raise 100 million Israeli pounds in order to help in the absorption of the 1972 immigration which, the government and Jewish Agency predict, will reach a sum total of about 65,000, including about 35,000 from the Soviet Union. Although this figure is based on projections from past experience, and in the case of the Soviets this is a highly risky method, it does seem to be a reasonable, though perhaps overly optimistic assumption, as most immigration predictions have been in the last few years. There is little doubt that Israel will be able to absorb such a wave without experiencing severe economic and social dislocations, especially if foreign governments and Jews living abroad step up their assistance and if the military and international situations remain more or less as they are. Increased assistance from abroad will help supply housing for the poor and for young couples, and will ease the social pressures which negatively affect the immigrants.

There is not much information available about the number of immigrants who leave the country. According to the Absorption Ministry, only 9 percent of all immigrants leave the country for good, and of those, 70 percent came as "potential immigrants," a category which receives all the rights of immigrants, but delays some of the responsibilities of citizenship. Clearly, the attrition rate is higher among some groups than others. Conservative estimates say that 30 percent of the American immigrants (84 percent of Americans come as "potential immigrants") who came in 1968 have left the country. It is difficult to measure the amount of re-emigration since many of those who leave the country do not declare themselves as leaving for good. For example, when doing its survey on the 1970 immigrants, the Central Bureau of Statistics found that 2,560 immigrants of that year had "disappeared"—that is, had left the country without declaring themselves emigrants. Furthermore, Israel is very sensitive on the question of *yordim*, or emigrants, and until recently it was not considered a topic for discussion in polite company, except to vilify the yordim as traitors, opportunists and the like. The Ministry of Absorption claims that the percentage of yordim among Soviet immigrants is less than the 9 percent general figure, and there is no doubt that the over-whelming majority of Soviet immigrants have stayed in Israel. A handful have gone back to the Soviet Union, where the Soviet media have used them in the campaign to paint Israel in the darkest colors and to discourage applications for emigration. Another small group, numbering around 50, has left Israel in an attempt to return to the Soviet Union, but has landed in Vienna where the Soviet authorities refuse to let them return to the Soviet Union. This may be another way of showing Soviet Jews the high costs of emi-gration—not only is life in Israel intolerable, but it is by no means certain that Soviet Jews will be allowed to return to the Soviet Union once they have left it.

While the prospects for continued immigration from the Soviet Union are uncertain, it seems that Israel's capacity to absorb them is certain, despite all the problems described here. For all their doubts and complaints, responsible people in Israel are aware of the historical significance of the Soviet immigration and of its im-portance to the scientific, demographic and economic growth of Israel. With some help the difficult task of integrating people "from another planet" can be successfully accomplished by the Israeli people and their government.

91

THE KIBBUTZ
TODAY

6

Bruno Bettelheim

SOME REFLECTIONS
ON THE KIBBUTZ

The kibbutz can no longer be regarded as an experiment; it is now a way of life which its members regard as good and important. For some time the kibbutz has concerned itself with issues which are of tremendous importance in the world today: women's liberation, communal child care, the protection of the family, dissatisfaction with a production-oriented society, the problem of the way people should live. The kibbutz has dealt with these problems for almost 70 years and has tried to solve them.

The kibbutz has been active, in a more serious fashion than any other society I know, in the effort to deal with the inequality of the sexes so far as social organization and working arrangements are concerned. Today in the United States there are communes where the young and not so young, dissatisfied with city life and their living arrangements, are trying to develop a different way of living. These young people could learn a great deal from the kibbutz movement.

What is the difference between American communes and Israeli kibbutzim? What causes the short life span (often less than a year) of American communes in comparison with the three-generation kibbutz? Why do kibbutz children not suffer from the social ills that affect many American young people—dropping out, drug addiction, delinquency, serious psychological disturbance? Even in

American communes, the lives of many are so empty that drug use continues or increases. Certainly the basic ideas for new settlements have been the same in both Israel and the United States. The issue of consumption, of the objectification of all human relations—the basis of the capitalistic society—repelled those involved with the communal movement in America. The original kibbutzniks sought to build a different kind of society which would allow people to lead the good life. Those who would live in such a society had to be free from personal monetary considerations and strains. In addition, the founders felt, as do many Ameriican communards, that the good life can only be lived close to the soil, close to nature and in step with nature. What young Americans are discovering now, young Zionists learned three generations ago.

So far the similarities in the movements are impressive. But there are obviously some important differences. The Israeli founders knew that production, though not of the capitalist variety, is the keystone of survival. They all worked together for the benefit of the whole community and toward a defined goal. True socialism marks an important way in which Israeli kibbutzim seem to differ from American communes, where exploitation of the weaker members is now being exposed. The sense of overwhelming purpose, known and unchallenged, plus an impressive unity, has made the kibbutz the permanent institution it is today.

So influential has the kibbutz been on its members that a new type of man has emerged. From shtetl Jews, bookish, weak, non-aggressive, came sabras—strong, hard, practical, self-assertive Israelis. Today Jews from diverse backgrounds come to kibbutzim —and their children become sabras with similar personalities and academic achievements. The special organization of family life in kibbutzim, in addition to the experience of living in the constantly endangered Jewish homeland, have worked together to produce this new breed.

A look at kibbutz family life reveals some of the reasons that a new type of Jew was able to emerge. The founders of the kibbutz realized that women must be as free to contribute to the society as men are. This socioeconomic equality could not be established unless someone took care of the children. Thus the idea of communal child care was accepted and implemented. It was thought that communal care would guarantee happy family life. But in the early kibbutzim people either didn't marry or had unsatisfactory marriages which frequently ended in divorce. In the course of development the early kibbutzniks realized that even when the children are taken care of by the community and are in school at the kibbutzim men and women must be able to form intimate one-to-one relationships if they are to have satisfying lives. Possibilities for this kind of intimacy had not been considered originally, but kibbutzniks discovered that the stability of human relationships and the intimacy between people were intimately woven and interconnected.

Now marriage is common and very stable in the kibbutz—certainly as stable if not more so than in American society. The great and extraordinarily important demonstration of the kibbutz is that there is far more to the family relationship than we originally thought. It had always been assumed that the family was created out of the need to take care of children, but child care is taken care of communally on the kibbutz—yet the family (and marriage) persists and flourishes. And kibbutz children flourish, too.

To consider this question psychoanalytically, two interrelated factors must be considered: the first relates to the child's knowledge that he has a rightful place in the world—in negative form the problem of alienation; the second factor is the Oedipus conflict.

An individual's loneliness is essentially an existential state, and to a very large degree develops when he does not feel he belongs or has a rightful place. Not so long ago everybody had a rightful place. One was born into it. The role of the father was clearly defined as head of the family; the role of the mother and wife was clearly defined; the oldest son had status; various occupations and professions carried with them defined roles.

In the kibbutz, as a member of the community, everybody has his rightful place that cannot be threatened by anyone. This is not always true in the United States. Some of the conflicts in middle-class American homes, and the complete dissatisfaction of children there, have a great deal to do with parental anxiety about their child's future. I think the pursuit of academic achievement and some conflicting factors in socialization ("Do this and don't do that; mind your manners or don't hold back"—depending on exactly what at this moment is fashionable. "Use four-letter words" so that you are unafraid of such language, or don't use four-letter words "so that you don't offend anybody") make for high amounts of parental anxiety. Such anxiety about a child's future work, role and status causes unbearable stress on children, too. I think that all children would have a much better life if parents could manage not to be so anxious that the child will fail.

97

This anxiety is totally eliminated from kibbutz education because the future of whoever lives in the kibbutz is assured—for better or for worse. The individual will be a comrade and the community will find something for him to do that is in line with his interests, the community's needs and his abilities. Therefore, the anxiety that interferes with a successful relationship between parents and children does not exist in the kibbutz. And with the emphasis on the high prestige of physical labor, academic achievement is not as important as in the United States even though the number of sabras going to the universities and Technion is increasing. But even with one anxiety removed, and with the child's knowledge that he need not depend on his parents for his place in the world, the Oedipus complex remains a further impediment to development. The Oedipus complex according to Freud and psychoanalysis, is universal, and I agree with this view. The Oedipal conflict is a result of the degree of the dependency of the child on its parents, and the degree to which the child is in the power of the parents. Since children in all societies are dependent, there will be some Oedipal conflicts in all societies. Because of the inability of the young of the human animal to take care of itself, they must be in the power of somebody, and to be in the power of somebody—as Dr. Star, the British analyst, has pointed out—always creates either depression or paranoia or both. The kibbutz child, being a young human animal, is dependent and therefore subjected to these stresses and strains. But since he is not in our society the stresses and strains are mitigated. He does not have to come to terms with his parents if he can see others around with whom he can come to terms—which reduces or mutes the conflict, although it does not do away with it.

Each society has a different problem and a different social structure. While the universality of the Oedipus difficulty comes from the child's immaturity, his delayed sexual development, the impossibility of attaining his forbidden goal, the particular form it takes depends entirely on the society.

In our society the child of age two and three only knows, "If my parents do not take care of me until I'm grown-up, I will perish." So there is a tremendous bondage, and every bondage of course brings resentment, striving for independence and anxiety about what the consequence of such fighting for independence might be.

In the kibbutz, on the other hand, from an early age on, the child knows that the community will take care of him. Everything that means security to a child: shelter, a bed, a cover, food—all of that is provided by the community—and no child in the kibbutz can have the erroneous notion that he depends on his parents for these essential ingredients of his security and livelihood.

From an early age on, the kibbutz child eats in a communal kitchen and carts the food into the children's home, so that he knows his sustenance comes from the community. He is not beholden to any particular parent for his food. He is not beholden to them for his clothes; they come from the clothes storage, and he is taken care of by the metapelet who is assigned to him by the community.

These children have a sense of security because they do not feel that they have to depend absolutely on their parents for their existence; and the parents do not have to worry about the child's future and therefore do not shape and reshape him from birth on.

The kibbutz has no policemen, for it has no need for private police. There is no criminality, there is no drug addiction, there are no dropouts, there is no homosexuality, there is—in our terms— no sexual delinquency. Kibbutz morality is of the highest sort, despite the fact that, until very recently boys and girls roomed together until age 18, even showering together.

The kibbutz example shows that in one generation an entirely different personality type can be created, but it also shows that this is not easily transplanted. The kibbutz succeeds because of the incredibly high devotion to duty, the incredibly high work morality, the incredibly high degree of cooperation between all members. Together they constitute a method of education that has achieved amazing results.

7

Michael Curtis

UTOPIA

AND THE KIBBUTZ

The vision of utopia has always lent direction to efforts to create more desirable communities. Cultures which have no such utopian vision remain, in Paul Tillich's words, "imprisoned in the present." Throughout history, attempts, usually on a limited scale and in simple fashion, have been made to implement the vision, but all have failed because the ideals quickly became perverted or because the practical problems encountered were too great to overcome. In the twentieth century attempts to create new forms of society have been made in the Soviet Union, Yugoslavia and China. But the most successful contemporary attempt to realize the ideals of socialism and to implement the principles and life style of a new social order has clearly been the Israeli kibbutz.

Some of the ideological principles of the kibbutz have been qualified, albeit reluctantly; some issues once regarded as difficult to resolve for ideological reasons have been settled; some desired results have not materialized; some new, unanticipated or neglected problems have emerged. As a result of the changes in the Jewish community both before and after the establishment of the state of Israel, proponents of the kibbutz have realized that there are no permanent solutions for the problems of men and society, and kibbutzim have changed accordingly. In spite of, or because of, these changes, the kibbutz exemplifies in practice the hopes of social

101

reformers and best illustrates the possibility of a desirable life in a collaborative and democratic setting. As the hopes of terrestial paradise in the communist countries have turned sour, the kibbutz remains the institution that has most successfully implemented the dreams of the socialist visionaries.

The essence of the kibbutz has been its combination of moral principles, spirit of messianic pioneering and dedication to public service in combination with a keen appreciation of and response to the requirements of practical reality. The vision of the new society for Jewish settlers was based on the convictions that work was honorable and the foundation of a desirable and healthy life; that social egalitarianism was the proper basis for human relations; and that individual emanciaption and self-relization could be attained simultaneously with the national renaissance, the redemption of the Jewish people and the transformation of social relationships.

The ideological stance of the kibbutz stems largely from its intellectual inheritance. It is firmly grounded in an institutional and practical heritage of socialist Zionism and the labor movements of Central and Eastern Europe with their combination of nationalist and socialist ideals, Poale Zion, Socialist Zionist Workers Party and youth organizations. But it also draws on the ideas and outlook of the Utopian Socialists of the nineteenth century in their opposition to the deficiencies of bourgeois society and their rejection of an inegalitarian system in which exploitation occurs through the existence of private property, the employment of others and a preoccupation with material success. The moral passion of the kibbutz and its antagonism to false standards and values stem from radical ideology and antibourgeois conviction.

Ideologically the kibbutz has based itself on collective ownership, the abolition of private ownership of the means of production, equality of persons regardless of function or occupation, equality of distribution, satisfaction of the needs of its members and the end of exploitation of others, self-reliance for survival and refusal to hire outsiders. The founders assumed that mutual aid, the pooling of labor and group solidarity would replace competitive behavior without the need for differential incentives. Life would of necessity be simple, if not austere. Medical, educational and social benefits would be available for all; expenses would be borne by the whole community.

Men and society would be reformed together through cooperative relationships and democratic self-administration. Production, consumption, education and social relationships would all be organized on a communal basis and be cooperative in nature. Group rather than individual projects would be emphasized. The socially egalitarian community would end the historic antagonisms and status distinctions between intellectual and physical labor. A cooperative community settled by people with no experience of the soil or of individual property rights would work on land belonging to the whole entity. A community of intellectual farmers would end the divorce between town and country. Human relations would be improved by the liberation of women, occupationally and sexually, by the removal of patriarchal authority in family relationships, and by the elimination of coercion as a method of obtaining acquiesence.

But the kibbutz has not only been based on a vision of the new society, provided a model for an egalitarian, socialist and democratic society, and set a standard by which existing society could be judged; it also has been conditioned by and serves to implement the practical needs of the Jewish community. Its complex and unique nature has included the functions of military defense, the need to settle uninhabited areas by establishing agricultural settlements, the creation of territorial bases for absorption of immigrants and for the learning of Hebrew (the new common tongue), sufficient production for self-sufficiency or for the reduction of imports, the provision of work for all, mutual aid to deal with malaria, educational training and a socialization process for children and cultural expression. Its agricultural organization and ability to transfer resources fostered the introduction of new fruits and vegetables and also led to greater mechanization. Communal eating arrangements served the purpose of economy as well as of ideological conviction.

Unlike the historic experience of unsuccessful attempts at communal settlements, the kibbutz has not been an isolated, cloistered island in a hostile environment nor an institution with principles contrary to those of the rest of society. The kibbutz has always been part of the general labor movement, has been linked to the structure and behavior of political parties, and has been generally admired for its belief system in addition to regarding itself as the instrument or the model through which more widespread change might be made in society at large.

The kibbutzim have been closely attached to four federations, to the political parties with which the federations are associated, to Histadrut, and to the pioneer youth movements which influenced their organization and behavior and prepared volunteers for work,

103

communal living and the task of nation building. The kibbutzim have supported their national federations with manpower for the central organizations which represent all collective settlements; decide which settlements should be increased; maintain a central fund for financing investments; grant loans; and provide norms for guidance on almost all issues, including the personal and domestic. All the kibbutzim are represented by the Kibbutz Industries Association through the Kibbutz Movement Alliance in their relations with the government, industry and technological institutes.

Relations between the kibbutzim and political parties have been close. Much of the manpower and strength of Mapam has come from the 74 kibbutzim of the Kibbutz Artzi movement, which supports the party by dues and subscriptions to its newspapers. The 58 kibbutzim of Kibbutz Hameuchad have been linked with Ahdut Haavoda, as the 76 kibbutzim of the Ichud group have been linked with Mapai. Voting and political behavior in the kibbutzim have been strongly along party lines, and ideological splits in the kibbutz movement have followed those of the political parties. Members share similar political views, mostly of a socialist and secular nature, though a small number of the kibbutzim are religious. Traditional adherence and the maintenance of a common and ideological point of view in a kibbutz remain, even when, as in recent years, ideological intensity has been reduced.

The kibbutzim are part of a nation in which landed property belongs to the entire community, in which the desire to eliminate or reduce social inequalities is widely held, and which has always had a government dominated by left-of-center parties. Though there is a strong sector of private enterprise, planning and priorities are laid down by public authorities. Some 45 percent of total investment comes from government sources. Government controls—through price fixing, credit policy, interest rates, subsidies, development loans, import and export duties—inevitably condition agricultural and industrial activity in the kibbutzim no less than in the general economy.

The labor movement as a whole is imbued with values similar to those of the kibbutz itself—values such as mutual aid, equality of treatment, socialist philosophy and democratic control, and lack of ostentation. Kibbutzniks are included in the 60 percent of all Israeli workers who are in some sense employed in the public economy, which accounts for a quarter of the national product and of the employed. The kibbutzim constitute a part of the Hevrat Ovdim, which controls 23 percent of the national economy.

They are part of the whole cooperative network, their produce being marketed by Tnuva, which is responsible for two thirds of all farm produce in Israel, and their supplies being obtained by the purchasing cooperative, Hamashbir Hamerkazi. Indeed, the immediate needs of the settlements and of the kibbutzim were the main reason for the creation of a number of Histadrut enterprises, marketing and supply cooperatives, the Workers' Bank, transport cooperatives, the public water company and some industrial enterprises.

Even acknowledging the aid provided by this practical assistance and communality of values in a large part of the population and public apparatus, the success of the kibbutz has been remarkable by any standard—economic, social, educational or political. The kibbutz is a fact of Israeli society, not simply a hopeful experiment. After 50 years of existence, routine has replaced glamor and romanticism.

The productive record of the kibbutzim in both agriculture and industry has been outstanding. Agricultural production, more than self-sufficient for the kibbutz, never has been less than 27 percent of the total in the country and now, with one fifth of the manpower in agriculture, it is 32 percent, productivity increasing annually by 10 percent. The kibbutzim, partly because of their large size and their members' desire to avoid hired labor, have been in the forefront of agricultural modernization and mechanization and the development of new crops. Industrial production in the kibbutzim belatedly undertaken in any substantial way is currently about 7 percent of the total in Israel.

The kibbut has constituted a complete welfare system for its members. Medically it has registered almost the lowest infant mortality rate in the world. Culturally it has been active in literature, art and drama, and responsible for publishing both journals and books. Not surprisingly for communities whose founders and settlers include many intellectuals, the kibbutz members are better read than the average citizen.

Similarly, the educational expenditure of the kibbutz per capita has been greater than the national average. Collective rearing of children has been successful in reaching its desired goals in socializing children to be effective kibbutzniks and to become worker-intellectuals. Children's training in democratic participation and fellow-criticism in their *kvutza* (peer group) meetings are preparation for adult membership in their community. Even the children's games illustrate the group and cooperative nature of relationships. Group care of the young and the role of the *metapelet* as collective mother has freed the natural mother from part of the customary domestic yoke, though more recently there has been greater cooperation between educators and parents as well as between parents and children.

The original pioneers tended to minimize formal education and in former years higher education was not encouraged in the kibbutz, but this has changed with the growing need for specialists and trained experts in the kibbutz and elsewhere in Israeli society, and kibbutz children now get at least a high school education, which entails a considerable financial burden. As a compromise between national secondary schools (which would call for removal of children from the kibbutz) and individual kibbutz secondary schools (which would be too small to provide a satisfactory secondary educational pattern), regional secondary schools have been established in a limited area by both the Ichud and Hameuchad federations. The present generation is less convinced ideologically that agricultural labor and rural life are automatically preferable to intellectual, cultural or specialized activity and urban life.

The kibbutz has been an extraordinary example of noncoercive communal existence, a community without police, judicial system or prison, and with only occasional cases of dishonesty. Restraint has come only from the force of public opinion and the ultimate fear of expulsion. Unlike the Soviet *kolkhoz*, paying wages in proportion to output, based on coercion and subject to the will of central authorities, the kibbutz, with its democratic general meetings once a week, committee structure and officials rotating on a regular basis, has attempted to prevent an elitist, entrenched bureaucracy or oligarchy from developing. In general the attempt has been successful. The kibbutz has been an open society in which no one has any claim on any position or privilege, though sometimes the offices have rotated among a small group of individuals, and in recent years the role of the secretariat has increased.

The place and prominence of the kibbutz has resulted not simply from its evident material success, but also from national appreciation of its moral worth, its outstanding record of public service and contribution to the public welfare and its weaving of individual and communal good in democratic fashion.

The kibbutz has long played a disproportionate role in the activity and leadership of public bodies, left-of-center parties, Histadrut, the diplomatic service and military organizations. It provided the core of the Palmach, the commando units of the Haganah, a significant percentage of the officers and NCOs of the Israeli army and of the elite parachute corps. In 1948 it provided four fifths of the officers on the general staff and two thirds of its field officers. In 1967 it still contributed 22 percent of officers and sustained 25 percent of all casualties suffered.

Politically, the kibbutz contribution has been equally significant. Almost one third of all cabinet ministers, three of the four prime ministers and about one third of the present Knesset are or have been members of kibbutzim. Members of kibbutzim have also been prominent in the ranks of the youth movements, Nahal, border settlements and reserve officers. Not surprisingly their prominence in all these different organizations has caused them to be regarded as an aristocracy, an elite group without wealth or material possessions.

CHANGES IN THE KIBBUTZ

Though some of the writers proposing utopias have provided for change in their ideal societies, utopian speculation in general has tended to possess an air of finality. Defenders of the kibbutz have in a similar manner tended to regard their principles as inviolate and to thus adhere to them in fundamentalist fashion. But change has inevitably come to the kibbutz as to the national society in which it is located. In a society which has rapidly increased its population from heterogeneous sources, developed economically and seen its private sector controlling 47 percent of industry and 82 percent of trade and services competing with the public sector, and taken over the functions of absorption, defense, social welfare and technological development, the kibbutz has seen change in both its internal organization and in its role in society. The new problems of Israel as both a developed and developing society have influenced the behavior of the kibbutz.

Membership of the 232 existing kibbutzim constitutes a diminishing percentage of Israel's total population: it is now 85,000 or 2.8 percent of the total. To overcome the effects of this relative shrinkage, efforts have been made over the last decade to consolidate the medium-sized kibbutzim of between 200 and 600 people, which have increased from 127 to 163. But the kibbutz population has grown slowly, partly because of the low birth rate. While the Jewish population grew by 170 percent between 1948 and 1961, that of the settlements increased by only 40 percent. Recent immigrants from both the Middle Eastern countries and the Soviet Union have, for different reasons—patriarchal domination of the family in one case and a dislike of collective life in the other—not regarded the kibbutz as a congenial or desirable place in which to live. Unlike the early days when the kibbutz was regarded as the major alternative to private farms, other forms of settlement, the moshav ovdim and the moshav shitufi, have now become more generally available. Originally the kibbutz recruited more from among bachelors than from family units, now the normal form of immigrant pattern, and it has always been more attractive to people from European than from Oriental backgrounds. The latter group constitutes no more than 7 percent of the kibbutz population. Moreover, the kibbutz is no longer unique in serving the double purpose of development and military protection. Between 1948 and 1955 over 70 percent of new kibbutzim built were in the Negev or Galilee, both underdeveloped regions. But Ben-Gurion's settlement in Sde Boker on the edge of the desert has been more admired than imitated.

Supporters of the kibbutz have been troubled by the possibility of dilution of ideological principle and reduction of moral force as a result of contemporary developments in Israel. Attention has been focused on a wide range of issues: the growth of industrialization; the hiring of outside labor; the dissatisfaction of women, especially older women; the greater importance of the family; the gap and difference in perception between the generations; the stress on education; the rise in the standard of living; the greater prominence and status accorded to production; the need for expertise; the resources that must be devoted to the handicapped and the elderly; the concern for privacy; the reduced interest in democratic participation; and the incompatibility between individuality and equality.

The kibbutz is troubled by the tension within itself between socialist ideology and the requirements of economic growth as well as by the seeming reduction of that socialist ideology and pioneering spirit in society as a whole, with the changing composition of the population, the need to attract foreign capital and the growth of private investment. As an operating entity the kibbutz is less conscious of its missionary role. With its members secure, affluent, inbred and practical, it is less preoccupied with providing cells for the future socialist society.

The kibbutz has struggled to accommodate itself to the increasing degree of industrialization that has been the logical development of the physical limits of land and irrigation, the increasing mechanization of agriculture, the need to provide less strenuous work for an aging group, the desire to provide more technologically oriented work for the second and third generation, and the necessity of employing labor and absorbing immigrants for national reasons.

But the requisites of the industrial process may logically require qualification of some of the fundamental principles on which the kibbutz is based. Lack of manpower—due to the fact that the kibbutz must provide personnel for a large variety of services such as education, health and security from among its members—has required hiring workers from outside the kibbutz. Though this has always been opposed as a form of exploitation, outside workers now constitute some 60 percent of the labor force, and in the kibbutzim with the largest factories it has been as high as 70 percent.

The kibbutz principle of rotation of office runs counter to the need for specialization of function, especially in production and managerial matters, and for technicians and engineers. Efficient operation and cost accounting are now of as much concern as democratic participation. The stress on efficiency has meant not only the need for specialized skills and the possible rise of a managerial group as the general assembly of the kibbutz becomes less capable of making detailed decisions in the industrial field; it has also led to a higher status being given to production over services, another qualification of ideological principle. In addition, specialization has induced educational change as people have been sent to training and vocational courses.

This desire to maintain principle as much as possible has affected the industrialization process. The small membership of the average kibbutz—350—has meant small-scale industry. Nevertheless, kibbutz industry, which employs 5 percent of the nation's industrial workers, now accounts for 7 percent of the industrial production of the country. Its value of $300 million is now about 30 percent of the total income of kibbutzim, which employ 22 percent of their labor force in industry; in some cases the value of industrial output exceeds that of agriculture. Industrial labor has been efficiently organized, and capital has been productively invested. Industrial increases have been particularly striking in light industry in general, and in areas such as plastics, metal work, food processing and electronic equipment in particular. The kibbutzim are no longer agricultural communities, but are mixed occupational entities in a rural setting, a phenomenon argued for by Marx in *The Communist Manifesto*. The communities' desire to obtain the advantages of industrialization while remaining small has led to cooperation among the kibbutzim through joint ownership, regional enterprises and elimination of overlapping projects, pooling of labor and shared marketing arrangements.

The primary aim of the kibbutz has never been the greatest possible economic return, and not until 1937 did the kibbutzim show a profit. Now there is a greater interest in collective success and profit. A kibbutz member is still usually employed according to his preference and skill. But the concern for efficient organization and management has meant the development of efficiency norms, the use of concepts such as marginal profitability, first branch accounting and then accounting for the whole farm, program and linear planning, and collective profits. The desire to avoid hired labor and yet obtain the advantages of specialization and economies of size has led to regional cooperation, common purchasing through Tnuva, processing plants, cotton ginning plants, laundries, bakeries, packing houses, fruit-ripening installations, cooperatives for heavy and expensive machinery and joint production enterprises.

The ideology of the kibbutz also meant a system of mixed farming, which would provide self-sufficiency, allow rotation of work and not require hired labor. Often this resulted in less than maximum possible productivity. Only slowly did industrial crops such as tobacco, sugar, cotton and ground nuts come into production and take advantage of the relatively large size of the kibbutz farm. Special stress has been put on export crops such as cotton, the production of which has increased tenfold during the last decade.

A rising standard of living, industrialization, efficient organization and regular agricultural surpluses constitute a situation far different from the days of dependence on long-term, low interest loans and aid from the Jewish Agency, Histadrut and the government. Critics have speculated that the style of life of the kibbutz and the personality of its members would be adversely affected by growing affluence and security. Efficiency and better coordination of work have perhaps reduced the more exuberant behavior of members and the legendary spontaneous dancing and singing, though it has not brought an accompanying resurgence of the property instinct. It would be absurd to argue that the improvement of living, private showers, occasional meals at home, more colorful clothes and the general alleviation of austerity are automatically destructive of the basic principles of the kibbutz or that the secular asceticism of the founders is essential. The basic values remain: communal ownership, collective consumption, communal organization of work, democratic participation in decision-making, elimination of personal budgets and money, and noncompetitive education. At the same time, not all would agree that the individual produced by the kibbutz: self-assured, secure, communally minded, devoted to his peer group, collaborative in behavior, effective participant and contributor to the life of the country, conforms with the anticipated model of the new person.

A major continuing problem in the kibbutz is the tension between individual and communal values. The kibbutz is a very public place in which communal arrangements and activities have been preferred to solitude. Though opportunities are available for members to maintain distance from their fellows on many occasions, the limitations on privacy are still troublesome. The kibbutz has escaped internal tyranny through its voluntary basis and ethic of mutual trust, though the pressure of public opinion and of peer groups on behavior is strong. The kibbutz has always had to balance individual autonomy with the requirements of collective well-being. Individuals have agreed on the supremacy of group interests and living experiences, the acceptance of communal decisions and identification with the community, but this has not meant the elimination of individual liberty or loss of autonomy.

Some ideological issues that caused anxiety in the past now seem of less importance. The employment of hired labor is still seen as a violation of common and equal ownership of property, and though the type and size of kibbutz industry is affected by that ideological belief, dislike of that type of employment is no longer an insuperable obstacle. Nor has the nature of a society in which money plays a minimal part been seriously qualified by the introduction of personal expense budgets and clothing allowances. The troublesome problem of where children should sleep, communally or with their parents, has now been settled in many cases in favor of the latter without undermining the essential nature of the kibbutz. Though the antifamily attitude of the past has not entirely disappeared, the role of the family, both in housekeeping and the socialization of children, has increased. But this has not destroyed the extended family relationship of the whole community, although there has definitely been strain caused by the changing composition of the kibbutz, the heterogeneity of members and the three generations present in the family unit.

But women, as Suzanne Keller argues in her chapter in this

111

book, clearly have not obtained the degree of liberation originally anticipated, they have not been freed from all but a minimum of domestic chores, nor have they been employed in an equal number of senior positions as men. They have tended to be employed in the nonproductive service jobs and have consequently been accorded a lower status, though some of the left-wing kibbutzim have planned industry suitable for women. Family relationships have been changing. Formerly work was assigned to husband and wife at different times, leaving little opportunity for family social life. Relationships have been affected by the greater division of labor between husband and wife, the increase in the number of children, the greater role of the family in the socialization process, the fact that many children now sleep in the family home and the existence of three generations. All this, while creating a greater family solidarity, has put a heavier domestic burden on the woman.

An equally difficult, if new, problem to resolve is that of the aged. Concern has been produced by their growing dependence on the community, their lack of specialized training useful for productive purposes, their occasional blocking of occupational opportunities for younger members and the inevitably increased strength of family ties. The problem is particularly acute for older women who, in addition to occupational difficulties, have in general also been less concerned with civic affairs, a possible occupational alternative. For both men and women the kibbutz ethic of work has meant less concern with the problem of leisure. The existence of the older generation has led in recent years to the organization of leisure activities, special health care, convenient housing arrangements and regular pensions. But anxiety about the proper life for senior citizens in the kibbutz still remains.

The kibbutz is now into its third generation, and there are necessarily differences of perception between the generations. The younger generation has tended to remain; in the Kibbutz Haartzi federation no more than 5 percent and in all kibbutzim no more than 20 percent leave the kibbutz. But the intensity of ideological belief has declined as the educational level has increased, the strongest change being among the younger generation.

For the older generation the kibbutz was to be an ideal community, the implementation of the vision of future society. To the second generation it is a natural home and form of existence in which individual aspirations can be fulfilled and less stress put on self-sacrifice. The impact of A. D. Gordon's views of the dignity of manual labor, of work as a basic value and of self-labor being the solution to both the Jewish social and national problem is now less pronounced. There is more participation in the economic aspects of the kibbutz and less in those of a political nature, or those requiring group activity, on the part of the second generation. There is also less occasion or desire to see asceticism as a virtue or an ideal, and less fear of the undesirable effects of consumption. There is now more stress on the desirability of a longer and more advanced education. Some observers have seen the second generation as rather conservative in its behavior and sexual attitudes, and thus rather different from the original pioneers of the first generation with their view of a much looser form of sexual relationship and their antagonism to the bourgeois concept of marriage. But such a comparison does not sufficiently take into account the heritage of Jewish tradition, which opposes promiscuity.

The kibbutz has to be seen as an institution in a society which is not only developing rapidly from an economic point of view, but which also has governmental institutions that now perform functions once performed by the kibbutz, such as absorption of immigrants, defense and social welfare. A growing educational system and knowledge industry and the highly competent Israel Defense Forces have reduced the glamor of the kibbutz.

The prominence of its members in public bodies and its elitist place in society will probably be reduced as other institutions produce figures worthy of admiration and a pattern of activity regarded as desirable. Necessarily, the kibbutz has had to adapt to increased immigration and outside competition.

Despite changes in ideology, population (numbers and structure) and economic needs and values, the kibbutz remains a unique institution with a remarkable record: self-sufficiency without greed or materialist spirit; cooperation without a coercive apparatus; equality without a reduction of cultural or intellectual standards; freedom without disorder; work with neither boredom nor need of incentives: self-expression without license; specialization without stratification; guidance of public opinion without repression; moral concern without dogmatism; industrialization without urbanization; rural life without idiocy. Georges Friedmann is not alone in believing that the kibbutz is the biggest and most successful utopian experiment in the world. It is not paradoxical that the realization of prophetic anticipation of the future and a fascinating institutional example for other peoples should have come from the ancient land of Israel.

8

Suzanne Keller

THE FAMILY

IN THE KIBBUTZ:

WHAT LESSONS FOR US?

More than 60 years have passed since the first kibbutz was founded by young idealists fleeing anti-Semitism and oppression in their homeland. Imbued with the goals of nineteenth century socialism, Jewish nationalism and Tolstoyan morality, they sought to start afresh in a new land and create a just and humane society.

One of the settlers' initial aims was to dispel the crippling stereotype of Jews as superintellectuals incapable of working with their hands. As socialist idealists, the pioneers also hoped to prove the superiority of cooperative social forms over competitive ones. In a context of cooperation and justice they sought to demonstrate the true worth of every individual regardless of creed, age or sex. Individuals would work for and be rewarded by the community directly. Women would no longer have to depend upon men economically, legally or spiritually, and patriarchal power over the young and the women would be broken forever. The harsh conditions and priorities of pioneer life focused collective attention and commitments on communal needs. The family, whatever its form,

The author wishes to thank Marie Syrkin, Malcah Yaeger and Lucille Pevsner for their helpful criticism.

had to take second place. Since few of the young founders were married and even fewer had children, this posed no special hardships. The relationship between the family and the collective only became an urgent problem later, when the founders themselves became parents. Later still, as the founders became grandparents, personal and family concern would not always coincide smoothly with collective priorities.

In this chapter I will concentrate on findings from some of those settlements which were founded and developed on those ideals— those kibbutzim which have made the most radical attempts to change family and child-rearing institutions. For it is in these communities that the costs, benefits, achievements and failures of sexual equality, communal child rearing and an altered division of labor are most apparent.

SOME KEY INNOVATIONS IN THE FAMILY

In their desire to alter the relations between the sexes and the generations, the pioneers were led, through trial and error, to a redefinition of marriage, work and motherhood. The bourgeois model of marriage which prevailed in nineteenth century Europe, with its disadvantages for women and children masked by romantic illusions and filial pieties, was rejected in favor of a more personal and private one. The woman was no longer to depend on her husband for any of the usual support. She could earn her own living; she did not maintain a private household for her mate; she did not assume his name; and she did not exclusively care for their children. Hence the relations between the couple could rest on intrinsic considerations of affection and compatability rather than on status and security. And since each partner was to have a distinct legal identity, neither a woman's social status nor her standard of living depended on her husband's failures or achievements.

In the very early years there were attempts to do away with monogamous marriage altogether by experimenting, informally, with polygamy and polyandry and by abandoning such terms as husband, wife and marriage. But monogamy soon became the accepted form, though with some important innovations. Although a man and a woman could now join together on the basis of desire uncontaminated by mundane needs for economic security or social status, the couple as an entity was somehow to keep itself in the

116

background. Couples were discouraged from spending their leisure time together and kept friendships, work schedules and vacations separate. Marriage was considered a private affair; public displays of affection were kept to a minimum, and divorce was relatively painless.

Given the pressures and problems of building a settlement in the desert, communal loyalty was placed above family loyalty. The kibbutz assumed many of the functions formerly assigned to the family and developed many ingenious devices to prevent "the consolidation of the family as a distinct and independent unit." [1] Husbands and wives were allotted separate jobs, and there was a strict ban on assigning members of the same family to the same place of work. And with both men and women laboring long, hard hours in the fields, dining and household services had to be organized communally.

Initially, too, because of the difficulties of building a community from scratch and under extremely unfavorable conditions, children were not especially welcome. It was feared that children would divide rather than unite the community by deflecting energies and loyalties from the communal to the personal sphere.[2] Later these attitudes changed, and children were hailed as a treasured link to the future, but the highest acclaim continued to be reserved for productive work. Collective nurseries, one of the key social contributions of the kibbutz, were initially developed as much to free the mothers for needed labor as to free the children from the worst features of traditional family life.

From the start, therefore, we notice a curious contradiction. Adults were expected to marry and live in a sustained partnership with a member of the opposite sex. But at the same time they were not to put conjugal ties above their ties to the community. How to walk the thin line between conjugal and communal commitment was a source of unresolved tension from the very beginning. As the community grew, moreover, so did a concern with the birth rate, which was far below replacement level. Hence there was an early stimulus to family and procreative concerns.

The kibbutz has made extraordinary achievements in the sphere of family life, and has accomplished a large part of what its founders set out to do:

1. It broke the power of the father, or of the patriarchy, over women, children and household.
2. It eliminated the legal, economic and personal dependency of the wife on the husband.

3. It developed an effective method of child rearing.
However, the promised equality of the sexes has failed to materialize to the extent envisaged, and this remains one of the major
contemporary problems of the kibbutz.

THE DIVISION OF LABOR BY SEX

Contrary to ideology and public pronouncement, a fairly pervasive and clear-cut division of labor by sex has emerged in the
kibbutz, both within the household and in the wider community.
It is true that the context of household care has been communally
organized, but there are now tendencies towards a more traditional
household organization with women responsible for its operation.
The reasons for this are complex: housework grew more time-
consuming as apartments became larger and better appointed; more
time could be spent with the children; and some meals could be
taken at home rather than in the communal dining hall. The
couple continues to share some household duties, such as afternoon
tea or play with the children, but essentially the woman has the
main responsibility; the husband is her temporary stand-in or assistant.[3] Even child care, a pleasant duty focused mainly on affection and attention and devoid of most onerous disciplinary
aspects, has assumed certain sex-typed characteristics. Fathers are
active outside of the apartment in yard, farm and community,
whereas mothers prevail within the home. Mothers tend to be
more involved with very young infants and with the bodily well-
being of children, while fathers attend to older children and to
matters of their moral education. So the parents divide along a
number of lines, and the children gradually come to see mother
as representative of "the family in the kibbutz" and father as
representative of "the kibbutz in the family." All of this takes
place in a generally egalitarian context, however, and without sex-
based patterns of authority. But as is often the case, the ideology
of equality is more pronounced in theory than in practice.

The sexual division of labor, though extensively modified on
the domestic level, has not been effaced entirely. Still, there is far
less separation than in the larger kibbutz community, where occupations are clearly and extensively sex-typed.

Initially, as much as possible, work was assigned without sexual
consideration, and women participated extensively in traditionally

118

masculine tasks, while men, though even then to a smaller degree, did some of the traditional feminine tasks within the household.[4] But now a clear-cut sex-patterning of work exists. Men are associated with agriculture, production and central public administration and women with services and education. Closer inspection reveals a fairly detailed sex-typing of work, with women entirely absent in some fields (fishery, carpentry, machine maintenance) but not in others (poultry raising). One wonders about the rationale for this. It cannot be only the oft-cited difference in physical strength of women which assigns them to orchards but not to carpentry or, conversely, which sees men teaching the higher but not the lower school grades. Surely we note here the operation of some system of belief about men's and women's inherent or traditional capacities and aptitudes.

The result is that the overall division of labor by sex is not radically different in the kibbutz from what it is outside. The vast majority of kibbutz women are engaged in non-income-producing activities and in fields traditionally assigned to women. The majority of men, on the other hand, are engaged in occupations considered masculine. A survey of 818 members of 18 kibbutzim showed that there were very few cross-overs.[5]

As a result several writers have made the point that women did become free from individual household and child-care responsibilities only to find themselevs doing these same tasks on a communitywide basis. The *metaplot* (communal nurses) are all women (most of them young), and the same holds true for kindergarten teachers, cooks in the communal dining halls, and functionaries in the central kitchens and nurseries. Rabin contends that objective needs compelled women to take up the very jobs from which the kibbutz had promised to liberate them.[6] And Spiro observes that women used to participate in a variety of family and household tasks, but now they have become specialists who do nothing else for eight hours a day.[7]

Women are also underrepresented in the managerial and leadership positions of the community. They are altogether absent from some committees and are predominant in those dealing with concerns defined as feminine, such as health, education and services. Talmon found that men predominate in the central offices as well as in committees devoted to planning and security. In three committees—those in charge of work assignments, social relations and cultural activities—men and women were proportionately represented. Most committees do have both sexes represented, though not proportionately, but community leadership is largely in male hands.

Part of the reason for this imbalance has to do with the occupational concentration of women and men, each gaining experience in some areas but not in others. Hence, committee work will favor those who know something about the areas involved—which takes us right back to occupational sex-typing and its carryover into other spheres. Moreover, women do not seem to be keen to serve on committees, and therefore avoid being nominated. Given their growing responsibilities in the home, combined with full-time work outside it, committee work would be yet a third obligation to cut into their limited free time.[8]

All in all, then, we note a growing differentiation of the sexes in work, leadership and family. Women have less opportunity for the most prestigious and rewarded positions in the kibbutz economy and polity, a fact not lost on them. One survey of 300 high school seniors [9] showed that while girls identified their future with the kibbutz they felt that there were not enough interesting jobs for women there. And a sharp sex difference was noted on a question about feminine propensities for household care, with the girls disclaiming and the boys insisting on a strong affinity between the two. Despite their joint upbringing, they clearly possessed different conceptions of femininity.

There has, indeed, been a basic reorganization of work in the kibbutz, but it affects husbands and wives rather than men and women generally. Husbands do not have to support wives, and wives do not have to cook and keep house for husbands. Both are members of the community on their own, and neither derives status from the other. On a deeper level, however, the equation of man as worker and of woman as mother remains intact. Whatever else women may do, however hard they may work, they are still first and foremost mothers. This has created some of the same problems of time allocation and cross-pressures between jobs and maternity which beset women in noncollective societies. Partly in response to this, women will forgo more prestigious and demanding employment in favor of the unskilled manual and service work which combines more easily with their maternal duties. Thus the kibbutz has succeeded in freeing wives from dependence on their husbands but it has not substantially altered the division of labor or rank between men and women.

The rank and prestige hierarchy in the kibbutz is more closely related to the situation and opportunities of the sexes than appears at first glance, for the differential distribution of rewards which it reflects readily lends itself to the creation of permanent status divisions. Raising a cash crop is considered more important than cooking the food or doing the laundry, even though the latter are clearly essential and even indispensable services. The problem is a familiar one in social stratification. It stems from the assessment of the contribution made to the wealth as distinct from the welfare of the community. Raising a cash crop adds something of value that was not there before. It can be exchanged. Cleaning and mending cannot be—at least not until we use more adequate yardsticks of collective well-being and communal wealth. Raising cash crops, irrigating the desert, developing economic and technical resources are, of course, also more difficult than cooking or cleaning. Thus the cash crop raiser is likely to be considered as making the more significant contribution to communal prosperity on both counts. Productive work will thus be ranked above service work, and by association, men will rank higher than women. Even though the woman's role of producing children adds "something of value that was not there before," men's productive work still ranks higher than women's reproductive work.

The discrepancy between the ideal of equality between the sexes and the reality must pose special hardships for women. Financial nondependency on husbands and the right to self-support are, of course, important gains for kibbutz women, but these are advantages only if opportunities for self-support are favorable. We have seen that they are relatively less so for women than for men. In addition, women have a double burden of job plus familial obligations. Hence they face the same problem women face in the outside world as they try to find a way to combine motherhood with status-conferring and meaningful work outside of the home. Should they fail to do so, they might choose to forgo the right to self-support in favor of full-time motherhood, a prospect which some are evidently seriously contemplating. Thus, in the work arena, women in the kibbutz confront two key problems: lower status in the community stemming from the lesser value attached to the work assigned them; and the absence of work satisfaction which becomes "an essential—and unfulfilled—need once economic independence has been achieved." [10]

For these and other reasons the woman question has reemerged in the kibbutz in full force. Women experience and express dissatisfaction with their relatively lower status and their double load of work, and they are among the chief instigators when couples leave the kibbutz.[11] Spiro considers this a problem of the first order. "With the exception of politics," he writes, "nothing occupies so much attention in the kibbutz. . . ." He goes on to note that "if Kiryat Yedidim should ever disintegrate, the 'problem of the woman' will be one of the main contributing factors." [12]

REASONS FOR THE PERSISTENCE OF
THE WOMAN QUESTION

The kibbutz experiment has made extraordinary contributions in a number of areas. Sexual equality, in the full meaning of the term, is not, however, one of them. Women did achieve freedom from domestic bondage, but this freedom did not bring full dignity and status.

Communal child care does free women from most, though not all, of the tasks of child rearing, but it frees them for work which may not be as gratifying. Women are still concentrated in kitchens, laundries and nurseries. Femininity is still focused on a nurturant, service ideal. But now, instead of doing one family's dishes and laundry, women do those of hundreds. And instead of service to one household, service now extends to the entire community. Not surprisingly, many women fail to see these developments as proof of liberation, emancipation or equality, by any definition.

As discussed earlier, the goal of economic equality between the sexes, sincerely, even passionately proclaimed and pursued, has been blocked by two unexpected developments in kibbutz life. One was the renewed emphasis on reproduction as population growth became necessary; the other, the need for specialization of work (and of leadership) as the community grew larger and more heterogeneous. The one reenforced the social importance of motherhood; the other the necessity for male political leadership and full-time work specialization.

There are three levels one must consider in tracing the implications of the increased birth rate, scale and specialization of work. On the community level, women's procreative contribution accentuates their maternal image, while also promoting a growth in service work and preoccupation with the welfare of children. It thereby changes the balance between productive and nonproductive work.

On the domestic side, more children, higher living standards, larger households to care for, accentuates a domestic division of labor in the familiar direction—which is also the line of least resistance. Childbirth, childcare and household care form part of a complex yet coherent whole.[13]

On the subjective level still other factors come into play. With an increased emphasis on childbearing and maternity, deeply rooted biopsychological needs and desires, repressed in the early pioneer days, reemerge and turn women away from the masculine work arena. Then there is the impact of childbirth itself and the special ties fostered between infant and mother. These lead, at least for some women, to a demand to take care of her own infant for a time. Whether or not this desire is natural, it has obviously not been culturally erased by the radical changes in child rearing over the past several decades. And as women spend more time anticipating the arrival of their progeny and later in caring for them, work interests and concerns change also. Pregnant women are transferred to lighter tasks, and nursing mothers may work only part-time in order to be near their infants. This creates job disruptions, loss of time for seniority and other discontinuities which the more specialized or essential tasks can ill afford. Thus men come to predominate in these activities, and women gravitate to the less-skilled, less-demanding work which they can more readily combine with their family concerns and time schedules. But the development is neither smooth nor simple as women find themselves aspiring to incompatible goals of maternity and child rearing as well as participation in the highest and most valued activities of the community.

The problem is not, however, only one of type of work, or of rank available, nor even of the time allocation between two compelling responsibilities. It goes deeper than that. It lies in the fact that the kibbutz endeavored to change the status of women without basically revising its stereotypes of male and female. Nor was there sufficient awareness that by assigning primacy to productive work it gave primacy to the male role and, by derivation, to men. This had as one unintended result the fact that women would be more eager to perform men's work than men to do that of women. The stipulated changes in the relations between the sexes were thus headed primarily in one direction. Equalization proceeded along a one-way street.

We realize now that the early kibbutz conception of equality between the sexes rests on turning one of the sexes into a partial version of the other. For this is what happens when women gauge their emancipation by their opportunities to do men's work rather than by their contribution in their own right. The occupational similarities fostered thereby are deceptive. They do not erase the basic sex differentiation, nor the values attached to it, but merely push it out of sight. Thus women, engaged in proving their equality, have tacitly accepted a male yardstick for it. With the renewed emphasis on procreation, the reproductive division between the sexes comes to the fore once again and women are caught up in cross-purposes from which escape is difficult. Under such conditions dissatisfaction is unavoidable, role conflict virtually inescapable. Equality must mean something more than and different from submerging one sex into the other. But to achieve this, equality must be defined differently. In this vein, one writer suggests that achievement "of equality is not a matter of getting women into one occupation or another, of having more women in the Knesset . . . but of conscious education toward a full partnership of the sexes in household management and raising a family— and in this respect we are still back in the bush." [14]

The notion that equality should mean neither the loss of identity nor the adoption of male patterns and objectives may lie behind the resistance to this conception of emancipation among women in many parts of the world. In the kibbutz this expresses itself in a noticeable generation conflict between militant feminists of the pioneer generation, with their denial of the conventional insignias of femininity, and an equally militant generation of granddaughters who insist on their right to be different from men, to be feminine, to accent beauty, eros and the creation of life.[15]

At the same time, however, the present generation of women feel relatively secure about the rights and opportunities won for them by their feminist forebears. Their demands for finery and flirtation thus rest on rights previously attained by the matriarchs of old. Not having won these rights, they also do not fear to lose them, a confidence not, however, shared by the pioneer women who are apprehensive about the young women's indifference.

One of the key problems confronting the women of the kibbutz, then, concerns the partial as well as only partially realizable conception of equality between the sexes which prevails there. This, combined with the unmistakable if tacit pressure on women to become "equal," meaning like men (plus the improbability of attaining equality), gradually results in their more or less passive resistance and a turning back to traditional feminine preoccupations, a rejection of masculine prizes and values, and a return to a modified form of familism. The women thus reject an equality that implies giving up their identity. When, in addition, maternity becomes socially desirable and necessary again, the one-sided equality and formal "de-differentiation" between the sexes recedes in favor of separateness and differentiation.

EGALITARIANISM

Granting the limited conception of equality in the kibbutz, based as it was on hard productive labor, minimal family involvement and particular occupational activities, how could women possibly achieve equality? Only by working hard in agriculture, in central administration and in specialized jobs involving machinery and manual skills; by not having children, because this takes time away from production; not doing service work, because this ranks lower than productive work; and by stressing a style of strength, sobriety and collective responsibility. Anything short of that must reduce their chances for equal access, equal honor and equal achievement.

But we already know that they cannot compete on these terms since they do have children, do concern themselves with their offsprings' care and growth, do concentrate on service work and do exhibit a different expressive style. Were they not to do these things, they would not be women, but men or quasi-men. And since these activities are also essential, men would have to find ways to do them or, where naturally incapacitated (such as in bearing children), would have to find substitutes for them. But for some reason, this basic imbalance in the prevalent definition of equality is not acknowledged. And women, having accepted a male value system, feel and actually are relatively inadequate to meet its demands.

Kibbutz society, according to a number of observers, "is first and foremost a society of men." [16] Its values and projects reflect male more than female concerns. And the ideology of sex equality does not penetrate very deeply. Talmon found that lip service was paid to the ideal of equality but that in practice "the effects of former socialization" and the impact of growing differentiation in household and community limited its realization. She also stressed that "covert conventional role images underlie the attitudes to many other tasks." [17]

Indeed one notes that the creed of economic and social equality by sex has stopped short of challenging the basic stereotypes of male and female. These were somehow to remain intact and not radically affected by economic self-reliance, the independence of spouses and the new nondomestic focus of women. Old stereotypes persist. "The conception of women as reticent, passive, and placating has not disappeared." [18] Drive, self-assertion and strong involvement in public life are considered unfeminine, and women exhibiting these traits are regarded with ambivalence.

In truth, the masculine bias that prevails in the kibbutz is striking. The yardstick against which individual contributions are measured is geared to the capacities and achievements of men; hence the tendency to interpret the failure of sex equality as the fault of women's lesser ability to do heavy physical labor, or needing to take time out for pregnancy and infant care, or otherwise being women. But this roster of relative inadequacies is in itself a reflection of a hidden hierarchy of values. These are values which rank one type of contribution to collective survival categorically higher than the other, with the result that those performing these activities will likewise be ranked unequally. Unless the basis for this ranking is changed, therefore, inequality between the sexes is inevitable.

The same bias is reflected in the ambivalent attitudes towards pregnancy and childbirth about which kibbutz culture, like other male-oriented cultures, is of two minds. Even though these major female events are essential to social survival, they nonetheless are considered secondary to economic productivity. Indeed, the pioneering founders, radical though they may have been on other grounds, were quite conventionally male in their designation of pregnancy, childbirth and lactation as "the biological tragedy of woman." Instead of seeing these as the fundamental life forces they are—or perhaps because the truth caused them jealousy—they designated the female capacity to bear children as something of a deficiency and limitation. Thus were early priorities expressed and apparently accepted by men and women alike.

The pervasive masculine bias in the kibbutz must create considerable psychological strains for women. They are members of a society that plays down feminine capacities without ceasing to emphasize their necessity. Motherhood and femininity, while important, are not important enough. This sets up a current of relative deprivation and discontent with which we are all too familiar.

Given these contradictions and frustrations, women may well seek to revert or escape into the tried and true domain of home, family, children. Not only would this make life easier in the sense of fewer cross-pressures, but it would also permit women to play starring rather than subordinate roles. And while a return to "familism" would probably accentuate the sex division in kibbutz society, it would also help women to recoup a lost self that has left them literally in no man's land.

Thus, gradually, if reluctantly, women begin to concentrate on children, services and quality of life, while the men become engrossed in the wider community. The traditional dichotomy of the industrial nuclear family begins to reemerge. At first, according to Polani,[19] the women struggled terribly against these developments: "Enraged and bewildered they saw a breach forming in their common front with the men." That rage suggests that the return to familism is not totally voluntary, not totally a reflection of women's natural disposition towards motherhood and child care. Part of that rage must have reflected their awareness of a loss of status, of a partial return to the gilded cage. For in the value system of the kibbutz, participation in public life is valued above domestic commitments, raising crops over bearing children. Women thus lose on both grounds.

The problem is not simply one of service versus productive labor, or of individual versus shared maternity, important though these be. It concerns the self-esteem of women in a society that does not sufficiently appreciate their contribution as women. This, combined with contradictory messages as to where women's primary goals lie—in service work for the community or in bearing and caring for children—creates special hardships for women, hardships as yet insufficiently appreciated.

The question that arises is: Why are kibbutz settlers ambivalent about femininity and activities traditionally labeled feminine? In part it may be a rational response to needed priorities in community building. But in part it seems to reflect irrational and unexamined fears. One author has suggested that the deprecation of femininity has its source in the lack of self-esteem among men. The male founders may have had serious anxieties about their own self-worth. Their manhood undermined in the society that rejected them, they became intent on securing it in the society they would create.[20]

The emphasis on masculinity entered the self-conceptions of women as well as of men and resulted in their playing down femininity as traditionally defined. Hence when women, in the pioneer days, rejected makeup, attention to dress and personal appearance, it was not only because there were more important things to worry about, but also because they sought to prove themselves equal in style to their masculine models. This has to be expected when a culture draws an erroneous equivalence between being equal and being masculine.

Thus the problem of the woman in the kibbutz turns out, in part at least, to be a problem of men. The woman question conceals another, more fundamental one, having to do with male self-doubt and male self-deception about their feelings and fears concerning women. Yet virtually no one has inquired into men's difficulties and dissatisfactions in the kibbutz. Everyone has been so busy investigating women's trials and tribulations that we are quite ignorant about the men and their problems as men.

Developments in the kibbutz demonstrate a pattern familiar from other social experiments where women became "free" to do work previously reserved for men. At first there is the lure of novelty and the challenge to prove oneself, but both become less compelling in time. And since sex-typing persists in areas other than work participation (where, ideally, it is effaced), in time men and women will gravitate to different spheres of interest and activity. So, for example, men have increasingly found their way into leadership positions in kibbutz society. There they will likely as not remain, as the women shuttle back and forth between their procreative and their productive undertakings.

Moreover, there is a heritage of unconscious prejudice and past traditions which help perpetuate the relative inferiority of women in the kibbutz. True, this inferiority is not personal or domestic—a genuine advance over other modern societies—but its link to occupational participation threatens to make it communitywide. For in the kibbutz, too, "the less talented man will sometimes be preferred to the more talented woman." [21] To be equal a woman must be exceptional.

Hence I must disagree with those who assert that civic and economic equality has been achieved by the women of the kibbutzim and that what remains are psychological survivals and lingering prejudice. In my view women have the dubious freedom to have two lifetime preoccupations: low-ranking jobs and part-time motherhood.

In sum, the kibbutz has not eliminated sex inequality though it has substantially reduced sex differentiation in marriage, ideology and work. As a result the woman question cannot be put to rest: first, because the original ideals to abolish the sexual division of labor and to create equality of status have been imperfectly realized;

and second, because the basic conceptions of what is masculine and what is feminine remain relatively unchanged. All of this occurs in a culture which contains elements of defensive masculinity and the downgrading of feminine capacities and contributions to which this typically leads. In the long run this must lead to a growing divergence between ideal and reality in the kibbutz.

The divergence between ideal and reality in sexual equality, and the strains it engenders, are already apparent. The dilemmas created thereby have led to countermeasures in the kibbutz to halt the trend toward the growing normative and institutional sex differentiation for fear that it would eventually undermine communal solidarity.[22] Hence "ingenious" intermediate mechanisms have emerged to bridge the gap between ideal and reality. These are most prominent in the occupational sphere where sex differentiation is also most pronounced. They include the rationalization and mechanization of services, which makes them less labor-intensive and thus releases some women for other kinds of work. They also raise efficiency and output, and make the service sector altogether more attractive and prestigious as a calling. Professionalization, another such mechanism, endeavors, via scientific and tested techniques, to turn housekeeping and child care into semi-professions, which increases the expertise and standing of those engaged in them. Some effort is also devoted to expanding the occupational opportunities of women into new areas such as counseling, arts and crafts, and social work.

In addition the kibbutz endeavors to discourage symbolic and actual sex differentiation by exerting pressure on women to join as many committees as possible, to develop new and non-sex-typed branches of occupational activities, and to favor women candidates in areas where they are now underrepresented. There is even an attempt to make men engage in specifically feminine occupations on a short-term basis, in kitchen and dining hall which have high communal visibility. These symbolic denials of sex differentiation are considered only a "token interchangeability" by Talmon, however; almost a kind of atonement for the way the community is structured. And then there are always the exemplary women who have achieved "equality in spite of serious difficulties" or, as I would say, equality on masculine terms, who serve as proof of the absence of deliberate discrimination as well as inspiring examples to others.

As yet then there is neither a rigidity of pattern nor a crystallization of sentiment and habit. I have described central tendencies, major pressures and contradictions, and sources of strain that are moving the community to greater sex differentiation in work and in life. However, the situation is in flux, and there is much room for experimentation and variation. There is also a changing config-uration of emphases at different stages of the life cycle. When young and without children, women are engaged in masculine or joint occupations. When children appear they become engrossed in feminine services of all kinds. Later in life they return to less feminine pursuits. And similarly, men past their productive prime will perform lighter, less "masculine-type" work. Mobility and cross-overs between sex-typed spheres of life are possible, even frequent, but the spheres are valuated unequally.

CHILD REARING IN THE KIBBUTZ

Patterns of childrearing in the kibbutz are important for at least two reasons: the impact of a different kind of mothering on women and children, and the degree of sex differentiation in childhood.

Mothering in the Kibbutz

Two features strike the observer of kibbutz child rearing. One is the fact that like all pioneer societies, the kibbutz is extremely child centered. Children represent the future, the vindication of one's struggles and sacrifices. The other is that kibbutz child rear-ing is performed by communal agents, an innovation of consider-able significance. Communal child rearing, whatever its difficulties, has proven itself an effective method of raising children. This is attested to by numerous studies that show the superiority of kibbutz-reared children in a number of areas—including their idealism, autonomy, cooperation, capacity for leadership, courage and loyalty to the community. In fact, the kibbutz seems to have managed to combine individual and collective aspects of child care in admirable fashion. A child not only knows and loves his own mother but also forms close and enduring ties with other adults and with children of his own age. This peer group, varying between eight and 16 members at different points during childhood, is part of the child's life from the time he enters the infant house at the age of four days until high school.

Altogether at least four adult women are involved with child care. There is, of course, the child's biological mother, who is joined by the chief communal nurse (the metapelet) and her two assistants. The biological mother remains the child's alone, whereas the social mothers must be shared with the other children. This, then, forms the setting for socialization of the child as he moves through the toddler's house, kindergarten, primary grades and on to high school at 12 years of age. From their age-mates, who form their most continuous membership group, and from the women who care for their needs, children learn the fundamentals of the world in which they will live.

The division between biological and social mother, between family and nursery, is present from the earliest days. The child develops somewhat different relations to each. With his biological mother, the child develops especially warm relations despite disrupted contacts because he knows that this is the woman who gave him life. In addition this is the woman who represented the whole world during the first four days of life and who is the source of nourishment during the first six weeks. Thus a child's first impressions, nurture, warmth and love come from his biological mother.

This mother is not the only source of security for the child, however. There is also the metapelet, who actually spends more continuous time with the child; while less romantic a figure, she has more actual influence on the child's day-to-day life. But while the mother can focus wholly on her child, the metapelet must divide her time among several children and in that sense she may have a less concentrated impact on any one of them. It is she, however, who becomes the focus for sibling rivalry and competition for attention among the children. She is also the one who is in charge of disciplining them. Thus, whereas the mother can be totally nurturant, loving and nonpunitive, the nurse must combine affection with discipline.[23] Like the mother in a conventional family, therefore, she becomes an ambivalent figure in the child's life. She has the power of punishment and reward.

Thus the communal nurses exact demands, can threaten and thwart, thereby creating dependencies and anxieties. The mothers, by contrast, can play a highly positive role. Freed from economic worries for themselves or their children, not having to discipline them, and associated from the earliest days with warmth, nurturance and survival itself, they can be extremely loving and supportive fig-

131

ures in their children's lives. Only their classification as females may make them targets, by association, for some of the ambivalence felt towards the metapelet.

The child views his father as special, too, and sees him as the husband of his mother, as a worker in the kibbutz, and as playmate and giver of gifts. Unlike the father in a typical Western family, however, the kibbutz father can be an even more permissive and nurturant figure than the mother, for in the household shared by the couple, even in a kibbutz, it is still the woman who must keep things in order and make demands for cleanliness and comportment. Since living quarters are small such demands are unavoidable, but they do fall to the mother. The father is not considered responsible for household activities. "His occupational role makes him a hero in the eyes of the growing child. Most of the occupations are known even by small children, and among the first words a child learns are the names of his parents' occupational roles. . . . According to the existing pattern of the division of labor, his father will be the one who is recognized as responsible for the farm . . . in the eyes of the child, the wider world." [24] Thus in a sense the father's role has changed more dramatically in the kibbutz than elsewhere, although most studies, imbued with the motherhood mystique, have paid very little attention to him.

Kibbutz fathers should, in fact, represent the epitome of selfless, loving parenthood. Unlike the mother who as a woman may be partly identified wtih the ambivalently regarded nurse, the father has no such association to fight against. I would expect, therefore, that the good father should be a developing archetype in the kibbutz. This may be linked in subtle ways to the longing for the ideal father which patriarchal systems implant in the young. Paradoxically, in successfully breaking patriarchal power, the kibbutz may also have succeeded in reinstating the paternal ideal. If this is carried over to the more prestigious occupational roles of men, the male role can emerge in a very positive light, purged of its major negative features.

The biological family is thus less complex a system for the kibbutz child than for children generally, since the mother and father roles are relatively undifferentiated in their emphasis on affection, permissiveness and nurturance towards the child. The family is expressive rather than task-oriented, and the child can use the family setting for reinforcement and support, since it is and remains an unconditional source of love and diffuse acceptance.

What about mothering, then? Have any of the dire effects of

multiple mothering and communal child rearing been demonstrated in the kibbutz? Bettelheim notes how reluctant American psychologists and psychiatrists were to find value in the kibbutz experiment. Their objections to separating children from their parents, especially from their mothers, blinded them to some of the considerable advantages of such an upbringing. Among these are the division of labor among mothers, the voluntary assumption of motherhood in its more delimited form by those specially gifted for it, and the absence of those debilitating struggles between the home and the world of housebound mothers in industrialized societies. There is also the positive influence of peer group socialization and the confidence, trust and cooperation it helps develop. Indeed, with regard to the basic values of the kibbutz, the experiment seems successful since the children seem socialized into the values of the community, are self-reliant, idealistic and committed to the group and its goals.

Bettelheim saw as one positive gain for kibbutz children the freedom from ambivalence towards parents that the small family usually engenders. Not dependent on their parents for economic security or social destiny, they are freer to develop emotional relations untainted by resentment, anxiety and self-interest. As a consequence, however, he also noted a comparative lack of emotional intensity in the relations between parents and children. "Blood simply is not thicker than shared emotional experiences" and it is the latter which binds people together—which means that parents must here compete with peers and nurses.[25]

Since dependency is shared or diffused in the kibbutz, the child has a number of different models, all important in their own way but none as exclusively and uniquely important as parents in the Western nuclear family. There is multiple mothering, the good father and the same-age peer group. There are also siblings to whom one is linked via one's biological parents.

The absence of the biological mother did not cause the maternal deprivation expected. Mothering was not abolished, but increased and divided among several figures. Everyone has remarked on the mother's intense emotional involvement with her children. And though the mother's visits are rationed she constitutes a continuous presence in the child's life. "Collective education has . . . proven that the existence of more than one image in infancy is not only not harmful for personality development, but, on the contrary, may be a very important psychohygienic factor."[26] Another observer notes that the kibbutz belies the assertion that what babies need most are a father and a mother in a house—in other words the conventional Western nuclear family.[27] He also admits that the practice of multiple mothering worked out better than he expected. Indeed, it has been suggested that the solutions hit on in the kibbutz "inadvertently exploded all Western notions about the sanctity of maternal care. If there was one belief cherished by educators and psychiatrists, it was the doctrine that an infant removed from his parents, particularly his mother, and raised together with other children in an institution, was doomed to warped and disastrous results." [28] This has patently been disproved by the kibbutz and the new generation of human beings it has created.

Of course here, as elsewhere, ideal and reality may not always go hand in hand. The kibbutz was an experiment under trying, insecure and very difficult conditions. Poverty, hardship and uncertainty marked the early years, and innovation proceeded through trial and error. Not all communal nurses were devoted and capable rearers of children, and not all children responded to the training and attention they received in a favorable way. Every form of training is a way of mistraining; every discipline creates its rebellion; all supervision is a constraint. Growing up is problematic by definition, since children are forced into channels they have not chosen or been free to choose. But taking into account these general difficulties of socialization and the specific hardships of the kibbutz, the experiment has worked remarkably well.

Finally, not all women respond positively to sharing child rearing responsibilities with nurses and peers. Some, especially those working at unfulfilling jobs, might well prefer to raise their own children. Some may even "romanticize the family" [29] that the pioneers strove so hard to revamp. Freedom *from* child care may seem like an infringement "on motherly rights" for those women who long for an exclusive relation to their children. One such woman recalls a terrible struggle against her conditioning when she let her baby go, fighting the baby house authority all the way.[30] Only later did she relax and appreciate the freedom this made possible and the ensuing harmonious relations between herself and her children. This same woman had occasion to find herself in a conventional family set-up at some later point, while away from the kibbutz, and came to appreciate its virtues more than ever before. She ruefully recalled the free time available, secure in the knowledge that her child was well taken care of, and the complete devotion to the child in the period set aside for her. The minor annoyances of her children in the kibbutz days were "only pinpricks compared to the great wounding rows we have here, in a so-called normal family set-up." [31]

The desire to return to such a setup may be motivated as much by the lack of interesting enough work or by too few chances for conspicuous achievement as by a natural maternal possessiveness. There is the suggestion that "women who hold public office in the kibbutz are less 'family conscious' than women who do not hold office in the community." [32] And the aforementioned witness of her own conversion to communal child care also notes a connection between interesting work and preference for communal child rearing.

All in all, the study of the successes and failures of kibbutz child rearing suggest that in principle children may derive considerable benefit from an upbringing that stresses peer relations, a merging of home and community and voluntary mothers.

Sex Differentiation in Childhood

Despite the changes in the family that have been brought about in the kibbutz, sex-typing has not been abolished there. The couple continues to be a distinctive social, sexual and emotional unit as well as a cultural ideal. Whether sex differentiation is natural or not, the kibbutz, as is true of societies generally, did not try to establish. Instead, it organized the development of appropriate sex identities, interests, and male and female roles in the earliest years of life. Indeed, according to Spiro, the culture's stake in survival made a concern for progeny and procreative roles mandatory. "A proper sexual identification is among the most important tasks of childhood," he observed, and if individuals fail to "identify themselves clearly as either male or female, then they cannot establish differential relationships to adults of the same and opposite sex." [33] Should they fail in this the society is endangered at a crucial point.

Since most adult roles in kibbutz society continue to be sex-typed, to be considered a normal, functioning adult one must conform to the cultural script as written for men and women respectively. Thus, adults might be expected to emphasize the attainment and maintenance of socially sanctioned heterosexual relationships, including parenthood.

In view of the continued focus on heterosexual intimacy and identity, children cannot avoid sex-typing in their own upbringing. There is likely to be some inconsistency in this, however, as the need for male-female differentiation on behalf of reproduction must be reconciled with the proclaimed irrelevance of such differentiation in the running of the community.

Another point of interest is the fact that women continue to be the key figures in the lives of children of both sexes. For, in the kibbutz as in societies with differently organized family systems, children are not only born of woman, but their earliest and deepest impressions gained prior to and at birth are experienced inside of and in close association with a female. Later, it is still females who dominate the child rearing process for boys and girls alike. Thus we note two distinctive attributes of kibbutz society which are shared with other societies around the world: each child is exclusively classified as a member of a given sex, and each child is born of and has its earliest as well as its later experiences of nurturance and care with only one, the female, sex.

Bases of Differentiation in the Kibbutz

Gender identity, sexual identity and sex differentiation of personality and of interests and activities start in early childhood. What, then, do we know about the treatment of kibbutz children according to their gender and sex? How similarly or differently are girls and boys raised? What are their role models? From where do they acquire their identities as future parents, a destiny strongly exalted in the kibbutz?

From infancy onward boys and girls are socialized by the same techniques, taught the same games and treated very much alike in a variety of respects. They eat, sleep, shower and play together. Since they are nonetheless expected to identify with a different sex category, how does this come about? How do they manage to make reliable sex discriminations and tell the sexes apart so as to identify with the "right" sex, especially since the social differentiation of the sexes is not very evident in the children's houses?

A number of clues are used to build up a construct of the opposite sex. One is perception of different anatomies since there is no taboo on nudity among the children. Another is clothing, especially the clothing worn on afternoon visits to parents. Ordinary clothes worn in the nurseries are not sex-typed, but non-play clothes are. Hairstyles also are different for boys and girls, with girls having ribbons and being generally fussed over more regarding their appearance. Then there is language, highly significant in Hebrew, in which every speaker must learn language appropriate to his or her sex. All nouns are either masculine or feminine, and gender affects the declensions of nouns and adjectives. In learning to speak each child also learns to identify itself as male or as female.

Closely allied to language is the area of personal names. These, too, are sex-typed, and since there are fewer names than there are individuals, the same name occurs several times, reenforcing the symbolic division by sex.

By age three a kibbutz child is generally expected to be able to discriminate between the sexes, learn sex-typed names, label others and itself correctly, and have some notion of the absolute and permanent division of these two different classes in human society.

One factor absent in kibbutz society is strong parental differentiation by sex, since the parents perform similar functions for the child and are not, in the very early years, perceptibly differentiated occupationally.

Thus kibbutz children experience differentiation by sex in two principal forms in their childhood years: by being classified as a member of an exclusive gender group, and by learning to differentiate the sexes by name, label, appearance, dress and speech. Every child must go through some such process as this: I am a boy and my metapelet is a woman and I will never be a woman. Or, I am a girl, my metapelet is a woman, and I will also be a woman someday. The sex categorization extends to dress, speech, name, but not to family, economic roles or to occupational activities in the community.

Despite the tendency to minimize sex differentiation in childhood, we note that it nonetheless constitutes a major part of the learning process. By high school age, however, it becomes more explicit and extensive. School curricula become sex-typed, with boys doing heavier labor in the student work assignments and also engaging in competitive sports and the girls turning to other interests and activities.[34] Each sex seems here to prepare itself for the different tasks it will assume in the community later on, though the way in which this is achieved awaits detailed study.

During these years biological maturation at puberty brings sexuality to the fore. Specific heterosexual interests emerge at this time, but heterosexual pairing is not encouraged until after army service and the return to the kibbutz. Then sexual experimentation is more common and continues until couples fall in love and decide to get married. Marriage constitutes a key relationship for adults and is a prerequisite for the procreation of the next generation.

A number of researchers have noted that while the sexes are reared jointly, freely sharing bedrooms and bathrooms, sexual relations in the sibling peer group are discouraged and "the incest taboo is in full force. . . ." [35] This stems from a rather deep-seated sexual puritanism and a sexual repressiveness in childhood which stands in marked constrast to the ideology of nonrepressiveness. This is particularly trying for adolescents who are expected to maintain rather strict control over their sexual impulses at a time of heightened awareness of sex. "They are unrestricted until they get into high school, at which time educators let them know that sexual relations are not desirable and the children themselves erect a shame barrier which up to this time has not seemed to exist." [36]

Not surprisingly, sex seems to be a rather confusing area which readily arouses anxiety. Some of this has been documented by means of Thematic Apperception Tests, protocols in which kibbutz-reared children were shown to differ sharply from other Israeli children. Sex taboos appear to be stronger among them, as is their provisional rejection of heterosexual themes and relations.[37]

Problems in Sex Identity

Since sexual identity is learned, every society must cope with culturally engendered learning problems. The kibbutz has its share. There is, first of all, the significance of the female in the lives of both boys and girls. This must create different problems for each, since boys will not grow up to be adult women. And studies show that boys do have special identity problems. Rabin, for example, found that boys identify less strongly with males than girls do with females (16 percent versus 47 percent). Boys also identified with females twice as frequently as girls identified with males. Some boys reject their male identity altogether and "express their feminine strivings openly" rejecting their maleness in fantasies of self-mutilation.[38] This syndrome, which has been described for other societies, [39] was frequently reported to one researcher in the kibbutz she studied.

Both boys and girls, it appears, identify most strongly with the metapelet, the woman who is most directly and continuously involved in their upbringing. Since they come into contact with a number of these women in the course of childhood, one wonders which one is most significant for them. Or perhaps they all add up to one composite image. Her power to reward and punish seems to make her the principal adult role model for all the children and underscores the significance of power for childhood identification.

Although on none of these questions is there a plethora of information, the role of the father in sex-role identity seems particularly neglected. As was pointed out earlier, the father represents an extremely nurturant, loving, unambivalent figure with considerable prestige for his work role in the kibbutz. This should help boys, though how much is not clear, since the father is not highly differentiated from the mother in early childhood. It should also facilitate the heterosexual adjustments for girls, since the male is both benevolent and nurturant whereas the female, as chief disciplinarian, is an ambivalent figure.

Boys do appear to have more psychological problems in childhood than do girls, a pattern that is fairly widespread in industrial societies. They have less continuity of experience with the same sex-role model, hence less reenforcement in masculinity via their contacts with mother and metapelet. But there is also the suggestion, stemming from the work of Rabin, that kibbutz children tend to identify less with same-sex parents than children not so reared.[40] If this finding is more widely confirmed, it raises a fairly fundamental question about the significance of parental role models for gender identification, which is something of an article of faith today; for it suggests that kibbutz children develop their gender identities by other means.

Still, heterosexuality may well be a focus of anxiety and confusion for kibbutz adolescents. One test asked fourth graders, aged 9 to 11, to draw a male and a female figure. Kibbutz children made far fewer sex differentiations than did other Israeli and American children with whom they were compared.[41] A clear-cut sex identity may be difficult to achieve for children raised in a situation where sex differentiation is minimized in official ideology and in public display, while being emphasized on the personal and private level.

Assessments regarding the family in the kibbutz depend in part on one's definition of the family. If this includes the economic interdependence of the spouses or children's exclusive dependence on their parents, then the family cannot be said to exist. This is Spiro's reason for considering the family to have been essentially eliminated in kibbutzim. The domestic unit in the kibbutz includes neither economic cooperation nor common residence between parents and children nor exclusive parental responsibility for rearing children. Moreover, considering the pioneers' goals of destroying patriarchal family power, the father's role has been reduced, his power and authority annulled. The kibbutz also makes it possible for women to combine motherhood with outside work with the approval of the community. And the children are independent of their parents for subsistence, educational attainments or social standing. The main function remaining to the family unit is reproduction in a context of lifetime companionship and erotic intimacy. Its main contribution is parenthood freed from the burdens of child rearing and child support. This should make parenthood extremely attractive to kibbutz couples.

A number of observers disagree with the view that the family has been disbanded.[42] Talmon-Garber notes that the family always remained a distinct unit, with a line drawn between serious and nonserious sexual relationships. Parents had definite responsibilities toward their children and watched their development with concern and pride. Children were closely attached to their parents. And while the family unit may have spent less time together than a conventional family—though even this is doubtful given the modern suburban household—relations were less strained and less ambivalent. Parents had the blessings of parenthood without its burdens. Children could be loved unconditionally without the sting of discipline. Indeed from this perspective, the original division between family and community responsibilities freed the family from the usual tensions, thereby strengthening its emotional and symbolic hold. The result is that children often become the emotional center of their parents' lives and, in turn, may become overdependent on them.

In one sense, then, the nuclear family has been eliminated in the kibbutz, but in another it has not. It lives on in the fact that the kibbutz does, approvingly, set apart two adults of opposite sex, living in a socially condoned sexual relationship, and closely relating to their own children. Part of the confusion surrounding this question stems from some contradictory objectives entertained by the founders, who simultaneously believed both that the family could be dispensed with and that it was "the basic cell of human society."[43]

Given the growing need for progeny, the original claims dispensing with the family were somewhat premature. In time, moreover, the second generation makes its appearance and causes major social redefinitions in the kibbutz. It promotes a core of specific family duties and loyalties and gives substance to marriage beyond the emotional feelings of the couple. And with the grandparental generation a sense of social and biological continuity develops that may set entire lineages apart as distinctive foci of interest and sentiment.

In time, also, the couple reemerges as an important collective focus. Its union is celebrated, its affection publicly demonstrated, its activities joined. Rituals symbolizing the union—tea with the children, some regular meals taken separately—develop. Gradually kibbutz architects take cognizance of the family's separateness by designing semidetached dwellings as physical symbols of the change. More and more, the couple exists as a sexual, emotional and conjugal entity, sharing living quarters, memories and a destiny through its children.

There is also a growing division of labor within the household, although parental roles continue to be flexible and overlapping. Still, the mother tends to be more involved with household and child care even in their attenuated form. The home is still more the woman's domain.

It is well to keep in mind, however, that the kibbutz has achieved its major aims of destroying the patriarchal family and of liberating the wife from domestic confinement and total dependence on her husband. Indeed, practically none of the traditional functions of the nuclear family remain intact except the one most underestimated at first—procreation of the next generation. For the rest, the family is neither a producing nor a consuming unit, does not socialize or educate its offspring except indirectly, and is not a source of security in old age. Even the couple, refurbished though it be, has been transformed by the equality built into the marriage bond. With traditional dependencies and patterns of authority eliminated, there is ample room for deep bonds of intimacy and affection between mates and the generations.

Increasingly, however, tensions do develop between the family and the collective, as the family claims more rights and a greater voice in the education of its children. There is a basic rivalry, but the collective continues to be preeminent. If the family accepts the primacy of the collective, it is an ally. If it disputes that collective authority, it becomes a danger. The collective still comes first.[44]

141

In sum, there is much we can learn from these small cooperative settlements and their achievements of a new form of family, communal child rearing and equality between the sexes. Beset by danger, lack of resources and inexperience they have made impressive headway in achieving their aims.

One of these objectives, however, equality between the sexes, has been attained only in part. For a number of reasons, overt and covert, subjective and collective, reality has fallen short of the ideal. Some of these reasons are easy to understand though not easy to deal with—for example, the increased sex-typing of work due to the reemergence of a focus on maternity and the activities and preoccupations surrounding it. The birth of a child makes all the difference, in the kibbutz as elsewhere.

But there are also less tangible reasons. They comprise all those beliefs and myths, facts and half-truths, that shape the images of the sexes and their importance in any society. Ultimately, it is the differential importance attributed to the contributions of men and women to survival which underlies the inequality between the sexes in kibbutz life. Given its basic priorities and values, greater equality between the sexes may not be realizable in the foreseeable future.

NOTES

1. Yonina Talmon-Garber, "Family vs. Community—Patterns of Divided Loyalty in Israel," *Comparative Perspectives on Marriage and the Family,* ed. H. Kent Geiger (New York: Little, Brown, 1968), p. 49.

2. Herbert Russcol and Margalit Banai, *The First Million Sabras* (New York: Dodd, Mead, 1970), p. 201.

3. Yonina Talmon, "Sex-Role Differentiation in an Equalitarian Society," *Life in Society,* eds. Thomas Lasswell, John Burma, and Sidney Aronson, (Glenview, Ill.: Scott Foresman, 1965), p. 142.

4. Ibid., p. 146.

5. A. I. Rabin, "The Sexes: Ideology and Reality in the Israeli Kibbutz," *Sex Roles in Changing Society,* eds. G. H. Seward and R. C. Williamson (New York: Random House, 1970), p. 297.

6. Ibid.

7. Melford E. Spiro, *Children of the Kibbutz* (Cambridge, Mass.: Harvard University Press, 1958), ch. 10.

8. Talmon, "Sex Role Differentiation," p. 151.

9. Leslie Y. Rabkin and Karen Rabkin, "Children of the Kibbutz," *Psychology Today,* vol. 3, no. 4 (Sept. 1969) pp. 40-48.

10. Emil Hurwitz, "The Family in the Kibbutz" in *Children in Col-*

lectives, ed. Peter B. Neubauer (Springfield, Ill.: Charles C. Thomas, 1965), p. 361.

11. A. I. Rabin, *Growing up in the Kibbutz,* (New York: Springer, 1965) p. 299.

12. Melford E. Spiro, *Kibbutz; Venture in Utopia* (Cambridge, Mass.: Harvard University Press, 1956), p. 221.

13. Talmon, "Sex Role Differentiation." op. cit.

14. Ruth Bondy, "Granddaughter Wants Conservative Femininity," *Hadassah Magazine* (May 1972) pp. 9, 38.

15. Jacqueline Kahanoff, "Grandmother was a Militant Feminist," *Hadassah Magazine* (May 1972) pp. 8-9, 30-31.

16. Judith Gilan, "Discussion on Women's Role" in Neubauer, *Children in Collectives,* p. 239.

17. Talmon, "Sex Role Differentiation," p. 149.

18. Ibid., p. 153 Menahem Gerson, "Women in the Kibbutz," *American Journal of Orthopsychiatry,* 41 (July 1971): 566-73.

19. J. Ron Polani, "From Collective Education towards Education in Collectivism," in Neubauer, *Children in Collectives,* pp. 330-41.

20. Gilan, "Discussion on Women." op. cit.

21. Dan Leon, *The Kibbutz, a New Way of Life* (Oxford: Pergamon Press, 1969), p. 130.

22. Talmon, "Sex Role Differentiation," pp. 154ff.

23. Rivkah Bar-Yoseph, "Assisting Kibbutz Parents in the Tasks of Child-rearing," ed. Geiger, *Comparative Perspectives,* p. 166.

24. Ibid., p. 173.

25. Bruno Bettelheim, "Does Communal Education Work?," *Commentary,* 33 (Feb. 1962): 123.

26. Neubauer, *Children in Collectives,* p. 70.

27. Gideon Lewin, "Infancy in Collective Education" in Neubauer, *Children in Collectives,* p. 69.

28. Russcol and Banai, *The First Million Sabras,* p. 201.

29. Polani, "From Collective Education," p. 339.

30. Lynne Reid Banks, "Motherhood Kibbutz Style," *Hadassah Magazine,* (May 1972), p. 28.

31. Ibid.

32. Polani, "From Collective Education," p. 339.

33. Spiro, *Kibbutz: Venture in Utopia,* pp. 236-37.

34. Rabin, *Growing Up in the Kibbutz,* pp. 285-307.

35. Edith Buxbaum, *Troubled Children in a Troubled World* (New York: International Universities Press, 1970), p. 285.

36. Ibid., p. 295.

37. Menahem Gerson, "Family Problems in the Kibbutz," in Neubauer, *Children in Collectives,* pp. 233-37.

38. Buxbaum, *Troubled Children,* p. 228; Mordecai Kaufmann, "Compara-

tive Psychopathology of Kibbutz and Urban Children," in Neubauer, *Children in Collectives,* pp. 261-69.

39. Bruno Bettelheim, *Children of the Dream,* (New York: Macmillan, 1969).

40. Rabin, *Growing Up in the Kibbutz,* p. 204.

41. Ibid., p. 110.

42. Uri Bronfenbrenner, "The Dream of the Kibbutz," *Saturday Review,* (Sept. 20, 1969), p. 84.

43. H. Darin-Drabkin, "Collective Agricultural Settlement-Kibbutz Socio-Economic Structure," *International Seminar on Rural Planning,* (Tel Aviv, Oct.-Nov. 1961).

44. Talmon-Garber, "Family vs. Community," p. 56.

9

Menahem Rosner

WORKER PARTICIPATION
IN DECISION-MAKING
IN KIBBUTZ INDUSTRY

Worker participation in decision-making is a central feature of the ideology and the formal authority structure of kibbutz industry. Both can be understood only within the broader framework of the kibbutz social system. Although the kibbutz economy is run as a single economic unit, organizationally it is divided into several autonomous branches. Most of the branches are agricultural, but recently a growing number of kibbutzim have added to their economy one or two industrial plants. We have investigated ten of these mixed-economy kibbutzim.

Between 1960 and 1970 the number of industrial plants in kibbutzim increased from 108 to 170. The industrialization of the kibbutz has been rapid even relative to the general pace of industrial-

The findings presented in this essay are based on data collected by an international research project on "Members' Reaction to Hierarchy in Industrial Organization." The research team was composed of A. S. Tannenbaum (U.S.A.), B. Kavic (Yugoslavia), M. Vianello (Italy), G. Wieser (Australia) and M. Rosner (Israel).

This research was sponsored by the National Science Foundation (U.S.A.). The Israeli data were collected by the Center for Social Research on the Kibbutz, Givat Haviva.

ization in Israel: the kibbutz contribution to total Israeli industrial output grew from 3.1 percent in 1955 to 6.2 percent in 1966. Kibbutz industry is concentrated mainly in a limited number of branches. Of the 157 industrial plants in kibbutzim in 1968, 117 were in four industries: 43—metal works, 23—plastics, 29—food, 18—furniture and wood. Two social factors made this fast pace of industrialization possible:

—the peculiar characteristics of kibbutz manpower;

—the managerial abilities of many kibbutz members.

The educational and cultural level of kibbutz members is relatively high. Most kibbutz founders and all those born there have had an opportunity to complete secondary school. The kibbutz movement set up a vast network of adult education and vocational training institutions. Kibbutz members entering industry from previous agricultural work usually have a technical background because of the high technological and agrotechnical level of kibbutz agriculture.

The democratic principles of the kibbutz make for a relatively wide distribution of managerial skills. Every year about 50 percent of kibbutz members take part in management, on the basis of rotation in committees and various functions of the organizational structure, and thereby acquire managerial experience and ability in various social realms. Education for performance of various social and managerial functions is integrated into the general system of kibbutz education. Hence managerial skills are widely shared by a high proportion of the members.

A major limitation to industrialization is the size of the industrial plants. The limited number of members of a kibbutz community prevents the development of large industrial plants. This limitation is bolstered by the prohibition against the employment of hired workers which originates from the socialist ideology of the kibbutz society. As a result of these limitations most of the kibbutz plants are rather small. In 1968, 72 percent of the plants employed less than 50 workers. Only 18 plants out of 157 employed more than 100 workers.

The organizational structure of kibbutz industrial plants has been determined both by the egalitarian and democratic principles of kibbutz ideology and by the functional requirements of industrial organization. It has been shaped by the general principles of kibbutz ideology, by experience in other work branches, and by the advice of production engineers who provided practical guidance. Only at a later stage was an organizational model formalized by one of the four kibbutz federations. This model can be seen as a crystalized expression of the patterns which emerged in most of the kibbutz plants and as a normative model.

THE NORMATIVE MODEL

In this model, workers' participation in decision-making at the plant level is both direct, through the worker assembly, and indirect, through the election of the different committees and of the management board by plant workers. The normative model recommended the establishment of different committees, such as for professional and technical problems and for marketing. Other committees which exist in plants are appointment committees for plant offices and training committees nominating the plant workers to be sent to different vocational training courses. The management board typically has three components:

1. The central officeholders in the plant, such as the plant manager, the production manager, etc.
2. The central officeholders in the kibbutz, such as the economic coordinator and the treasurer.
3. Workers' representatives, like plant officeholders, are elected by the plant workers' assembly, while the kibbutz officeholders are elected by the kibbutz general assembly. Some decisions, such as election of the plant manager and approval of the investment plan, are usually taken by the general assembly of the kibbutz, where the plant workers participate along with all other kibbutz members. Only technical and professional matters are definitively decided upon by the management board. In almost all other matters the role of the management board and of the different committees in the decision-making process is according to the normative model —the preparation of proposals as input to decision-making sessions of the worker assembly or the kibbutz general assembly.

In contrast to the rather high degree of formalization and institutionalization of participation in decision-making on the plant level, there are no formal rules regarding the patterns of participation in decision-making on the department or work group level. The assumption probably was that because of the relatively small size of the departments and groups, participation would take place on a spontaneous and informal basis, as a result of the general par-

ticipative and egalitarian character of relations among kibbutz members. The roles of the different plant and kibbutz institutions in
the stages of the decision-making process in different areas are shown
in Table 1.

As shown in Table 1, some issues are discussed both by plant
committee and by kibbutz committees. The usual procedure is that
the plant committees establish the different needs of the plant, such
as for investments or the training of plant workers. The workers'
assembly reaches tentative decisions that are again discussed by the
kibbutz committees in the general framework of the kibbutz investment plan or training plan, and finally approved by the kibbutz
general assembly. The pattern for the election of the plant manager
is different. Candidates are discussed by the kibbutz committee dealing with appointments to all kibbutz offices, which nominates one
candidate. After discussion of this nomination in the plant final
appointment is made by the kibbutz assembly. All other plant officeholders are elected by the workers' assembly. The reason for the exception with respect to the plant manager is that he is not necessarily
selected from among the plant workers as are the other plant officeholders.

The nonconventional features of the organizational structure of
kibbutz plants are not confined to the decision-making process.
The hierarchical division of authority among officeholders seems
quite conventional. But a series of deviations from the conventional
bureaucratic model of industrial management can be observed. Of-
fice-holders, from first-line supervisor to production manager, are
elected by plant workers and not appointed by management. The
election to office is based not only on professional abilities but also
on broader personal qualities. The staffing of managerial positions is
based on a system of rotation. The time period for holding the different offices varies, according to the normative model, from two
to three years for the supervisor to four to five years for the plant
manager. Some deviations in this area were uncovered by research,
but many plants conform to the model.

Contrary to the strict formal definition of the rights and duties
and the impersonal rules which characterize the bureaucratic
model, the definition of offices in kibbutz plants is quite flexible and
depends often on the personality of the officeholders. Most officeholders, especially first-line supervisors, take part in production
work, and only a part of their time is dedicated to supervision and
other managerial functions. The social relations among the kibbutz
members who perform different functions are not limited to the
work hours spent in the plant but are a part of the more general

Table 1. THE ROLE OF PLANT AND KIBBUTZ INSTITUTIONS
IN THE DECISION-MAKING PROCESS ON
DIFFERENT TOPICS AS STATED BY THE NORMATIVE MODEL

The Topic	The Institution				
	Plant Committee	Plant Management	Worker Assembly	Kibbutz Committee	The General Assembly of a Kibbutz
Production Plans		Suggestion	Decision	Discussion	Approval
Investment and Development Plans		Suggestion	Decision	Discussion	Approval
Work Arrangements		Suggestion	Decision		
Technical and Professional Problems	Discussion	Decision	Information		
Choice of Candidates Training	Decision	Suggestion	Decision	Discussion	Approval
Election of Management Team		Discussion	Discussion	Suggestion	Decision
Election of Other Offices		Suggestion		Decision	

network of social relations in the kibbutz. The participation of workers in decision-making in kibbutz plants, then, is not only a result of ideological principles and organizational decisions but a part of a broader philosophy and style of life.

IMPLEMENTATION OF THE NORMATIVE MODEL

An attempt to measure the degree of implementation of the normative model was made in 1969 in the framework of a larger research project dealing with the social and organizational problems of kibbutz industry. A sample of ten kibbutz plants in four industrial branches—metal, plastics, furniture, and food canning—was studied by survey-research methods. These plants were chosen as samples of kibbutz industry to be included in an international comparative study, but they do not comprise representative samples.

These ten plants are among the largest kibbutz plants that do not employ salaried workers. The number of workers varies between 50 and 80. Relative to Israeli industry in general they can be considered as technologically advanced and economically successful.

The degree of implementation of the normative model on the plant level was measured by checking the effectiveness of the workers' assembly in each of the plants. The workers' assembly is the expression of the workers' direct participation in decision-making. This is the major distinctive feature of the kibbutz system of participation vis-à-vis other systems of indirect participation by workers' representation in management.

The effectiveness of the workers' assembly was measured by:
—the frequency of assembly metings; and
—the influence of the assembly on different areas of decision-making.

In three plants the assembly met every week. In one plant there were no workers' assemblies. In six other plants the workers' assembly met less than once a month. (Additional data from a later survey of 24 other plants has shown that in 11 plants the assembly met once a month or more, in 10 plants it met less frequently, and in three plants there were no meetings at all. In the normative model a frequency of once a month was recommended.)

The degree of influence of the assembly on the areas of decision-

making was measured by separate questions for each:
1. The yearly production plan.
2. The yearly investment and development plan.
3. Work arrangements.
4. Technical and professional problems.
5. Choice of candidates for vocational training.
6. Election of management board.
7. Election of committees.

The respondents were asked how the assembly dealt with each area. Answers varied on a five point scale: the assembly does not deal at all with area 1; it obtains information on area 2, approves of decisions on area 3, and discusses and makes recommendations on area 4; it has the final decision on area 6.

An index of general influence in the decision-making process was computed on the basis of these questions and a correlation coefficient of .79 (p=.001) was found between the frequency of assembly meetings and this index. The three plants where the assembly meets every week were also the highest on the index.

To complete the picture, we present the following table:

Table 2. PATTERNS OF WORKERS ASSEMBLY
INFLUENCE IN DECISIONMAKING

Areas	The Patterns				
	A	B	C	D	E
Committee Election	+	+	+	+	+
Management Election	+	+	+	+	
Work Arrangements	+	+	+		
Choice of Candidates for Training	+	+			
Investment Plan	+	+			
Production Plan	+				
No. of Plants	1	2	2	3	2

151

The combination of patterns forms a sort of Guttman scale. The plus sign (+) was assigned to plants where the majority of respondents said that the workers' assembly had the influence called for by the normative model. For example: according to the model, the assembly is supposed to make the final decision on work arrangements but not on the investment plan, which has to be approved by kibbutz institutions. For a plant to be marked + on work arrangements it was necessary for 5 to be the most frequent score, while for investment plan the parallel score was 4. Table 2 shows an apparent order of importance in the areas. In five plants the assembly conforms to the normative model only in the area of election. Its influence in other areas in three plants is less than that stated by the model.

Two other plants conform to the model also in work arrangements, two more on choice of members for training and on investment plans, and only one accords to the model in all areas.

The three latter plants are those with the most frequent meetings. The ordering of the areas seems meaningful. A conventional explanation for the fact that only in a minority of plants does the assembly have much influence on economic matters may be that generally workers are less competent and less involved in these matters than in the area of work arrangements, which touch them directly and personally. But contrary to this assumption is the finding that in the three plants where the assembly has most influence on economic matters the assembly meetings are also the most frequent. We know that between the workers of the different plants there are no basic differences in demographic characteristics such as education, age, sex, etc., which may explain why in these three plants workers should be more interested and involved in economic matters than in the others. It seems reasonable, therefore, to assume that the higher influence of the assembly on economic decisions in these plants is a result of a higher degree of conformity to the normative model by the management, which is responsible for the frequency and content of assemblies. The finding in the other seven plants that the desired frequency of the workers' assembly is significantly higher than the actual frequency also shows that workers are generally interested in participation.

A strong correlation was also found between the general index of assembly influence on decision-making and an index formed from two Likert-type questions dealing with the perceived degree of participation in general plant matters and in work related matters ($r=.91$, $p=.001$).

As stated above, there was no formal normative model for participation in decision-making on the work group level. The degree of participation on this level can be seen therefore as dependent on the degree of participativeness of the supervisor. This variable was measured by an index composed of two questions. For each work group the average score was computed. The distribution shows that 26 supervisors were seen by their subordinates as highly participative, six as nonparticipative, while 42 had an intermediate position.

THE IMPACT OF PARTICIPATION

The impact of the degree of participation on a series of psychological and organizational variables was studied by correlational methods on both levels, the plant and the work group or department. The index of the influence of the workers' assembly was chosen as an independent variable on the plant level. The degree of participativeness of the work group supervisor as seen by his subordinates was chosen as an independent variable on the group level. The dependent variables were two individual psychological attitudes (satisfaction with the plant and commitment to plant goals) and two organizational characteristics (the trust of members in management and the attitude of workers toward management). Members' collective or personal influence was seen as an intervening variable between the degree of participation and the individual or organizational outcomes. The rationale for this assumption is that it is not participation itself but the increase of members' influence resulting from it that may cause the differences in outcome. On the other hand a direct relationship was assumed between members' participation in decision-making and the flow of communication in the plant or the work group. This seems reasonable because the existence of work assemblies or the fact that the supervisor asks for the opinion of his subordinates are themselves acts of communication and should therefore add to the overall amount of communication.

The correlations among the independent, interviewing and dependent variables are presented in Table 3.

All the variables were measured by taking the average for the plant and for the work group of respondents' scores.

Because of the different situation there were differences between the measures used for variables on the plant level versus the work group level: (1) on the plant level member influence was measured by a

Table 3. CORRELATIONS BETWEEN MEMBER PARTICIPATION
IN DECISION MAKING ON PLANT AND WORK GROUP LEVEL,
MEMBER INFLUENCE AND DIFFERENT OUTCOME VARIABLES

Correlations Between:	Plant Level	Group Level
1. Participation and Member Influence	.90[c]	.56[d]
2. Member Influence and Satisfaction with Plant	N.S.	.27[b]
3. Member Influence and Commitment to Plant Goal	N.S.	.60[d]
4. Member Influence and Trust in Management	.59[a]	.28[b]
5. Member Influence and Perception of Worker Attitude to Management	.76[b]	—
6. Participation and Flow of Communication	.85[c]	.74[d]

a- p .10.
b- p .05.
c- p .01.
d- p .00¹

question asking how much influence workers have as a group in the plant while on the group level we questioned how much influence the worker had personally; (2) on the plant level members' trust in management was measured by an index composed of questions dealing with the attitude of management toward workers as perceived by the respondent (on the group level the parallel index is composed of questions dealing more directly with the personal trust of the respondent in his supervisor); (3) on the plant level the measure of the flow of communication deals with communication between departments while on the group level the parallel question deals with frequency of communication on work matters between the respondent and his supervisor; (4) on the work group level we had no measure of the perception by the respondent of workers' attitude toward management.

On the plant level a clear pattern seems to occur. While no correlation was found between participation or workers' influence and the variables measuring personal attitudes, significant correlations were found with the measures of organizational characteristics. In

154

plants where workers have more influence, based on a high degree on members' effective participation in decision-making, they also have more trust in management and the general attitude toward management is more favorable. When participation is more effective there is also more communication among work groups in the plant. In contrast to the lack of significant relationship between effectiveness of participation, members' influence and personal attitudes on the plant level, strong positive correlations between these variables were found on the group level. Especially strong is the correlation between member influence and commitment to plant goals. The correlation between participation on the group level and communication is also very high.

By comparing the impact of participation on the two levels we found that at the plant level this impact is mainly on organizational and collective variables, such as members' attitude and trust toward management and the influence of workers as a group, while on the group level the impact is also on individual and motivational variables. These differences can be seen as related to the more formal and impersonal character of the workers' assembly where general organizational issues are discussed and decided versus the more informal and personal nature of participation at the group level. The decisions at the group level are also more related to personal conditions of work and work content and may therefore trigger more personal involvement.

It is important to specify some of the limitations on and possibilities of generalization from the specific kibbutz model of worker participation in decision-making in industry.

1. Each kibbutz plant is part of the larger kibbutz social system, a community which encompasses all aspects of a member's life. The social relations in the plant are therefore part of a more comprehensive system of relations.
2. The workers in kibbutz industry are co-owners, and their attitude toward the plant is not like that of wage and salary workers.
3. Kibbutz plants are relatively small, but relatively capital-intensive.
4. There are no material incentives in the kibbutz and there is no direct relationship between the individual contribution of a member and his standard of living.

But despite these limitations some important lessons can be learned from the experience of kibbutz industry:

1. Technologically advanced industrial plants can be managed effectively on the basis of direct democracy by means of decision-making within the framework of the workers' assembly.

2. Beside the mechanism of direct democracy there still exists a hierarchical organizational structure; but this hierarchy is limited by the fact that a high degree of participativeness prevails in the relationships among hierarchical levels, and supervisors engage in production work.

3. A rotation system functions not only for higher management, as in Yugoslavia, but also for managers and supervisors on the line. The system of rotation stimulates a large dispersion of professional and technical knowledge and of leadership skills.

4. Our findings stress the importance of worker participation in decision-making both in smaller work groups and larger workers' assemblies and the specific and different impact of these two forms of participation.

APPENDIX
THE MEASURES OF VARIABLES

The Variables	The Measures
A. On Plant Level	
Influence	How much influence do the workers as a group have on what happens in this plant?
Satisfaction with Plant	An index formed from five questions:
	a. How much satisfaction do you get from your job in the plant compared to what you do after leaving the plant?
	b. Do you like working for this company?
	c. Do you like the work you do in this plant?

d. Are you interested in continuing working in this plant?

e. How good is this plant compared to the other branches in the kibbutz?

Commitment to Plant Goals

An index formed from five questions: To what extent do you feel really responsible for the success of:

a. Your own work group?

b. Your department?

c. The whole plant?

d. In your kind of job, is it usually better to let your supervisor worry about producing better or faster ways of doing the work?

e. How often do you try out on your own a better or faster way of doing the work?

Trust in Management

An index out of three questions:

a. Do you think the responsible people here have a real interest in the welfare of those who work here?

b. Do the responsible people in this plant improve working conditions only when forced to?

c. When a worker in this plant makes a complaint about something is it taken care of?

Attitude toward Management

a. How frequently do the workers in the plant suggest innovations and new approaches?

b. Do the workers in this plant encourage each other to contribute their best for the plant's success?

c. What are the attitudes of the company's members toward plant management?

Communication

Do the workers in the different departments communicate with each other on what happens?

B. On the Work Group
   Level

Influence	How much influence have you, personally, on what happens in this plant?
Satisfaction with Plant	The same as on plant level
Commitment to Plant Goal	The same as on plant level
Trust in Supervisor	An index formed from two questions: a. Do you have trust in your superior? b. Would you like to have your superior changed?
Communication	How frequently do you speak to your superior on work matters?

10

Uri Leviatan

THE INDUSTRIAL PROCESS IN ISRAELI KIBBUTZIM: PROBLEMS AND THEIR SOLUTIONS

During the last few years there has been a revolutionary change in the economic structure of the kibbutz movement in Israel. Until several years ago, farming was the sole source of income for most kibbutzim. Now many kibbutzim have established industries and the number of new plants is growing at an ever faster rate.

In 1971 industrial workers constituted 25 percent of the labor force in production in the entire kibbutz movement. This overall number conceals the fact that in several kibbutzim the industrial workers already constitute 50 percent of all production workers and that the output of industry in some kibbutzim is about 90 percent of the value of total output. At the moment 146 of the 232 established kibbutzim have at least one industrial plant. These data clearly indicate that the industrialization process is expanding in the kibbutz movement. What are the reasons for this particular phenomenon?

Several conditions, in different combination, have been responsible for the growing emphasis on industry in the kibbutzim.

First, agrotechnical and agrogenetical developments[1] in farm products have enabled the kibbutzim to produce more and more with the same amount of labor. Farm production in the last ten years has increased by an average of 3.7 percent while the number of workers has remained constant. In one of the three large kibbutz movements 1,087 million work days were put into farming in 1961 and 1,098 million work days in 1970, while production increased by 120 percent over the same time span. In view of the growth of the kibbutz population, it seems obvious why the kibbutz had to look for other sources of income and employment for its members. Yet the industrial plants that were established had to be relatively small in terms of the number of workers employed, because the number of workers released from farming is only a percentage of the total production labor force, which ranges from 50 to 400 workers per kibbutz.

Second, farm work, even with its technological advancements, still calls for physical fitness and is not appropriate for most older persons. However, the kibbutz population, on the average, is getting older every year. This is because the kibbutz movement was established by young pioneers but is now a three generation society with an aging population of founders. Thus, jobs more appropriate for physically disabled or elderly members are needed. Industry is one solution. Indeed, in one study we found that industrial workers were five years older on the average (42 years versus 37 years) than farm workers.

Third, women, in particular, are a disadvantaged group with respect to work in a society such as the kibbutz, which values production work more than services.[2] At the present technological stage few farm jobs are appropriate for women in view of their physical demands. Industry may offer women a larger choice of jobs. Although women constitute a minority even in industry (about 30 percent of the total industrial work force) they are still a much larger minority than they are in agriculture.[3]

Fourth, farming is a less profitable enterprise in Israel than industry. Due to governmental policies, the average income of farmers vis-à-vis the average income of workers in general has been smaller for the last 12 years and in the last seven years that gap has continued to grow at an even faster rate.[4] In 1970 farm owners, on the average, had an income which was only 68 percent of that in Israel in general. The kibbutz, being an organization that has to cope efficiently with the economic market of the state, had to adapt itself to these conditions and look for more promising alternatives. Industrialization may be one such answer.

And finally, second generation kibbutz males are technologically oriented and desire jobs which are technologically sophisticated. At its present stage of development farming is limited in its technological sophistication compared to some industries. Indeed, at the present moment 59 percent of the second-generation men work as farmers, 31 percent work in industry or workshops, and 10 percent in various services; however, the distribution of desired jobs is different: 38 percent want farming, 36 percent industry and workshops and 26 percent various services.[5] Young kibbutz members also aspire to jobs that demand more education and training. While at their present jobs only 8 percent of them need formal education above the high school level, at their desired jobs 31 percent will need that level of formal education. [6] Industry may have a larger selection of jobs which demand high formal education.

To summarize, many conditions have made it necessary for the kibbutzim, the larger and older ones in particular, to turn to industrialization. Indeed, many have taken action in this direction, as the following tables indicate.

An additional set of requirements became relevant for those kibbutzim that decided to industrialize. The first type of requirement concerns the adherence to the ideological and value principles of the kibbutz society: a minimum use of outside hired labor, which means that a plant cannot be larger than 50 to 100 workers (because of the relatively small size of the individual kibbutz); managerial practices that would be based upon values and principles of democracy and participation of workers in decision-making; rotation of offices among workers, including the rotation of the highest offices in the managerial hierarchy; vesting of the final authority, related to major decisions in the industry, in the general assembly of the kibbutz.

The second type of requirement deals with the individual members who are the proposed workers. Their needs must be satisfied to at least an acceptable level; attention must be paid to possible effects of work on the well-being of the worker, such as feelings of alienation, loss of self-esteem, and other negative symptoms of mental and physical ill health. Such negative effects of work in industry upon the individual worker have been found in many studies conducted in the United States, Europe and the developing countries.[7]

Table 1. INDICATORS OF INDUSTRIAL GROWTH
IN THE KIBBUTZ MOVEMENT OVER THE LAST DECADE

Year	Number of Workers	Percent Compared to 1960	Number of Plants	Percent Compared to 1960	Output in Millions of Israeli Pounds	Percent of 1966
1960	4,860	100	108	100		
1966	6,980	144	148	137	247.7	100
1969	8,390	173	157	145	418.2	169
1970	9,080	187	170	157	505.9	204
1971			185	171		

Source: S. Stanger, *The Kibbutz Industry*, Kibbutz Industrial Association, 1971 (Hebrew).

Table 2. SHARE OF OUTPUT AND LABOR OF FARMING AND INDUSTRY
IN THE LAST DECADE IN ONE KIBBUTZ MOVEMENT

Year	Percentage of Total Output		Percentage of Total Labor in Production	
	Farming	Industry	Farming	Industry
1960	73	20	66	18
1966	64	29	60	22
1969	58	35	55	24
1970	50	40	54	25

Source: Y. Nachtomi "Trends and Developments in Production Branches," Hedim 96, 1971, pp. 70-84 (Hebrew).

Note: This movement accounts for one third of the total kibbutz population and farm production, and 40 percent of the total industrial production of the kibbutzim.

Two questions are now to be asked: (1) Can the kibbutzim cope simultaneously with all the requirements of the industrialization process? and (2) How do the criteria, requirements and individual needs relate to each other? It seems that in order to establish plants that would satisfy the demands of and reasons for the new trend towards industrialization in the kibbutz movement and the requirements related to this process, the following would be necessary: these plants would have to be very profitable; small, in terms of the number of workers; able to provide jobs for the physically disabled; able to provide jobs that are challenging; not intensive in the use of labor; and managed according to kibbutz ideological principles.

Though this is an almost impossible list of requirements, the kibbutzim have been fairly successful in fulfilling them. Most of the data and findings reported here are from a series of studies conducted by the Center for Social Research on the Kibbutz at Givat Haviva. Of particular relevance here is the kibbutz industrialization research program which was begun in 1969 and has been sponsored by the Kibbutz Federation, the American Council for the Behavioral Sciences in the Kibbutz and the Fritz Naphtali Foundation.

Two phases of the industrialization research program have been completed. The first was part of an international study that compared industries in three European countries, the United States and Israeli kibbutzim. The major dimensions of comparison were managerial and organizational practices and values as well as workers' behavior and attitudes. The second phase of the research program focused upon a representative sample of kibbutz industries, their managerial and organizational practices, structures and technologies, and the ways in which these variables affect workers' behaviors and attitudes, and the organizational and economic efficiency of the industries. Another focal point of the study was the comparison, on relevant dimensions, of industrial plants and their workers to farm branches and their workers. The third phase of the research program is being designed as a set of sociotechnical field experiments in several industries where we will apply some of the conclusions derived from our findings in previous phases.

Another study conducted at the Center for Social Research on the Kibbutz dealt with intergenerational relations and differences within the kibbutz movements. Some of the results of that study are incorporated in the following material.

What do the findings show?

Goal A: Economic Viability. A fairly clear finding is that kibbutz industry has proven its success economically. Even though the kibbutz population is only 3.6 percent of the total Jewish population of Israel and about 5.4 per cent of the national industrial work force, its industry produces between 6 and 7 percent of the national industrial output. Another index of economic viability is the rate of growth of industrial exports. This rate has been 28 percent per year for the last four years. It was 25 percent in 1970 as compared to 13 percent for Israeli industry at large (excluding diamonds). In a comparative study of kibbutz and nonkibbutz industrial enterprises, Melman [8] has also shown that kibbutz plants were more efficient and profitable economically.

Goal B: Small Size. It is a fact that kibbutz industry is composed of relatively small plants—90 percent of them with less than 100 workers, and 73 percent with less than 50 workers.

Goal C: Avoiding Hired Labor. The kibbutz movement has failed to adhere to the ideal of self-labor. This has been one of the more important values in kibbutz ideology and its abandonment has been very painful to many members. In the farm branches the percentage of hired workers (wage-earning nonmembers employed by the kibbutz) has been kept relatively low, ranging (in 1970) from a minimum of 6.5 percent in one of the three large movements to a maximum of 20 percent in another of the large movements. In industry the percentages are much higher, ranging from 14.5 percent to 76 percent. In the kibbutzim 55 percent of all industrial workers are hired from outside the kibbutz. However the above summary numbers are a bit misleading since 80 percent of all the hired workers are concentrated in only 18 percent of the plants while 72 percent of the plants have only 20 percent of the hired labor (in one third of the plants there is not even one paid worker).

Goal D: Employment for Older Members. We have pointed out that kibbutz industrial workers are on the average five years older than farm workers. In the intergenerational study we found another indication of the same trend: 36 percent of the young kibbutz members (age 19 to 35 years) work in agriculture but only 17 percent of the older members do. However, in industries and workshops (e.g., garages, carpentry, shoemaking, etc.) percentages of the two age categories employed are the same (17 percent). This means that older persons are less likely to work in farm jobs than are young persons, while there is no such difference in jobs related to industry.[9]

We have seen that kibbutz industries have been quite successful in achieving the economic objectives of industrialization and also in solving to an acceptable degree the demographic and manpower problems related to the process of industrialization. The only sphere where industrialization has created problems is the ideological: in regard to hired labor. Does the employment of hired workers also have an effect upon profitability and productivity of industrial plants in the kibbutzim? We do not have a conclusive answer to the question, but two independent studies have tended to show a negative relationship between the employment of hired labor and indices of profitability and productivity. One study has used industrial plants as the unit of analysis and the other used the whole kibbutz as the unit of analysis. Both showed that, on the average, kibbutzim or industrial plants with a larger percentage of hired workers were less profitable. In our industrialization study we sampled plants employing 30 percent or less of hired workers, restricting the range of the variable "percentage of hired workers employed in the plant." Nevertheless, we found that the plants with no hired labor were on the average more profitable than those with even some hired labor. We do not know as yet the exact explanation for this finding, and many hypotheses have been offered. Future analysis will be directed toward finding the intervening variable that may explain this relationship.

We turn now to the question of whether or not kibbutz industries have been as successful in carrying out their other objectives as they have been economically. Two questions arise in this connection. First, Are the managerial methods and other organizational practices in accord with kibbutz values and norms? Second, Do the jobs and the settings offered by the industries meet the expectations and needs of the individual kibbutz members who work in them?

We will review the relevant findings against two frames of reference: farm work in the kibbutzim; social organizations outside the kibbutz.

Goal E: Rotation in Managerial Offices. It was found that rotation of workers in offices in kibbutz industries is as prevalent as in the farm branches. Industrial managers, in our study, held their offices, on the average, between three and four years. This was also the term in office for farm-branch managers. Using another indicator, we found that in the last five years about 60 percent of the workers in our industrial sample had served in a managerial position at least one year.

Goal F: Workers' Participation in Decision-making. Compared to industry in other countries, including plants managed by workers' councils in Yugoslavia, the workers in the kibbutz plants participate to the highest degree in the making of decisions related to their own work and to general plant policies.[10] Similarly the style of supervision is most participative and supportive in the kibbutz plants. Positive relations among coworkers and group cohesiveness were strongest among workers in the kibbutz plants. However, in all the above dimensions, the industrial plants are consistently further away from kibbutz ideals than are the farm branches.

Goal G: Offering Job Satisfaction and Mental Health. The extent to which kibbutz industries offer opportunities for the satisfaction of the needs and aspirations of the individual worker is relatively high compared to industrial organizations outside the kibbutzim. Four surveys conducted in the kibbutzim in the last three years have indicated that the general level of job satisfaction among kibbutz members is very high. Between 55 and 70 percent of the workers said that they were very satisfied with their jobs, about 9 to 11 percent said that they were dissatisfied with their jobs; the rest were satisfied only to a small degree. There were no differences in job satisfaction between farm and industrial workers, nor were there differences between farm and industrial workers in measures of mental health, alienation and illness behavior. The level of job satisfaction was higher than that found for any occupational group in a survey of employed American workers and workers in other countries.[11]

Although there were no differences between farm workers and industrial workers with respect to the general measure of satisfaction with the job, differences do appear with regard to particular aspects. Farm workers often report that in their work they have more opportunities for self-actualization, for the exercise of influence and more access to relevant information. On the other hand, being an industrial worker offers a greater chance for self-development by way of formal academic education. About 59 percent of young kibbutz men work in farming, but they provide only 7 percent of the young men currently studying in academic institutions, while the industrial workers, who comprise about 31 percent of the young men, provide about 40 percent of the number studying at present. This last finding means that industrial jobs are, on the average, more sophisticated than farm jobs and call for more training.

In summary, one may conclude that the industrialization process in the kibbutzim has been less successful in achieving objectives related to kibbutz social values and individuals' needs than in meeting economic and demographic demands.

At present we have no research data to account for this discrepancy. One plausible explanation is based on the fact that industry was introduced into the kibbutzim in a special way. Farming has been in the kibbutzim from the very beginning, and the kibbutzim have always been the pioneers in Israel in the introduction of new techniques and products. There were no outside models from which to learn organization and administration, and therefore no constaints were put on the freedom to adapt and adjust organizational methods and principles to the kibbutz social values.

With industry the history was different. Many of the plants were imported into the kibbutz framework from the outside. Their technology, know-how and market were bought intact. In many cases, package-deal-type importation carried with it the belief that the organizational principles used with a particular technology outside the kibbutz were an inseparable part of the successful operation of the industry within the kibbutz. These imported organizational principles were, of course, alien to kibbutz social values and led to relatively less positive results in terms of adherence to kibbutz principles and to individual need-satisfaction.

Our final concern is with the interrelations among the three spheres that compose the total set of normative requirements and criteria for kibbutz industry. In particular, How do organizational principles and management methods affect individual behavior, motivation, satisfaction, and health? How does job satisfaction relate to behavior which is relevant for economic success? What is the importance of workers' behavior and motivations for determining the economic efficiency level? What is the role of organizational practices? Finally, are the relationships among the variables mentioned here the same in the kibbutz setting as in societies such as the United States, Europe and other developed areas? Indeed, the basic question in the minds of many kibbutz members is whether the economic success of the kibbutz industries is a result of the adherence to kibbutz social values or *in spite of* the restrictions imposed by these values?

Our data show that the workers' sense of responsibility to their work and their initiative-taking behavior, together explain about 33 percent of the variance of performance indices in 21 kibbutz industrial plants for which economic data are available. This number is impressive when considered in light of the fact that the plants were different from each other on almost every relevant dimension:

branch of industry (food, textile, metal, electronics, plastics, paper), size (nine to 60 workers), number of years in business (three to 30 years), political movement, affiliation and geographic location.

The relationship between human behavior and motivation and economic success was expressed in two efficiency indices: in seven plants, where the workers were highly motivated and behaved in an initiative-taking manner (solving problems, trying new ways and approaches, etc.), rate of return on investment was 43.3 percent and the profit per member's work day was 102 Israeli pounds. In the eight plants where the workers' scores on both variables of motivation and initiative-taking behavior were low, the rate of return on the investment was 18.5 percent and the profit per member's work day 30 Israeli pounds. In the middle group of six plants, either high on motivation, or high on initiative-taking behavior but not on both, the respective scores were 19.5 percent and 46 Israeli pounds.

At the individual level of analysis, we have found that the more opportunities one has at work for the fulfillment of psychological needs, the more likely he is to behave in a way conducive to the economic efficiency of his work organization. Workers with a very great deal of opportunity for influence at their work were three times as likely to show up for work as workers who had no such opportunity at all.[12] Workers with more opportunities for influence were also more likely to feel responsible for the success of their plants (as Figure 1 illustrates), and more likely to behave in ways conducive to the success of the work organization, such as avoiding tardiness, solving problems, putting more effort into their work and the like.

The opportunities for social interaction offered by the job are strongly related to the worker's illness behavior pattern, as expressed by the frequency of his visits to the physician. People with few such opportunities were about three times more likely to visit a physician than those who had many such opportunities. Feelings of alienation were also negatively related to the extent to which a work place offered opportunities for the satisfaction of the psychological needs of the workers. The same is true of other mental-illness behavior and symptoms. Satisfaction with the job was, on the one hand, a function of the level of the opportunities for fulfillment of psychological needs—as in the example illustrated by Figure 2. On the other hand, job satisfaction was negatively related to tardiness.

Organizational climate variables, such as the degree of participative management, coworkers' cohesiveness and support, supervisor

Figure 1. FEELING RESPONSIBLE FOR THE SUCCESS
OF THE PLANT AS A FUNCTION
OF THE EXTENT TO WHICH OPPORTUNITIES
FOR INFLUENCE ARE OFFERED TO THE WORKER

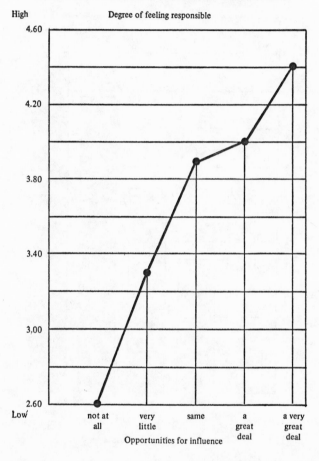

support and trust and other human-relations skills, were all related positively to the satisfaction and the motivation of the individual workers.

In view of the findings reported above, one may conclude with a great deal of confidence that adherence to kibbutz values contributes to economic success. The economic efficiency of kibbutz industry is a result of the attention paid to the human needs of its workers, and the employment of organizational principles based on

Figure 2. SATISFACTION WITH JOB AS A FUNCTION
OF THE EXTENT TO WHICH OPPORTUNITIES
FOR SELF-ACTUALIZATION ARE OFFERED

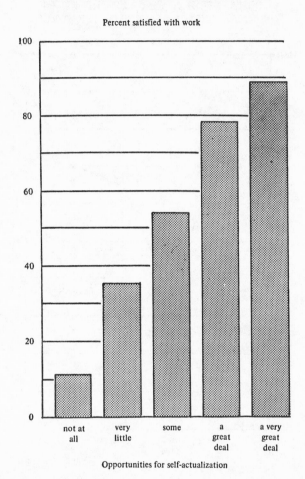

Percent satisfied with work

Opportunities for self-actualization

kibbutz values. In the more successful plants organizational practices keep up with kibbutz norms.

Another conclusion that may be drawn from the data is that
the kibbutzim differ from each other in the application of organizational principles and in their adherence to kibbutz values and
norms. There exists great variation in kibbutz industrial plants in
all areas.

The third, and perhaps most optimistic, conclusion is that kibbutz society is aware of the problems that industrialization brings.
It is aware of the need for research and for the application of re-

search results in solving these problems. The very fact that resources are put into this research activity may lead the kibbutz society to become among the first where planning precedes action and the prevention of social ailments obviates the need for cure.

A last conclusion that may be drawn from these studies is that some principles of human behavior transcend cultural boundaries and are fairly general. The relationships among organizational, psychological and behavioral variables found in our study have also been found in studies conducted in Europe and the United States, although the kibbutz stands higher on the various dimensions than social organizations in the United States and Europe (the least participative industrial plant in the kibbutz movement is still more participative than the most participative plant in the United States). This is very encouraging to a social scientist because it means two things: kibbutz researchers may consider sociopsychological and organizational theories developed in the Western world as valid tools to be used within the kibbutz framework; and the outside world may use kibbutz society as a natural laboratory and gain from its experience ideas relevant to its own conduct.

NOTES

1. Most kibbutzim could not expand in farming much beyond their present rate of growth because of restrictions imposed by the scarcity of land and water. Therefore, the only possible direction for expansion was by agrotechnical and agrogenetical means.

2. M. Rosner, "Women in the Kibbutz," *Asian and African Studies,* 3 (1967): 35-68.

3. Most of the women work in education and other services.

4. Y. Nachtomi, "Trends and Developments in Production Branches," *Hedim,* 96 (1971): 70-84 (Hebrew).

5. These data come from an unpublished study conducted in 1969 by the Center for Social Research on Kibbutz Givat Haviva.

6. This trend toward jobs that require higher formal education is true also of young kibbutz women. In the women's present jobs 27 percent need formal education beyond the high school level, while in their desired jobs 47 percent will need that level of formal education.

7. A. Kornhauser, *Mental Health of the Industrial Worker* (New York: Wiley, 1965); R. Blauner, *Alienation and Freedom* (Chicago: University of Chicago Press, 1964).

8. S. S. Melman, "Managerial vs. Cooperative Decision Making in Israel," *Studies in Comparative International Development,* 6(1970-1971): 3.

9. The greatest concentration of older persons is in the local, regional and movement services.

10. For detailed exposition about the participation in the decision-making process of kibbutz industrial workers, see the chapter by M. Rosner in this book.

11. N. Morse and R. S. Weiss, "The Function and Meaning of Work and the Job," *American Sociological Review,* 20(1955): 191-8.

12. U. Leviatan, "Status in Human Organization as a Determinant of Mental Health and Performance" (Ph.D. diss. University of Michigan, 1970).

ECONOMIC
AND LABOR
DEVELOPMENT

II

Howard Pack

INCOME DISTRIBUTION AND ECONOMIC DEVELOPMENT: THE CASE OF ISRAEL

Successful economic development is an unusual phenomenon. Outside of Western Europe and some areas of British overseas settlement, only Japan, Israel and one or two other countries have reached per capita income levels equal to those of the middle rung of European countries such as Italy and Austria. Economists have made considerable efforts to estimate the quantitative importance of a number of factors—physical capital, labor (including skilled labor) and "technical progress"—in the growth in per capita income. (Technical progress is determined as a residual after calculating the contribution of the other tangible factors.) However, the growth in tangible factors such as capital and labor does not guarantee growth in either gross national product (GNP) or GNP per capita. Thus, in some countries high levels of investment (measured as a percentage of GNP) may result in limited per capita growth, while countries with considerably lower levels of investment may be much more successful. Substantial investment in inefficient industries can undermine the impact of high aggregate investment, while efficient use of smaller investment can have substantial payoffs.

Such differences in performance are often attributable to government economic policies, which, in almost all underdeveloped countries, exert a pervasive influence on the evolution of the economy. Among the instruments used by governments are foreign trade restrictions (including tariffs), taxes and subsidies, government expenditure and monetary policy. A number of recent studies by economists have indeed shown the harmful impact of particular incorrect government policies. Such policies may completely abort the growth process, as in Argentina during the Peron regime. Alternatively, growth may occur in such a manner as to contain the seeds of its own demise because of imbalances in the process itself, particularly a skewed distribution of its benefits. This type of growth process is exemplified by the recent experience of Pakistan, in which the benefits of rapid aggregate growth accrued mainly to one area of the country, and led to substantial internal dissension and an eventual breakup of the country. The possibility of significant growth in either part of what was Pakistan is now doubtful.

Whether we analyze the reasons for a total failure to grow or the self-destructive distribution of the benefits of growth, the immediate cause is likely to be the particular set of economic policies which a government pursues.[1] However, these policies are only proximate causes: they are themselves the result of the resolution of conflicting objectives of groups within individual countries, be they organized along regional lines as in Pakistan or in terms of rural-urban differences as in Argentina. Conflicts between interests will be present in some degree in every society. The critical question for the economic development process is whether the resolution of such clashes leads to a set of economic policies which is consistent with those required for continued income growth.

The following is an attempt to suggest why Israel's growth was not aborted by such conflicts and why, at least until recently, Israel's development contained little that would slow the growth process because of unacceptable distribution of resources. We shall analyze the distribution of income by sector, region and individual families, then consider the extent of income differentials by birthplace of immigrants. Throughout, the concern is with the distribution of income among Jewish families. This is not to imply that developments in the Arab sector are unimportant. However, including the Arab population would require an extended discussion of a large variety of factors which would take us considerably beyond the present chapter. On the other hand, much of the economic analysis about the position of the Asian-African Jewish immigrants is, with modifications, relevant also for the Arabs.[2]

THE IMPACT OF DEVELOPMENT ON INCOMES

Sectoral and Regional Effects

Two major themes underlay government economic policies from 1948 to 1967 [3]:

1. Encouragement of agriculture, partially as a fulfillment of the Zionist ideology of returning to the soil, but also as a way to absorb new immigrants, especially those from North Africa and the Middle East.

2. Protection of industry in order to promote replacement of imports and then a slow shift to the encouragement of exports.

This agricultural policy had several economic benefits: the augmentation of national income; a reduction in the importance of agricultural imports; and a considerable increase in exports. In addition, substantial employment was generated.[4]

There is evidence that, viewed from a perspective of maximizing national income, the encouragement of agriculture went too far in comparison to that given other sectors, particularly before 1960. There may also have been some unfortunate decisions about particular agricultural products. Part of the excessive encouragement was no doubt due to the disproportionate influence of the various farm groups within the major political parties. The need to conciliate particular interests resulted, in Israel, as elsewhere, in policies not consistent with a strategy which would have led to a maximum economic efficiency.

However, in comparison with experience in other less developed countries, such sectoral favoritism had a relatively brief life, at least partly because many of the national leaders had backgrounds in agriculture. While they remained interested and influential in agricultural development, they did not view themselves solely as its representatives but as members of a government responsible for national development. Indeed, their earlier experience in farming had represented an attempt to strengthen the economic viability of the state at a time when industry was relatively unimportant. It is not surprising, then, that policies in the national interest became dominant rather rapidly.

The second major area of government intervention was in the active encouragement of industries which replaced imported commodities. After the potential for substituting domestic production for imports had been exhausted, government policy shifted toward the encouragement of exports. Import substitution policies have been typical of most less-developed countries in the postwar period. Economists have devoted substantial effort to evaluating such policies, and their conclusions have been pessimistic.[5] All studies have shown extreme inefficiency within manufacturing. Also of considerable importance has been the impact of such policies on income distribution. The wages of industrial workers are raised relative to those in other sectors, as well as the price of manufactured goods relative to others. This results in a redistribution of real income to workers employed in industry and a decrease in incentives to other sectors. In Argentina this led to such a reduction in agricultural output that the national growth rate fell.[6] In Pakistan the conflict manifested itself regionally, industry being located mainly in one wing of the country.

In Israel, the emergence of a rural-urban conflict was limited because of the simultaneous encouragement of agriculture and industry, while a regional clash was not an important possibility because of the considerable dispersion of industry. Obviously, in a country such as Israel, in which most residents are recent arrivals, only limited regional identification is developed and this is strongest among those in agriculture. Dwellers in particular towns often viewed themselves (sometimes correctly) as being transient. In such a situation, grievances which might arise would tend to be about relative sizes of income rather than regional differences. Moreover, the government, to decrease the population density of the Tel Aviv-Haifa coastal strip, encouraged industry to relocate in poorer regions and increased social overhead capital in these areas. Residents in poor areas thus perceived that something was being done to improve their position, though perhaps less than they desired.

What could have occurred, though, was growing dissatisfaction within urban areas, particularly between workers in manufacturing and those in other sectors (construction, utilities, services) who had not benefitted from the import protection strategy. What prevented industry from reaping undue advantage was the complicated parity system by which wages of all economic groups within the country are closely interrelated, *de jure* or *de facto*.[7] Thus, the wage of an unskilled worker in manufacturing is ultimately tied to that of project evaluator in the Ministry of Finance. Service workers in both the public sectors (government, Histadrut and the "national institutions" such as Hadassah) and private sectors thus have their incomes at least partially tied to workers in manufacturing, who were the beneficiaries of tariff protection. This system can cause difficulties, especially if it blocks the efficient flow of labor among sectors in response to changing economic forces. However, the fact that the system was able to prevent differences in sectoral wage levels from growing, especially given the import substitution program, was of considerable importance. Of course, wage linkage has itself become a source of controversy, indeed one which is often acrimonious.[8] But such conflicts were resolved in such a way that the tendency towards sector inequality was not strengthened.[9] Conflict between economic sectors was avoided, or at least highly muted, in Israel.

The Size Distribution of Income

The absence of serious sectoral or regional conflict was an important factor in Israel's growth. We have yet to consider the question of the distribution of income by size. This can be approached in two ways. On the one hand, it may be viewed in terms of the distribution of monetary income, using either a summary measure such as the gini coefficient or examination of particular deciles. Alternatively, one can examine changes in the absolute standard of living of various income groups. Both are needed, as simple measures of income inequality provide only one dimension of a meaningful measure of distribution. Clearly, even if a gini coefficient (the measurement of multivariables in one formula, an index of inequality) remains constant, rapidly rising GNP per capita implies that the welfare of the lowest income groups is likely to be growing at the same rate.[10] Their perception of their welfare may be absolute, not relative, and the relevant measure will be the growth in absolute standards.

Consider first the size distribution of income which is useful for obtaining information on relative income levels.[11] In 1951 this distribution was more equal, as measured by the gini coefficient, than that of any other country, at that time, for which data are available.[12] The only country close to Israel was Sweden, where distribution is well known to be relatively unskewed.[13] The lack of skew undoubtedly reflected the strong egalitarian beliefs of much of the leadership and its institutions, such as Histadrut,[14] and was made possible by the wage-tying arrangement described earlier, the absence of private land ownership, Histadrut ownership of heavy industry and a substantial percentage of highly educated people which reduced market pressures toward higher wages for the educated.[15] There is considerable evidence that inequality increased in the 1950s. In a sense this was inevitable as the initial relatively homogeneous, highly skilled population increased threefold, becoming far more heterogeneous as a result of the immigration of less educated, lower skilled groups. Though market forces could have been withstood, labor allocation would have become almost random. On the other hand, taxes could have redressed market determined prices, but the incentive effects of such pricing would have been lost.

Thus, an implicit decision was made to allow inequality to widen in the fifties. However, it is hard to compare the relative welfare of groups in a rapidly changing population; those in the bottom decile in 1950 could easily have moved up considerably, especially since there was substantial immigration.[16] In Israel, because of substantial immigration even in the 1950s, the use of data on income distribution is likely to be a less reliable index of changes in welfare than it is in other countries. However, since the late 1950s, changes in distribution probably reflect changes in welfare for relatively stable groups; i.e., those in the bottom three deciles in 1959 are likely to be similar to those in the same position in 1968.

Distributions of family income are shown in Table 1 for the period 1957-1958 to 1968-1969. There is remarkably little change over this period despite considerable shifts in the structure of the economy, levels of education, and so on. The data allow for differences in family size which decrease the amount of inequality a bit (compared to raw data used in other countries), as the lowest deciles of the distribution contain a large number of single-person households.

To obtain some perspective on the extent of inequality reflected in the table it is necessary to refer to data from other countries. Table 2 presents data for six less developed countries, Israel and the United States. A striking feature is the relatively low concentration of income in the top decile, a percentage matched only by Taiwan.[17] Similarly, the gini coefficient for Israel is equalled only by Pakistan. Nevertheless, it remains true that even a good performance by international standards still implies a considerable degree of inequality. Thus, the top decile in Israel receives almost three times the total income of the lowest three deciles. Stating this another way, the top 10 percent of all Israeli families has about

Table 1. DISTRIBUTION OF GROSS INCOME AMONG JEWISH URBAN FAMILIES*

Deciles	1957-1959	1963-1964	1968-1969
Lowest Decile	1.9	2.1	2.2
Second Decile	3.5	3.7	3.6
Third Decile	5.0	4.9	4.9
Fourth Decile	6.3	6.3	6.0
Fifth Decile	7.5	7.5	7.3
Sixth Decile	9.0	8.8	8.8
Seventh Decile	10.6	10.4	10.4
Eighth Decile	12.9	12.4	12.8
Ninth Decile	16.5	16.2	16.5
Highest Decile	26.9	27.7	27.5
Gini Coefficient	.367	.369	.372

Source: *Report of the Committee on Income Distribution and Social Inequality* (Tel Aviv, 1971) p. 21.

*Data have been adjusted to allow for differences in family size. These adjustments change the raw data mainly in the lowest decile (from 1.5 in 1969 to 2.2) and the highest (from 26.8 to 27.5).

Table 2. CUMULATIVE SHARE OF TOTAL FAMILY INCOME

	Lowest 30 Percent	Lowest 60 Percent	Highest 20 Percent	Highest 10 Percent	Gini Co-efficient	Highest 10 Percent/ Lowest 30 Percent
Argentina (1961)	17*	30	52	39	.392	4.1
Brazil (1960)	10	26	56	41	.440	7.0
Mexico (1963)	6	21	59	42	.500	
Pakistan (1963-1964)	12*	33	45	30	.348	2.5
Phillipines (1965)	12	23	56	40	.468	
Taiwan (1964)	20	37	41	26	.384	1.3
U.S. (1961)	11	31	48	34	.376	3.0
Israel (1968-1969)	10	33	43	27	.356	2.7

Source: Israel, *Report of the Committee on Income Distribution and Social Inequality* (Tel Aviv, 1971) p. 47. These data do not reflect adjustment for family size as do data in Table 1. Data for other countries was taken from Ian Little, Tibor Scitovsky and Maurice Scott, *Industry and Trade in Some Developing Countries* (London, Oxford University Press, 1970) referred to hereafter as *Industry and Trade*. Gini coefficients calculated by author using quintiles.

* Lowest 40.

nine times as much income as the "typical" family in the bottom 30 percent of this distribution.[18]

In a rapidly growing economy which exhibits per capita consumption growth of 6 percent per annum, these data may not provide much insight into the possibility of conflict. As suggested earlier, if the distribution was not changing very much, one could assume that absolute living standards were rising for all groups. Moreover, it is not unreasonable to assume that lower-income families would value such growth quite highly given their initial low absolute living standard. Such absolute growth may be as important as relative standings when someone thinks about whether he has benefitted from the growth process. Consider, then, the percentage of Jewish families owning major durable goods in 1960 and 1970.[19]

Year	Electric Refrigerators	Gas Stoves	Electric Washing Machines	Television Sets	Automobiles
1960	51%	64%	17%	2%	(1966) 11%
1970	96%	88%	46%	53%	(1970) 17%

Widespread ownership of such durable goods surely suggests that aggregate growth has filtered down through the entire spectrum of the income distribution. Auto ownership is limited, but in a country with a per capita income of about $1,500 car ownership could hardly be more widespread. On the other hand, ownership of such a highly visible, high-status commodity could engender considerable jealousy.

Two other statistics are also of interest. An important measure of living standards is the adequacy of housing. Between 1960 and 1970 the percentage of Jewish families in which there were three or more persons per room declined from 21 to 8 percent, and the percentage in which there were one or fewer per room increased from 7 to 18 percent.

Thus, the material living standard for the population was increasing quite rapidly, even in the lowest deciles of the population. Per capita income of the lowest decile rose at the same rate as that of the general population, i.e., about doubled between 1960 and 1970 with income distribution remaining roughly constant.

None of this is meant to imply that the poor are well off. Obviously, even though housing density is lowered, housing itself may not be of high quality. And a family which owns a refrigerator may not be able to afford to stock it with beef. Nevertheless, by any reasonable standard, the benefits of growth seem to have been fairly widely dispersed. Moreover, the government budget and quasi-public service institutions have undoubtedly redistributed income still further; income taxes are progressive and social expenditures also benefit the poor disproportionately. Available data suggest that the lowest 30 percent of wage earners experienced an increase from 13 to 18 percent in their total income as a result of the combined effect of taxes and government expenditures in 1959/1960, while the upper 16 percent suffered a decrease from 33 to 26 percent of total income.[20] Finally, the national health service (or its functional equivalent) is likely to be of greater relative importance to the poor.

No serious conflict over the size distribution of income,[21] has occurred in Israel, because the benefits of growth have been widely dispersed. Although income is far from evenly distributed, rapid growth of absolute living standards has overshadowed any concern about relative deprivation. Moreover, the absence of extreme inequality in relative terms has contributed to a reduction in potential conflict. Adding to this the lack of marked sectoral and regional imbalances in growth and income distribution helps to explain the absence of problems which might have obstructed the growth process as it has done in countries cited earlier.

DIFFERENCES BY AREA OF ORIGIN

In 1970 and 1971, a phenomenon appeared, which given the calm of preceding years, was surprising. A group of youths of North African or Middle Eastern parentage staged demonstrations about income inequality and, having carefully learned the lessons of the mass media, called themselves the Black Panthers. Though there had been some demonstrations in the past, they had occurred mainly in new towns and often had specific objectives such as pro-vision of jobs or changes in public housing characteristics. The new demonstrations were more general in import, questioning the distribution of the benefits of growth between the Asian-African groups on the one hand and those of European origin on the other. The lower income of Asian-African groups has long been recognized,[22] though not acted upon by the government.

What is the income level of the Asian-African group or "Ori-entals," as they are often called? Data on relative incomes by area of origin are shown in Table 3. The Asian-African-born have con-siderably lower incomes than those of Western or Israeli parentage. Data not included in the table indicate that substantial differences exist within the Israel-born category between those with European parents and those with Oriental parents. The widening of the dif-ferential in the early 1950s reflected the impact of the substantial immigration of persons possessing relatively low skills and literacy from North Africa and the Middle East. However, since 1954 relative incomes have not deteriorated. Nevertheless, differentials on the order of 100 percent exist between Orientals and those of European background. This situation has existed for a long time and has been a concern of a number of individuals and groups. Nevertheless, there was only limited overt tension along area-of-origin lines. Why has behavior changed so suddenly? What are its implications for future stability of the growth process? [23] Both noneconomic as well as economic factors must be considered.

Table 3. INDICES OF RELATIVE INCOME BY AREA OF ORIGIN*

Continent of Birth of Head of Family	March 1951	1954	1959 -1960	1963 -1964	1970
All Families	100	100	100	100	100
Asia-Africa	88.8	76.2	75.7	63	69
Europe-America	101.2	107.9	112.1	124	126
Israel Born	102.9	103.7	111.5	125	119

Sources: 1951 to 1959-1960, Hanoch, op.cit., p. 57. 1963-1964, 1970, *Committee on Income Distribution*, p. 13.

*Data for 1963-1964 and 1970 reflect an adjustment for family size and are thus not directly comparable to data for previous years. Similar adjustment for earlier years would presumably have increased relative differentials to about the levels of the later years.

It could be argued that the sense of security following success in the Six Day War in 1967 has allowed the voicing of complaints which had earlier been suppressed in the interest of national unity. Though there may be some truth in this view, it is necessary to note that there had been numerous sit-ins and other demonstrations in earlier years directed at specific objectives, particularly in housing. Though they were not as carefully planned with respect to the impact on domestic and foreign communications media, they were often quite effective in obtaining publicity.

Almost certainly more important than voluntary restraint is the fact that by 1970 and 1971 there were youths of Asian-African parentage who had been born in Israel (or had arrived at a very early age) and did not feel insecure or grateful for an emergency haven. Their interest was no longer only "What can I do for my country?" but inevitably, and not unjustifiably, also "What can my country do for me?" Indeed, the fact that their first language was Hebrew rather than any European language still used by many "veteran" settlers undoubtedly strengthened their own sense of identity.[24]

It is likely, however, that even such a fundamental change in self-identity and the presence of income inequality might not have led to public demonstrations had not two catalysts been present: namely, a small, but easily observed growth in luxury consumption (including a related rapid rise in the price of apartments); and an influx of American and European immigrants who immediately achieved relatively high consumption standards.

A rapid growth in luxury consumption is noticeable to any observer who has been in Israel both before and after 1967.[25] This ranges from the proliferation of expensive restaurants, to increasingly frequent vacations taken out of the country, to the often fantastic sums (by Israeli standards) paid for apartments. While growth of this type of consumption is inevitable if reliance is placed on market incentives, the presence of such luxuries is certain to draw attention in a society as physically small and ideologically committed to egalitarianism as Israel. Not only has the current generation of Asian-Africans matured in Israel—they have been repeatedly inculcated with the social democratic ideology of the founders. Even if Oriental immigrants did not necessarily share the social-democratic aspirations of the East European elite, the deviation between semi-official ideology and the real world was increasingly apparent.

Although the growth of luxury consumption was surely important, it was aggravated by the contrast with the living standards of new immigrants. During the years of Israel's mass immigration (1948-1952) most immigrants were housed in tents and then in relatively primitive, but more permanent structures. These maabarot emptied only slowly. Even in 1960, 49 percent of post-1948 Asian-African immigrants lived in densities of three or more people per room, though this rapidly declined to 17 percent by 1970.[26] However, American, Russian and other immigrants who came after the 1967 war were helped to obtain spacious quarters.

The official rationale has been that "Western" immigrants are, in any case, voluntarily taking a reduction in living standards, and "luxury" housing at least cushions the drop. While this is to a large extent true, and there is a need for the skills which new immigrants have brought, this is little comfort for Orientals who still view their own conditions as inadequate.

Another key to the current tension may lie not in current income or asset differentials, but in perceptions of the long-run possibilities of adaptation to Israeli society and mobility within it. Even if current Asian-African living standards are not low, even by comparison with the new Western immigrants,[27] it may well be true that the latter have much brighter prospects because of their stock of skills. The crystallization and reinforcement of this perception may then be a critical factor in the new tensions. To see why, it is necessary to note that the sources of the observed income differentials between Orientals and Westerners appears to be due mainly to differences in education.

A careful examination by Hanoch in the 1950s suggested that much of the income differential in that decade could be explained by differences in education level and occupation structure.[28] Recent data gathered for the 1968-1969 family expenditure survey lead to similar conclusions (see Appendix).

The education-income relation involves a relatively sophisticated conceptualization. Members of low-income groups are hardly likely to ask questions about how their lower education is reflected in their lower income. Yet in a geographically small society in which the physical separation of the U.S. city-suburb type is relatively rare, in which all men between 18 and 45 spend 40 days or more per year in the close contact of the army reserves, the characteristics of those with high incomes are bound to be discerned. Those with less education, mainly of Asian-African background are likely to perceive how slowly (in their terms) the education differential is being removed.[29] Though both secondary and university attendance differentials are decreasing, the current disparity implies that income differentials will persist for another generation, if market forces are allowed full latitude. The contrast with many of the highly trained American and European immigrants cannot help but lead Orientals to doubt their economic future. The more general question of the usefulness of the individual in an increasingly technical society is also underscored. This is particularly acute if news reports are accurate about the relative youth and lack of schooling of the Black Panthers. For them, birth, maturation, identification and military service in Israel are of little worth, and their resentment is inevitable. Added to their limited economic prospects relative to that of Westerners is their consciousness of the alacrity with which Israel has responded to Western immigration in the hope of maintaining a strong Western cultural orientation.[30]

How do the current and prospective differences in income affect the growth process? So far there have been few overt manifestations such as strikes or slowdowns. Yet the absence of such acts until now should not lead us to naively forecast similar future behavior. One lesson of the 1960s has been the difficulty of predicting the particular form in which dissent will be expressed, and it is foolhardy for social scientists to try, though novelists may have more success.[31] Indeed, it may even be possible that continued growth of absolute consumption levels may eliminate much of the current tension. However, growth as rapid as that of the past is unlikely, for consumption's share of national output will have to be reduced to allow an increase in exports to reduce the unfavorable balance of trade.

If the government chooses to play an active role in the reduction of inequality, several methods are available. A long-term solution requires, at the least, increased education for Orientals.[32] Although many ad hoc statements have been made that families from the Islamic countries lack an orientation toward education, the data cited in a previous footnote indicate substantial increases in attendance in secondary schools, and rising university enrollment. Given the fact that until recently high schools charged tuition, and school expenses may loom large in a poorer family's budget, in addition to more prosaic problems such as overcrowding, the frequent assertion that Orientals have demonstrated less interest in school must be seriously questioned.[33] While cultural differences may exist, differences in behavior are small enough to warrant additional effort to reduce differential enrollment rates. Such programs already exist in the form of scholarships, but family income supplements would constitute an important element of any program.[34]

Even if there is a change in education patterns, the impact on income distribution is necessarily slow. In the interim, redistribution through the budget should be considered, whether in the form of changes in the allocation of existing receipts or in alteration of the tax structure. Indeed, even if reallocation of the existing budget allows redistribution, particularly in the form of increased provision of public housing, changes in the tax structure may still be warranted.

Two arguments can be made for this restructuring. First, in terms of the distribution questions considered above, heavier taxation of high incomes can slow the further spread of conspicuous consumption. Second, it is clear that Israel must restrain domestic consumption in order to realize a sufficient rise in exports to redress the trade balance. Although this latter position has been argued for a decade and a half,[35] there has been only limited response to it. Unfortunately, when in 1964 the balance of payments deficit on current accounts became quite large, the policy response was a planned recession,[36] in which unemployment fell disproportionately on the Oriental community. Thus, both current redistribution and long-term macroeconomic policy dictate increased taxation, and the logic of the argument suggests that much of such an increase should be levied on high-income recipients.

Opposition is inevitable, since Israelis view themselves as highly overtaxed. This assertion must be analyzed, and there are two separate questions which need to be considered: First, in international terms is Israel's GNP highly taxed? Second, do individual Israelis pay high rates?

International comparisons show that Israel is not among the most heavily taxed nations: most western European countries exhibit ratios at least as high and a number considerably higher.[37] Moreover, the Israeli ratio contains an upward bias insofar as the substantial import surplus allows domestic use of resources to be greater than it would be otherwise.[38] Regardless of which of many possible indices of the burden of taxation are used,[39] the tax burden is less than in Western European countries. On the other hand, it is true that Israel's per capita income is about 60 to 75 percent of the middle-range countries such as the Netherlands and Belgium, though at the level of Austria and Italy. However, these countries exhibited their current high tax ratios even when their per capita incomes were considerably lower. Thus, if international comparisons are used to obtain a benchmark against which to measure what is socially feasible, Israel could raise taxes still further.

However, in looking at individual tax schedules the stated progressivity of the personal income tax rates is impressive. The *average* tax rate paid by those in the top decile was 25 percent [40] in 1968-1969, and rates have since been raised. Indeed by 1971, scheduled rates indicate that a family of four with 36,000 Israeli pounds per year, the average income in the top decile (roughly $7,800) will pay 45 percent of total income in taxes (52 percent if a compulsory loan is included).[41] These, of course, are schedules, and it is not clear what their realization will bring. If they are roughly indicative of actual rates paid by those who are salaried, much higher levels may lead to incentive problems, and sole reliance on "soaking the rich" may not be desirable. However, there is a good possibility that, as in other countries, loopholes for capital gains and other property income exist, and much luxury consumption is probably financed with this income. While this may not yield the amounts of revenue required for serious redistribution, its morale-boosting effect would be considerable.

Substantial additional revenue could be generated if the average rate of personal tax levied on the top five deciles were increased by, say, 3 percent. As these households receive 73.1 percent of net income (net of direct taxes) [42] this would, if transferred, represent 8.5 percent of the after-tax income of the lowest groups.[43] The direction of such resources to housing and income supplements, particularly to encourage more education, could be of major importance in redressing existing inequality and preventing future differences. Such measures would help the Oriental community most as its members constitute a disproportionately high percentage of the bottom half of the distribution, and would also help, as it should, the poorer members of Western background.

Lest it appear to impose an onerous burden, it is worth noting that direct taxes paid by the upper deciles (except for the highest one) are not particularly high. For example, families in the eighth decile paid about 15.5 percent of their gross income, and this includes a substantial payment for social security, so that the income tax per se is only about 10 percent. An income tax of 13 percent (10 percent on current income plus a 3 percent surcharge on gross income) levied on such an income does not seem inordinate.

Since independence, Israel has exhibited rapid growth coupled with relatively widespread distribution of its benefits. For most of the period it is likely that the entire population experienced considerable growth in consumption standards. Moreover, there was limited inequality along regional or sectoral lines. On the other hand, there was a widening of personal income differentials, mainly during the 1950s, from the relative egalitarianism of the pre-state and early post-state years. I have argued that the general sharing in the benefits of growth precluded the rise of frictions whose resolution would have required policies inimical to continued development. However, this line of reasoning runs the risk of committing the *post hoc, propter hoc* fallacy. One cannot be certain that the relatively equal income distribution was the source of the general equanamity as there were many pressures, from that of received ideology to the existence of international tensions, which tended to make sustained and open economic disputes an activity to be entered upon with trepidation. To the extent that relative income equality has been a causal factor, there is a basis for concern about recent shifts toward highly visible luxury consumption among a few, and the continued low incomes of Orientals. While it would be foolhardy to assert that failure to reduce current inequalities will inevitably result in conflicts which slow the entire development process, such a possibility cannot be ruled out, especially in view of a number of recent experiences in other less developed countries. Moreover, failure to execute such redistribution would be to deny now a fundamental principle which contributed to the vigor with which an independent state was pursued and achieved.

NOTES

1. The reference point here is a country which has the preconditions for growth in terms of public and private capital, sufficient skilled labor and so on. In very underdeveloped countries which lack such material factors, governments can exert only limited influence.

2. For a thorough analysis of the Arab labor force, see Yoram Ben-Porath, *The Arab Labor Force in Israel* (Jerusalem: The Falk Institute, 1966), particularly chap. 5.

3. These issues are considered in detail in my *Structural Change and Economic Policy in Israel* (New Haven: Yale University Press, 1971), chaps. 4-6.

4. There were, of course, many noneconomic benefits ranging from the morale-boosting effects of transforming barren land to green belts to the defense purposes served by new agricultural settlements in border areas.

5. For a survey see Ian Little, Tibor Scitovsky and Maurice Scott, *Industry and Trade in Some Developing Countries* (Cambridge: Oxford University Press, 1970), referred to hereafter as *Industry and Trade*.

6. See Carlos-Diaz Alejandro, "The Argentine State and Economic Growth: A Historical Review," *Government and Economic Development*, ed. G. Ranis (New Haven: Yale University Press, 1971).

7. For a detailed description of the linking process see Milton Derber, "Israel's Wage Differential: A Persisting Problem," in S. N. Eisenstadt, Rivka Bar Yosef, and Chaim Adler, *Integration and Development in Israel* (New York: Praeger, 1970).

8. Ibid.

9. Indeed, attention was focused on the minutiae of particular tying formulae rather than any basic changes in income distribution. This emphasis probably reflects the acceptance of the broad distribution outline and an attempt to change only relatively small details.

10. Moreover, with rapid structural change and heavy immigration, those in the bottom deciles may not be the same people over time, suggesting even greater advancement for the formerly poor. Simon Kuznets, "Economic Growth and Income Inequality," *American Economic Review*, March, 1955.

11. We ignore here differences by area of origin as these will be considered in detail below.

12. The data and an admirable analysis are presented in G. Hanoch, "Income Differentials in Israel" in *Fifth Report 1959 and 1960* (The Falk Project for Economic Research in Israel, Jerusalem, 1961).

13. Ibid, p. 46.

14. For a more detailed discussion see Pack, *Structural Change and Economic Policy*, chap. 8.

15. Hanoch, *Fifth Report*, p. 51.

16. Halevi and R. Klinov-Malul, *The Economic Development of Israel* (New York: Praeger, 1968), pp. 115-23.

17. The authors of the *Industry and Trade* study emphasize the uncertain quality of their data, particularly omission of income in upper income groups. On the other hand, the Israeli data are quite inclusive and of high reliability. Thus, the data presented probably understate the difference in income concentration among the countries.

18. Adjustments for family size slightly changes these conclusions. The Israeli data in Table 2 do not reflect such adjustments in order to allow comparisons with other countries.

19. *Report of the Committee on Income Distribution and Social Inequality* (Tel Aviv, 1971), p. 18 (referred to hereafter as *Committee on Income Distribution*).

20. Halevi and Klinov-Malul, *The Economic Development of Israel*, pp. 196-97.

21. Again, this is not to discount continuous fighting by specific groups, such as professionals, to change the relative distribution. It was, however, limited in its impact by the small size of the group. Moreover, the intensity of the conflict was undoubtedly reduced by the continuous growth in absolute incomes.

22. See, for example, Hanoch, *Fifth Report*, for an early analysis of income differentials of the groups.

23. This is not meant to suggest that the only reason for concern is the possible slowing of the growth process. Clearly, the level of income inequality is of intrinsic importance.

24. The favorite epithet directed towards Westerners involves a parody of a frequently used German (and Yiddish) expression.

25. This can occur without any change in relative incomes, simply as those in the highest deciles receive quite high absolute incomes.

26. *Committee on Income Distribution*, p. 15. The comparable percentages for European-American immigrants were 12 and 2.

27. In 1970, 92 percent of Asian-African families owned electric refrigerators, 89 percent owned gas stoves, 46 percent owned washing machines and 48 percent owned television sets (*Committee on Income Distribution*, p. 18); these percentages are not substantially different from those for the European-American group. Only in automobile ownership is there any substantial difference. New Russian immigrants are likely to possess far lower amounts of durable goods.

28. Hanoch, *Fifth Report*, chaps. 3-6.

29. Although there is a narrowing of differentials in school attendance between the two area-of-origin groups, they are still significant. Thus, between 1963 and 1970 the percentage of 14- to 17-year-old Asian-Africans attending high school increased from 27.3 to 44.5 percent while the corresponding rate for European-Americans rose from 60.6 to 76.6 percent. In 1970, university attendance of the Asian-African born or those whose father was born in Asia-Africa was about a quarter of that of Westerners. (Education data from *Committee on Income Distribution*, p. 29.)

30. For a discussion of the general problem of cultural conflict see Terence Prittie, *Israel, Miracle in the Desert* (London: Penguin Books, 1967); or Amos Elon, *The Israelis, Founders and Sons* (New York: Holt, Rinehart and Winston, 1971). An earlier, insightful work is Raphael Patai, *Israel, Between East and West* (Philadelphia: Jewish Publication Society, 1957).

31. The best "prediction" of the form of U.S. urban disorders came not from sociologists, but from Ralph Ellison's *The Invisible Man*.

32. A question may be raised about whether additional education actually increases productivity and warrants the expense from the viewpoint of the national interest. This is irrelevant for the income distribution question as long as income continues to be closely related to education. For an insightful interpretation of this relationship see H. Gintis, "Education, Technology and the Characteristics of Worker Productivity," *American Economic Review*, May, 1971.

33. See, for example, Amos Elon, "The Black Panthers of Israel," *New York Times Magazine*, September 12, 1971.

34. To the extent that status is a function of education *per se,* and status differentials are a source of friction, it will be necessary to reduce education differentials regardless of other income-redistributing measures.

35. See Don Patinkin, *The Israel Economy: The First Decade* (Jerusalem: Falk Project, 1960).

36. See Pack, *Structural Change and Economic Policy*, chap. 7.

37. See Pack, *Structural Change and Economic Policy*, p. 182, for data for the 1964-1966 period. The Israeli data for 1970 do not change the conclusion.

38. It is important to note in this connection that foreign capital inflows appear to substantially exceed direct imports attributable to defense.

39. For a number see *Bank of Israel Annual Report, 1970*, p. 129.

40. *Committee on Income Distribution*, p. 23.

41. Ibid, p. 45.

42. Ibid. p. 23.

43. To the extent that these groups currently receive transfers, the percentage increase would be smaller. The calculation is $(.03).(73.1)/26.9$.

APPENDIX

Table 4 shows the relationship between area of origin, education and income. Each column shows the distribution of family income given the education of the family head.

There are two questions: first, how does increased education affect the income position of the Asian-African? Second, does greater education change his status as much as it does that of the European-American group? The latter question is of interest in analyzing the existence of discrimination.[1]

The first and most important inference to be drawn is the large decrease in the incidence of low incomes (taken as the two bottom quintiles) as education increases. Among Orientals this percentage declines from 68.3 among those with zero to four years of education to 23.9 of those with 13 or more years of education; conversely, the percentage of those within the top 40 percent increases from 14.2 to 66.2. Of course, similar movements also occur among heads of households born in Europe, America and Israel.

Answers to the second question, that of the existence of discrimination are much more ambiguous. However, some rough generalizations are possible. In every education category, the percentage of Orientals in the highest two quintiles is somewhat smaller than it is for the other two groups. Moreover, the percentage in the highest quintile is with one exception substantially smaller. On the other hand, for each education level, the percentage in the bottom 40 percent is roughly the same. Such results initially suggest that although higher education helps to increase the incomes of Orientals, it may not help them as much as it does others. However, there are a number of factors which necessarily modify the initial conclusion.

Perhaps the most obvious is the fact that Asian-Africans in the more highly educated groups (nine to 12 years, 13 years and over) are likely to be quite young, as there were relatively few people in this category in earlier years. It is well known that labor income and age are related, especially in higher level jobs, and thus the smaller percentage of Orientals in the top quintiles may well be

---

1. It is obvious that a simple chi-square test can be used on the data from which the table is drawn to test the discrimination hypothesis. For reasons given in the text, I do not believe such a test yields much information in this context.

Table 4. DISTRIBUTION OF URBAN JEWISH FAMILY HEADS BY CONTINENT OF BIRTH, YEARS OF SCHOOLING AND INCOME QUINTILE, 1968-1969

Income Quintiles	Years of School			
	0-4	5-8	9-12	13 or more
Asia-Africa Born Family Heads				
Lowest	39.3	16.3	10.8	15.4
Second	29.0	30.4	21.5	8.5
Third	17.5	26.9	26.0	9.9
Fourth	9.1	19.7	24.7	36.6
Highest	5.1	6.7	17.0	29.6
Europe-America Born Family Heads				
Lowest	54.4	24.5	12.0	7.4
Second	20.5	19.7	16.4	9.8
Third	10.2	24.4	17.3	13.0
Fourth	10.2	22.4	24.8	23.3
Highest	4.7	9.0	29.5	46.5
Israel-Born Family Heads				
Lowest	56.9	12.6	5.9	7,4
Second	22.4	9.4	6.7	16.7
Third	0	37.2	31.8	11.1
Fourth	10.3	14.2	22.4	17.3
Highest	10.4	16.6	33.2	47.5
All Families				
Lowest	45.6	19.6	10.9	8.5
Second	25.9	24.6	16.5	11.4
Third	14.0	26.6	21.5	11.9
Fourth	9.3	20.4	24.4	23.3
Highest	5.2	8.8	26.7	44.9
Total	100.0%	100.0%	100.0%	100.0%

Source: Calculated from *Committee on Income Distribution* Table 10.

related to this factor. Second, the role of property incomes must be considered. As the data include such income, one would expect those with higher assets to exhibit higher total incomes. As the previous working life and accumulated savings of the Asian-African group is lower due to lower average age, this factor exaggerates differences.

The differences in the distribution of the 13 year and over groups (and the same is true of the nine to 12 year groups) are surely not strong enough to allow us to ignore age, assets and other factors as a potential source of income differences among this group. Finally, one must consider the participation rate of women. Everything else being equal, a household in which the wife is employed will have a higher income than one in which this is not the case. It is well established that female participation rates in the Asian-African group are much lower.

Given all of these qualifications it is difficult to argue that there is any obvious discrimination. The differences in income distribution within education groupings is simply not large enough to warrant the conclusion, though certainly there may be some. What is outstanding in Table 4 is the strong association between income and education.

12

Oded Remba

INCOME INEQUALITY
IN ISRAEL: ETHNIC ASPECTS

The emergence of the Black Panthers in Israel early in 1971 has produced a spate of scholarly studies and popular articles on the social gap between Israel's Oriental and Western Jewish communities. The voluminous output of academic and journalistic writing has no doubt contributed to a greater awareness of a whole range of related problems which until recently had received relatively little attention. But the most striking feature of these publications is that they arrive at diametrically opposed conclusions on the trends of poverty and inequality in Israel.

Is the gap widening or narrowing? Representatives of the Sephardic-Oriental community have argued repeatedly that the social gap has been widening. A detailed report issued at the end of 1971 by the World Sephardi Federation claims that one third of Israel's population, or 200,000 families representing 970,000 people, are living in conditions of deprivation and that poverty is still growing. "The sons and daughters of the generation of immigrants from the Arab world, and in some instances the grandchildren of these immigrants, are even more deeply mired in the swamp of poverty and distress than were their parents and *it will be even harder to help them and their children to extricate themselves*," the report asserts.[1] It suggests that little improvement has been made in the areas of housing, education, social welfare and income maintenance.

199

Similarly, Israeli author Amos Kenan is quoted as having written that in "twenty years, the inequality has doubled, and in the young, so-called progressive Israeli society, the rich become richer, and the poor, poorer." [2] In an essay published in 1972, an Israeli sociologist concludes that "far from shrinking with time," the income gap between the two ethnic groups "is even widening." [3]

On the other hand, a study by Itzhak Kanev, director of the Economic and Social Research Institute in Israel, found that the "social and economic policies of the State and its public and private bodies succeeded in warding off poverty and want to a large degree," particularly during the 1967-1970 period when there was a substantial reduction in the incidence of poverty, due to full employment and increases in social insurance benefits.[4] Late in 1971 Welfare Minister Michael Hazani stated confidently that "this year we will reach a state in which no family in Israel lives under the poverty level. In several more years, no family will be residing in sub-standard housing." [5]

The Minority Rights Group, a London-based international organization that maintains a watch on the conditions of minorities all over the world, noted in a report released in August 1972 that in the last 25 years the economic status and educational level of Oriental Jews have "greatly improved," adding that this has not been accidental but the result of hard work by various governmental agencies.[6] Another study, by the Horowitz committee—appointed by Israel's Prime Minister, the Finance Minister, the Secretary General of Histadrut and the governor of the Bank of Israel to examine developments in social inequality during the 1960s—concluded that "the standard of living of families of Asian and African origin improved relative to the standard of living of all families. This improvement found expression in higher income levels, in better housing, in a higher rate of ownership of consumer durables, in a decline in the proportion of Asian-African immigrants among low-income families, and an increase in the proportion of these families in the higher income brackets." [7]

These widely divergent interpretations of trends arise partly because of differences in ideology and vested interest. But what further confounds the picture is that there are any number of ways of looking at such broad concepts as social gap or living standard differentials and even at the more readily measurable notion of income inequality. All too frequently, Israeli leaders, editorial writers and others making statements about the widening or narrowing of the gap do not specify the particular indicator used, whether the statement applies to income groups in the population as a whole, or more specifically to the two ethnic communities, or to specific groups within these communities (such as urban employees). Even if specific indicators are used, such as differences in educational attainments or housing conditions between Oriental and Western immigrants, they frequently apply to a given point in time only, without any indication of significant changes over time. Selection of particular time periods, either accidentally or deliberately, can also lead to conclusions which are not completely valid or representative; some unusual factor such as a major recession or a large immigration wave from a given geographic region can seriously distort the results.

Finally, none of the studies on the social gap point out that all Israeli government statistical publications give a *geographic* rather than an *ethnic* breakdown; i.e., the data are broken down by continent or country of birth of family heads (Asia-Africa, Europe-America and Israel), not into Sephardic and Ashkenazic or Oriental and Western groups. The problem here is that while virtually all Jews born in Asia and Africa are Oriental or Sephardic, a small but nonetheless significant number of those born in Europe are Sephardic. In fact, some scholars distinguish between Middle Eastern or Oriental and Sephardic Jews, pointing out that the majority of Sephardic Jews are European. The Sephardic Jews from such countries as Bulgaria, Greece, Italy and Spain have higher incomes than Middle Eastern Jews, yet they are included in the European-American group. The importance of this can be seen in the fact that the Bulgarian community, which was middle class in its country of origin and immigrated almost completely in the early years of statehood, today boasts a higher percentage of doctors and dentists than any other group in the population; of the two Sephardic-Oriental cabinet ministers (out of a total of 18), one—Minister of Health Victor Shemtov—is Bulgarian.

Similarly, the Israel-born group includes a small but growing proportion of families of Asian-African origin as well as patrician, upper-middle-class Sephardic families long established in the country. These Israel-born families enjoy living standards which are generally comparable to those of the European-American immigrant group and, in the case of those ranging in age from 45 to 54 years old, their incomes are higher than those of veteran European-American immigrant families in the same age group. Therefore, where the data give a breakdown of Asian-African, European-American and Israel-born families—with no further subdivision within each of these categories—they probably moderately over-state the gap between the two ethnic groups.

THE RISE IN OVERALL LIVING STANDARDS

Given the disagreements, it is best to begin with two basic state-ments of fact which are beyond dispute: first, Israel's living stand-ards have risen rapidly since the establishment of the state; and second, all three population groups, including Oriental families which arrived during different periods, shared in these gains in significant though in varying degrees.

Per capita private consumption in real terms (i.e., adjusted for inflation—the most reliable indicator of living standards) more than doubled in the 1950-1970 period, rising at an average annual rate of 4.4 percent.[8] Per capita income or gross national product—admittedly not an ideal measure of living standards but the only one readily available for international comparisons—nearly tripled, from $563 in 1952 to $1,544 in 1971 (in constant prices of 1970); it rose at an average annual rate of more than 5 percent. This rate of growth in per capita income has been among the highest in the world, exceeded only by about a dozen countries (major oil-pro-ducing countries such as Saudi Arabia and Libya, centrally planned Soviet bloc economies and a number of other countries such as Japan with unusually high economic growth rates and relatively stable populations). In terms of per capita income, Israel ranked 21 among 65 countries in 1971.[9]

The real gross income of African-Asian families rose markedly throughout this period. The rate of increase in family income was greater in the 1960s than in the 1950s and was in fact greater during the past decade than the rate of increase for the European-Ameri-can and the Israel-born families. Important and interrelated as these trends are, the critical question is not so much what has happened to the income of Asian-African families in absolute or relative terms during their residence in Israel or compared to average income in their countries of origin. The critical issue, as it has typically been presented in discussions of the social gap, is how the income of Asian-African families compares with that of European-American families, both at a given point in time and over different periods of time.

INCOME DIFFERENTIALS BY ORIGIN GROUP 1951-1971

Table 1 gives income ratios for the two groups of Jewish immigrant families for those years during the 1951-1971 period for which data are available. It should be pointed out, as so many of the discussions on the subject fail to do, that no consistently comparable data are available on income distribution for Israel's entire Jewish population by continent of birth since the establishment of the state in 1948. The data that are available for the entire period refer to the urban population and more typically to urban employee families, which constitute about two thirds of all families in the country. It is evident from the table that one can show that the gap is widening or narrowing, depending on the specific years or periods selected. A glaring illustration of this type of distortion appears in a May 1972 issue of an American-Jewish publication which carries the following statement: "The oriental Jew earned 89 per cent compared to the European Jew in the early years. This went down to 74 per cent in 1957, and it dropped to 69 per cent in 1969." [10]

The basic trend is fairly clear, however. The income differential between Asian-African and European-American families widened substantially in the 1950s and early 1960s, but stabilized around the 70 percent mark in the second half of the 1960s except for the recession period of 1966-1967. The high unemployment rate which prevailed during the recession hit Oriental families—especially those living in development towns—much harder than other population groups, bringing the gap to its widest level. But as the economy attained full employment in the boom following the Six Day War, the ratio quickly approximated its pre-war level and by 1971 reached its narrowest point since 1951.

The scope of the income survey for 1951 exaggerates the degree of equality which existed in Israeli society during this period of mass immigration. The survey for that year was confined to families of permanent Jewish employees living in eight cities, thus including a relatively larger proportion of veteran and European families than their actual share in the population. Had the survey included the thousands of new immigrants in transit camps and other unemployed individuals, the degree of income inequality would have been greater even as early as 1951.[12] Starting in 1954, it is possible to compare years for which sample surveys are gen-

Table 1.[11] RATIOS OF AVERAGE GROSS INCOME
AND PER CAPITA INCOME OF URBAN EMPLOYEES FAMILIES
BY CONTINENT OF BIRTH OF FAMILY HEAD

Income Ratios by Continent of Birth of Family Head	1951	1954	1956-1957	1959-1960	1963-1964	1965	1966	1967	1968	1969	1970	1971
FAMILY INCOME												
Asia-Africa as percentage of Europe-America	88*	71	73	68	62	72	69	60	71	69	73	74
Asia-Africa as percentage of Israel Born	86	74	74	68	68	66	64	61	68	70	71	73
Asia-Africa as percentage of All Families	89	76	78	76	73	79	78	71	80	79	82	83
PER CAPITA INCOME												
Asia-Africa as percentage of Europe-America	61		46	45		45	43	39	47	45	47	48
Asia-Africa as percentage of Israel Born	67		57	53		46	44	44	51	53	54	57
Asia-Africa as percentage of All Families	66		58	59		63	62	58	65	66	68	70

*All figures are percentages,

erally consistent in regard to definitions and coverage. But only the data for the 1965-1971 period are strictly comparable in all respects; they are based on annual income surveys conducted within the framework of the Labor Force Survey of the Central Bureau of Statistics.

While attention has usually focused on the European-Oriental gap, it may be of interest to see how the growing Israel-born group fits into the picture. Israel-born families consist of three subgroups: family heads whose fathers were born in Europe-America; in Asia-Africa; or in Israel, with no further breakdown for the last category. There were significant differentials in income among these subgroups, but average income of the Israel-born group as a whole was higher than that of the European-American immigrant group for five out of seven years during the 1965-1971 period, even though Israel-born family heads were more than 15 years younger on the average than European-American family heads in 1971 (see Table 2). Thus the income gap between Asian-African and Israel-born families was somewhat wider than that between Asian-African and European-American families; but by 1971 the gap was similar to the level which prevailed in the mid-1950s.

The ratio of average income of Asian-African immigrant families to average income of all families (Asian-African, European-American and Israel-born) shows a narrower gap than the Asian-African/European-American ratio. Since the European-American group includes many higher-income Sephardic families and the Israel-born group includes a significant number of families of Oriental-Sephardic origin, this overall ratio may well be more meaningful than the other two. This indicator reveals widening income differentials in the 1950s and early 1960s, with stability achieved in the second half of the 1960s around the 80 percent mark (again with the exception of the recession period), followed by a trend toward a narrowing of the gap in 1970 and 1971; in 1971 average income of an Asian-African family was 83 percent of the overall average, its highest level except for 1951.

This indicator also reflects more accurately the major changes which occurred in the relative size of the three population groups during the past two decades, an important aspect ignored in nearly all recent discussions on the subject. The size and composition of these groups changed dramatically over the years, mainly as a result of immigration, but also because of the formation of new families headed by young people entering the labor force and the influence of mortality, emigration and retirement. The proportion of Asian-

African immigrant families among the total number of urban Jewish employee families increased sharply, from 12.0 percent in 1951 to 41.5 percent in 1971; the proportion of European-American families declined from 80.3 percent to 42.6 percent, and that of Israel-born families rose from 7.7 percent to 15.95 percent in the same period. These demographic shifts contributed in themselves to the widening of income differentials on the basis of origin. The differentials between average incomes of Asian-African and European-American families would have widened even if their relative size in the population remained exactly the same throughout the period. But the rising proportion of the generally poorer families from the underdeveloped countries of Asia and Africa brought about a further widening of the income gap or slowed down its reduction. Put differently, even if the relative income of the two main groups had remained exactly the same throughout the period, the income gap would have widened due to the changes in their relative size in the population.

CAUSES OF GAP

This gap can also be seen by comparing the 1971 average income of Asian-African families by period of immigration: 11,900 Israeli pounds for family heads who immigrated prior to 1947; 11,500 Israeli pounds for 1948-1954 immigrants; 9,800 Israeli pounds for 1955-1960 immigrants; and 8,500 Israeli pounds for family heads who immigrated since 1961 (Table 2). The large number of North African and Middle Eastern immigrants who arrived since 1955 pulled down the average for all Asian-African families to 10,700 Israeli pounds in 1971. On the other hand, three times as many European as Oriental family heads arrived prior to 1947, and the very high incomes of these veteran families pulled up the average for all European-American families.

These figures suggest two conclusions: first, the income gap has not been created in Israel, as has sometimes been alleged, but has largely been imported; second, there is a strong positive correlation between duration of residence in Israel and income. Indeed, no discussion of the income gap is very meaningful without an examination of its underlying and often interrelated causes. In addition to period of immigration, the major factors which influence the level of income include education, occupation, age and sources of income abroad.

Table 2.[13] AVERAGE GROSS ANNUAL MONEY INCOME PER EMPLOYEE'S FAMILY,
BY CONTINENT OF BIRTH AND PERIOD OF IMMIGRATION
OF FAMILY HEAD (1971)

Continent of Birth and Immigration Period of Family Head	Gross Income (Israeli Pounds)	Years of Education Family Head	Average Age of Family Head	Average Size of Family	Percentage of Families, by Continent and Immigration
TOTAL	12,800	9.9	42.5	4.0	100.0
JEWS	12,900	10.0	42.7	3.9	97.2
Asia-Africa, Total	10,700	8.1	39.2	4.8	40.3
Immigrated:					
Up to 1947	11,900	8.3	44.5	4.2	4.6
1948-1954	11,500	8.4	39.0	4.9	21.6
1955-1960	9,800	8.0	38.3	4.9	6.9
Since 1961	8,500	7.0	37.5	4.9	7.2
Europe-America, Total	14,400	10.9	49.4	3.2	41.4
Immigrated:					
Up to 1947	16,100	12.1	52.6	5.3	14.2
1948-1954	14,900	10.2	47.8	3.3	15.5
1955-1960	12,900	10.6	49.2	3.0	4.5
Since 1961	11,000	10.6	46.9	2.8	7.2
Israel Born, Total	14,600	12.3	33.9	3.7	15.5
Father born in:					
Asia-Africa	11,100	9.3	32.2	4.1	3.3
Europe-America	16,300	14.0	32.5	3.5	8.8
Israel	13,600	10.9	39.1	3.7	3.4
NON-JEWS	8,600	6.4	34.0	6.4	2.8

Substantial disparities exist in the educational attainments of the various groups. In 1971, family heads born in Asia-Africa had 8.1 years of education; European-American family heads had 10.9 years; and Israel-born family heads 12.3 years. But these figures say nothing about differences in the quality of education both in the countries of origin and in Israel. The figures relate to urban employees only. For the Jewish population as a whole, as recently as 1970 24 percent of persons over 14 years of age who were born in Asia-Africa had no schooling at all, and an additional 8 percent had one to four years of schooling; i.e., they were functionally illiterate; comparable data for European-American immigrants were 3 percent and 8 percent and for native-born Israelis 1 percent and 1 percent.[14]

These educational disparities are explained in large measure by the sharp contrast between the forcible mass migration from the Middle East and North Africa and the selective immigration from the West. Immigrants from the pre-industrial Islamic countries were for the most part poorly educated and unskilled; with such notable exceptions as the Iraqi and Yemenite communities, the elites of the Oriental communities either stayed behind or fled to France and other Western countries. Both the pre-1948 and post-1967 immigrations from Europe and the Americas were largely selective and voluntary; most immigrants were highly motivated and relatively well educated, with a large component of professionals. According to Hanoch Smith, head of the Manpower Planning of the Israel Ministry of Labor, the "best description of Israel's pre-1948 population is that it was 'select': over 90 percent of them were of European extraction. The average education of the adult population—measured in number of years at school or by the proportion of those with higher education—was perhaps the highest in the world, even higher than that of the U.S. at that time." [15]

The educational disparities which the immigrants brought with them have not narrowed more rapidly, partly because the outlay of Western families on education and culture has been twice as high as that of Oriental families, even after allowing for their lower income and larger family size. But the educational gap is also due in part to the fact that schools in development towns and slum areas inhabited by Oriental families are inferior to schools in long-established towns or relatively prosperous suburbs.[16]

The educational backgrounds of the three groups have largely determined their occupational distribution in the labor force. In 1969 more than half of all Asian-African immigrants were employed as industrial or service workers, as compared with one third of

European-American immigrants and Israel-born workers. Only 17 percent of all Asian-African immigrants were employed in high-paying professional, scientific, technical, administrative, executive, managerial and clerical occupations; 38 percent of European-American immigrants and 44 percent of Israel-born workers were employed in these occupations.[17] Israel's development as a modern industrialized economy, and particularly the growth of science-based and other sophisticated industries, have put a premium on the services of those with the requisite skills. The pattern of high incomes earned by professionals and managers can be found in practically all countries today regardless of economic system, including such collectivist economies as the Soviet Union and Yugoslavia.

Still another factor explaining the income differentials is age. The average age of Asian-African family heads was 39.2 in 1971, compared to 49.4 for European-American family heads. The ten years separating the two groups of family heads are the prime years of life in which incomes can be expected to rise significantly. On the average, Israel-born family heads were only 33.9 years old, but they had the highest income because their educational attainment was the highest of the three groups.

Education, occupation, age and duration of residence in Israel explain a large part of the differentials in income, although the relative importance of each of these causes varies, and a special study would be necessary to measure them separately and jointly. But the income differentials stem from many other factors, some of which are not susceptible to quantitative measurement. These factors include the following: personal differences in ability and intelligence, insofar as they are not already expressed in educational and occupational levels; the degree of economic, social and geographic mobility of workers; the importance attached to leisure and nonmonetary factors such as comfort and prestige; discrimination; and the elements of luck and chance as well as personal contacts and political influence.

One other factor, which is particularly important in Israel's case, is access to sources of income abroad. The Jews from Arab countries left behind them most of their property and assets, receiving no compensation whatsoever. But tens of thousands of European families received personal restitutions from Germany in the form of current pensions and lump-sum grants totaling more than $2 billion during the 1954-1972 period. More recent immigrants from affluent Western countries were able to bring substantial amounts of funds, property and equipment. In the 1966-1970 period alone, individual transfers (pension payments from abroad other than restitutions, family support payments, personal gifts and other cash and property brought from abroad) totaled $666 million. These transfer payments have increased the income of European-American families both directly (as in the case of current pensions and regular support payments) and indirectly by enabling these families to finance the cost of education and training.

If poorer, older or less educated Jews had arrived from Western countries, while the elites or even a cross-section of the Oriental communities had come to Israel together with their personal funds and possessions, the income data would have been quite different.

The Oriental and Western immigrants also brought different demographic syndromes, usually reflecting the conditions prevailing in their countries of origin. The average Asian-African family consisted of 4.8 members in 1971, compared with only 3.1 members for the European-American family. This means that the differences in per capita income were much greater than those in family income (Table 1). But the trend toward narrowing in overall family income by continent of origin noted above is also evident when a comparison is made on a per person basis. Income per person of an Asian-African immigrant family was 45 percent of that of a European-American family in 1965, rising to 48 percent in 1971, the highest ratio since 1951. While family income per person may be a meaningful indicator statistically, it does not take into account the fact that a four-member family does not need twice as much income to maintain a certain level of consumption as a two-member family, but less than twice as much (60 percent more to be exact). When an adjustment is made on the basis of actual consumption patterns using the concept of "income per standard equivalent adult," the Asian-African/European-American ratio shows a rise from 51 percent in 1963-1964 to 55 percent in 1970, the Asian-African/Israeli ratio rising from 50 percent to 58 percent, and the ratio of Asian-African families to all families rising from 63 percent to 69 percent in the same period.[18]

Not only has the income of Asian-African families risen in direct relation to duration of residence in Israel, but the size of the family has tended to decline. Family size was smaller (4.2 members) for Asian-African family heads who immigrated prior to 1947 and still smaller (4.1) for family heads born in Israel whose fathers were born in Asia-Africa than for Oriental family heads who immigrated since 1948 (4.9).

210

The foregoing discussion has dealt with gross income before deductions of direct taxes imposed on income such as income tax, defense levy and national insurance premiums. But in reality it is net or after-tax income which determines a family's ability to buy goods and services in order to sustain a particular standard of living. As a result of Israel's highly progressive tax system (with top marginal rates rising up to 80 percent at income brackets which would not be considered particularly high in Western countries), the differentials in net incomes between European and Oriental families are significantly less than the differentials in gross income.

The way income is defined also has an important bearing on the results. The gross monetary income of urban employee families includes the income of all family members from employment and all other sources, including private and government pensions and grants. But it excludes the value of services given by employers to their employees without payment as well as payments which constitute a refund of expenses. These nontaxable benefits cover the cost of maintaining a car and a telephone or of travel expenses; they are available to senior personnel in the private, Histadrut and government sectors—such as officials, managers and engineers— most of whom are of Western origin. The definition of income also excludes the value of free or subsidized social services—such as education, medical care and housing—provided by public institutions to low-income families, which are mainly Oriental. Also excluded are all nonrecurrent payments (e.g., legacies and severance pay). No accurate estimates are available of the monetary value of all the exclusions; on balance, they probably do not simply cancel out but widen the true income differentials between Asian-African and European-American families.

A survey of the total urban population—including employers, the self-employed, employees, retired persons and welfare recipients —might show somewhat greater income differentials by continent of origin as compared with a survey of urban employees only. But one such comparison, for 1963-1964, showed surprising similarities. The income gap between Asian-African and European rural families is probably greater than that between urban families, since the veteran settlements have been largely populated by families of European origin. But these qualifications do not alter the basic trends, particularly because families of wage and salary earners constitute the vast majority of all urban families and because the proportion of rural families has been declining.

CONCLUSIONS AND PROSPECTS

Perhaps the most obvious conclusion which emerges from this discussion is that one cannot make facile generalizations about the social gap in Israel. The subject is immensely complex, for the numerous factors which influence the gap include the scope of social insurance and social services, changes in the tax structure, wage policy, the unemployment rate, ethnic intermarriage, consumption patterns, the size and sources of future immigration, and the defense burden. Some of these factors are largely beyond the control of the state.

Just as there are sharp disagreements about past and present developments, there are divergent forecasts on future trends. Israeli leaders, both in and out of the government, have tended to express optimistic views. Finance Minister Pinhas Sapir stated in May 1972 that within one generation all socioeconomic gaps between the Western and Oriental communities will disappear; he noted that the main problem was education, which by its very nature is a prolonged process. Yitzhak Ben-Aharon, Secretary General of Histadrut and a champion of a more egalitarian society, suggested on a number of occasions that the problem of the social gap *can* be solved and that such a task is within the financial and institutional capacity of the state. The Minority Rights Group also concluded that Israel will successfully bridge the social and economic gaps that separate the various segments of its population.

Whether these optimistic assessments or the alarming warnings of the World Sephardi Federation's report about growing poverty and imminent social disintegration will be borne out is a matter of conjecture. It will take at least ten to 15 years more before many of the forces now operating in various spheres of Israeli society, particularly those resulting from immigration, can shape a stable, long-term trend. In the case of the United States, for example, income distribution remained basically unchanged during the 1950-1970 period, after major movement toward less inequality in the previous 20 years of depression and world war. What can be said about Israel at this stage is that the pattern since 1967 has clearly been in the direction of a sharp reduction in the incidence of poverty and a moderate lessening of income inequality.

NOTES

1. Edward Geffner, *Sephardi Problems in Israel* (World Sephardi Federation, Executive of Israel), p. 7.

2. Amos Kenan, "Poverty as Treason," *ACIID* (*A Critical Insight Into Israel's Dilemmas*), vol. 2, no. 5-6 (Aug. 23, 1971): 13. ACIID is a student publication of Washington University, St. Louis, Mo.

3. Dan Soen, "Aspects of Israeli Society: The Communal Gap," *New Outlook* (March-April 1972), p. 28.

4. Itzhak Kanev, *Israel's War on Poverty and New Approaches to Rehabilitation* (New York: American Histadrut Cultural Exchange Institute, 1971), pp. vi, 8.

5. *The Jerusalem Post Weekly Overseas Edition*, October 26, 1971.

6. Alfred Friendly, *Israel's Oriental Immigrants and Druzes* (London: Minority Rights Group, 1972), p. 7.

7. *Report of the Committee on Income Distribution and Social Inequality* (Tel Aviv, 1971), p. 4. The Committee was headed by David Horowitz, governor of the Bank of Israel at the time.

8. State of Israel, The Economic Planning Authority, Ministry of Finance, *The Israel Economy: 1950, 1960, 1970, 1980*, p. 6.

9. Agency for International Development, *Gross National Product: Growth Rates and Trend Data by Region and Country* (Washington, D.C., May 1972).

10. *The Jewish Post and Opinion* (New York), May 26, 1972; reprinted in *Palestine Digest*, vol. 2, issue no. 3 (June 1972). The statement was made in an interview with Dr. Kenneth R. Kattan, an Iraqi Jew who is now associate professor of radiology at the University of Cincinnati College of Medicine. Dr. Kattan prefaced his statement by saying that "the gap was created in Israel."

11. The data for Table 1 were computed from the following sources: for 1951 to 1959-1960—Giora Hanoch, "Income Differentials in Israel," in *Fifth Report: 1959 and 1960* (Jerusalem: The Falk Project for Economic Research in Israel, 1961), pp. 57, 63; for 1963-1964—*Statistical Abstract of Israel 1966*, p. 188; for 1965-1971—*Statistical Abstract of Israel 1971*, p. 182, and Israel Central Bureau of Statistics, *Monthly Bulletin of Statistics, Supplement* (Hebrew), May 1972, p. 41. For the 1965-1971 period, the data cover settlements with a population of 2,000 or more; excluded are employees' families living in small villages, kibbutzim, moshavim and institutions. Data for a given year relate on the average to income at the beginning of the year.

12. Hanoch, "Income Differentials in Israel," pp. 60 and 126; Nadav Halevi and Ruth Klinov-Malul, *The Economic Development of Israel* (New York: Frederick A. Praeger, 1968), p. 119. The Hanoch study is the classic work on income differentials in Israel in the 1950s.

213

13. Source for Table 2—*Monthly Bulletin of Statistics, Supplement,* May 1972, p. 50.

14. *Statistical Abstract of Israel 1971,* p. 543.

15. Hanoch Smith, "Israel's Employment Potential," *The Israel Economist* (January 1969), p. 12.

16. Hayyim Cohen, "Integrating Israel's Underprivileged Immigrants: The Jewish Migration from Africa and Asia," *The Wiener Library Bulletin,* vol. 25, no. 3/4, (1972):6.

17. Ernest Krausz, *The Making of a Community: The Ethnic Factor* (London: Anglo-Israel Association, 1972), p. 6.

18. The concept of "income per standard equivalent adult," which uses a scale of differential weights per person by family size, was first developed in the United States. It was adapted to the Israeli population using the consumption patterns obtained from the Survey of Family Expenditure for 1968-1969. Thus the weight for a one-person family is 1.25 standard equivalent adults, for a two-person family 2.00, for a three-person family 2.65, for a four-person family 3.20 and so on. See *Report of the Committee on Income Distribution and Social Inequality,* pp. 38-9.

13

Yoram Ben-Porath

ON EAST-WEST DIFFERENCES IN OCCUPATIONAL STRUCTURE IN ISRAEL

In social structure analysis the occupational distribution is determined by various social variables and in turn helps determine other variables—the distribution of income and social status. The aggregation of individual jobs into occupations and the classification of the latter into major occupational categories expresses some implicit weighting of the determinants and consequences of certain job affiliation.

The nature of occupational distribution is such that there is a measure of vagueness and a wide margin of error attached to inferences based upon it. The "continental" breakdown which we follow in this chapter, i.e., the distinction between Jews born in Asia and Africa and Jews born in Europe and America is dictated by the nature of the published statistics; it is certainly imperfect, given the large differences between the characteristics of immigrants who came from individual countries. Still, there seems to be enough variation to justify this exercise.

This research was financed by NSF Grant GS-2762. I am indebted to Simon Kuznets, Zvi Griliches and Nachum T. Gross for their helpful comments; needless to say they are absolved of any responsibility.

Table 1. JEWISH EMPLOYED MEN BY OCCUPATION, PLACE OF BIRTH AND PERIOD OF IMMIGRATION, 1969
(PERCENTAGES)

Major Occupation	Total Jews	Born in Israel	Born in Asia and Africa					Born in Europe and America				
			Total	-47	48-54	55-60	61+	Total	-47	48-54	55-60	61+
Prof., Sci., Tech.	11.4	16.9	5.7	7.5	5.7	4.2	6.1	13.7	14.2	11.3	19.9	15.3
Adm., Exec., Manag., Clerical	16.4	15.6	9.5	10.8	10.1	9.5	5.8	22.7	30.3	19.7	14.0	13.0
Traders, Agents, Sales	8.2	4.7	7.9	12.5	8.7	4.4	5.5	10.0	10.6	11.0	7.1	6.6
All White Collar Workers	36.0	37.2	23.1	30.8	24.5	18.1	17.4	46.4	55.1	42.0	41.0	34.9
Farmers, Fishers	9.0	10.8	10.8	7.0	10.6	14.0	10.4	6.6	6.9	6.3	6.6	6.9
All Blue Collar Workers	55.0	52.0	66.1	62.2	65.9	67.9	72.2	47.0	38.0	51.7	52.4	58.2
Workers in Trans. & Communication	7.4	10.8	6.4	11.3	7.0	4.7	2.7	6.6	7.0	8.3	3.7	2.1
Construc., Miners	8.7	5.6	13.1	10.4	14.4	12.4	10.6	6.3	6.3	6.7	5.4	5.7
Craftsmen, Prod. process	30.3	31.6	33.7	26.0	32.1	35.9	43.6	26.9	20.2	27.9	34.5	41.3
Services, Sport, Entertainment	8.6	4.0	12.9	14.5	11.4	14.9	15.3	7.2	4.5	8.8	8.8	9.1
Total–in percent	100.0	100.0	100.0	100.0	100.0	100.0	100.0	100.0	100.0	100.0	100.0	100.0
Total–in thousands	591.6	117.2	215.8	24.2	123.3	38.8	29.5	258.6	103.3	101.7	25.7	27.9

Source: Labor Force Surveys of the Central Bureau of Statistics, *Statistical Abstract* No. 21, pp. 280-281.

The distinction and the analysis of differences by origin are interwoven with immigration. The Israeli labor force (men) is at the present 80 percent foreign born, and the majority of the native born have foreign-born parents. This fact has affected not only the personal status of those involved but has shaped the whole economy to which they belong. This should affect the way one describes the differences between the various groups.

OCCUPATIONAL STRUCTURE IN 1969-1970

Of the currently employed men in Israel only about one fifth were born in the country. A little more than two fifths were born in Europe and America, and a little less than two fifths in Asia and Africa. Of those born in Europe and America about two fifths immigrated before 1948 and a little less than that in the period 1948-1954. Of the Asian-Africans only about one tenth immigrated before 1948, and more than half immigrated in 1948-1954.

The main characteristics of the present (1969) occupational distribution of men are the following:

1. Almost half of the men born in Europe and America have white-collar occupations, but less than a quarter of those born in Asia and Africa.

2. Within the white-collar category European-American men have higher incomes than Asian-Africans.[1]

3. The proportion of farmers is larger in the Asian-Africans, and so is the proportion of blue-collar workers (approximately two thirds against one half).

4. The Israel born have a comparatively high share of professional and technical workers. They have a somewhat higher proportion of farmers than the rest. If the Israel born are distinguished by their father's continent of birth, there are still wide differences between those of Oriental and Western origin.

Within each of the origin groups there are differentials by period of immigration:

5. Within the Asian-African group the proportion of white-collar occupations is larger for the earlier immigrants. The proportion of blue-collar workers is higher for the more recent immigrants and there is a marked difference in the internal distribution—the longer-resident group having higher proportions in transport and communication (the highly

217

paid category of blue-collar) and lower proportions of craftsmen and production process workers. There is also a tendency toward lower proportions of farmers among the longer-term residents.

6. Within the European-American group the differentials tend to be in the same direction. There is however almost no difference between European-American immigrants from the early and late fifties in terms of the three broad categories (white-collar, farmers, blue-collar).

Table 2. OCCUPATIONAL DISTRIBUTION OF JEWISH MEN,
AVERAGE OF 1969 AND 1970–EXPECTED EARNINGS
BY 1969 AVERAGE URBAN WORKER EARNINGS

Place of Birth and Period of Immigration	(1) Expected Earnings	(2) Indexes –47=100	(3) $(\frac{EA}{AA}-1)100$
Asia-Africa (AA), Total	6,962		13.9
Immigrated:			
Up to 1947	7,188	100.0	14.2
1948-1954	7,033	97.8	10.4
1955-1960	6,830	95.0	15.2
Since 1961	6,665	92.7	13.2
Europe-America (EA), Total	7,930		
Immigrated:			
Up to 1947	8,212	100.0	
1948-1954	7,764	94.8	
1955-1960	7,872	95.8	
Since 1961	7,548	91.9	
Israel Born	7,881		
All Jews	7,564		

Source: Distribution by occupation–Table 1, and CBS files. The earning figure used– 11800, 9700, 6400, 400, 8800, 6700, 6400, 5700 IL per occupation in the order of Table 1. The figures are taken from Central Bureau of Statistics, *Statistical Abstract of Israel 1970* No. 21, p. 296.

Summary measures of the average of occupational distribution of men in 1969 and 1970 are presented in Table 2. I use here and in the rest of the essay a measure based on the average annual money earnings per urban wage earner in each occupation (in 1969). Thus a distribution by major occupation, in e.g. 1960, of Israeli-born men, will be represented by the average earnings that Israeli-born men would have had in 1960 if the 1969 average earnings by occupation prevailed in 1960.[2] When I talk about "higher" or "lower" occupational distributions, the ranking is in terms of this

metric. Also, when individual occupational categories are ranked, it is in terms of average earnings. The limitations of this procedure are too obvious to merit amplifications. It is particularly important to note that the occupational distributions are of all employed men, including non-urban and non-wage earners. The figures that we use here for earnings of farmers which play an important role in some of the findings do not correspond to the figures that would be required. In Column (2), one can observe again the systematic relation between the occupational level and period of immigration among AA * and the somewhat less systematic relation among EA.†
The expected differential between EA and AA (Column 3) is much smaller than the actual. (The actual differentials are more than three times larger.) This gives an idea of how partial is the picture presented here if one is interested ultimately in exploring the income distribution.[3]

A FRAMEWORK

I shall not attempt here an explanation of the causes or even an interpretation of these occupational distributions. All that I shall do is try to present some of the evidence on the occupational distribution in a manner that may help clarify some of the questions and that subsequent explanatory treatment will have to answer.

The occupational structure of an origin group defined by place of birth (with or without native-born offspring) in a context where immigration as an important current or recent phenomenon can be usefully viewed as the combination of snapshots taken at one chronological time but at different phases over the occupational life cycle of several cohorts of immigrants who came at various dates in the past. In order to be understood it should be decomposed along such lines.

Let us take a group of immigrants coming to the country in a given year, e.g., immigrants born in Poland coming to Israel in 1950. Most of the adult men would have come equipped with some education and occupational experience acquired abroad in the country of birth or elsewhere. Some would have had education abroad but would not have accumulated any work experience because of age, sex, economic reasons or the vicissitudes to which this genera-

* Asia-Africa
† Europe-America

tion of Jews was exposed. Some would have been too young even to get any education abroad. These, together with other demographic, economic and cultural traits constitute what we may call imported characteristics.

At the time of immigration there is a certain demand structure, government policies with respect to employment in general, and absorption of immigrants in particular, including housing and residential policies. These local conditions, in conjunction with the set of imported characteristics, determine the initial occupational structure, and initial geographical dispersion (in particular urban-rural partition).

The further change in occupational distribution of this group of immigrants depends upon and reflects several factors.

First, a "learning" or adjustment process through which immigrants become acclimatized—learning the language, getting to know the market and institutions better, and trying to move to better positions.

Movement to a better position may entail, in the short run, further differentiation from the majority of the population, when immigrants move to utilize the comparative advantages emanating from their "imported characteristics." In a pluralistic society the "short run" phenomenon may last for a long time (or the other way around).[4] Most groups of immigrants tend however with time to lose some of their imported characteristics and to converge to some kind of a majority standard. In a country where immigrants of any given period are a small proportion of the total population, absorption of immigrants can be described in terms of their behavioral and structural convergence to the majority. However, when the immigrants constitute a large proportion of the population, the "veteran" population may be so greatly affected that its characteristics cannot be taken as given anymore, and one should describe absorption in terms of a convergence to a new equilibrium.

Second, the aging of the immigrant group means that those who are in the labor force from the start will experience some of the normal occupational mobility associated with age. Also, the old ones will retire, while those who immigrated very young will, depending on general and family condition, get some education and start their occupational careers.

And third, economywide changes occurred in the structure of demand and the supply of other labor. Rapid economic growth with its associated structural change affords more opportunities for mobility. Subsequent waves of migration affect the structure of demand; they also alter the supply of labor and thus, together with other sources of labor (non-Jews) affect the demand which any particular group of past immigrants faces.

EVIDENCE

The evidence to be surveyed here applies mostly to men. The increased employment of women and the difference between the EA and AA in the nature of female employment are an important element of the total problem and should be surveyed as well.

Imported characteristics

A consistent feature of all waves of immigration is that AA are on the average much younger than EA. Children up to age 14 constitute about two-fifths of AA and only about one-fifth of the immigrants from EA. This is one major reason why the proportion of "earners" is about two-fifths of AA men and three-fifths of EA men.[5] These differences mean of course that whatever the economic position attained by "earners" the per capita real income attained would be appreciably lower among AA. It also means that even if there were no other differences AA came more like a raw material embodying less human capital than EA.

The main source of information on the educational and occupational background of immigrants up to 1961 is the 1961 Census of Population. A special set of tabulations describes the education and occupation abroad of men who were under 60 in 1961 and between the ages of 25 and 54 at the time of immigration.

There are several obvious questions as to the meaning of this information, putting aside questions of accuracy in the crude sense. The questions refer to the comparability of categories across countries and continents either in the absolute or the relative sense, and to the transferability of characteristics to Israel. To illustrate: eight years of schooling in Yemen versus eight years of schooling in France meant very different absolute levels of real income in the respective countries, and presumably meant something else in terms of relative income and social status within the respective Jewish

Table 3. 1961 DISTRIBUTION BY YEARS OF SCHOOL OF FOREIGN BORN MEN
UNDER 60 WHO WERE 25-54 AT IMMIGRATION
BY CONTINENT OF BIRTH AND PERIOD OF IMMIGRATION

Continent of birth and period of Immigration	Total N	%	Years of School					Expected Earnings IP*	%	$(\frac{EA}{AA}-1)100$
			0 %	1-4 %	5-8 %	9-12 %	13+ %			
Asia-Africa (AA),										
Up to 1947	3,860	100.0	20.7	9.1	44.6	21.6	4.0	6,505	100.0	25.4
1948-1954	41,345	100.0	27.9	12.0	34.0	19.8	6.2	6,462	99.3	14.3
Since 1955	17,190	100.0	30.9	10.6	33.0	19.1	6.5	6,441	99.0	20.3
Total	62,395	100.0	28.3	11.4	34.4	19.7	6.2	6,463		18.8
Europe-America (EA)										
Up to 1947	34,145	100.0	0.8	2.8	32.5	41.7	22.2	8,163	100.0	
1948-1954	62,530	100.0	2.0	10.8	44.7	29.4	13.1	7,387	90.5	
Since 1955	20,425	100.0	1.8	10.7	40.1	26.1	21.3	7,751	95.0	
Total	117,100	100.0	1.6	8.4	40.4	32.4	17.2	7,678		
Average Earnings 1969*			4,800	5,700	6,200	8,200	11,400			

Source: Distribution by years of school, Central Bureau of Statistics, *Population and Housing Census 1961 Labor Force Part IV, Occupation Abroad*, Publication No. 27, pp. 50–55.

Earnings by years of school, Central Bureau of Statistics, *Statistical Abstract No. 21*, p. 295.

*In Israeli Pounds per annum.

or general communities. On top of this there is the question of the value of these characteristics in Israel. In other words, one would want to evaluate the imported human capital on the basis of relative prices in the respective countries, according to some international set of prices and in domestic Israeli prices, arriving in this way at different concepts of the capital loss (or gain) incurred through immigration. At this stage we are able to present just the classifications with one undifferentiating set of constant Israeli prices.

Education. The level of education of the Jewish population in Israel in 1948 was relatively high. Most of the population was of European origin with a large element of educated voluntary immigrants, plus the refugees from Germany in the 1930s. Together with the developed Israeli system of education, this created a relatively high overall level. The immigrants, particularly of the 1948-1954 period, generally imported lower levels of education. The immigrants of the first few years were either Jews from Yemen and other Arab countries or refugees from World War II Europe.

The major points that emerge from Table 3 are:

1. AA of all periods have a very low level of education with more than a quarter reporting no schooling and only about a quarter reporting 9+ years of school. EA have almost no men without schooling and approximately half of the men had 9+ years of school. In money terms (using the earning of men in 1969 by years of school) the difference between EA and AA is approximately one-fifth.

2. AA of all periods have approximately the same level of education in spite of wide variations in level between individual countries.

3. The EA group shows significant variations by period of immigration. The 1948-54 immigrants have less education than the pre-state immigrants. The late fifties immigrants, with a large element of Eastern Europe professionals, were more educated than the early fifties immigrants. Consequently, the lowest differential in "imported education" among EA and AA is in the 1948-54 group, the period of mass immigration.

Occupation abroad. As shown in Table 4, the main characteristics of the occupational structure abroad are the following:

1. All immigrants, AA and EA, had almost no background in farming.

Table 4. DISTRIBUTION BY OCCUPATION ABROAD
AND OCCUPATION IN ISRAEL OF MEN UNDER 60
WHO WERE 25-54 AT IMMIGRATION

Continent of birth & period of immigration	(1) Professional Managerial Clerical	(2) Traders Agents Sales	(3) All White Collar	(4) Blue Collar	(5) Farmers	(6) Percent Who did not change main group
Occupation Abroad						
Asia-Africa						
Total	17.2	33.6	50.8	47.4	1.9	47.9
Up to 1947	14.5	40.4	54.9	43.5	1.4	53.0
1948-1954	18.0	34.1	52.1	45.9	2.1	48.3
Since 1955	16.0	30.9	46.9	51.5	1.5	45.9
Europe-America						
Total	28.5	27.9	56.4	42.0	2.6	59.9
Up to 1947	31.1	29.2	60.3	35.2	4.5	57.0
1948-1954	22.8	33.9	56.7	42.0	2.3	58.6
Since 1955	41.2	11.5	55.7	46.4	0.8	67.9
Occupation in Israel						
Asia-Africa						D*
Total	14.6	9.1	23.7	51.6	24.8	27.1
Up to 1947	17.2	19.0	36.2	52.7	10.9	21.4
1948-1954	15.6	9.4	25.0	51.6	23.5	27.1
Since 1955	11.8	5.8	17.6	51.5	30.8	33.1
Europe-America						
Total	29.7	12.3	42.0	50.5	7.5	15.1
Up to 1947	37.9	12.6	50.5	42.9	6.6	16.6
1948-1954	25.9	14.3	40.2	51.7	8.1	19.1
Since 1955	28.9	6.2	35.1	57.8	7.0	17.6

Source: CBS, Population and Housing Census 1961, *Occupation Abroad*,

*D is half of the sum of differences, ignoring the sign between the distribution by occupation in Israel and abroad, for each group.

2. The proportion of blue collar workers is 40-50 percent among both AA and EA, being somewhat higher among AA.
3. The large difference between AA and EA is more in the composition than in the overall proportion of white collar workers. AA have less professional, management and clerical workers.
4. Both within EA and AA more recent immigrants tend to have a higher proportion of blue collar workers. The differences by period of immigration within AA are not large,

224

except that the pre-state immigrants show large proportions of "traders, etc." Within EA there is however broader variation: the 1948-54 group is "low," while the 55+ group is even "higher" than the pre-state immigrants, having a much higher proportion of professional and management than sales (perhaps partly a reflection of the communist transformation of the East European countries) people.

It is interesting to note that the difference between EA and AA implied by the distribution by schooling (Table 3) is significantly larger than that implied by the distribution by occupation abroad (Table 5) using in both cases the earning figures for 1969. This probably reflects the much lower educational "requirement" of white-collar occupations in the AA countries of origin.[6]

Early Allocation

To discuss the early allocation within Israel of the immigrants, it is important to remember something of the general context. Immigration has been a relatively important phenomenon over most of Israel's existence, but very unevenly distributed in time: about half of the total number of immigrants that came during the twenty-three years since 1948 came within the first two and a half years—August 15, 1948 to December 31, 1951. During that limited period, net immigration was 666,000 people. The Jewish population in 1948 was 650,000. In two and one half years, then, the population grew at a rate of 24 percent per year.[7] After a short cessation, immigration was resumed at a much more moderate rate.

The initial flooding of the labor market meant that the main problem was finding some kind of employment for many people rather than worrying about what kind of employment. There were grave imbalances between the imported skill composition as just described and the structure of demand. As is well known and again shown here, Jews in the diaspora were disproportionately concentrated in white-collar occupations. The Israel economy, faced with the task of absorbing what amounted in relative terms to huge waves of immigration, was demanding labor in the goods-producing rather than the services sectors and could allocate surpluses of labor only to unskilled, menial jobs. The industrial emphasis was on construction and agriculture. To the continued ideological commitment to agriculture were added food shortages, the balance of payments problem and the availability of Arab agri-- cultural land as motivations for emphasis on agriculture. Obvi-- ously a lot of the occupational background of the immigrants had become obsolete, and large numbers had to change their occupa-- tions. The amount and nature of the changes involved differed among the groups.

There is no information on the first jobs of immigrants in Is-- rael. I therefore use the data on occupations in 1961, recorded for the same people for whom occupations abroad were reported. The distribution in 1961 is thus to a varying degree a combination of the initial allocation and some subsequent mobility. The main features of the 1961 allocation are listed in Tables 4 and 5.

Table 5. SUMMARY MEASURES OF
OCCUPATION ABROAD AND IN ISRAEL IN 1961
OF MEN UNDER 60, AGED 25-54 AT IMMIGRATION

Continent of birth & period of immigration	(1)	(2)	(3)	(4)	(5)	(6)
	Expected Earnings		Index		$(\frac{EA}{AA}-1)100$	
	Abroad	Israel	Abroad	Israel	Abroad	Israel
Africa-Asia						
Up to 1947	6,751	6,629	100.0	100.0	9.3	14.3
1948-1954	6,882	6,338	101.9	95.6	3.7	11.1
Since 1955	6,782	6,032	100.4	91.0	15.0	18.5
Total	6,850	6,273			7.4	14.9
Europe-America						D*
Up to 1947	7,382	7,575	100.0	100.0	19.6	20.6
1948-1954	7,139	7,041	96.7	93.0	4.5	15.4
Since 1955	7,799	7,150	105.6	94.4	25.2	23.8
Total	7,356	7,206			11.5	18.4

Source: Table 4. The 1969 Earnings figures used are: Prof. & Manag. & Clerical-- 10300, Traders etc.−6400, Blue Collar−6000, Farmers−4400 (based on the figures cited in Table 2).

*D is defined in Table 4 and is applied here to the difference between EA and AA abroad and in Israel.

1. Less than a quarter of AA are in white collar occupations, compared to about half abroad, with most of the decline concentrated among traders, etc. Farmers increased from almost nothing abroad to about a quarter in Israel.
2. The share of white collar workers among EA was cut by approximately a quarter, the increase being distributed among blue collar workers and farmers.
3. Correspondingly, a larger proportion of AA than EA were

226

in a different occupational category in Israel than they had belonged to abroad, and the difference between the distribution abroad and in Israel is again larger for AA than for EA (Table 4, Column 6).

4. By 1961, the time at which occupation is recorded, sharp differences by period of immigration had already been created within the AA group—a lower proportion of farmers and a higher proportion of white collar workers for the more veteran immigrants. The more recent immigrants are more "distant" from the occupational structure abroad and have a "lower" occupational structure in Israel.[8]

5. Within the EA group the picture is more complicated. The pre-state EA have a clear superiority over later immigrants in terms of the proportions in professional, managerial, and clerical jobs. The late fifties immigrants are in a higher position than the 1948-54 group, i.e., their superiority in terms of "imported characteristics" compensated for this "learning" advantage of the 1948-54 group. The "edge" over the 1948-54 EA immigrants (Table 5, Column 3) of approximately 9 percent abroad (using the 1969 earnings) was reduced to about 1.5 percent in terms of occupation in Israel (Column 4). Their position was still lower than that of the pre-state immigrants.

6. Comparing EA to AA by subperiods one can see that the 1961 superiority of EA in Israel is greater than was the edge abroad. This is particularly true of the 1948-54 immigrants.

There is reason to believe that the retrospective data on occupations abroad are upwardly biased, perhaps more so for AA. On the other hand, the 1961 Census is believed to have underestimated the proportion of farmers, the group that plays a crucial role in all these comparisons.

As already indicated, no group of immigrants imported agricultural skills. A much larger proportion of AA than EA, however, went into agriculture, as we just noted. Residentially in 1961, 40 percent of the labor force which immigrated in 1948-54 lived in the three large cities (Tel-Aviv, Haifa, Jerusalem), the corresponding proportion among AA was 25 percent. Of the 55+ group, the respective shares are 26 percent and 16 percent. The reasons for this difference calls for study beyond the scope of this essay. Agriculture, subsidized and protected, subject to special care by the

227

Jewish Agency, may have provided a shelter more important and attractive to the immigrants from the less developed countries of Asia and Africa than those coming from Europe. While the specific occupational experience of large factions of both groups had become obsolete through immigration, the European immigrants may have been more adaptable to the demands of the relatively modern Israel economy. The fact that the absorbing population was composed mostly of Jews of European origin who, in many cases, had family relations or common origin with new EA immigrants, may have facilitated the absorption of the latter in the urban economy, even when the exact necessary skills were not present.[9]

Even the data for 1961 that were presented suggest that the main aspect of "learning" was the exit from agriculture, and out of the rural areas. It is interesting to note that in the period 1955-1961 (we do not have earlier reliable estimates) the overall proportion of Jewish farmers among all employed Jews almost did not change, hovering in the range of 14.7-16.2 percent. In part, it was sustained by becoming the entry occupation of immigrants, particularly for the AA group, from which they tended to exit quite rapidly.

An interesting question, with implications transcending our particular problem, has to do with the role of education acquired abroad in the allocation of people in Israel. The data (not shown) indicate that for a given number of years of schooling the occupational distribution of EA is "higher" than that of AA. However, people with higher education acquired abroad have "higher" occupational distribution also in Israel both among AA and EA. More interesting—of those with a given occupation abroad those with more education acquired a higher occupational distribution in Israel. This was in fact more so among AA than EA. The question is whether in a labor market in which ordinary sources of information are scarce or irrelevant, a large measure of reliance was put on education as a "labeling" device.

Learning during the Sixties

I now proceed to compare occupational distribution around 1960 with more recent distributions. Apart from technical problems involved in such a comparison (such as small changes in the classification of major occupations) note that when we examine groups of e.g., AA who immigrated in 1948-54, by 1960 and 1970 they are not the same people. In 1970 we do not have all those who retired or died between 1960-1970 and, on the other hand, we have all those who in 1960 were too young to work. The proportion of the 1960 and 1970 overlap will be different in AA and in EA because, as noted earlier, AA came with proportionately more children. Also, the age for starting employment is lower among AA. The difference in that respect between the two groups is in fact so large that the employed AA 1948-60 group is larger in 1970 than in 1960 while the corresponding EA group is smaller in 1970 than in 1961.

The processes that determine the occupational mobility of those who come as adults are likely to be different from those determining intergenerational mobility, while our data will contain the combined results. Bearing this in mind let us turn to the evidence.

Table 6. PERCENTAGE INCREASE IN VALUE
OF OCCUPATIONAL DISTRIBUTION 1960/61–1969/70

Place of birth and period of immigration	1969/70 / 1960/61	1970 / 1960	1969 / 1960	1970 / 1961
Asia-Africa	8.3	8.9	7.6	9.3
Up to 1947	2.8	1.4	2.4	3.2
1948-1960	10.1	11.6	8.9	11.3
Europe-America	4.6	5.0	3.8	5.4
Up to 1947	3.0	3.8	3.0	3.1
1948-1960	7.9	8.3	6.6	9.2
Israel Born	3.1	5.3	4.7	1.6
All Jews	5.0	5.7	4.4	5.5

Source: Occupational distribution, see Table 7. Earning figures, see Table 2.

Starting with the summary measures of expected earnings on the basis of the 1969 urban earnings by occupation, let us compare the experience over the sixties of the pre-1948 and the 1948-60 immigrants. The rates of improvement (not annual but total) using different end points are presented in Table 6.

Because of the small group of pre-1948 AA all that one can say about that period is that the rate of improvement for both AA and EA was lower than the average for all the Jewish population and

Table 7. OCCUPATIONAL DISTRIBUTION OF JEWISH MEN 1961, 1970

Place of birth and period of immigration

	Asia-Africa				Europe-America				Israel Born		All Jews		Asia-Africa Since 1961	Europe-America Since 1961
	Up to 1947		1948-1960		Up to 1947		1948-1960							
Year	61	70	61	70	61	70	61	70	61	70	61	70	70	70
Total	100.0	100.0	100.0	100.0	100.0	100.0	100.0	100.0	100.0	100.0	100.0	100.0	100.0	100.0
Professional Scientific, Technical	4.4	6.7	2.9	6.4	14.9	15.0	9.3	15.1	15.2	17.9	9.0	12.3	3.4	14.7
Admin., Exec. Managerial														
Clerical	12.0	13.4	6.4	10.1	24.2	32.3	11.4	18.7	16.9	16.2	14.9	17.1	6.8	13.4
Traders, Agents, Sales	17.3	10.0	6.0	7.7	10.8	8.5	10.6	9.4	3.2	5.0	8.5	7.7	4.9	8.8
All White Collar	33.7	30.1	15.3	24.2	49.9	55.8	31.3	43.2	35.3	39.1	32.4	37.1	15.1	36.9
Farmers	11.3	8.9	23.3	8.5	8.3	8.0	10.4	5.6	16.8	11.9	14.7	8.4	9.6	5.3
Blue Collar	55.0	61.0	61.4	67.1	41.8	36.2	58.3	51.2	47.9	49.0	52.9	54.5	75.3	57.8
Transp., Comm.	7.0	9.0	3.6	8.1	6.7	5.8	5.8	6.8	10.7	10.4	6.4	7.4	3.8	2.6
Const., Quarry., Miners		7.6		15.7		6.0		7.4		6.0		9.2	11.2	5.5
Craft., Produc., Proc.	36.9	30.1	45.5	31.4	30.6	20.3	43.7	29.6	32.6	28.6	28.4	29.7	44.2	40.9
Service, Sports, Enter.	11.1	14.3	12.3	11.9	4.5	4.1	8.8	7.4	4.6	4.0	8.2	8.2	16.1	8.8
D*-Ratio	8.2	9.7	15.1	15.1	8.2	8.2	14.1	14.1	8.4	8.4	7.1	7.1		

Source: Labor Force Survey *Special Report* No. 162, pp. 96-98, and CBS files.

*D—as defined in Table 4.

that it was roughly similar for AA and EA. The rate of improvement of the 1948-60 immigrants was more than twice as high as
the rate for the Jewish population as a whole and it was clearly
higher for the AA group by approximately one-fourth (Table 7).
Because of the larger weight of pre-1948 immigrants in EA, the
overall rate of improvement of all AA is almost twice as large
as that of all EA.

Examining the occupational distribution, the amount of change
is striking: the AA 1948-60 immigrants left farming and reduced
it to almost a third of its 1961 share, increasing the share of white
collar occupations by a factor of 1.6 and also increasing the blue
collar share. Among 1948-60 EA the pattern of improvement is
from farming and blue collar occupations into white collar occupations, particularly the "higher" ones. In contrast to the fifties,
the overall proportion of farmers in the total Jewish labor force
has decreased (from 14.7 to 8.4) mostly to the advantage of the
"high" white collar occupations.

It would be interesting to compare the two subperiods of the
fifties. This can be done by comparing the end points either with
the 1961 Census or with labor force surveys since 1962. It seems
that the main source of the edge in the rate of improvement in the
sixties that 1948-60 AA had over 1948-60 EA comes from the
1955-60 rather than from the 1948-54 immigrants [10] (Table 8).

Examining now the differentials between EA and AA we observe
of course some narrowing of differentials as implied by the difference in rates of improvement. Two additional features should be
noted (Table 9).

First, the rate of improvement of 1948-60 AA over the sixties
is approximately the size of the present differentials between AA
and EA, i.e., 1948-60 AA are a little more than a decade behind
1948-60 EA. But as EA are also improving, the closing of the gap
is a much longer process.

Second, the gap between EA and AA who immigrated during the
sixties (1961+) at the end of the period (13.2 percent) is similar
to that observed in 1961 for the 1948+ immigrants.

There is an interesting difference between the 1970 occupational distribution of the 1961+ immigrants and the 1961 distribution of the 1948-60 immigrants: while among AA the proportion
of white-collar workers is almost identical (15 percent) the immigrants of the sixties are to be found excessively (compared to
earlier immigrants) in blue-collar occupations, while the AA immi-

231

Table 8. RATE OF IMPROVEMENT OF OCCUPATIONAL STRUCTURE, ASIA-AFRICA AND EUROPE-AMERICA 1948-1954 AND 1955-1960

Continent of birth and period of immigration	1969/70 (LFS) 1962/63 (LFS)	1969/70 (LFS) 1961 Census (corrected)
Asia-Africa 1948-1954	6.3	9.2
Europe-America 1948-1954	5.8	8.1
Asia-Africa 1955-1960		13.4
Europe-America 1955-1960		9.9

Source: Occupational structure:
    1969, 1970—CBS files.
    1962, 1963—CBS *Special Reports*.

Earnings: See Table 2.

Table 9. EUROPE-AMERICA/ASIA-AFRICA— PERCENTAGE DIFFERENCE IN OCCUPATIONAL LEVEL

	1961 Census	1960/61 LFS	1969/70 LFS	1970 LFS
Total	16.4	17.9	13.9	13.7
Up to 1947	13.7	14.0	14.2	15.2
1948-1954	11.5		10.4	10.3
1955-1960	19.0		15.2	12.9
1948-1960	13.1	13.8	11.5	11.0
Since 1961			13.2	13.9

Source: See Table 8.

grants of the fifties were excessively in agriculture. This most likely reflects a difference in the initial allocation as affected by the different pattern of demand.

Summary and Indications of Further Study

Differentials in occupational distributions between "Western" and "Oriental" Jews should be decomposed to reflect the following:
—differences in imported characteristics
—differences in initial allocation in Israel
—differences in the shape of "learning" or mobility processes in the course of time in Israel.

The evidence suggests that as far as imported characteristics are concerned, the two groups came to Israel wtih very wide differences in educational background. The occupational background abroad also differed, but had some common features—the absence of farmers and a large proportion of white collar workers. The background of both groups was quite incompatible with the structure of demand and both groups underwent change in their occupational structure. The initial occupational allocation in Israel in the fifties emphasized farming (and rural or semi-rural residence) proportionately more among the Oriental compared to the Western immigrants, implying a greater occupational change (from their occupations abroad) of the AA group. In the sixties the economy shifted away from agricultural employment, which ceased to be an important entry occupation for AA immigrants. Education acquired abroad improved the shift from occupation abroad to occupation in Israel.

Over a period of time, between 1960 and 1970, the immigrants of the fifties show high rates of improvement in occupational structure, higher than the improvement of the total Jewish population. The rate of improvement of the Orientals (AA) was higher than that of the Western (EA). The advance of AA took the form of rapid exit from agriculture. There has thus been some narrowing of differentials between AA and EA. The rate of advance of AA over 1960-1970 is roughly equal to the 1970 gap.

Given the preliminary nature of this discussion, I conclude by indicating what I consider to be some necessary extensions of this work.

Of primary importance is the distinction between generations

and the description of the path followed by those born or educated in Israel and the identification of intergeneration mobility.
Other important elements in the descriptive scheme are the analysis
of the occupational structure of women, control for age differentials and—what may be more difficult—a refinement of both the
occupational and "continental" classifications.

Second, one should move to a more general study of causes and
implications where the interrelationships with education and income
are first on the agenda.[11] It is important not to begin such a study
with too strong restrictions, and insert restrictions only after some
familiarity with the data has been acquired.

The initial treatment of immigrants and the continuing attention to earlier, disadvantaged cohorts of immigrants are at present
at the center of a policy question in Israel. The nature of past
policies and their interactions with private motivation in determining initial allocation and subsequent improvement should therefore
be studied. It is particularly important to assess the role of initial
allocations in determining future development. Policy is probably
relatively most important in determining initial allocations, particularly through the provision of housing. It is quite natural that
this power will be used to further some general objectives (such
as the dispersion of population) and not only the optimization of
the private absorption process. A study of the sort indicated here
should be able to indicate what were the implications in the long
run for the absorption process of the policies that were followed.

NOTES

1. Unfortunately clerical occupations are put in the same category with
executives, managers, etc. This precludes a meaningful distinction between
"high" and "low" (clerical and sales) white collar workers.

2. Economists are likely to be reminded of Griliches's quality index of
labor; sociologists are permitted to view it as a degenerate form of the
occupational index used by Duncan and Blau.

3. This is approximately the share of explanation of differentials between
whites' and non-whites' earnings provided by the classification according to
major occupations. See A. Wohlstetter and S. Coleman, *Race Differences
in Income*, (Rand, R-578-030, October 1970).

DIFFERENCES IN OCCUPATIONAL STRUCTURE

4. A framework for analyzing such phenomenon is suggested by a recent unpublished manuscript by Simon Kuznets on the economic history of U.S. Jewry.

5. Central Bureau of Statistics, *Statistical Abstract* No. 13, p. 104.

6. One would naturally be suspicious of the accuracy, and not only the meaning, of data on occupations abroad. There is one reassuring comparison

	Asia-Africa 1961 Census	Up to 1954 1954 LFS	Europe-America 1961 Census	Up to 1954 1954 LFS
Prof., Mgmt., Clerical	17.8	14.7	25.5	28.9
Sales	34.9	30.8	31.6	29.0
Blue Collar	45.3	52.6	39.7	39.7
Farms	2.1	1.9	3.1	2.5

Source: 1959 Central Bureau of Statistics, *Special Report* No. 56, Table 25. 1961 Census of Population *Occupation Abroad, op. cit.*

that one can make. In 1954 the first labor force survey was conducted. The Central Bureau of Statistics later dropped this survey from all its time-series comparisons because of doubts as to its reliability. This was, however, the only labor force survey in which occupation abroad was investigated. The results are quite similar to the 1961 census: (the pre-1947 and 1948-54 groups are combined in this comparison).

7. Central Bureau of Statistics, *Statistical Abstract* 1970, No. 21.

8. This is indeed a reflection of movement over time and is corroborated by comparison with the Labor Force Survey of 1954.

9. In the first few years there was also the factor that the EA group came somewhat earlier than AA and of the deserted property of the Arab refugees settled mostly in the cities and towns (Jaffa, Ramleh Lydda, etc.).

10. This is based on the following evidence: Comparison of 1969, 1970 with 1962, 1963 for the immigrants of 1948-54 (no comparison is possible for 1955-60) show a smaller (and even reverse) difference compared to the over 2 percentage points observed for the slightly longer period for the immigrants of 1948-60. Also, if one takes the 1961 census and makes a uniform correction for the underestimation of farmers (by comparison with the 1961 labor force survey) the difference in the rate of improvement of the 1955-60 immigrants between AA and EA is 3.5 percentage points compared to 1.1 for the 1948-54 period (Table 8).

11. Here one can draw on a recent study by Haim Levi for the Bank of Israel and the earlier study by Giora Hanoch for the Falk Institute of Economic Research in Israel.

14

Fred M. Gottheil

ON THE ECONOMIC DEVELOPMENT OF THE ARAB REGION IN ISRAEL

ARAB-JEWISH DUALISM IN ISRAEL

The creation of the state of Israel in 1948 produced a geographic division among the Arabs in Palestine, with 700,000 of the population of 1,300,000 locating within the borders of Israel. These numbers were quickly reduced to 156,000 during the 1948-1949 conflict when 550,000 Arabs emigrated to the West Bank and Gaza regions. By 1969, however, the Arab population in Israel had increased to 414,000, recording a remarkably high 5.2 percent annual rate of increase. This represented 14.3 percent of the total Israel population and is expected to reach, by conservative estimate, 18 percent by 1985.[1]

The dispersion of population in Israel is determined, in part, by ethnic origin. Israeli Arabs, for example, are located in 104 distinctly Arab towns and villages and in six towns with large Jewish majorities. For the most part, these towns are clustered in three areas of the country: the Galilee, the Little Triangle[2] and the Negev. Sixty percent of Israeli Arabs live in towns situated in the Galilee. An additional 20 percent live in a set of villages in the Little Triangle, and 7 percent more are located in the Negev. These three centers of Arab population compose the Arab region. A common characteristic of these towns and villages is their proximity to the land borders of Israel and the adjoining Arab states.

The Arab region can be identified not only by ethnic origin but also by economic structure and performance. Unlike the rest of the economy, the Arab region is characterized by the predominance of agricultural output and employment and by the use of traditional techniques of production. In terms of economic activity, it contrasts sharply with the more advanced and more rapidly expanding Jewish region.

Historical inheritance. This regional contrast or dualism predates Israel. Under the British Mandatory system, Palestine was already divided into noncompeting Arab and Jewish regions. Such a duality, although not exclusive,[3] served Arab and Jewish interests alike. For Jews, the *raison d'être* of immigration to Palestine was to create a self-sustaining community. To achieve this end, a concerted effort was made to produce an independent Jewish economy based upon Jewish ownership of land, and more important, upon the creation and employment of Jewish manual labor. At the same time, Arabs founds the duality convenient for their own purposes. The British administration of Palestine provided the Arab population with both employment and public services which complemented the traditional economic system. Moreover, they had access to the greater Arab economy of adjacent Syria, Lebanon, Trans-Jordan and Egypt and in this wider market held a more favorable competitive position than they would have held had the Jewish and Arab regions of Palestine been fully integrated.

Arab-Jewish dualism, then, was already a feature of the pre-Israel Palestine economy, and the experience during the Mandate period was one of growing disparities of economic structures and performance.

Post-1948. After the creation of Israel, the focus of attention among Jewish political leaders was no longer expected to be upon an exclusive Jewish community but upon the administration of a nation composed of a Jewish and Arab population. Nonetheless, the extension of pre-state interests into the post-state environment was accentuated by the highest priority given by the state to the immigration and absorption of Jews from Asia, Africa and Europe.

Although the inheritance of Arab-Jewish duality was clearly under-stood and unacceptable, it did not materialize into an explicit policy of preferential regional economic development. This is not to suggest that regional development programs did not exist. On the contrary, investment funds have been allocated through the development budget for the 21 development towns that had been established primarily for the absorption of new immigration. It is also true that development funds were allocated for the Arab region. As early as 1949, the government supported the establish-ment of marketing, consumer credit, irrigation, housing and pro-duction cooperatives in the Arab region. In 1961 the Arab Department of the Prime Minister's Office prepared and the govern-ment financed a five-year agricultural plan for the Arab region. More recently in 1970, the Pan Proposal, submitted by the Tech-nion Group, emphasized the introduction of industrialization and mechanization of agriculture in the region via government in-struction.

Nevertheless, implicit in the government's development policy was and continues to be the underlying assumption that aggregate investment is the critical variable, and that the spread effects of such investment, no matter where placed, would generate income and employment throughout the economy, including the Arab region.

Indeed, statistical evidence has been offered to support the contention that Israeli Arabs have shared fully in the rapid eco-nomic growth of the nation. Ben-Porath, for example, demonstrated that from 1950 to 1960 the rate of increase in Arab incomes was higher than the corresponding rate for Jews.[4] Even Arab writers, critical of Israel's development policy, conceded the advances made in Arab standards of living.[5] The argument is confidently made that the traditional Arab-Jewish dualism that had characterized Palestine and Israel will disappear as the Arab region integrates with the rest of the Israel economy.

Such an argument, however, is open to question. Distinction must be drawn between the consuming and the producing aspects of the Arab region. Although it is clear that Arab incomes and consump-tion have increased considerably since the formation of the state, it is also clear that the Arab region, as a producing region, has de-clined relative to the rest of the economy. Arabs are increasingly leaving their villages for employment opportunities in the Jewish sector, and although their consumption of houses, automobiles, re-frigerators, television, food and clothes has increased, construction of factories, expansion of agricultural acreage and the development of local services in the Arab region have not. This circumstance, incidentally, contrasts with the experience of the Mandate period. While the Jewish economy during 1922 to 1931 was expanding rapidly (e.g., capital stock increased by 327 percent and net domestic product by 410 percent [6]), the development of the Arab economy in Palestine was also substantial. The extent of Arab participation in the industrialization process is reflected in the growth, from 1918 to 1928, of 1,373 new Arab-owned enterprises. Although clearly of smaller scale than the Jewish enterprise, they nonetheless represented over 60 percent of the total Arab enterprises.[7] But since 1948 disparity between the Jewish and Arab regions in Israel has increased rather than diminished.

THE DUALISM HYPOTHESIS

The persistence of the Arab-Jewish dualism in Israel, it can be argued, reflects the general hypothesis offered by Gunnar Myrdal concerning economic development and regional inequality.[8] Myrdal rejects out of hand the hypothesis that the spread effects of development in any region will operate in all regions. Yet this hypothesis seems to underscore Israeli thinking on regional development. Myrdal offers the alternative hypothesis that unbalanced development tends to produce greater imbalances in the economy. He argues that for developing countries, the spread effects of development tend to be weak and secondary to the backwash effects created by the development process. The net result is a reinforced regional economic divergence. By spread effects, he means that no matter where the investment occurs, the interregional economic relations will more or less diffuse its impact throughout the system.

The backwash effects have the opposite result. Investment in the more developed region of the economy tends to attract both productive labor and capital out of the less developed region thereby reducing the development potential in the poorer region. The process is cumulative. With selective emigration producing an increasingly less qualified labor force in the poor region, the chances of attracting industry to the region diminish. At the same time, the development of the banking system and capital market in the poor region make it possible for the limited savings available in that region to shift to the more advanced and developing region where prospects for higher rates of return are better.

240

Kuznets, Williamson, Chenery, Hirschman and Dziewonski provide supporting evidence to Myrdal's dualism hypothesis.[9] Chenery, for example, noted the negative impact of northern Italy's substantial development on the southern regions. Williamson's study of 24 nations showed that the relationship between the level of development and the degree of regional inequality are both significant and widespread.

A cursory reading of the Israel case suggests the applicability of the Myrdal argument. The 1961 Census Bureau of Statistics Report on the Arab population emphasizes some of these backwash effects. For example, while the occupational distribution of the Arab labor force shows a convergence with the Jewish labor force (see Table 1), the migration of Arab workers from the Arab region is substantial and disproportionately composed of the most skilled, i.e., industrial and construction workers (see Table 2). Some 50.3 percent of the Arab labor force worked outside the Arab region. For industrial workers and artisans, the percent rises to 59.8. For machinery production workers it rises to 67.4 percent. For those in public works and the construction trade, it rises to 76.5 percent. The suggestion offered by these numbers is that the backwash effects are indeed operative.

Of course, the migration out of the Arab region may reflect not only the demand-pull of the Jewish region, but also the supply-push of high population growth and limited resource capacity. The growth in population, the 1953 Land Requisition Act and the founding of Jewish semirural communities adjacent to Arab ones had contributed to a decrease in per capita agricultural holdings from 6 dunam in 1952 to 4.2 in 1965.[10] Moreover, the Arab peasant who has always cultivated his land by traditional methods found it increasingly difficult to compete with the mechanized and irrigated kibbutzim and moshavim. The result has been a dramatic shift of Arabs out of agriculture, from 50 percent of the labor force in 1950 to 31.5 percent in 1969. A substantial labor surplus was thus created. Moreover, this excess labor supply was augmented by surplus labor from Arab cities in the region, e.g., Shfar'am and Nazareth, so that most of the Arab workers from the region made their way to such producing centers as Petah Tikva, Ramat Gan, Tel Aviv, Natanya, Hadera, Afula, Haifa and Acre.

But it is worthwhile to emphasize again that while the Arab region had been undergoing fundamental and painful change, the income and consumption impact of this change on the Arab population had been both positive and substantial.

Table 1. DISTRIBUTION OF EMPLOYED ARABS
ACCORDING TO CATEGORY OF EMPLOYMENT 1931-1969

	1931	1950	1969	Jews 1963
Agriculture	57.0%	50.0%	31.5%	12.1%
Industry and Handicrafts	10.0	10.0	18.8	25.5
Construction	3.0	6.0	21.3	9.1
Electricity and Water	–	–	0.6	1.8
Transport	6.0	6.0	6.6	7.2
Commerce and Banking	8.0			
Public Services	7.0	28.0	8.1	13.3
Personal Services	9.0		13.1	31.0
Total	100.0%	100.0%	100.0%	100.0%

Source: S. Zarhi and A. Achiezra, *The Economic Conditions of the Arab Minority in Israel*, (Givat Haviva: Center for Arab and Afro-Asian Studies, 1966), p. 4. *Statistical Abstract of Israel, 1970* (Central Bureau of Statistics, 1970), p. 273.

Table 2. ARABS OCCUPIED AWAY FROM THEIR PLACE OF RESIDENCE
ACCORDING TO CATEGORY OF EMPLOYMENT (1961)

Category of Employment	Total No. of Employed Arabs	No. Working in Place of Residence	No. Working Away	Percent of Total Working Away
Agriculture and Afforestation	20,460	12,790	7,670	37.5
Mines and Quarries	945	415	530	56.1
Industry and Artisans	7,135	2,865	4,270	59.8
Building and Public Works	6,995	1,645	5,350	76.5
Electricity, Water Sanitation	385	230	155	40.3
Commerce and Banking	3,270	2,235	1,035	31.7
Transport	2,020	1,315	705	34.9
Public and Commercial Service	5,425	3,595	1,830	33.7
Personal Service, entertainment	1,915	1,045	870	45.4
Unknown	4,960	455	4,505	90.8
Total	53,510	26,590	26,920	50.3

Source: S. Zarhi and A. Achiezra, *The Economic Conditions of the Arab Minority in Israel* (Givat Haviva: Center for Arab and Afro-Asian Studies, 1966), p. 20.

FRED M. GOTTHEIL

So the question posed by the economic events in Israel is the following: Must the economic betterment of the Arab population lead to the disintegration of the Arab region as a producing region?

The resolution of this issue, which is the issue of economic development and regional inequality that Myrdal describes, is of critical importance in formulating an approach to the development and modernization of the Arab region. If the Myrdal hypothesis is valid and is applicable to the Israel situation, then one conclusion we can draw—and is drawn by the Technion Group—is that much of Israeli thinking on development planning will have to change. For one thing, regional priorities will have to assume much greater importance than they presently do. And priorities within the existing regional programs will have to be broadened to include the Little Triangle as well as the Negev and the Galilee.

But it is not clear by any means that the prevailing priorities are, in fact, misplaced. First, it is less than clear that Myrdal's observation concerning economic development and regional inequality, however interesting and pregnant with recommendation, is a valid statement of development experience. Second, even were his observations true for those countries analyzed by Chenery, Williamson and others, it still does not follow that such a condition represents the situation in Israel.

For one thing, Israel is not the Italy that Chenery describes. Israel is no more than 8,000 square miles and only 30 percent of Italy with the exclusion of the Negev, which is both relatively underpopulated and of minor importance as a producing region. Israel, from Beersheba north, is a particularly small geographic area which holds over 90 percent of the total population. Its regions are separated by tens of kilometers rather than hundreds of miles. It may be more accurate to describe the Arab villages as suburbs of the larger ethnically mixed cities than as a distinct producing region. The time spent travelling between these villages and the main producing centers would be, in most cases, less than the time required to travel from the Loop area of Chicago to Evanston. Arab workers, with less inconvenience than Chicago commuters experience, can combine residence in the Arab region with employment in the Jewish region—and most, in fact, do.[11] In other words, the issue of Israeli development and regional inequality is as complex and uncertain as it is important. Whatever development strategy is adopted will decide the economic character as well as the social, political and cultural patterns in the Arab region. Should the development policy as practiced now continue, the likelihood

244

is that the Arab region, as a producing region, will become Israel's Appalachia. The main difference between the deprived areas of the United States and Israel is that in the case of Israel, the standard of living among the region's population can be expected to increase.

But the development alternative that follows from Myrdal's analysis may still be preferred to this acceptable existing state of affairs. The alternative is to direct the development to the population, rather than the population to the development.

The six points that follow relate directly to this alternative:

First, and perhaps most important, there exist no real obstacles to the development of the Arab region—other than money.

The second point, which is implied in the first, is that the problems associated with the retraining of the Arab labor force are neither insurmountable nor as difficult as some of the economic literature suggests. Admittedly, they are important, but they have been in the past a much overemphasized concern. Israel's leaders and populace have coped with this kind of problem before. The economic absorption of the relatively unqualified Asian-African immigration has been more than moderately successful—in spite of persisting problems. The founding of 21 development towns with government support was based on a population of 80 percent Asian-African immigrants. With rather uneven success these towns have managed to survive, some dropping the development town status, and have virtually retrained a whole population to economic advantage. Similar successes can be cited for the Arab population. British demands for skilled labor during World War II transformed in relatively short time thousands of *fellaheen* into masons, carpenters, electricians, etc.

Third, the development of the Arab region would preserve whatever entrepreneurial, managerial and administrative talents exist and would attract others back to the area. The occupational distribution among Arab workers and the distribution between the employed and self-employed would more closely resemble the rest of the Israel economy. The political and social by-products of such an outcome are equally important.

Fourth, the technical assistance, that is, the human expertise required to initiate and oversee the early stages of the development are available. Israel has already accumulated a rich experience with the founding of 21 development towns and a network of industrial estates.[12] This experience represents capital stock that can be transferred to the Arab region.

Fifth, the development of the Arab region opens a new alternative in Israel's relations with the West Bank economy [13] and with the possibilities of resolving the Arab refugee problem.

Finally, development funds may be available on the most attractive terms if such development incorporates a positive response to the problem of the refugees. U.S. policy since 1955 has emphasized a willingness to underwrite to some degree the resettlement of the Arab refugees.[14] One of the consequences of the Six Day War was to give Israel a much greater flexibility in dealing with the resettlement issue.

Because of the proximity of the Arab region to the land borders of the West Bank and Arab countries, the implications for such regional development can be expanded to include such policy issues as refugee settlement, the economic cooperation between Israel and the West Bank and, most important, the interregional migrations of population. The integration of the Arab region with the West Bank could create a more self-sustaining overall market and resource base. In other words, the resolution of the Arab refugee problem could be designed in terms of regional economic development where job opportunities and economic independence are substituted for individual compensation.[15]

The modernization of the Arab region is both desirable and economically feasible. Of course, the development of the region would require substantial outlays of money—always a first item of concern. A most conservative estimate would be about a billion Israeli pounds for a ten-year program to absorb the surplus labor in the Arab region.[16] This sum does not include the basic social overhead capital that would be demanded for increased housing and other needs. Such expenditures would raise the figure by at least 25 percent. This totals about 125 million Israeli pounds per year for ten years, or about an annual expenditure of 1 percent of 1969 GNP.

As a long-term investment policy in nation-building, such a development scheme must be ranked with other priorities in the system. The problems that Israel faced on its very first day of statehood—security and massive immigration—have persisted. The post-1967 defense needs and the more recent acceleration of immigration from the Soviet Union and the West have forced cutbacks in already committed social and economic development programs. Poverty among Israeli Jews is no longer a muted issue, and its solution—housing, education, employment—taxes not only the imaginations of planners, but also their budgets.

It is most unlikely that commitments of the magnitudes described above will be forthcoming in the near future. Perhaps by default rather than design, the development strategy concerning the Arab region will be simply a continuation of the past—that is, the integration of the Arab and Jewish labor forces in the Jewish region and the decreasing importance of the Arab region as a source of income and employment.

But whatever the policy outcome, the Myrdal hypothesis remains a very real issue and its applicability to the Israel case should be a matter of continuous discussion and research. After all, the highest priority in Israel has always been to change the existing priorities.

NOTES

1. *Projections of the Population in Israel Up to 1985* (Jerusalem: Central Bureau of Statistics, Special Series No. 242, 1968).

2. The Triangle was part of the Samaria District enclosing Nablus, Tulkarm and Jenin. The Israel Triangle, or Little Triangle, refers to that area of the Triangle that falls within Israel's borders. It is more a thin stretch of villages about 25 miles east of Tel Aviv running north along the Israel-West Bank border.

3. In the years prior to World War II the Jewish sector absorbed approximately 30 percent of the Arab agricultural output. "The Influence of the Jewish Colonization on Arab Development in Palestine," memorandum submitted to the Anglo-American Committee on Inquiry in Jerusalem by the Jewish Agency for Palestine, March 1946, in *Palestine Year Book,* vol. 3, 1947-1948 (Washington: Zionist Organization of America, 1948), p. 193.

4. Y. Ben-Porath, *The Arab Labor Force in Israel* (Jerusalem: The Maurice Falk Institute for Economic Research in Israel, 1966), p. 81.

5. For example, Ibrahim Shbat, "Economic Situation of Israeli Arabs," *New Outlook,* March/April, 1967; Muhammad Watad, "Unemployment Haunts the Arab Village," *New Outlook,* September 1966; and Elias Tuma, "The Arabs in Israel: An Impasse," *New Outlook,* March/April, 1966.

6. R. Szereszewski, *Essays on the Structure of the Jewish Economy in Palestine and Israel* (Jerusalem: The Maurice Falk Institute for Economic Research in Israel, 1968), p. 82.

7. S. Himadeh, *Economic Organization of Palestine* (Beirut: American Press, 1936), p. 172.

8. Gunnar Myrdal, *Economic Theory and Under-Developed Regions* (New York: Harper and Row, 1957), chap. 3.

9. S. Kuznets, "Quantitative Aspects of the Economic Growth of Nations. VIII. Distribution of Income by Size," *Economic Development and Cultural Change,* II (1963): No. 2, Part 2; J. G. Williamson, "Regional Inequality and the Process of National Development: A Description of the Patterns," *Economic Development and Cultural Change,* 13 (1965): 3-45; H. B. Chenery, "Development Policies for Southern Italy," *Quarterly Journal of Economics,* 76 (1962): 515-47; A. O. Hirschman, *The Strategy of Economic Develop-*

FRED M. GOTTHEIL

ment (New Haven: Yale University Press, 1958) chap. 10; K. Dziewonski, "Theoretical Problems in the Development of Economic Regions," *Regional Science Association Papers*, 8 (1962).

10. Shbat, *Economic Situation of Israeli Arabs*, p. 37.

11. This circumstance is not peculiar to the Israel period. During World War II, the increased economic activity in Palestine brought about by British demands for food and military supplies and British investments in buildings, roads and fortifications attracted substantial numbers from rural areas into the much increased Arab labor force. The number of wage earners employed by the British increased from 15,578 in January 1939 to 76,548 in December 1942. ". . . thousands of workers, who were hitherto employed on their own land in their village were transformed into wage-earners working for the government. Thousands of them were trained as skilled workers." Z. Abramovitz, "Wartime Development of the Arab Economy in Palestine," *The Palestine Year Book* (Washington, D.C.: Zionist Organization of America, 1945), pp. 130-44.

12. Thirty-six estates were constructed and financed by the central government between 1955 and 1967 and among them, estates in the newly developing areas of Kiryat Shemona, Safed, Nazareth, Migdal-Ha'emek, Carmiel, Ashdod, Beit-Shemesh, Shderot and Dimona. These estates were established in advance of demand. *Industrial Estates in Europe and the Middle East* (New York: United Nations, 1968), p. 5.

13. See Oded Remba, "Israel and the Occupied Areas—A Common Market in the Making," *New Middle East*, November, 1970, p. 34.

14. Addressing the Council on Foreign Relations, on August 26, 1955, John Foster Dulles made the following statement: "Compensation is due from Israel to the refugees. However, it may be that Israel cannot, unaided, now make adequate compensation. If so, there might be an international loan to enable Israel to pay the compensation which is due and which would enable many of the refugees to find for themselves a better way of life. President Eisenhower would recommend substantial participation by the United States in such a loan for such a purpose. Also he would recommend that the United States contribute to the realization of water development and irrigation projects which would, directly or indirectly, *facilitate the resettlement of the refugees*."

15. Such a proposal has already been offered by a number of Israeli economists and government people. Minister of Defense Moshe Dayan, for example, has proposed the establishment of a semi-autonomous Arab canton within Israel for the Arabs on the West Bank. Also, a team of economists from the Hebrew University and the government headed by Dr. Ranaan Weitz of the Settlement Department of the Jewish Agency undertook a study in 1968 of the development of the West Bank areas in association with the development of the Arab region in Israel.

16. The estimate is derived by assuming 25,000 Israeli pounds capital stock per worker (compared to 28,000 Israeli pounds in industry for the 1965 Israel economy. See Gaathon, *Economic Productivity in Israel*, p. 101) and an out-of-region Arab labor force of 40,000 (from a 1969 total Arab labor force of 91,000, see *Statistical Abstract of Israel*, 1970, p. 267).

248

15

J. Joseph Loewenberg

HISTADRUT:

MYTH AND REALITY

Few phenomena in the phenomenal country of Israel cause as many curious and contradictory comments by outsiders as Histadrut (the General Organization of Workers in Israel). Even people knowledgeable about labor and friendly to Israel, have discussed Histadrut in terms such as the following:

—The Histadrut—that's the workers' organization that owns everything in Israel.

—Doesn't the Histadrut really run the country politically?

—The Histadrut is positively irresponsible; strikes are constantly interrupting industry and services in Israel.

—The Histadrut embodies the ideal form of workers' participation in enterprise.

—Clearly a group that is capitalistic and owns the means of production cannot truly represent workers' interests in collective bargaining.

In fact, some people in Israel share one or more of these views about Histadrut. It is not coincidental that the headquarters of the Histadrut in Tel Aviv is popularly nicknamed "the Kremlin."

Much of the confusion surrounding Histadrut results because in many ways it is unique. Certainly someone coming from the United States or Western Europe has preconceptions about what a trade union movement should be and how it should act. Since the origin, organization, function and operations of Histadrut do not fit the classic pattern, it becomes difficult for the outsider to place Histadrut into perspective. (Incidentally, it is just as difficult for Israelis to understand labor organizations and industrial relations in our country). In this chapter I hope to dispel some myths and to instill an understanding of Histadrut and its role in the development of Israel.

THE ORIGIN AND DEVELOPMENT OF HISTADRUT

The typical pattern of labor organization in Western industrial societies has been first, uniting workers in a particular trade and in a particular locality to combat exploitation by industrial employers, then expanding the labor organization to regional and national levels, and finally, establishing a federation of national trade unions into an overall umbrella group. In Western Europe, the affiliation of unions with political labor or socialist parties frequently occured before the labor federation stage, but now the federation and the political party are closely identified.

The pattern for Histadrut had to be different. Palestine was as lacking in capital and capitalists as it was in excess labor. The problem of livelihood was not a matter of exploitation. Jewish settlers who came to Palestine more than a half century ago held a multitude of socialist philosophies that quickly became institutionalized into social and political forms. Each group formed its own employment service, its own communal agricultural settlements (kibbutzim), its own welfare funds, its own unions composed primarily of agricultural workers, since agriculture was then the main industry of the country—and of course its own political party. In 1920, a number of these socialist organizations pooled their resources—with the exception of their party identification—to found Histadrut. In this process, Histadrut reversed the Western pattern described above. It was formed essentially in an agricultural environment, prior to the establishment of strong national unions, and by (if not in spite of) a number of political parties. This formative process has continued to play an important role in the function and organization of Histadrut.

The purposes of Histadrut were identified in the constitution adopted in 1923:

1. To organize workers according to their trades into respective unions.

2. To establish and develop enterprises in all branches of agriculture and industry in city and village; to set up credit institutions and funds for settlement and other economic activities; to unify economic and labor groups; to supply workers through its Labor Exchange; to contract and execute efficiently various public works; to further the establishment of labor consumers' and producers' cooperatives with the object of extensive reciprocal exchange of supplies.

3. To persist in conducting the struggle of hired workers for improved labor conditions until the complete liberation of the working class.

4. To provide for the revival of the Hebrew language; to publish newspapers and literature on professional, technical and general subjects; to set up cultural, educational, and technical institutions.

5. To care for the organization and expansion of labor immigration; to maintain contact with the pioneering movements "Hechalutz"; to receive immigrants and care for their employment and organization.

6. To promote comradely relations with Arab workers in Palestine and to foster the link between the Jewish labor movement and international labor movements all over the world.

7. To establish and develop mutual institutions (sick fund, life insurance, credit unions, unemployment assistance, etc.).

Clearly only some of these goals are traditional labor movement objectives, namely organizing workers, seeking improved working conditions and establishing mutual benefit funds. The remainder are a consequence of an underdeveloped economy, Zionist philosophy and an absence of strong representative government. It becomes obvious that the role assigned to Histadrut goes far beyond trade union activity as the Western democratic societies have come to know labor organizations. Rather, Histadrut was to be a principal instrument in the economic, social, cultural and political development of the Jewish people in Palestine.

Perhaps the surprising thing is that Histadrut succeeded so well. Each of the objectives mentioned in the 1923 constitution was subsequently carried out by Histadrut. Thus, trade unions were organized as soon as there were sufficient workers in an industry or profession; most national unions were a product of the late 1940s. Histadrut organized and financed numerous enterprises in agriculture, industry and services, both to provide needed goods and services and to provide employment. It operated employment service offices to match workers and jobs, and it started insurance programs to cover sick and retired workers. Kupat Holim, the country's major health-care program, is of Histadrut origin. Histadrut also controlled a newspaper, publishing houses, cinemas and a repertory theater. Its educational activities included an elementary and secondary school system and a wide-ranging adult education program. Histadrut organized and supported Haganah, the major defense group prior to the founding of the state of Israel. In many ways, Histadrut was the representative body of the Jewish community in dealings with local authorities and in international relations.

The establishment of the state of Israel in 1948 altered the role of Histadrut and therefore affected its functions. To be sure, some of these changes did not come about immediately or easily. The national government had to assume control over certain areas, such as defense, education, employment services and social insurance. Support of theater and similar activities became less necessary as other sources of supply filled the need. Arab workers became eligible for Histadrut benefits and eventually were entitled to full-fledged membership; indeed in 1966 the label "Jewish workers" was dropped from the full title of Histadrut in recognition of the enlarged scope of membership. Perhaps the most difficult—and most critical—change for Histadrut in the transition years was the need to share power with a new institution, the national government. At least Histadrut had the consolation of knowing that it provided much of the leadership of the new government from among its own ranks and that it retained close ties with the government through the political party system of the country.

HISTADRUT TODAY

Despite the paring of functions, Histadrut is still a major institution in Israel and is involved in an unusually varied number of activities.

To begin with, an overwhelming majority of Israel's citizens are members of Histadrut. Over 80 percent of all wage earners are members, and Histadrut unions represent almost 90 percent of the country's employed population. In addition to wage earners, Histadrut membership is open to self-employed and professional workers, members of kibbutzim and moshavim, and, perhaps most surprising of all, housewives working at home. To be sure, membership is not always a matter of ideological conviction. Many persons have joined because of the benefits conferred by membership.

While Histadrut is the major worker organization in Israel, it is not the only one. Several professional organizations and Histadrut Haovdim Haleumit (National Workers' Organization) which organizes in industry, are outside the ranks of Histadrut. In order to compete for membership, each organization has its own system of benefit funds and attendant activities.

Among the varied Histadrut activities, the one that creates the most interest and astonishment among non-Israelis is that of Histadrut enterprises. Some of these were actually undertaken prior to the establishment of Histadrut. Even more were added as the economy developed, the labor force increased, and economic and social requirements mounted. Histadrut is now involved in over 2,000 economic activities ranging over the entire gamut of industrial classifications. Among the more significant enterprises are Solel Boneh, the country's largest building contractor; Koor Industries, a conglomerate of some three dozen companies engaged in the manufacture of cement, glass, steel, rubber, plastic and electric appliances; Tnuva, Israel's leading processor and distributor of agricultural products; Hamashbir Hamerkazi, a countrywide retail chain; Supermarket, whose name is self-explanatory to English-speaking peoples; and of course the cooperative settlements and bus companies.

The organization in charge of these economic activities is Hevrat Ovdim (Workers' Association), which is essentially a holding company. Hevrat Ovdim originates, funds and controls some companies completely; in other cases, it may provide capital support but does not direct the venture; and it also supports affiliated cooperative groups. Every Histadrut member has one share in Hevrat Ovdim and is therefore an owner in all of Histadrut enterprises. But effective control and direction is in the hands of the managing executive board of Hevrat Ovdim, whose members also happen to be members of the executive board of Histadrut.

As large and as important as Hevrat Ovdim enterprises are, they account for only about one fifth of the net domestic product and employ a similar portion of the labor force. Of course in some industries the percentage is more significant than in others. Moreover, Histadrut influence extends beyond those enterprises it controls outright.

Despite Histadrut control over a number of enterprises and the nominal worker ownership of these enterprises, there has been little effective worker participation in management in Israel. Workers in Histadrut companies are not happy when their interests are sacrificed to enterprise needs. But, except for the cooperative enterprises, Histadrut companies tend to be operated as those in the private sector, with the managers directing workers and being responsible for results. Histadrut leadership is currently attempting to introduce greater worker participation in its enterprises, but meaningful results await the future.

The lack of difference in practice between the Histadrut and private sectors of the economy is also applicable to collective bargaining in Israel. The size of the country and the dominance of Histadrut militate toward centralized bargaining on major economic matters. Frequently the government is an active or hidden intervenor in the negotiations between Histadrut and private employers. In the 1969 "package deal" negotiations, for instance, Histadrut agreed to curb wage demands while the Manufacturers' Association, representing private employers, agreed to limit price increases and the government agreed to obtain indirect taxes through forced loans.

The need to sustain a continually hard-pressed economy, the self-image of "responsible national institution" espoused by Histadrut and the close political ties between the leadership of Histadrut and the national government result in Histadrut's supporting government economic policies unpopular with large parts of its constituency. At times Histadrut has been willing to accept wage freezes and tax increases "for the good of the country." Such sacrifices cannot be sustained interminably. Moreover, the standard of living has risen dramatically in Israel. Indeed, average family income in current money rose 150 percent in the decade of the 1960s.

It is easy but dangerous to overplay the centralization of bargaining and the control of Histadrut in employer-employee relations. All workers in an enterprise elect representatives to workers' committees. While these committees are nominally authorized by Histadrut, they are frequently quite independent of Histadrut and its local union agents. Especially in critical skills and industries, these workers' committees possess considerable bargaining power; and they exploit this power, regardless of the constraints imposed by Histadrut agreements or the consequences for the country. Most of the minor strikes that plague Israel are those called by worker committees without the authorization of Histadrut. These strikes often occur during the life of an agreement and are short in duration. One reason suggested for the Israeli view that worker strikes are sacrosanct is that such strikes were political weapons in the independence movement prior to 1948. Whatever the reason, time lost to strikes as a proportion of total work time is considerably less in Israel than it is in the United States.

In describing the founding of Histadrut and collective bargaining at the national level, mention has already been made of the influence of politics. Indeed, politics is an integral feature of Histadrut structure and Israeli industrial relations today.

Histadrut elections, on national and local levels, are conducted on a political basis. All political parties registered in Israel regularly appear on Histadrut ballots. Members cast their votes for a given party, and each party appoints representatives to Histadrut conventions and councils in proportion to the vote it received. The fact that Histadrut elections are conducted in the same process and in close proximity to national government elections enhances the possibility of similar results. As a result, political party representation in national government leadership is invariably reflected among Histadrut leadership. And since the political parties take positions on issues and can expect to exercise strict discipline, the views as well as the personal ties between Histadrut and the government are close.

SOME PROBLEMS FOR THE FUTURE

Having provided this generally favorable review of Histadrut, I want to make a few concluding comments on unresolved problems still facing the organization. It is very understandable from a historical perspective to see why Histadrut is what it is, is organized the way it is, and acts the way it does. But times change, and organizations need to adapt. There are three areas which Histadrut leadership needs to think through critically and take conscious steps to alter if Histadrut is to play a continuing useful role.

First of all, Histadrut's activities are still wide-flung. The reduction in scope has been gradual and, at times, unwilling. Histadrut needs to ask itself whether maintaining all of its present activities is necessary and desirable. For the sake of the country as well as for trade union members, it may be that a number of Hevrat Ovdim projects should be curtailed or that the entire organization be made independent of Histadrut control. If so, it would be better for Histadrut to plan such steps now rather than have them enforced by others at a later date.

Second, the problem of worker control is far from satisfactory. Even if total strike activity is lower in Israel than in the United States, it seems to occur at the wrong times among the wrong workers for the wrong reasons. A 1972 change in the labor laws of Israel now makes it illegal to strike during the life of a collective bargaining agreement. But changes in the law and enforcement of the law are only part of the answer. Another may be in strengthening grievance procedures. But probably the most important would be a change in the relation of the workers' committees to Histadrut and in the Israeli view of the strike weapon.

Third, the role of politics in Histadrut is troubling, even to some Israeli industrial relations scholars. The closeness of Histadrut leadership to government leadership and the dominance of the same political parties in both makes it difficult for Histadrut to be an independent institution, which is important not only for industrial relations but for maintaining a democratic society in Israel.

16

Milton Derber

HISTADRUT AND INDUSTRIAL DEMOCRACY IN ISRAEL: AN INTERPRETIVE ESSAY FROM AN AMERICAN PERSPECTIVE

A central question about the labor movement of any democratic country is, How much has the movement contributed to the development of democracy within industry? This is an appropriate question because the labor movement itself invariably regards some form of industrial democracy as a major goal; and because democratic societies legitimize labor movements in large part for their promotion of industrial democracy. In Israel, where the labor movement (the labor parties, the collective agricultural settlements, the buying and selling cooperatives, a number of trade unions

This chapter is to be published in *Labor and Society*, edited by Isaiah Avrech and Dan Gilaldi, Histadrut Department of Higher Education, Israel.

and, finally, Histadrut) preceded and was a principal factor in the establishment of the state, ideas about industrial democracy were imbedded in the earliest thinking on work relations.

Since the term "industrial democracy" means different things to different people, it might be helpful to adopt a working definition. The definition of democracy used in this essay is derived from American, rather than Israeli, experience and thought, but it is still relevant and applicable to the Israeli scene. The definition is based on nine principles [1] relating to nine dimensions which I regard as essential to democracy within industry. They are in brief:

1. *Representation.* Employees, like employers, have the right, if they so desire, to form organizations and to choose representatives who will act on their behalf in the government of an enterprise or industry. Employee representatives are chosen by majority vote of an appropriate constituency on the principle of one man, one vote. (Where industry is privately owned, employer representation is determined by financial rather than electoral considerations.)

2. *Participation.* Employees have a voice, directly or through their representatives, in determining the rules relating to their terms and conditions of employment.

3. *Equal rights and opportunities.* All employees have equal rights as citizens of the enterprise and equal protection under the rules. Discrimination because of race, religion, sex, nationality or other personal characteristics unrelated to the requirements of a job is prohibited.

4. *Right of dissent.* The rights of freedom of speech and orderly opposition to the formal leaders are protected.

5. *Due process.* Individuals or groups may raise complaints over the interpretation or application of existing rules and are to have ready access to effective procedures which assure them of a fair hearing and a just decision.

6. *Responsibility.* The parties live up to their contractual duties and responsibilities in an orderly and lawful manner.

7. *Minimum standards.* Socially acceptable minimum terms and standards of employment are provided.

8. *Information.* All needed information, including an accounting of funds, consistent with the external relationships of the enterprise, is provided to the interested parties.

9. *Personal dignity.* The dignity of every individual in the enterprise is respected.

The character of industrial democracy may vary somewhat in different industrial contexts. For example, the potential participation of workers in a textile factory would appear to be more restricted than that of professionally trained secondary school teachers. The process of selecting representatives in publicly owned enterprise may be based more on political considerations than in privately owned enterprise. Providing information to workers in the shop may involve different communication channels than providing information to union officials at the top level of an industry. In this essay Histadrut's contribution to industrial democracy will be discussed within these three contexts—industrial level, ownership and occupation.

The focus of this discussion will be primarily on relations between Histadrut as an organization and the membership in the work force rather than on relations between Histadrut and the employer or on employer-employee relations. The reason for this emphasis is simply that Histadrut is the center of power in Israeli industrial relations. It is a widespread belief among Israelis that Histadrut's power has declined in recent years and that government officials, employers and managers, and professionals, are assuming more responsibility. Nevertheless, the web of industrial rules is still determined mainly by Histadrut, with private employers largely acceding to the pattern. This does not mean that employers exert no influence on industrial government. At the national level the Israel Manufacturers Association, the largest and most important organization among private employers, is regularly involved in governmental considerations of labor legislation; its views on national wage-price policies are offered with increasing vigor; and its negotiations with Histadrut on an industry basis are serious and often prolonged. Spokesmen for the association have acquired an expertise on labor relations which merits respect and carries definite influence. At the enterprise level the employer's financial stake obviously entitles him to a principal role in determining where an enterprise will be located, what and how much it will produce, how production will be carried out, and who will manage the enterprise. In short, Histadrut leaders cannot and do not impose their views without careful consideration of the views and concerns of numerous interest groups, including private employers. Israel remains, however, a labor-oriented rather than an entrepreneurial economy and its industrial relations system is shaped much more by organized labor than by private employers.

MILTON DERBER

INDUSTRIAL LEVEL: NATIONWIDE AND WORKPLACE·

Representation

Union membership in Israel as a proportion of the labor force is among the highest in the world. In 1966, at its tenth general convention, Histadrut reported that it had 915,000 members, who, with their dependents, consistuted about 60 per cent of the total population.[2] About 80 percent of the members were wage and salaried workers. Each employee member is assigned to one of 35 national trade unions responsible for his occupation or industry so that he is assured organizational representation in the collective bargaining and rule-making process.

For a number of years, however, many members have been dissatisfied with their representational status because the national union officials who have spoken for them were appointed by the Histadrut executive rather than being elected by members or delegates from their own occupation or industry. Some of the unions, like the teachers, agricultural workers and building workers, had achieved a relatively high degree of autonomy, with the members electing their officials, but these were exceptional. Responding to a growing dissatisfaction, Histadrut leaders acknowledged the validity of the complaints and slowly moved toward reorganization. Thus at the 1966 general convention, Secretary-General Aharon Becker laid down the following guidelines: [3]

> a. We shall deepen the process of democratization at all levels of trade union organization in order to strengthen the individual member's attachment to his organized community. To that end:

> b. A different composition of the central authority for trade union affairs will be set up so that half will consist of people elected for that purpose by the national organizations and trade unions directly representing them, the other half to be delegated by the General Executive Committee.

> c. The same pattern of organization will apply to the trade union affairs departments of the labor councils—50 percent to consist of representatives elected by the trade unions, and

260

50 percent delegated by the labor councils. It is my opinion that we should aim to have such general institutions as the General Executive Committee of the Histadrut and the labor council plenary memberships composed partly of members elected directly from the trade unions.

d. Within the coming year, national industrial workers' organizations will be set up.

e. Elections to the national conventions of the trade union organizations will be held once every four years in accordance with the Constitution.

f. The secretaries and secretariat members of the trade union organizations and associations—national and local—will be elected by the authorized institutions of their organizations. The Histadrut will encourage and foster the growth of elected officials from the ranks of the workers themselves.

g. Preliminary discussions on the question of wage policy will take place in the national trade union organizations and at the labor council plenaries.

h. The national organizations and trade unions will be authorized to fix their demands for wage hikes within the over-all wage policy of the Histadrut.

i. Local shop committees within the jurisdiction of any given labor council will maintain regular liaison and cooperate in accordance with the accepted rules.

j. With the establishment of the national industrial workers' organizations, their locals will be set up within the jurisdictional areas of the labor councils and they will function under the supervision of the labor councils.

k. It is our opinion that the time has come to endow our academic workers with full citizenship status and residence rights in all phases of the Histadrut's existence through one comprehensive Academic Workers Union within the General Federation. This should be done in all sincerity, without reservations, and with the full awareness that this community has its own distinct shade, where professional matters are concerned, and therefore merits systematic attention—and not solely in times of crisis.

1. The Histadrut will strive to maintain a general committee at every place of employment representing all classes of workers and vocations. The Histadrut will define the rights of local and national shop committees, their duties, and the manner of their election, in a detailed statute, and it will serve as their liaison with its own national and local institutions. The Histadrut's institutions will re-examine the system of elections to shop committees.

But Histadrut is a large and unusually complex organization and reforms come slowly. It was not until the beginning of 1969 that the Clerical and Administrative Workers Union held a reorganizational meeting (its last general meeting had been nine years earlier) and elected its national secretary. The Government Employees Union was then being served by an interim appointed secretary, a long-time Histadrut official who was an able and experienced trade unionist but not connected with governmental employment. The Trade Union Department had still not been able to agree on appropriate organizational lines for the manufacturing unions, including the 60,000 member Metal Workers Union.

In one sense Histadrut follows optimal democratic procedures in the selection of its officialdom. Its general convention (801 delegates in 1966), which has met on the average every four and a half years (the range has been from three to nine) is elected in a manner similar to the election of members of the Knesset—by a vote of all eligible members in favor of one of the organized political parties. Indeed, Histadrut elections are often a good predictor of the national elections. The number of delegates to which each party is entitled at the convention is roughly proportionate to the number of votes received. The vote also establishes the party "key" which is applied to positions all along the lines of the national organization—to the council of some 350 delegates elected by the convention to serve as the supreme policy-making body between conventions, to the executive committee of 133 members (most of whom are full-time officials in one or another Histadrut agency) and to the central executive bureau (19 members) which is responsible for daily administration. The more than 500 full-time operating officials in the headquarters are, for the most part, also selected on the basis of party-key lines. Thus the leaders of the party which commands a majority (and one party has throughout the post-war period held a clear majority) can determine the controlling personnel in each Histadrut agency. The minority parties, however, are assured a proportion of the available positions and thereby have access to information and an opportunity to press their views. The same party-election approach applies to the worker representatives on each municipal labor council as well as to most national union councils.

As the secretary-general and others have come to recognize, however, this system of selecting representatives, except for the national unions themselves, fails to give adequate weight to the specific industrial and occupational interests of workers. Moreover, the electorate at large includes substantial numbers of housewives, members of kibbutzim and moshavim, and other non-employees. The problem is particularly acute in the case of those trade union officers who are appointed by the Trade Union Department rather than being chosen by elected delegates of the union concerned or by direct membership vote.

At the workplace level, the problem of representation is rather different. The workers committees (usually separate committees for production and office workers) are generally elected in a plant or office on a nonpartisan basis, that is, as individuals, although party politics often intrude. Some Histadrut factions contend that a proportional representation system based on party lists would be fairer to the minorities. The Manufacturers Association has argued that worker representatives should meet three tests—education, seniority and disciplinary record—to assure experience and responsibility. Histadrut has preferred to leave the choice to the workers themselves.

Participation

Wages, hours and working conditions are determined, for the most part, through collective bargaining on a national industry basis. The plant agreement is the exception, although not a rarity. Wage agreements must conform to the national wage policy jointly formulated by the Labor Party leadership in the government and Histadrut to foster national economic growth and to restrain price inflation. Basic hours patterns and certain fringe benefits, like annual vacations, are bargained for within the frame of national legislation which Histadrut helped to formulate.

Union participation in rule-making about wages, hours and conditions of employment, as revealed by collective bargaining agreements and national laws, is therefore substantial. However, in those areas of management which relate to product choice, production and engineering methods, plant location, selection of managerial personnel, marketing and accounting, union participation is extremely limited or nonexistent, at least as far as private employers are concerned. (The public and Histadrut sectors will be discussed later.) Histadrut was responsible in the early days of the state for the establishment of joint labor-management production committees in plants with more than 50 employees, but these committees have largely been confined to the administration of wage incentive plans and have failed to contribute significantly to other aspects of productivity and efficiency. Some private companies not using wage incentives have discarded their joint production committees.

At the workplace, the elected workers committees are responsible together with management for the administration of the collective bargaining agreement. Strong committees may exercise considerable influence over hiring, the level of discipline, the manner of handling redundancy, the manner in which new technology is introduced and in some cases even the choice of first-line supervisors. But worker participation in management rarely extends beyond direct personnel matters, other than in a negative sense when worker fear of job displacement or a reduction in working conditions exists.

Equal rights and opportunities

Discrimination because of national origin, sex, age, color, or other ethnic and personal characteristics is regarded as contrary to fundamental Jewish principles. Although personal favoritism and political influence are not uncommon, and rivalries among the diverse ethnic groups are sometimes strong, the equal rights and opportunities principle is accepted by all parties and reinforced by Israel's defense situation and tight labor market conditions. Employees of European background often have advantages of education and industrial or professional experience in comparison with the newer immigrants from North Africa, and Histadrut officialdom is overwhelmingly of Russian, Polish and German descent. But Histadrut policy is firmly based on principles of nondiscrimination.

Right of dissent

Thanks to the multi-party system within Histadrut, the right of dissent has been provided a formal structure and is widely exercised. Israeli workers are vocal and do not hesitate to express their views about their jobs, their employers or union leadership. As with most generalizations, however, this one needs to be qualified to take account of individual local situations where a powerful union or management personality may dominate a plant and choke off opposition.

Dissent has frequently gone beyond the stage of talk. The then secretary-general, Aharon Becker, felt obliged to confront the issue in his major address at the tenth convention. He noted "a number of conflagrations" at some plants arising from "action committees" set up ("on more than one occasion it was the outcome of inter-party and supra-party connivances of devious kinds") to undermine the authorized local representatives of the workers and to humiliate the recognized shop committee which was responsible for implementing the agreement at the plant.[4] He also observed the finding of a Histadrut research project that most workers' committees regard themselves as Histadrut representatives on the spot but only a minority of them are prepared to accept Histadrut's authority. "To our regret, the inference was that the sense of connection between the local committee and the organization as a whole had, to a large extent, been lost."[5] This subject will be discussed later in this chapter.

Due process

All of the major collective agreements provide procedures for the settlement of personal and group grievances relating to the interpretation and application of the agreement, although procedures at the plant level tend to be highly informal. Arbitration by a neutral third party is available as the terminal point of such procedures, but this step is rarely necessary. If a grievance cannot be settled in the workplace by the management and the workers committee, an official from the local labor council will attempt to work out a settlement with the management. If this step fails, the matter will be referred to the national union secretariat for discussion with the employer association counterpart in what is referred to as a "parity committee." It is rarely necessary to go to the final stage of arbitration. Sometimes this procedure is short-circuited by the calling of an unofficial or wildcat strike. In these cases as well as in the more normal ones Histadrut officials often find themselves in the dilemma of trying to settle a demand exceeding the terms of an agreement without antagonizing the membership.

Responsibility

Histadrut prides itself on its sense of responsibility. Again quoting from Becker's 1966 address:

> Honoring a signed agreement is one of the fundamentals of any soundly functioning system. The unilateral violation of an agreement upsets mutual trust and frustrates all efforts made to arrive at any actual agreement. The Histadrut's signature has been honored up till now, and it will continue to be so honored.[6]

But there is another dimension of responsibility involved. Histadrut leaders see themselves (quite accurately) as much more than trade unionists, as indeed major factors in the building and progress of Israel. By playing the dual role of statesman and union leader, however, they regularly find themselves confronted with conflict situations of an exceptionally complex order. As statesmen they participate in the formulation of the national income policy to moderate inflation and to reduce the unfavorable balance of payments. As union leaders they must satisfy their members' desire for higher incomes. As statesmen they help plan the location and development of old and new industries with considerable emphasis on settling new immigrants or establishing strategic defense towns; as union leaders they must provide their members with a maximum of job security. As statesmen they are expected to contribute to increased productivity and efficiency and to eliminate costly work rules and practices; as union leaders they are pressed to support the workers' demands for restrictions on work speed.

The Israeli public, especially the professional and business segments, is often very critical of the manner in which Histadrut leaders discharge their responsibilities. It is alleged that their practices frequently do not conform to their principles, that they yield too much and too often to rank-and-file pressure. Whatever the validity of these criticisms, and there is evidence for them in the public service and on the docks, the Histadrut, throughout the state's 25 years, has performed a multiplicity of functions which no other democratic labor movement has attempted—and that these functions are to a considerable degree conflicting. In comparison, the typical Western-style trade union role of defending and furthering the economic interests of union members is a relatively simple one. In most Western countries the employer or the government, not the labor organization, is expected to assume responsibility for economic development, efficiency and profitability. The trade union "statesman" may be applauded by the outside world but is likely to be repudiated or dethroned by his members if he is overly concerned with the interests of the corporation or the public.

Minimum standards

As in other industrial societies, Israel has adopted a body of legislation to assure a socially acceptable code of minimum standards for workers. These laws cover such areas as the payment of wages, hours of work, annual holidays, employment of women and children, apprenticeship, factory inspection, severance pay, and insurance covering death and old-age, maternity, occupational injuries and diseases, and family allowances. Histadrut has been largely responsible for their enactment. But even more important, in contrast to some nations with equally elaborate labor codes, it has provided a mechanism for relatively effective administration and enforcement of these laws, at least in the larger establishments.

The chief gaps in the labor law code are in the areas of minimum wages and unemployment insurance, although the latter is partially offset by the severance pay law. Where national standards are low, as in the case of pensions, supplemental programs have been instituted through collective bargaining or through purely internal Histadrut financing.

Information

The problem of funneling industrial information to union officials and workers exists mainly at the workshop level. As an organization Histadrut appears to have effective channels of information to its national and local officials—with respect to both government and private data. The flow of information to workers, however, is far from satisfactory despite the existence of a variety of newspapers and magazines directed at workers and their families. At various times Histadrut and Manufacturers Association officials have toured the country to explain the terms of new collective agreements to workers. But such direct contact is only limited and occasional. Copies of agreements are not distributed to the mass of workers. Discussions between managers and union officials or worker committee representatives are not transmitted to the general membership in any formal or systematic fashion.

Communications in industry are greatly complicated in Israel by the fact that the work force is composed of diverse ethnic and language groups including many new immigrants inexperienced in industrial custom and thought. Histadrut leadership is, of course, aware of this problem and has attempted to cope with it. However its efforts have been only partially successful because the links between the national union officials and the workplace are tenuous and indirect. Whereas the union representatives on the local labor councils are in continuous contact with the workers committees in the plants, they do not always function as a smooth transmission line to the national union secretaries. In part this is due to the fact that the local representatives are usually on the payroll of the labor council rather than of the national union. Thus they have divided responsibility and loyalty. Although oriented to the problems of their industry, they are often more dependent on local political factors than on their national union ties for their jobs. Being subject to local pressures, they are less likely to accept the national point of view of problems. In turn the national union secretariat is usually understaffed and unable to provide the services which might strengthen their relations to local labor council personnel and to plant activists. The question of Histadrut structure as it bears on industrial democracy will be discussed in some detail later.

Personal dignity

This principle is firmly imbedded in Israeli life and thought. Histadrut has always been its staunch advocate. To say that there is no prejudice against individuals or groups in the industrial sector would be inaccurate. But ideologically and functionally the personal dignity of workers is given strong support.

OWNERSHIP AND MANAGERIAL CONTROL

Employment in Israel is provided by three principal types of employers—privately owned enterprise, the Histadrut-owned economy and public institutions, such as the national and local governments and nongovernmental agencies like Hadassah. A significant number of companies also have mixed ownership (e.g., private and government or private and Histadrut) but it is not necessary to pursue this added complexity in this essay. According to Becker's speech at Histadrut's tenth general convention in 1966, about a third of all Histadrut members and about a quarter of the total labor force were employed within Histadrut's labor economy.[7] Government and public agency employment covered another quarter, leaving approximately 50 percent in the private sector.

Most of our earlier observations were based on experience in the private sector in an industrial relations system determined by Histadrut and the Manufacturers Association. The question remains whether type of ownership and managerial control has any significant effect on the degree of industrial democracy that is achieved. Is there a difference between private enterprises and those operated by Histadrut or by a public agency?

Some Histadrut leaders have long argued that industrial democracy ought to be carried to its highest potential within that part of the economy belonging to Histadrut.[8] The kibbutzim, which have increasingly been engaged in small-scale manufacturing and service trades, have been advocated as the model for industrial democracy despite the very different nature of relations between the kibbutz member and his organization from those of the Histadrut factory worker and his organization. Although some of the kibbutzim have been troubled by the problem of "hired workers," both in theory and practice these cooperative systems must be

rated outstanding examples of democratically run enterprises. Indeed the kibbutim go considerably beyond the theoretical framework used in this essay. The one-man, one-vote majority-rule
principle is a basic axiom; the managers are elected by the total
membership; opportunities for participation in rule-making and
decision-making are available to all members at the weekly membership meeting; and information can be termed "total" for those
who wish to know.

The principal manufacturing division of Histadrut, however, is
operated on the model of private enterprise, not kibbutz com-
munitarianism. Koor, with its highly diversified group of 37
manufacturing establishments, is governed by a managing director
and a small board of directors appointed by the top leadership of
Histadrut through its economic wing, Hevrat Ovdim. Long dominated by political considerations, the selection process for Koor
management has given increasing weight to technical and pro-
ficiency factors. Hevrat Ovdim's general secretary and the managing director of Koor as of 1969 were far more conscious of cost
factors and much more inclined to emphasize cost and profit elements than their predecessors. The Koor work force elects local
worker committees and each enterprise sends one or two representatives to a national organization similar to the national unions
for bargaining with Koor management. The workers' organization
in turn has a representative on the Koor board.

Since the mid-1950s Histadrut has been gravely concerned about
the role of Koor workers in the government of Koor enterprises.
As the then secretary general, Pinhas Lavon, stated in 1958:

> The relationship between management and worker in a Hista-
> drut plant must differ fundamentally from the old conven-
> tional one in private enterprises. Unless it ceases to be that
> of employer and employee the enterprise is not genuinely a
> workers' concern, even if wages, working conditions and so-
> cial securities leave nothing to be desired. A Histadrut enter-
> prise must be a living cell of workers. They must conceive
> of their role within the enterprise not that of mere wage-
> earners, but they themselves must share responsibility for the
> future of the enterprise, its planning, efficiency, and daily
> management.[9]

Although the principle of worker participation in management
through joint establishment councils had been adopted by the eighth

general convention in 1956, it was almost universally opposed by the production managers and widely suspected by workers themselves. The managers regarded the idea as a restriction on their flexibility and expertise and a waste of time. The workers for the most part appeared to be uninterested in the managerial process as long as wages and work conditions were satisfactory. The experimental programs introduced in some 30 establishments between 1958 and 1960 proved to be failures for a variety of reasons, including internal political difficulties in Mapai, which led to the resignation of Histadrut's general secretary.

In 1963 and 1964, however, two important Histadrut meetings reaffirmed the need of and support for the workers' participation idea and resolved to implement a local joint management system in every Histadrut industrial enterprise. But implementation again proved contrary to rhetoric. Only one serious experiment was conducted and it failed. At the tenth general convention in early 1966 "participation" was once more endorsed and a department for workers participation in management was established in place of the previous unit. The new efforts, despite the department head's intense convictions and dedication, made little or no headway. As of January 1969 the managerial and worker attitudes in Koor were more closely aligned to private sector attitudes on participation than ever before. Thus far the experience has indicated that "worker participation" cannot succeed if the primary interest groups are not committed to the idea and are not prepared to make a major effort to overcome the natural obstacles which the technical structure of large-scale modern industry interposes.

Despite the lack of success in the participation program, Koor establishments satisfy the criteria of industrial democracy postulated in this essay more fully than do those in the private sector. Neither the managers nor the workers may be enthusiastic supporters of joint management, but they are thoroughly aware that their enterprises belong to Histadrut and not to private owners. The managers therefore maintain close ties with the workers committees. First-line supervisors are usually selected only after consultation with committee members. Information is more readily made available to workers and their representatives on new orders and new equipment. On individual and group complaints, the workers are able not only to pursue the normal grievance channels but also to exert added pressures on management through their political contacts within Histadrut. Although wage levels have not differed appreciably from the private sector levels, fringe-benefit standards have been somewhat higher. Finally, the workers have tighter hold on their jobs, as the experience at the Acre Steel Works during the 1966-1967 recession revealed.

Democracy in government and other public agencies is perhaps somewhat closer to the Koor pattern than to the private sector pattern although, as we have seen, the differences in practice are much smaller than the differences in ideology. Public employees are extensively and strongly organized. Those within the civil service system have the protections of both civil service regulation and unionism. Those who are outside of the civil service appear to be well protected by their organizations. The experience of the salary adjustment struggle between 1963 and 1966 revealed that public employee organizations can exert great economic and political pressures which the political leadership is unable to resist. Reduction in the public work force is extremely difficult to achieve even though the country needs more industrial workers and fewer employees in the bureaucracy.

Occupation

One might expect more highly developed democratic practices among the skilled and educated occupations than among the unskilled or semiskilled. In Israel, however, this is not the case. The history of Histadrut and of the socialist-Zionist tradition which preceded it help to explain this phenomenon. The labor movement in Israel, in contrast to that of virtually every other westernized country, began among intellectuals who were urged to forego their professional aspirations and to work with their hands— especially in agriculture and construction. Manual work was glorified to "normalize" Jewish life, to demonstrate that Jews could use their hands like all other peoples. Thus the principles of industrial democracy became imbedded at an early stage in sectors of the economy which involved a good deal of physical labor— unskilled as well as skilled—e.g., farming, road and building construction, the docks and bus transportation. The idealization of physical labor gradually disappeared after the formation of the state in 1948, but the industrial democracy heritage persisted.

Lest it be inferred that only manual work was organized at an early point, it should be stressed that nonmanual occupations, such as teaching and clerical work, also were unionized prior to the

272

establishment of Histadrut. And as the professions and semi-professions proliferated during the formative years of the state, they too became strongly unionized. Histadrut spread its wings across the entire economy and the principles of industrial democracy necessarily followed.

One of the paradoxes of Israeli industrial democracy is the conflict between the professional unions and Histadrut which has periodically flared up since the middle fifties and which led to the formation of an informal coordinating committee of academic unions outside of Histadrut's framework.[10] Strictly speaking, the issue is not one involving the nine aspects of industrial democracy. Yet it flows out of Histadrut's social-democratic heritage. Superficially, the conflict is over the size of the appropriate differential between wages paid to professionals and to industrial workers. At root it is a conflict over status and ideology. The differential has traditionally been very narrow, stemming back to the days when teachers, doctors and lawyers performing farm or road work could see no justification for higher pay for their colleagues who practiced their professions. The problem was aggravated during the early years of statehood when dockers and bus drivers in short or strategic supply conditions were able to achieve relatively favorable economic status while pay for professions in oversupply lagged. But as the professional role in Israeli society "normalized," the status and bargaining position of professionals improved. They began to argue the need for comparison based on training and education; they pointed to the differentials paid to professionals in Europe and the United States. They also stressed that their incomes should more fully reflect the rising importance and status of professionals in Israeli life.

Since Histadrut leaders in conjunction with their government counterparts were responsible for the national incomes policy, and since the bulk of their members were nonprofessionals, they had to bear the brunt of the professionals' attack. Caught between powerful opposing forces, both their rhetoric and their policy changed only gradually—not fast enough to satisfy the professionals. But the change has been in a realistic direction. The older egalitarian wage ideology had become incompatible with the evolving scientific-technological society. The professionals' desire for new status and prestige had to be met. Israel needed its professionals more than ever before, and the professionals were in an increasingly favorable bargaining position (particularly because the United States offered numerous attractive positons for the younger professionals). The difficulty, from an economic standpoint, was that the manual laborers were also in short supply and the country's national wage structure was one great interlinked web. No significant change in one sector could fail to stimulate changes in the rest. The natural tendency was to look for indirect escape valves, to improvise temporary solutions and to compromise.

From the standpoint of industrial democracy, the wage differential issue was serious but not crucial. Egalitarianism in income is not a prerequisite of democracy provided acceptable minimum standards exist and extreme differentials are avoided. Israel's wage structure remains one of the world's more compressed.

WITHIN HISTADRUT

In an economy like Israel's, where most power is in the hands of the labor movement rather than among businessmen, nonlabor politicians or technocrats, the major conflicts over industrial policy and administration are likely to occur within the labor movement itself. The wage differential struggle briefly referred to in the preceding section is illustrative. The basic question from an industrial democracy perspective which has confronted Histadrut with increasing intensity is whether its economic objectives and institutional structures are fully compatible with democratic procedure and, further, whether the latter is compatible with the economic needs of the society.

Histadrut has often been called a state within a state, but this is misleading. Its leaders see Histadrut as the primary institutional force in the economic development of the state while safeguarding and promoting the economic and social interests of its members. Thus they justify and point with pride to Hevrat Ovdim, the "labor economy": to Kupat Holim, the health and medical service; to the Israel Productivity Institute, which Histadrut initiated; to the vocational training program; to the Afro-Asian Institute; and to the cultural, recreational and educational programs—all in addition to the traditional union functions of conducting collective bargaining and proposing labor legislation.

Histadrut's critics (internal as well as external) have contended that, great as its contributions to the establishment of the state were, with the emergence of a strong and stable political entity, the old conception is no longer valid or workable. They urge the conversion of Histadrut into a conventional, Western-style trade union, with the "labor economy" set free and the health service transferred to the government, as was earlier done to the employ-ment exchanges, the labor schools and even the Haganah (the military organization). Some urge the rupture of ties between the political parties and Histadrut so that the latter can concentrate on industrial problems. They attribute the strains and stresses within Histadrut to the effort of the leadership to play incompatible roles —as co-maker of national policy, as employer and as worker representative.

Histadrut leaders agree that the complex of organizational goals and the resultant mix of roles inevitably produce strains. But they claim that the dismantling of Histadrut would weaken the organi-zation (it is believed that many workers retain membership solely because of the benefits of Kupat Holim) and would create strife and divisiveness within the state at a time when its very survival is still in jeopardy.

Histadrut leaders contend further that much of the internal conflict can be resolved by the correction of structural defects. The main defects, they perceive, are the faulty and inadequate communication channels and lines of authority between the workers in plants and offices and the national officials in Tel Aviv and Jerusalem. To correct these defects they propose to give all unions an electoral rather than an appointive basis and to allocate a sub-stantial proportion of the seats on Histadrut councils and com-mittees (both national and local) to representatives chosen by the national unions. In other words, workers would have directly elected representatives at all levels and would not be able to argue that the national decisions were made by persons whom they had not selected to speak for them. Presumably, also, the national secretariats would be sufficiently staffed to maintain continuing two-way communications with the local representatives and rank and file members.

If such structural changes were made, they would undoubtedly improve member-leader relations. Unfortunately there is currently a substantial credibility gap among the membership because of the long-time failure of the leaders to implement their reform rhetoric. Some participants think that the gap has widened rather than nar-rowed. Clearly, speedy structural change is necessary.

But even if the structure were effectively renovated, the struggle between members and leaders would persist—although perhaps at a more tolerable level. The chief reason lies, as described earlier, in the duality of roles which the policy-makers play. A lesser reason is the political party system which encourages local job action against disliked policies by providing minority parties with a mechanism for challenging or embarrassing the majority leadership. The recent alignment of the leftist Mapam and Ahdut Avodah with the centrist Mapai into a single labor party is seen as a counteracting force in this respect. By uniting the parties, they may be able to reduce the tendency to resort to local "action committees." On the other hand, as the Haifa and Ashdod dockworkers have demonstrated, strategically situated groups of workers can successfully challenge leadership decisions without a political nexus, although such challenges are otherwise more easily suppressed through the disciplinary machinery of the Histadrut.

What is involved in the last analysis is a problem of balance between gains and costs, not the achievement of one best way. Democracy has its costs as well as its benefits. One cost is the conflict which comes out of political opposition. Another is the cost from members challenging the decisions of leaders. At times it has seemed that these costs were becoming excessive. Despite the ability of Histadrut leaders to improvise settlements of one internal crisis after another during the past decade and a half, there is a widespread belief that the links between the membership and the leaders have deteriorated to a dangerous degree. On the other hand, the continuing dangers of Arab aggression have enabled the leaders to combat the factionalism by appeals for unity and moderation. Since the end of Arab hostility appears to be a long way off, the leaders still have time to make the structural and communication changes which they hypothesize can strengthen the traditional order that has made Histadrut the world's most complex and distinctive force for industrial democracy.

NOTES

1. The derivation of these principles has been discussed in detail in my book, *The American Idea of Industrial Democracy: 1865-1965* (Champaign, Ill.: University of Illinois Press, 1970).

2. As of January 1969, the voting membership was reported to be 1,129,589, which, with members' dependents, represented an estimated 56.76 percent of the total population (Chadashot Umeda Bahistadrut, June 1, 1972, no. 19, p. 1).

3. Aharon Becker, *Histadrut: Program, Problems, Prospects* (Tel Aviv International Department, Histadrut, 1966) pp. 56-8.

4. Becker, *Histadrut,* pp. 58, 61.

5. Ibid., p. 58.

6. Ibid., p. 60.

7. Ibid., p. 74. The Histadrut percentages in agriculture and building were much higher than in the total labor force; in manufacturing it was between 12 percent and 15 percent.

8. The recent history of this subject has been carefully traced and assessed in J. Yanai Tabb and Amira Goldfarb, *Workers Participation in Management* (Haifa: Technion, 1968) chapter 4.

9. "Histadrut Economy: New Ways for Old," *Jewish Frontier* (September 1958) p. 7.

10. This struggle led to the replacement in 1966 of the Academic Workers Department by a new section for professional unions designed to regain their attachment to Histadrut.

ETHNIC
RELATIONS
AND PROBLEMS

17

Shlomo Avineri

ISRAEL: TWO NATIONS?

Israel's problems of poverty and its struggles with agonizing issues of communal integration have figured quite prominently in Jewish welfare literature for the last 20 years. What United Jewish Appeal contributor hasn't seen those pictures and drawings, sometimes not in the best of taste, but very effective in loosening purse strings, of a Mediterranean-looking group of refugees seeking shelter in the old-new homeland? What reader of things Jewish and Israeli hasn't heard about the educational and economic gaps which separate most of the immigrants that have come from Arab countries from so many of the European Jews?

All this has for decades been part of the image of Israel. Yet when the "Black Panthers" of Jerusalem made the headlines, the shock among American Jews, old and young, conservative and radical alike, was enormous. Poverty and discrimination in *Israel?* Communal hatred among *Jews?* Social inequality in egalitarian, Histadrut-run Zion? Jewish police being stoned by Jewish demonstrators? Jewish police hitting Jewish demonstrators? Something must have gone wrong. And since poverty is such a popular and uplifting topic among the affluent intelligentsia in the West, no parlor discussion of Israel could now be complete without the inevitable question, And what about the Oriental Jews in Israel? There are many people around, in conventional living rooms and pot-reeking student dorms alike, who couldn't for the life of them name one Israeli political party, but *know* all about the Black Panthers.

Of course the Israelis themselves were surprised when the Pan-

Reprinted with the permission of *Midstream*.

thers burst on the Israeli scene, but for different reasons. Basking in the general euphoria and economic prosperity that have engulfed Israel since 1967, the more solidly established Israelis lulled themselves into complacency by thinking that the disappearance of unemployment and the universally felt rise in living standards meant that the major problems of immigrant absorption had been solved. Israelis are, of course, deeply aware that many economic, educational and sociopsychological gaps still remain, but since every indication tends to show that these gaps are being narrowed—and they are, as we shall see later—few Israelis were ready for the bitterness and venom of some of the Black Panther outbursts. Had there been mass unemployment, had those awful tent camps, the ma'abarot of two decades ago, still been the abode of hundreds of thousands of new immigrants, nobody would have been surprised if there had been demonstrations or even bloody confrontations. Nobody was surprised when demonstrators rhythmically clamoring for *Lechem! Avoda!* (Bread! Work!) filled the streets in the bad old days of austerity and mass immigration immediately after the establishment of Israel. But now? (Incidentally, those demonstrations never caught the public eye outside of Israel at that time. Israel was then still much of a backwater; few foreign newspapers had regular correspondents in Israel; and the messages of TV were seldom relayed out of the Land of the Book.)

Hence the initial Israeli reaction to the Panthers was one of sincere astonishment. Expressing, as usual, popular feeling in Israel, the Prime Minister dismissed the Panthers as "not nice boys." Newspapers picked on the criminal records of some of the youngsters involved, and pooh-poohed the whole thing as ordinary hooliganism; the police, which is very heavily Sephardic in its composition, vowed to maintain law and order. The Iraqi-born police officer who confronted the Panthers, Inspector Avraham Turjeman, was a prime example of the fact that there were Orientals on both sides of the police line; and dark hints were dropped into ears only too willing to listen that some nefarious political elements (who knows, perhaps even *Fatah*, which obviously gloated over the whole business) lurked behind those misguided kids from Jerusalem's Musrara Quarter.

What sometimes got lost in the controversy was that its very emergence bespoke a deep change in the social structure of Israeli society. The point about this change is that as a process its progress moves snail-like and does not render itself to catchy headlines. The ephemeral reporting of an itinerant correspondent may hardly take cognizance of the fact that any such process is under way—after all, how many people read those sociological tomes, political tractates and economic reports? Nor does a rendering of such a process sound convincing when channeled through the self-congratulatory rhetoric of Israeli officialdom. But it is to these processes that one must turn in order to understand both the relative achievements of Israel as well as its shortcomings, and it is in this context that the Panther phenomenon has to be placed.

In 1948, when Israel emerged as a state, less than 15 percent of its Jewish population was of Eastern, or non-Ashkenazi origin. Roughly, it could be divided into three main social groups: the Sephardic patriciate, the Sephardic masses and the Yemenites.

The Sephardic patriciate was centered mainly in Jerusalem and the powerful Sephardic Community Council. It was a typical business and white-collar community, mainly dating from pre-Zionist days, very well entrenched in its status of affluence and its upper-middle-class ethos. Though operating a number of charitable institutions for the Sephardic poor, its philanthropy, like all philanthropy, was a measure of its upper-class affluence. Under the British Mandate, members of the Sephardic patriciate were prominent in banking and business, in the legal profession and in government service. Many of the Jewish civil servants in the Mandatory administration were Sephardim. Their education, mainly in English and French, as well as their knowledge of Arabic, made them much more suitable for government service than the less well-educated and less sophisticated Eastern European *halutzim* (pioneers). Their social ethos was also better attuned to the genteel manners of a colonial administration than the somewhat plebeian background of the socialist revolutionaries or petty shopkeepers who were the predominant elements among the third and fourth waves of immigration from Poland and Russia in the 1920s.

For these reasons the Sephardic patriciate also tended to stand aloof from the overall Zionist effort, based as this was on notions of revolutionary socialism and romantic nationalism that were quite foreign to it. The Eastern European *halutz*, usually from a small town, Yiddish-speaking and Hebrew-singing, leading an unconventional existence, experimenting with communes and unheard-of ideas of life styles and family structures, was looked down upon by this established class. (Many old Jerusalemites still remember how unwelcome the Russian halutzim were when some of them presumed to show a healthy interest in the daughters of the Sephardic grandees.)

With the establishment of the state of Israel, the Sephardic patriciate managed for a couple of years to maintain its own parliamentary representation in the Knesset in the form of a separate electoral list which succeeded in electing one or two members in the first few elections. Ultimately they became amalgamated with their Ashkenazi peers and joined the bourgeois General Zionist Party. A lone member of the erstwhile Sephardic parliamentary group, Bechor Shalom Shitrit, who as police officer and later as judge under the Mandate in Tiberias had more contact with kibbutzim than other members of his group, eventually joined Mapai and served for many years as Israel's Minister of Police. Socially and politically this group is now well integrated and intermarried into the upper levels of Israeli society, and some of the more prominent names in Israel's law, banking and business life, like Reccanati, Molcho, Sassoon, Chelouche, Valero, Manny, Eliachar, Kukkia and the like, attest to the high status of these families in Israeli life. In Israel, as in England, France and to a certain degree the United States, the Sephardic elite belongs to the most genteel part of the Jewish establishment and lends it the charm and style which made even a sophisticated Central European like Herzl feel that they were the only true Jewish aristocracy.

The Sephardic masses, on the other hand, presented a totally different picture. The class structure of the Sephardic community was extremely pronounced: while the patriciate in Mandatory Palestine was sophisticated, Western-educated and socially well-placed, the Sephardic masses, mainly in Jerusalem but also in Tiberias, Safed and in clusters around Tel Aviv, were an under-educated, poverty-stricken group. For decades they were the objects of philanthropic aid from grandees like Sir Moses Montefiore and the Paris-based *Alliance Israelite Universelle*. Many were descendants of pre-Zionist immigrants to Palestine, and most led a highly religious and traditional life. Since the mainly socialist Zionist parties in Palestine emerged from the halutz waves of immigration from Eastern Europe, the Sephardic population, like the Ashkenazi religious pre-Zionist groups clustered around Meah Shearim in Jerusalem, remained outside the main stream of Zionism and its secular, nationalist ethos. But unlike the Meah Shearim ultra-Orthodox who stuck to their messianic passivism and hence viewed Zionism as a secular blasphemy, the populist religiosity of the Sephardic masses caused many of them to identify with the militant nationalism of the Revisionist Irgun Zwai Leumi and later with Beigin's right wing Herut party. The number of such

Sephardim in the Irgun was very high, and the numerous following which Herut's almost exclusively Polish-born leadership has until this day among a wide sector of the Oriental population in Israel dates from this period. Many labor movement leaders, especially Itzhak Ben Zvi, who became Israel's second president, tried to build bridges between Histadrut and the Sephardic populace during the Mandatory period, but the effort was not very successful—life styles, belief sytems and the elements of social cohesion were too disparate.

The Yemenites are another element again. Some of the first Yemenite immigrants came to the land of Israel around 1882 on the wave of a resurgence of messianic hopes among this almost completely isolated community tucked away in the southwest corner of Arabia. Later, around 1910, in one of the most incredible episodes of Labor Zionism, the leaders of the Second Aliyah sent one of their members, Shmuel Yavne'eli, to Yemen and Aden, and he was successful in inducing several thousand Yemenites to immigrate to Palestine. Most Yemenites were artisans and highly skilled craftsmen, and because their literacy rate was higher than that of any other Oriental community due to a very deep veneration for religious learning, their integration into the Jewish yishuv in Palestine appeared to have been much more successful than that of the Sephardic populace. Many Yemenites settled on land, became agricultural workers and artisans and, due to a long tradition of thrift and hard work, became relatively well established economically. Some of the best known popular artists of the yishuv were Yemenites: Esther Gamlielit, Shoshana and Saadia Damari, Beracha Zefira, Hannah Aharoni. Yemenite folk dances, together with the Hora and the Krakoviak, were paraded as expressions of the new folk culture of Zion.

Though highly traditional, religious and patriarchal in their private lives, the initial links of the Yemenites with the labor movement remained strong; later, some of the young Yemenites joined the more nationalistic underground groups, but it appears that the sophisticated and intellectual Stern group appealed to them more strongly than the more philistine Irgun (among the Sephardic populace it was the other way around). But the main link with the labor movement persists to this day: the first moshav, Nahalal, had a Yemenite member who doubled as the community's rabbi; one of Yigal Allon's most popular staff officers in the Palmach was a Yemenite, Yeruham Cohen; Ben-Gurion had a strong charismatic appeal among the Yemenite community; and the fact that the first non-Ashkenazi Secretary-General of the Labor Party, who still holds that powerful position, Yisrael Yesha'ayahu, is a Yemenite, harks back to the attachment forged in the 1910s.

When mass immigration from Arabic-speaking countries came in the 1950s, this picture changed completely. From less than 15 percent of the Jewish population in 1948, the Oriental population rose to about 50 percent in the sixties. While the number of Oriental Jews the world over is less than 15 percent of the total number of Jews, Israel's Jewish population is about half Oriental. In this, as in many other respects, Israel is highly atypical of the worldwide Jewish community. And though any generalization which identifies Oriental Jewish groups with underdevelopment, backwardness and a high degree of illiteracy is obviously wrong (the Sephardic patriciate is one, but not the only, proof), it is nonetheless true that the percentages of illiteracy, undereducation and low economic status are much higher among Oriental Jewish groups than among Western Jewish communities that have benefited from emancipation and enlightenment for a much longer time than any of the Oriental Jewish communities. Jewish groups, for better or for worse, reflect the characteristics of the general level of development of their host societies—though some illuminating exceptions, such as the Yemenites, should make one wary about sweeping generalizations.

The limitations of generalizations should always be considered when discussing the Oriental communities. We have seen how the so-called "Eastern" Jewish population in pre-1948 Palestine was far from being a homogeneous group. Even the term *Sephardim*, which is very much in current usage nowadays, can be misleading. Originally it referred to those Jews whose ancestors were expelled from Spain (*Sepharad* in Hebrew) during the heyday of the Catholic Inquisition and who usually spoke a Castillian dialect, Ladino. Gradually it came to encompass non-Western Jewish communities that had nothing to do with Spain. Iraqi Jews, for example, are usually referred to as Sephardim, and the present Sephardic Chief Rabbi of Israel, Yitzhak Nissim, is Iraqi-born. Strictly speaking, he is not, of course, Sephardic at all. Other appellations have been used, such as Orientals (which we shall mainly use in this chapter), Easterners, Jews from Arab or Islamic countries, and the like.

All this has a bearing on the central issue: there is no one Sephardic or Oriental community in Israel. There are Oriental communities, in the plural, and they differ markedly from one another. What distinguishes them are not only characteristics brought lock, stock and barrel from their countries of origin, like the difference between the high degree of literacy, an almost Calvinistic attitude to work (if one may pardon the expression in this context) of the Yemenite artisans, and the generally lower levels of literacy, professional tradition and economic motivation of some sectors of the Moroccan community. After all, there are many differences also among the Ashkenazi community—not only between the Central Europeans and the Eastern Europeans, but also among immigrants from Poland between the sophisticated, usually Polish-educated bourgeois from the wealthier areas of Warsaw and Cracow and those hailing from the *shtetls* of the Pale of Settlement, with their immediate *Yiddishkeit* and populist-egalitarian traditions.

But it is not only the countries of origin which determine differences, but also the mode of the communities' immigration to Israel which is of prime importance. Here the crucial variable is whether a community immigrated to Israel in its entirety, or whether only some sectors of it came, and if so, which ones. Thus, in the Yemenite and the Iraqi cases, though the communities come from quite different backgrounds, in both instances the community immigrated in its entirety, with its leadership and elite, both spiritual and socioeconomic. Hence after a few years of intense dislocation and hardship, the Iraqi community managed to achieve and regain its cohesion, its elite found its niche in the economy, mainly in banking, commerce and some sectors of the civil service. Certain comfortable areas of Ramat Gan, sometimes ironically referred to as Ramat Baghdad, attest to the existence in Israel of a bourgeoisie of Iraqi origin, very proud and conscious of itself. Thus, too, the Bulgarian community, which was middle class in its country of origin and immigrated almost completely to Israel, boasts today not only of a higher percentage of doctors and dentists than any other group in the population, but also has in the Jaffa Maccabee soccer team, almost entirely Bulgarian, a visible and highly popular symbol of its cohesion and place in the sun.

Other communities, and the Moroccans are a prime example, have a different history. Here the elite stayed behind. Most of the rich are still in Casablanca, and so long as King Hassan's liberal policy will protect them, they will probably stay there. The well educated, nurtured in French colonial schools on *Nos ancêtres les Gaulois*, are to be found all over the Parisian intellectual and professional establishment. Those who came to Israel were, until very recently, the less well educated, the poor and the economically less successful; apparently, a process of negative social selection was operating here. Thus the Moroccan immigration brought to Israel not only a group that was markedly less well placed educationally and socially than other Oriental groups, but also a community of about 200,000 people without an elite and without its traditional spiritual or economic leadership. It is this atomized, lopsided and leaderless nature of the Moroccan group which made this group much more of a problem than many other Oriental communities. Only recently has the picture began to change with the immigration, usually via France, of some well-educated and trained younger Moroccans who in some cases have suffered a traumatic shock by discovering, with the compliments of de Gaulle, that their ancestors hailed after all from Judea rather than from Gaul. This young group is giving the community a sense of self-assurance and an image it lacked in the past and has been instrumental in the last few years in changing many of the oldtimers' stereotypes about Moroccan Jews. But the overall picture has not changed much.

One has to consider all these elements when discussing the relative success of integration, educational and social mobility and general image of any of the Oriental communities, and any detailed account will have to discuss each community separately.

Any observer of the changing Israeli scene would probably ask how the influx of such a mass of immigrants affected the political structure of the country. With the examples of other immigration countries in mind, he may well make a number of revealing comparisons. The old European establishment, for instance, has managed to hold on to power; any observer must be struck by the fact that most Israeli political parties maintained their relative strength vis-à-vis each other since 1948, and no new ethnic parties ever succeeded in gaining a foothold in the Knesset. One would also note that the percentage of Oriental members in the Knesset, though slowly rising, is still very low (less than 13 percent) and no major breakthrough could be noted on the level of national representation.[1] Here, it would seem, the Black Panthers express a real grievance and appear as the first political expression of "Oriental Power."

But this is only part of the picture; the overall political scene is much more complex. The initial reaction of the Israeli political establishment to massive immigration—be it Western or Oriental—was to view the immigrants as mere pawns in the game. Work, housing and schooling were allocated with more or less efficiency by the existing power structure, and the newcomer was expected to be grateful, especially on Election Day. Since in the political structure of Israel political parties and their affiliate organizations fulfill central roles in the process of integration of new immigrants, this form of patronage became commonplace. (The Israeli humorist Ephraim Kishon, who is always very good at reducing every comic aspect of Israeli life *ad absurdum*, epitomized this phase of Israeli politics in the amusing Israeli film *Sallah*.)

But ethnic patronage is dialectical, as every henchman of Tammany Hall would acknowledge if he could speak Hegelian. It begins with the machine manipulators controlling their suppliers of blocs of votes; it ends with the suppliers becoming bosses and the clients becoming patrons themselves.

This is what happened in Israeli local politics, and it is to the level of local politics that one must turn in order to perceive the changes in the Israeli political structure. It has been repeatedly pointed out that, though far less visible, local politics is much more innovative in Israeli politics than the national scene.[2] And it is here that a process similar to the takeover of local politics in American life at the turn of the century by the new ethnic bloc vote is taking place. Its consequences for the future of Israeli politics will undoubtedly be as dramatic.

The pattern is unmistakable: wherever you look—to town halls, trade union councils (the powerful local Histadrut branches), local party committees—the number of Oriental members is steadily growing. In many places, where the Orientals now form a majority, they have ousted the European oldtimers' establishment and completely taken over the place politically.

The most outstanding case is Beersheba, Israel's fourth most important town, the seat of the University of the Negev and of some crucially important science-based industries. The first Israelis to settle in Beersheba after 1948 were a few hundred oldtimers of European background, and naturally, when a local government unit was organized, they controlled town hall as well as the local Histadrut council and the Mapai branch. With time, the population grew—from 8,300 in 1950 to 77,400 in 1970, most of the newcomers hailing from Middle Eastern countries. Initially a few Orientals were coopted by the European establishment into some of the representative bodies; ultimately the Orientals gained a majority in the executive body of the local Mapai branch, which controlled the city's politics, and eventually ousted the incumbent Ashkenazi party secretary, the Histadrut secretary and finally the mayor as well. Now Beersheba has a mayor of Iraqi origin. Mapai (or rather the Labor Party as it is now called), is in power in

1972 just as it had been in 1950—the change occurred within the party, but it was widely reported in the press, and its lesson was not lost upon the public. The observer who concludes that nothing has changed politically in Beersheba because Labor has continually been in power for the last 20 years misses the main point. The change was as significant as the shift in the fortunes of the Democritic Party in New York when the "ethnics" took over from the Hudson Valley aristocrats.

Though Beersheba was the most dramatic of cases, the pattern is universal: the whole composition of the municipal councils is changing. In 1950, only 13 percent of all Jewish members of local government bodies were Orientals; since then the figure has grown consistently—to 24 percent in 1955, 37.5 percent in 1959 and 44 percent in 1965. In the 1969 municipal elections the percentage remained the same, but since the number of Jewish local councillors grew from 951 to 1,081 (due mainly to the establishment of new municipal bodies in new development towns), the number of Oriental representatives actually involved has gone up.[3] With the Oriental population roughly estimated at about half of Israel's Jewish population, it may well be that a representation of about 44 percent may be the most that can be expected at the moment. It certainly shows a high degree of representative correlation between the electorate and the elected, though it is not equally distributed throughout the country. In Tel Aviv, for example, the Oriental population is still heavily underrepresented. It is also interesting to note that some parties have been more successful in integrating the new Oriental communities than others—or were more receptive to pressures from them. While the percentage of Oriental local councillors who were Labor members rose from 42 percent to 51 percent, the parallel percentage of Gahal Oriental local councillors went down from 48 percent to 38 percent in the same period. The religious parties seems to have the highest percentage of Oriental local councillors in 1969—68 percent of the religious local councillors were Orientals.

This process was accompanied by the replacement of mayors (or chairmen of local councils, as they are called in the smaller towns) of European background by Orientals in many of the cities and towns throughout Israel. In 1952, 1954 and 1955, one European mayor was replaced by an Oriental one, two were replaced in 1957, eight in 1959, again one each in 1961 and 1963, ten in 1965 and one again in 1966. Though there have also been some reversals, at present there are Oriental mayors in 30 percent of the municipalities in the country that have a Jewish mayor.[4]

The specific backgrounds of these Oriental mayors or chairmen of local councils are as follows: there are mayors of Iraqi origin in Beersheba, Ramleh, Or Yehuda, Kiryat Hacarmel, Mevasseret Zion, Kiryath Malachi and Rechasim; mayors of Moroccan origin hold office in Dimona, Ofakim, Beit Shemesh, Gan Yavneh, Hatzor, Yeruham, Mazkeret Batya, Netivot, Sderot and Shlomi; there are Yemenite mayors in Beit Dagan, Gedera, Yehud, Pardessiya, Kiryat Ekron and Rosh Haayin; the chairman of the local council in Kfar Yona is of Turkish origin, while the one at Maalot-Tarshiha is of Libyan background; the mayor of the Galilean city of Safed is an Israeli-born Sephard. If one were to add to this list also the Oriental deputy-mayors, who in the Israeli system of local government are full-time executives, the range of penetration of the Oriental groups into the real power structure of Israeli local government would be even more evident: Jerusalem, for instance, has a deputy-mayor, André Chouraqi, who is of Moroccan origin. Anyone looking through a roster of local government officials in Israel will thus be struck by the fact that Oriental names replace the European or Hebraized ones: Kazaz, Jeraffi, Ohayon, Hatukha, Sawissa, Danino, Aboudi, Arbeli—these are some of the new vintage of mayors and chairmen of local councils in contemporary Israel. Though, as noted, the picture is different in a place like Tel Aviv, even there the number of municipal councillors who are Orientals is going up.

A similar process has become apparent also on the level of Israel's regional councils, which group together the smaller, unincorporated villages. While a few years ago one hardly found Orientals as chairmen of these muicipal bodies, at present ten of the 48 regional councils in Israel are headed by Orientals.

It will obviously take some time before this shift will be as visible on the national level of politics as well—after all, it took two generations of urban politics to produce an Irish Catholic president in the United States. But political power grows out of provincial smokefilled backrooms; parallel developments are going on at Histadrut level, and the emergence of a Yemenite as secretary general of the Labor Party will certainly mean that more Oriental candidates will be included on the party's list of candidates in the next election. Moreover, political power in the form of patronage, which is extremely important to communities of relatively recently

arrived immigrants, is much more pronounced on the local level.
Due to Israel's system of proportional representation, decisions
about parliamentary candidates are taken at the center, and the
time lag between the changes in the composition of the electorate
and central party response may be longer than in the Anglo-Saxon
system of constituency representation. But given the jolt the Black
Panthers have dealt the Israeli establishment, there is little doubt
that the next Knesset will have a significantly higher number of
Oriental members.

A possible victim of such a development may, paradoxically, be
the archetypical Israeli-born sabra, usually (at the adult generation level we are talking about here) a child of European-born
parents. For years, many have expected that after the demise of the
generation of Eastern European founding fathers and mothers, political power would pass into the hands of sabras. But the old guard
is not only very tenacious; it is also blessed with extraordinary
longevity and resilience. Some of the sabra young Turks have been
waiting in the wings for decades and have become, like the young
and upcoming Dayan, grandfathers in the process. (One still refers
to Moshe Dayan, Yigal Allon, Arie Eliav and their like, all in their
late forties or early and mid-fifties, as the "young ones.") But it
may be that the immediate transition will not be—some charismatic names notwithstanding—from the Eastern Europeans to the
sabras of European background but from Eastern Europeans to
Orientals. It is just conceivable that the sabras, so visible now in the
higher echelons of the civil service, the army, the universities and
industry, may become the odd men out as far as politics is concerned.

This happened once before in Israel, to the German-speaking
immigrants, whose contributions to Israel's economic, technological,
academic and cultural life has been enormous, but who were left
high and dry politically. No two groups could be wider apart
than the German Jews and the sabras. The former, with his Ger-
manic inflection, European manners and sophisticated intellectual-
ism, has always been the butt of the humor of the down-to-earth,
rough-and-ready, and rather unintellectual archetypical sabra.
Nonetheless, the sabras, just like the German Jews, lack the organizational cohesion and patience of the dedicated Eastern European.
Their directness, bluntness and no-nonsense attitude do not lend
themselves very well to the arduous and painstaking work of political horse-trading, bargaining and back-slapping; they seem to
prefer to get a thing done rather than bargain over it and discuss

it in committee into the small hours of the night or build up a political machine of their own over the years. The Orientals, though they usually lack a democratic tradition in their countries of origin, have the patience, the knowledge that you have to cajole and argue and discuss again and again; the endless haggling of the Orient appears to be much more adaptable to machine politics than the bright straightforwardness of the somewhat spoiled sabra whiz-kids. There may be an element of exaggeration in this account, but one cannot but be struck by the fact that the one field where Israeli-born sabras are underrepresented is that of politics; within the Labor Party, the Oriental blocs are much more powerful than the perennial young guard, which has been trying to storm the bastions of the old machine-ridden politics, mainly in Tel Aviv, for the last two decades, but to no avail. That the first secretary general of the Labor Party who belonged to this young group, Arie Eliav, left his post after only two years in obvious disgust and impatience, and was replaced by a Yemenite, may be coincidental; but it may also be an adumbration of the shape of things to come.

The integration of the Oriental immigrant into the political structure of Israeli life thus shows remarkable similarities with the process through which Irish and Italian (and Jewish) immigrants became integrated into the American political structure at the turn of the century. None of the political alienation and exclusion which until very recently characterized the position of the American blacks can be found in the process which the Oriental communities are undergoing in Israel. Like the Italians and the Irish in America, they still are at the bottom of the economic ladder—though, as we shall see in a moment, they are moving up quite rapidly. It would be foolish to deny that there still exist many popular prejudices and generalizations about the Oriental immigrants—but these exist even with regard to non-WASP white Christian groups in the United States. But if one looks for American parallels, it is among the Italian and the Irish that one would find something akin to the position of the Oriental communities in Israel—not among the blacks.

There are obviously some areas of Israeli life where this penetration of the Oriental immigrants is less advanced than others. It may come as a surprise to some, but the kibbutzim have been generally not very successful in absorbing new immigrants from Arabic-speaking countries. The main reason for this appears to be that the universalistic and egalitarian ethos of the kibbutzim tends

293

to do away with most of the Orientals' cherished family traditions. The Oriental immigrants, with their emphasis on male dominance and the closely knit family, find kibbutzim alien and difficult to adapt to. But while the collectivist kibbutz has thus been less of a success than it expected to be with Oriental immigrants, the cooperative moshav, based on the family unit, appealed strongly to Oriental immigrants. The cooperative nature of the extended traditional clan could be easily adapted to the kind of links holding together the different families making up a moshav, and today the majority of moshavim are made up of immigrants from Middle Eastern countries. These moshavim have given rise to a whole new elite of young activists of Oriental background, very much integrated into the complex and interlocking structures of the moshavim movement, the Agricultural Center of Histadrut, the various Histadrut-run marketing organizations (Tnuva, Hamashbir Hamerkazi, etc.) and the Labor Party. One representative of this new brand of *moshavniks* of Oriental background, Aharon Ouzan, has served for several years as Deputy Minister of Agriculture, and it is from this sector that one may expect a further flow of young political leaders of similar background.

One of the major aspects of integration is of course that of intermarriage among the various groups. One should point out that the problem is not only how many Ashkenazim will intermarry with Sephardim, but also how many Iraqis will intermarry with Moroccans or Tunisians, and it is here that the traditional family structure of the Oriental communities tends to favor endogamy not only within the broad Oriental community, but also within specific and narrower groups: Iraqis tend to marry Iraqis, Moroccans to marry Moroccans, etc. Nonetheless, with rising economic and educational standards among the younger generation of the Oriental communities and the emancipation of the younger people from the oppressive parental tutelage characterizing some of the Oriental families, the level of intermarriage between the communities is steadily rising. In 1969, 17.5 percent of all Jewish marriages in Israel were intermarriages in the sense that one of the partners came from European background whereas the other came from Asian-African background. This percentage is steadily rising—the army and the universities appear to be the two environments most conducive to such intermarriages. One would find nothing like such a percentage when it comes to intermarriages between whites and blacks in America; it is my guess that there also does not exist a similar percentage of exogamy between WASPs and Italian-Irish groups in the United States. This emphasizes a fundamental fact: despite differences, the various communities in Israel regard themselves as belonging in fact, and not only in principle, to a single nation, and the consciousness of being Jewish is stronger than the much more abstract (and hence economically oriented) consciousness of being, say, American. With education and a modicum of social mobility, origins in Israel fade into the background and intermarriage becomes a reality. Given the relative independence of Israeli youngsters from parental opinions, it is the younger generation that makes the decision, and the prejudices of the older generation have little power to perpetuate themselves. These 17 percent of "mixed" marriages—and the ratio is now growing by about 1 percent every year—are one of the most fundamental indications of the direction social change is taking in Israel.[5]

But the crucial indices are the economic ones, and here we have a number of data prepared by a committee headed by David Horowitz, who was then governor of the Bank of Israel. Its findings[6] point to the unequivocal conclusion that on the basis of every criterion used, the gap between families of Asian-African origin and those of European-American origin has been visibly narrowing over the last decade. However there do exist some very obvious gaps and while Israel could congratulate itself on its achievements in narrowing some of the more glaring ones, much more effort has to be put into the disparate sectors of Israeli society in order to eradicate the remaining gaps.

The committee expressed this very succinctly:

In the period under review (1963-70), the standard of living of families of Asian and African origin improved relative to the standard of living of all families. This improvement found expression in higher income levels, in better housing, in a higher rate of ownership of consumer durables, in a decline in the proportion of Asian-African immigrants among low-income families, and in an increase in the proportion of these families in the higher-income brackets. However, even after the improvement in their relative position during the past decade, the average income per standard equivalent adult among families of Asian-African origins is still only 70 percent of the overall average for Jewish families.[7]

To obtain the perspective one should add that in 1963-1964, the corresponding percentage was 63 percent. The committee found

that the worst years for the Asian-African families were the recession years 1965-1967; the prosperity of post-1967 has given a tremendous boost to the lower rungs of Israel's society.

The Horowitz committee found that while the gross income per
standard equivalent adult of all Jewish families in Israel arose by
34 percent for the period under investigation, that of families of
Afro-Asian origin rose by 46 percent, that of European-American
families rose by only 36 percent and that of Israeli-born families
by a mere 27 percent, a clear indication that income distribution
is becoming more, not less, egalitarian with respect to country of
origin. Moreover, between 1963-1964 and 1968-1969 average real
income in the lowest decile of the population rose by 35 percent
as compared with an overall rise of 26 percent.

The committee went into some details to establish the social distribution patterns of ownership of durable consumer goods. Among
families originating from Asia-Africa, 92 percent owned electric
refrigerators in 1970 compared to 17 percent in 1960 (comparable
figures for European-American born families were 97 percent for
1970 and 69 percent for 1960); 89 percent of all Asian-African
families owned gas stoves in 1970 as compared to only 43 percent
in 1960 (88 percent in 1970 and 75 percent in 1960 are the figures
for Western-born families); 46 percent of Asian-African families
owned electric washing machines in 1970, compared to only 8
percent a decade ago. (Here the Oriental families not only progressed faster from lower levels of ownership but virtually over-
took Western-born families: only 42 percent of Western-born
families owned a washing machine in 1970 as compared to 21 percent in 1960. Smaller family size, as well as a higher incidence of
domestic help among Western families may help to account for
this.) As for TV sets, 48 percent of all Asian-African families had
one in 1970 as compared to merely 2 percent in 1960. (Western
families progressed to 55 percent in 1970 from a similar 2 percent
in 1960.)

Thus, while a very serious gap existed in 1960 between Asian-
African and Western-born families with regard to consumer durables, in 1970 this gap was almost entirely wiped out. There is one
exception: car ownership. Due to the vagaries of Israeli taxation,
a car is still a very expensive purchase, and it is here that the differences between Asian-African and Western-born families still remain pronounced, even though the Oriental families have managed
to double their ownership of cars during the decade under investigation. Only 8 percent of Asian-African families owned cars in

1970, compared to 4 percent in 1960: among Western-born families, the incidence has been 19 percent in 1970, compared to 14 percent in 1960. The highest incidence of car ownership is among Israeli-born families (30 percent in 1970, 23 percent in 1960), and since this category includes second-generation Israelis of both Western and Oriental background, this may somewhat mitigate these figures. But the gap in car ownership is there, and it visibly stands out when compared to the virtually equal distribution of other durable consumer goods.

A further dimension is that of housing. Here too, though the general picture is that of more crowding among families of Asian-African background, the emergence over the years of a lower density of persons per room is revealed by the report:

> During the past decade a significant improvement occurred in the housing conditions of the population as a whole. . . . The percentage of families living in a density of three or more per room dropped from 21 percent in 1960 to 8 percent in 1970.
>
> Among Asian-African born families who emigrated to Israel prior to the establishment of the state (1948), the proportion of families living in a density of three or more persons per room declined from 37 percent in 1960 to 12 percent in 1970. Among families of Asian-African origin who emigrated to Israel after the establishment of the state, the proportion of those living in a density of three or more persons per room declined during the same period from 49 percent to 17 percent.[8]

Though the last figure especially is most impressive, the committee eschews complacency even while pointing to dramatic progress. It adds immediately: "Despite this considerable improvement in housing conditions among families of Asian and African origin, the percentages of those families living in high density conditions is still relatively large."

The committee noted a similar picture of progress which, however, has not wholly eradicated differences with regard to education. Among the 14- to 17-year-olds in the total population the percentage of those attending secondary schools rose from 46 percent in 1963-1964 to 59 percent in 1969-1970. Among 14- to 17-year-olds of European-American origin, the percentage attending secondary schools rose from 61 percent in 1963-1964 to 77 percent in 1969, while among those of Asian-African origin it rose from 27 percent to 44 percent in the same period. At the university level, the increase in the percentage of 20- to 29-year-olds attending university has risen highest among those born in Asia-Africa—it doubled during the five-year period between 1964 and 1969. But the actual numbers involved are still rather low: this figure is, after all, a direct function of secondary school dropouts, and the break-through in secondary education among Asian-African immigrants occurred only in the last few years. While in 1964 only 0.8 percent of the Asian-African born of the 20- to 29-year-old age group attended university, their percentage rose to 1.6 percent in 1969; but the overall percentage for the entire 20- to 29-year-old age group was 4.1 percent in 1964 and 6.4 percent in 1970. Obviously higher education may be the last area of Israeli life where equality will be achieved, and looking at other immigration countries there is no doubt that integration in politics and economic activity sometimes precedes integration in higher education. Nonetheless, a marked increase in students of Asian-African backgrounds at the universities has been noticed in the last few years; while in the 1960s only about 5 percent of university students came from fami-lies of Oriental background, in 1969-1970 the figure was about 14 percent.[9] This is still too low, but progress is being made.

One reason for the increase has been not only better perform-ance on the part of the Israeli secondary school system, but also a special program, initially introduced by the Hebrew University and the army, by which several hundred soldiers from educationally deprived families were allowed nine months off from their military service to prepare for university study. During this time they con-tinued to receive pay and board from the army, but they partici-pated full-time in a specially designed reinforcement-oriented pre-academic year at the university, mainly aimed at increasing their general reading capabilities, mathematical skills and command of English. Even during the height of the "war of attrition" along the Suez Canal, when the strains on Israel's manpower were quite considerable, these courses were not discontinued. They have proved remarkably successful, having provided the university with highly motivated students from Oriental backgrounds and the pro-gram has now been adopted by other universities as well.[10]

Such then, is the backdrop against which the Black Panther phe-nomenon makes sense. Remarkable progress toward economic equality and political integration has been made by the Oriental communities in Israel, but a considerable gap still remains, and some visible pockets of poverty and underdevelopment plague the land-scape. For years one of the most outspoken advocates of a more active government policy in this respect has been the energetic director of the Institute of National Insurance, Dr. Israel Katz, who previously headed the School for Social Work at the Hebrew University. Claiming that welfare benefits have not caught up with the cost of living and that Israel has badly neglected the welfare of the poorest among its Oriental immigrants, Dr. Katz has been massively vindicated by the Black Panthers' emergence as a vivid testimony to the fact that though Israel was generally successful in closing the gap between Westerners and Orientals, this was not done quickly enough and left the utterly poor outside the general prosperity that engulfed most of the Oriental newcomers. Dr. Katz called for new priorities and bold new programs. Like many others in similar situations, so long as his critique was mainly incorporated in statistical reports, few people in government paid attention—they were only too naturally basking in what the overall statistics told them. But when the least favored took to the streets, every-body began to listen.

The ecology of the Jerusalem Black Panthers is of extreme sig-nificance. They did not come from the esthetically dismal, but nonetheless relatively decent though crowded housing projects on the western outskirts of Jerusalem—the Katamonim, Kiryat Hay-ovel or Kiryat Menachem. Their breeding ground was the Musrara Quarter, an erstwhile abandoned lower-class Arab neighborhood bordering on no-man's land on the old Israeli-Jordanian armistice line that cut Jerusalem in two prior to 1967. Even today the area remains scarred from the fierce fighting of 1948. Though only a couple of hundred yards from busy Jaffa Road, Jerusalem's main thoroughfare, this area was until 1967 a dead end. The population is almost entirely Oriental, and consists of some of the poorest families who somehow got left at the margin of Israel's social and economic development. Some couldn't afford even the heavily sub-sidized low-cost housing offered to new immigrants; others moved from development towns such as Beth Shean or Dimona, where they had been allocated housing, but preferred to live in Jerusalem for family reasons, or because they wanted to be in a large city rather than on the periphery. A high percentage of heads of fami-lies are disabled, or do not have any distinct occupation, nor have they acquired one since their immigration. In some families, the husband died or abandoned his wife and children. Musrara is thus the grimmest quarter, where the poorest element of Israel's population lives. And just as it would be misleading to generalize from conditions prevailing in Musrara about the position of Oriental immigrants in the country as a whole, so would it be overlooking the harsh truth to try to minimize the misery of places like Musrara because they are atypical and the great majority of Israel's Oriental immigrants live in conditions vastly different and better than those which prevail there.

A high degree of juvenile delinquency has been noted in Musrara over the years. The Israeli army as a rule does not draft youngsters with criminal records. This policy, which may or may not be justified on its own merits, created an unusual phenomenon in Musrara—a very high percentage of its young people have not served in the army. They have thus been deprived of the integrative impact military service has on young immigrants, and likewise deprived of the vocational skills which the army usually teaches very efficiently to recruits with a low educational profile. Their chances of upward mobility through getting a relatively well-paid job as skilled workers are consequently much lower than those of young people with a similar background who have served in the army. Moreover, prospective employers in Israel usually ask applicants for their military service record, and a blank on the form dealing with military service very often results in rejection of the job applicant as it implies either a criminal or psychoneurotic record. Finally, in a country where military service is very highly valued, being rejected by the armed forces tends to class one as a pariah. One of the Black Panthers' most adamant demands was to be drafted into the army—and it is this demand even, if nothing else, that should make any observer aware of the difference between the kind of grievance which motivated the Israeli Black Panthers and the "real" Panthers in the United States and elsewhere.[11]

In other words, the Panthers want to get *inside*. With Israel at the stage of often vulgar conspicuous consumption, in which Westerners and Orientals share alike, the small minority which is left outside consumerism feels very harshly hit. The introduction of TV in 1967, mainly aimed at trying to win over the Arabs under Israeli rule, has not been remarkably successful in its propagandistic mission. But it has been instrumental in heightening consumption expectations among all sectors of the population, and those who couldn't keep up with the Cohens became much more frustrated than they would have been without the goading influences of the TV set.

One should also add that the patterns of immigration to Israel have changed in the last few years, and add to the feeling of help-lessness and the perceptions of discrimination. So long as the new-comers were more or less of the same social group as the slightly older immigrants, the ever-increasing financial help that Israel could afford to give to new immigrants didn't visibly irritate the older ones. But when the new immigrants turned out to be relatively well-off Americans, or Russian Jews with pronounced middle-class tastes fostered by the traditional Soviet discrimination in favor of the intelligentsia, the new housing put up for these new immigrants, and the sometimes very liberal loans granted to them by a govern-ment that felt it had to attract professional people from the West, became a symbol of the gap between the way Israel neglected its "forgotten 10 percent" and the zest with which it catered to the more well-to-do European-type immigrants, whether from the United States or the Soviet Union.

These special tax benefits, housing loans and mortgages which the government has been offering to immigrants from the West have triggered off a number of protests from Israeli-born young couples as well. They pointed out that a young American couple, settling in Israel, is far better off in terms of government help than even a relatively comfortable Israeli-born young couple. The Ameri-can couple, for instance, can buy a car and other appliances with-out having to pay the crippling Israeli sales tax, which sometimes amounts to 200 to 300 percent of the purchase price; they don't have to pay income tax during their first years in the country; they don't have to pay travel tax when they travel abroad during their first years; and they get a much larger and cheaper mortgage for their house.

Paradoxically the Israeli sabras and the poorest among the Ori-ental communities found themselves likewise discriminated against by the government's policy of encouraging aliyah (immigration) from the affluent West. In recent months, under pressure from these two groups (in Tel Aviv young Israeli-born couples occupied some of the building sites of the Ministry of Housing), the authori-ties have decided to reduce some of the special benefits given to these groups of immigrants. It should be added that these benefits were technically open also to immigrants from Oriental countries, but in most cases they could not afford to make use of them.

One should also add that Israel has been so preoccupied in re-cent years with the aftermath of the Six Day War that the very fact that the country was having full employment in many cases lulled people into believing that the internal problems have been solved. How much ink and newsprint went into discussing the minutiae of where exactly the future boundary between Israel and the Arab countries should be—at a time when it appeared that no meaningful negotiations were in prospect? How much spleen was wasted in defending or denigrating the idea of a "Greater Israel?" In the last few years the Cabinet spent more time discussing and debating the touchy issue of future Jewish settlement in Hebron than in dealing with the existing quality of life of tens of thousands of Jews already in Israel.

From this point of view the Black Panther outburst had a salutary effect. Whatever damage it may have done to Israel's image abroad (and the damage, obviously, has been considerable), whatever illusions it might have kindled in the hearts of enemies and genteel skeptics about "Israel breaking up from within," it has also jolted the establishment into action. Hundreds of millions of pounds were mobilized for additional housing projects for lower-income groups; scores of remedial educational programs were introduced into the educational system; the nation's conscience has been aroused, and money—always a visible indicator of the workings of conscience coupled with the political instincts of self-preservation—is pouring into the more depressed areas of Israel's society.

But ultimately Israel will be able to achieve a solution only by reordering some of its priorities. There is no doubt that the easy opportunities for making big money which have been available since 1967 have to be reviewed in the context of the Israeli vision of an egalitarian and socialistically oriented society. Finance Minister Sapir, in his zest to develop Israel's economy, has been repeatedly accused that his policies upset the delicate balance between the predominant public sector and the private sector in the economy. There is no doubt that Israel's economic policy of attracting foreign Jewish investors has resulted in pumping vast amounts of public money into the private sector in the form of inducements such as loans, tax exemptions and rebates. This obviously stimulates the economy and created thousands of jobs which enabled numerous Oriental families to better their economic position. But it also tended to make Israel less of a socialist and egalitarian society. It may be that some of Israel's economic leaders do not have the sensibility which should tell them that if Israel were just to become another Brooklyn or Golders Green, the whole effort would not be worth the candle. Yitzhak Ben Aharon, secretary general of Histadrut, may not always be most politic in voicing his grievances; but it is obvious that many trends in the Israeli economy have to be halted and reversed if the social vision of Israel as a just society, and not only as a haven, is to be preserved.

In the last few years various prophets of doom have predicted a dire future for the Jewish state. If it would engage in unending war, it was argued, it would inevitably become the Prussia of the Middle East, a militaristic state, ultimately ruled by the army. The end of the war is not yet in sight, and Israel had the army at its center since 1948, and in a way had been fighting since the first attempts of the return to Zion. Yet the civilian nature of its army has not been undermined, and if the Spartan nightmare haunts some people's minds, one should point out that the Athenian golden age of democracy and the flourishing of the arts was accompanied by a warlike history as belligerent as that of Sparta. Some social structures manage to sustain civil society even under stress; others don't; and if today there are Spartans in the Middle East, they speak Arabic, not Hebrew. Even a most critical observer of Israel will have to agree that it is precisely among the army people—and in the universities—that one finds much milder views about the Arab-Israeli conflict than among the more ideologically inclined civilians of the older generation. Few doubt nowadays that the farmer and general from Nahalal is much more accommodating than many civilians in the government.

There is still another prophecy of doom: namely, that Israel holds together only because of external threat. Remove this, so the argument goes, and the Israelis will be at each other's throats: religious vs. secularists, European vs. Orientals, in short, *bellum omnium contra omnes.*

How much wishful thinking is implied in such views of Israel's future is beside the point. What is material is the ignorance manifested by such views. Obviously, internal differences are muted when the country is involved in deadly daily warfare. But this view implies that Israel has always been, due to the enormous external pressures, a nation united only in the aim of survival, and that the inner differences are only now beginning to raise their head.

Nothing could be further from the truth. Israel's President Zalman Shazar is reputed to have told President Johnson, who complained to him about the difficulty of being the President of two hundred million people, "I am, Mr. President, the President of two-and-a-half million Presidents." Few societies have been as divided as first the Jewish community in Palestine and later Israeli society. Under the British, the three Jewish underground organizations were not only disagreeing among themselves on how to fight the British, but were sometimes also fighting each other. In the 1948 war of independence, the legitimacy of the infant state of Israel was severely challenged by the *Altalena* affair. In the early 1950s, the then Stalinist Mapam was viewing the Soviet Union as the "Second Homeland," and at least once, during the debate on German reparations, it appeared as if Herut might be challenging the legitimacy of parliamentary democracy in Israel. And the early sixties saw almost all political debate embroiled in the aftermath of the Lavon Affair. Yet beneath all these sometimes violent disagreements, a basic consensus remained at work, and Israel's unity in adversity was never that of a regimented, uniform and conformist phalanx, but one achieved through trial and error, through debate and sometimes violent confrontation, between various sectors of a very individualistic and pluralistic society.

The present challenge of integrating the Oriental communities is not a new one. The recent outbursts only pinpoint those areas where it had misfired, and not its overall failure. With the takeover of local politics by the Oriental communities, with the economic gaps generally narrowing between Westerns and Orientals, the structure of Israeli society is definitely changing in the direction of further integration of the non-Western groups. That the process is not easy, that one tends now more than ever to see Israel as it is, warts and all, is a measure of Israel's growing normalcy. That Israel has to set its eyes on much higher achievements, and that it is responding to the internal challenges just as to the external ones, is a measure of the vitality of its social vision.

NOTES

1. See Avraham Brichte, "Ha-shinuyim beherkev ha-Knesset ha-shevi'it" [Changes in the Composition of the 7th Knesset] in *Medina u'Mimshal*, Vol. I, No. 2 (Jerusalem, 1971), pp. 150-153.

2. This claim has been recently most cogently argued by Daniel J. Elazar in his *Israel: From Ideological to Territorial Democracy* (New York: General Learning Press module, 1971).

3. See Shevach Weiss, *Typologia shel ha-nivharim he-lokaliyim ushe'elat ha-yatzivut bashilton he-mekomi* [*The Typology of Local Representatives and the Problem of the Stability of Local Government*] Jerusalem, 1970, p. 82. Dr. Weiss, who heads the department of political science at Haifa University, has compiled some extremely helpful data on local government in Israel.

4. We have disregarded in our survey the Arab local government bodies in Israel: this is an area where recent development has also been of extreme significance for future Jewish-Arab relations, but it merits a special discussion which is outside the scope of this article.

5. The Endogamy Index has thus come down from 0.78 in 1960 to 0.67 in 1969 (*Statistical Abstract of Israel 1971*, p. 70).

6. Report of the Committee on Income Distribution and Social Inequality (Tel Aviv, 1971).

7. Ibid., pp. 4-5.

8. Ibid., pp. 14-15.

9. Out of 33,383 students enrolled in all Israeli institutions of higher learning in 1969-1970, 3,307 were born in Asia and Africa, and an additional 1,040 were Israeli-born children of Asia-Africa-born parents (*Statistical Abstracts of Israel 1971*, p. 568).

10. As chairman of the department of political science at the Hebrew University, I was myself rather surprised to note when routinely going through the questionnaires of the departmental teaching assistants, that 9 out of 41 were of Oriental background. This was higher than the percentage of Oriental students at the university as a whole, and a similar ratio would probably not have been duplicated in other departments. Whatever the reasons for this phenomenon, it was *not* the outcome of any conscious policy of favoring students of Oriental background over other groups.

11. As a consequence of the Panthers' grievances about the draft, the army has now revised its policy with regard to youngsters with criminal or police records, and they are being drafted. It seems highly probable that this measure will considerably diminish the incidence of further similar outbursts.

18

Raphael Patai

WESTERN AND ORIENTAL CULTURE IN ISRAEL

There is a famous Talmudic anecdote about the pagan who came to the great Hillel and said to him: "I will convert to your religion if you can teach me your Torah while I stand on one leg." Unhesitatingly, Hillel answered: "Do not do unto others what you don't want others to do to you. This is the essence of the law: all the rest is commentary." Like Hillel, I think that the gist of what I want to say in this essay can be compressed into one sentence: Genetically, the Oriental Jewish population of Israel is rapidly absorbing the Ashkenazi Jews of the country, while culturally it is the Ashkenazi Jews who are absorbing the Oriental Jews. This is the essence of what I want to say: the rest is commentary.

The first part of the commentary that follows, then, pertains to the identity of the Oriental Jews. Who are they and what is their origin? Briefly, the Oriental Jews are those Jews who have lived in Asia and Africa ever since their ancestors were exiled from the land of Israel. From 732 BCE on, contingents of the population of Israel and Judah were moved into Assyria, Babylonia and Egypt. Subsequently, their children and later exiles went from these countries, as well as from Palestine itself, to other lands in Asia and Africa, including Turkey, Syria, Persia, the Arabian Peninsula and the entire North African littoral. The descendants of these exiles

307

remained in the various countries of the Near and Middle East and in contiguous areas of Central Asia, for two to two-and-a-half millennia. These, then, are the so-called Oriental Jews, whose masses returned to Israel after the Jewish state won its independence in 1948.

An offshoot group of these Oriental Jews moved across the Straits of Gibraltar when the Moors conquered Spain in the early eighth century. A few hundred years later, when the Spaniards and the Portuguese retook the peninsula, the Jews remained in their cities of residence, and exchanged their Arabic mother tongue for Spanish. After their expulsion from Spain in 1492 they retained their Ladino (medieval Spanish with an admixture of Hebrew words) in their new places of settlement, in North Africa, the Ottoman Empire and elsewhere. These Jews and their present-day descendants are called *Sephardim*, or Sephardi Jews.

As to the Ashkenazi (or "German") Jews, their origin goes back to the expansion of the Roman Empire into Central Europe, and to the settlement of Jews in the early Slavonic principalities to the north of the Black Sea. In the Middle Ages all these Jewish communities adopted a form of German ("Yiddish") as their language, and came to be called *Ashkenazi* (i.e., "German") Jews.

Hand in hand with the cultural ethnic differentiation went the processes of genetic differentiation among the Jewish communities. As an overall generalization one can state that the Jews exhibited a marked tendency to assimilate to the genetic configuration of their host peoples.

Another development that began around the year 1000 CE was the gradual historical process which can be called the "Ashkenization" of the Jewish people. This, too, came about as a result of the adoption of the major demographic and cultural traits of the non-Jewish environment by the Jews in every part of the globe. About the year 1000 CE, when the total number of Jews in the world was 1,500,000, some 95 percent of all Jews were Sephardi and Orientals. Thereafter, the number of the Sephardi and Oriental Jews remained roughly stationary (as did that of the Asian and African peoples), while that of the Ashkenazi Jews increased, at first slowly, then, from about 1800 on, rapidly, paralleling the increase of the European peoples in the wake of the industrial revolution. Despite the terrible setbacks suffered by the Ashkenazi Jews, such as the Chmielnicki massacres in the seventeenth century and other periodic bloodbaths, the numerical relation of the Ashkenazim to the other two divisions of the Jewish people has become practically reversed in the last thousand years. In 1939, before the German holocaust, the number of Ashkenazim was estimated at 15,000,000, while that of the Sephardim and Oriental Jews at 1,500,000, or about the same as it had been throughout the Middle Ages.

Following World War II the Ashkenazi rates of natural increase dwindled to a point of zero population growth. At the same time the very high infant and general mortality rates of the Asian and African peoples were gradually reduced, which resulted, among other things, in the increase of the Sephardi and Oriental Jewish communities whose numbers roughly doubled from 1945 (1,350,000) to 1973 (about 2,700,000). Those same years saw the ingathering of the most of the Sephardi and Oriental Jews in the land of Israel, where their number in 1973 was estimated at close to a million and a half, or about 60 percent of the total Jewish population of the country.

At present, one of the significant differences between the Ashkenazi and the Sephardi-Oriental sectors of Israel's Jewish population is in their basic demographic rates. The birthrate and the natural increase of the Ashkenazi sector are very low, while those of the Sephardi-Oriental groups are very high. The Ashkenazi sector, barring immigration, can be foreseen to remain stationary; the Sephardi-Orientals, on the other hand, are rapidly increasing. Their high birthrate, coupled with the low infant and general mortality (thanks to the excellent medical services available in Israel) resulted in the early 1970s in a natural increase which, if maintained, will lead to a doubling of their numbers within less than a generation. To this must be added the genetic results of the growing intermarriage rates between Ashkenazi and Sephardi-Oriental Jews (close to 20 percent of all Jewish marriages in the early 1970s). The total genetic effect of all these demographic factors and processes is that the Sephardi-Oriental sector is gradually, and not even too slowly, absorbing the Ashkenazi Jews of Israel.

Thus far the explanations of the first part of my Hillelian statement. Its second part will likewise be discussed only briefly.

As far as the cultural scene in Israel is concerned it has been pointed out by numerous observers that it is the Western culture, partly brought along by Ashkenazi immigrants and partly developed by them in the country itself, which has largely replaced the traditional cultures of the various Middle Eastern Jewish communities. Twenty years ago I wrote a study concerning issues of the meeting of the Oriental and the modern Western cultures in Israel.

In that study, entitled *Israel Between East and West,* I posed the question of what could be assumed to be the shape of things to come in Israel in the cultural arena, and I dwelt in particular on the possible contribution of the Sephardi-Oriental communities to the future cultural physiognomy of Israel. In the postscript added 18 years later (in 1969) to the second edition of the book I had to record that the intervening relatively short period has shown this contribution to be extremely limited, and that the dominant tone and quality of the new Israeli culture was unquestionably Western; or, to put it differently, that modern Israeli culture differed to no greater extent from a theoretical generalized Western culture than did, say, British, French or Italian culture.

This means that the Sephardi-Oriental majority of Israel's population, upon entering the mainstream of Israeli life, gave up all or almost all of its traditional cultural heritage. Space does not allow discussion or even enumeration of all these abandoned cultural features, but a few can be mentioned by way of illustration. In Israel today, there exists no polygyny, no child marriage, no female illiteracy, no itinerant peddling, no traditional handicrafts; the patriarchal, patrilocal, extended family is on its way out; the traditional uncontrolled fertility is rapidly being brought under control; the old costumes and utensils have disappeared; folk medicine, amulets, remedies, magic and the like are derided by the young; the traditional folk arts are almost gone except where purposely fostered by modern institutions; the rich oral folklore of the Oriental communities has become a matter for a few interested scholars to gather and record from the mouths of the oldtimers; the traditional communal institutions have been replaced by copies of their Western Jewish counterparts; the many and variegated traditional occupations are a thing of the past; and so the list could go on and on.

In all these areas and in many more, Western forms (i.e., their modern Israeli versions) have replaced the traditional features. The old people perhaps try to hold on to the traditions of their community, but the young ones, those who went through Israeli schools and were exposed to the great equalizing and modernizing influence of the Israeli army, do not want to hear of what they consider old-fashioned nonsense, and embrace wholeheartedly and eagerly anything and everything that modern Israel has to offer. Typically, when the Israeli Black Panthers want to have a full share of the advantages the Western immigrants receive in the country, all the benefits they claim are of a Western type. There is no

Israeli equivalent of the American Negroes' dashiki, Afro hairdo, Swahili language and the like. The typical demand of the young Oriental Jews in Israel is to be permitted to live like and be like the Ashkenazi Jews.

What all this boils down to is that the contributions of the Sephardi-Oriental Jews to the modern culture of the country can be enumerated on the fingers of one hand: the Oriental food is one; some Oriental jewelry, embroidery, basketry is another; Oriental musical influences, especially in popular song, is the third; the partly-Sephardic pronunciation of Hebrew can be added as the fourth element. I would be at a loss if I were pressed to find quickly a fifth one. Perhaps the religious field might yield some such features. It is thus clear that by the early 1970s the cultural absorption of the Sephardi-Oriental Jews by the Ashkenazi Jews in Israel has become an almost accomplished fact.

Looking forward to, say, the year 2000, I can foresee an Israeli population which will be genetically largely Sephardi-Oriental while culturally largely Western. Within the general Middle Eastern context this will mean that in the very midst of the Arab sea there will be a tiny island, Israel, which while genetically not too different from the Arab-Muslim world, will be a bastion of modern Western culture in the middle of a world area which at that time will foreseeably still be struggling to modernize, industrialize and democratize. And as far as the Jewish people as a whole is concerned, it will in the year 2000 consist of two main parts: a swarthy, Hebrew-speaking Oriental part living in Israel, and a lighter, English-speaking part, concentrated mostly in America. Both parts, however, will be united by a respect for Jewish religion and tradition, by a love for the land of Israel, and by a firm commitment to Western culture and values.

19

Celia S. Heller

THE EMERGING
CONSCIOUSNESS OF
THE ETHNIC PROBLEM
AMONG THE JEWS
OF ISRAEL

The rise of the *Pantherim Shehorim*, the Black Panthers of Israel, focused the attention of the Israelis on and made known to the world the presence of a problem that has been evolving since Israeli independence. The existence of the problem was obscured by the dazzling success in integrating large numbers of European immigrants. Even though there was some perception of "the problem of Orientals" it was overshadowed by the more basic problem that faced Israel from the very beginning of its independence, that of national survival in a sea of enemies. There may be significance in the fact that the "Oriental problem" came to the surface at a time when the war front was relatively quiet, and only now, since the emergence of the Panthers, are voices beginning to be heard that these two sets of problems—that of national survival and that of the Orientals—are closely connected.

Even now, despite its notoriety, the problem which the Panthers represent has been neither thoroughly acknowledged nor even defined adequately. Its ethnic character is often denied or minimized by influential Israelis. But from a sociological perspective it clearly constitutes an ethnic dilemma. And for the sociologist who chooses to address himself to it, it means focusing on a negative aspect of Israeli society rather than the positive features which have won such recognition as extraordinary accomplishments. In Israel—the country founded on the principle of the unity of the Jewish people—distinct ethnic groups have emerged among the Jewish population since independence, and processes now underway might transform it into an ethnically stratified society. The source of major tensions in Israel is not inequality per se but the fact that the inequality is closely pinned to ethnicity. The range of economic inequality is still rather narrow: income differentials, although widening, are among the narrowest in the world. The problem lies in the continuously growing coalescence of ethnicity and class in Israel, a reality that sharply contradicts the national ideology of the "ingathering of exiles" and their amalgamation into a unified nation. Unless the country mounts an all-out offensive of imaginative and effective programs on a scale that would counteract the processes which move in the direction of crystallizing a system of ethnic stratification, such a system will come into being. It will consist of two major ethnic strata (and some marginal groups)— Europeans and Orientals, light and dark—separate and unequal: one dominant and the other subordinate.

The historical irony is that such a system would develop without being willed into existence by either the founders, or the dominant stratum. On the contrary, such a result has never been anticipated by this stratum, whose ideology proclaimed and whose social policies were aimed at creating a unified nation. This is especially worth noting because, in surveying multi-ethnic societies, we find that in the great bulk of cases subordination is "the result of coercive subjugation by dominant groups. . . . Evidence shows conclusively that the overriding relationship has been one of force and compulsion."[1] And yet this historical fact is not likely to serve as a consolation for the underprivileged in Israel, the Jews from the Islamic countries, and particularly their children.

The very fact that the term "ethnic," affixed to one of the major problems facing Israel, is meant not to designate the relation between Jewish and non-Jewish groups, but the relation between different Jewish groups, is of utmost sociological and historical significance. Jews throughout the world have been regarded and continue to be regarded by sociologists as members of a single ethnic group.[2] Such is the case even in the United States, for example, where the three major waves of immigration—Sephardic, German and East European—showed marked cultural differences from one another.

The big post-independence *aliyot*, like the immigrations to Palestine that preceded them, consisted by and large of people who, in their native countries, were considered to be ethnically Jews, and who considered themselves Jews. There was some awareness among them that Jews of other countries differed in some respects, but the notions of these differences were rather vague. Also, these differences were thought to be relatively minor, compared with the joint fate, the shared historical past and the common religious faith that bound all Jews. And yet a process of fission, of splitting into two ethnic groups took place in Israel—the respective groups variously referred to as Ashkenazim and Sephardim, or Europeans and Orientals. This process could also be viewed from another angle: the fusion of multiple groups of heterogeneous background—hailing from many geocultural areas—into the above two ethnic groups.

It might be fitting at this point to note the element of error in the labels used for these groups. For example, "Sephardic" and "Oriental" are often employed in Israel as if they were antonyms to "European." The term "Sephardi" originally applied to all the Spanish Jews who, after the Inquisition, lived both in Europe—Greece, Turkey, etc.—and in "Oriental" countries, Egypt and North Africa. They were bound, in addition to country of origin, by a common language, *Ladino,* and common religious rituals. If the Sephardim differed in cultural characteristics from the bulk of European Jews who were Ashkenazim, they also differed thus from the bulk of Oriental Jews. And yet today the term "Sephardim" is applied to the masses of Jews from the Islamic countries, most of whom in fact are not Sephardic.

THE GEOCULTURAL COMPOSITION
OF THE JEWS IN PALESTINE

Even though the bulk of the Jewish community living in Palestine before the start of immigration from Eastern Europe in the 1880s consisted of Sephardim, most of the Sephardim came after World War I. Also coinciding with the main waves of Central and East European immigration was the arrival of Jews from Oriental countries. Thus, apart from the Eastern and Central European Jews, there were the following communities of Jews in the yishuv (settlement) of Palestine prior to independence: Sephardim, Persians, Kurds, Babylonians, Yemenites, Moghrebites (from Morocco), as well as Jews from Bokhara, Haleb, Urfa, Georgia and Afghanistan. Each group had some particular cultural traits which distinguished it from the others. But the Sephardim—regardless of whether they hailed from Europe or Egypt or North Africa—were especially marked off from the others.[3]

However most of the Jews who came to Palestine during the British Mandate were Ashkenazim, Jews from Eastern and Central Europe. As a matter of fact when Israeli scholars speak of the major waves of immigration prior to independence, the aliyot, they usually refer solely to these immigrants who were inspired by Zionism to return to Zion. The tenets of this secular ideology were imaginative responses to the bitter realities of East European Jewry; basically, Zionism was formulated by European Jews and for European Jews. (The knowledge that the early Zionists had of the Jews in Asia and Africa was very slight.) The realization of this ideology led to both the sought-after objective of the re-emergence of a nation and the unanticipated consequence of ethnic division within the nation.

THE RISE OF ETHNIC GROUPS AFTER INDEPENDENCE

An important factor in the formation of ethnic divisions among the Jews of Israel is the overall goal (inspired by ideology) that the oldtimers—those Ashkenazim who pioneered the country—and especially the governing elite, set for the large number of immigrants who came after Israel was established. The goal is to some extent implied in the much-used Israeli term "absorption" of immigrants: they expected the immigrants to shed the values and behavior in which they were socialized and to conform to the values and behavior of the existing secularized pioneering community. It was very similar to what has been characterized as the philosophy of "Anglo-conformity" in the United States.[4] The elite did not recognize that any of the non-European Jewish immigrants had a different overall goal, a pluralistic one. Their way of life was strongly traditional and they expected that, having held on to their traditional ways while living among Gentiles, they would find it much easier to practice them in a Jewish land.

> They came hoping to be able to follow their own way of life fully and securely and did not envisage any drastic change. They were not consciously prepared to alter either their economic and occupational structure or the basic tenets of the social and cultural life and their traditionally religious Jewish consciousness. They did not lack positive identification with the new Jewish community in Palestine—their traditional Jewish faith and Messianic aspirations embraced all Jews. . . . Most . . . intended to perpetuate their former ways of life, without social segregation or political subjugation. This, however, proved impossible within the framework of the Yishuv.[5]

The foremost Israeli sociologist, S. N. Eisenstadt, thus described the attitudes of the Jews coming from the Islamic countries prior to independence. However, these words also fit in a great measure the larger number of non-European immigrants who came after independence was won. One could trace the roots of the relative separation of the Sephardic and Oriental communities from the rest of the yishuv to the Mandate period. Unlike the Central and East European groups, the members of these communities were not institutionally dispersed. They formed separate neighborhoods in Jerusalem and in Tiberias. They also maintained their own schools. And one may note the beginning of separate political parties: the Yemenite Party and the Sephardic Bloc. Although the origin of the phenomenon could thus be placed in the Mandate period, its full development came after independence. Great numbers of immigrants arrived from the Islamic countries, and what was expected of them was conformity. That conformity was expected of the immigrants is even reflected in the "objective" analysis of Israeli sociologists—themselves members of the dominant group—who speak of the failure of absorption and integration of Oriental as compared with European immigrants. The main thrust of their analysis is on the characteristics of the Oriental immigrants which impeded their successful integration. Were these sociologists Orientals, they would more likely focus on the failure of the governing elite to be concerned with the goals of Jews hailing from the Islamic countries, the failure to recognize the goals and the ways of these people as legitimate alternatives in Israel. To give a simple example, the skills of the artisans coming from these countries were not sufficiently recognized, valued and exploited.

Prior to independence, Zionists argued the issue of selective versus indiscriminate immigration. Those who were bent on creating a utopian society favored the former. However, their argument proved irrelevant in the face of the holocaust. Thus, the right of return became the prevailing philosophy of post-independence immigration. First to be brought were the survivors of the displaced person camps and Eastern Europe, and then the Jews from the Islamic countries. In terms of numbers, the immigration was split almost equally: half of the immigrants (54.6 percent) came from the Middle East and North Africa. Conformity was expected of both categories, but neither worked out in accordance with this expectation. "Neither of the two types of new immigrants," says Talmon, "had much training, aptitude, or taste for the utopian collectivist endeavor." And yet in the first case, the Israeli scholars speak of successful absorption and in the latter of failures in absorption. The fact is that the European immigrants succeeded in transforming society and steering it away from the collectivist endeavor and along the path of modern development. As Talmon expresses it: "An extremely egalitarian society, based on voluntary teamwork, changed almost overnight." [6] The rhetoric of the governing elite remained egalitarian; the social structure was no longer so.

The immigrants from the underdeveloped Islamic lands had to adjust to a rapidly industrializing society. They were preached to in terms of egalitarian and collectivist ideals; they were often treated in terms of a divisive, rugged and impersonal individualism. The implementation of the goals of the "ingathering of exiles" was assigned to bureaucracies, which contrasted with the direct contact between oldtimers and newcomers so characteristic of the pre-state period. And how did the bureaucracies implement it? Upon arrival the immigrants were given financial aid, housing on easy terms and some help in finding work. But "after that they were left more or less to their own devices with little continuous guidance or help." [7] Left to themselves, the immigrants from Europe were able to cope comparatively well in the Israeli society that they were shaping along the lines of industrialization and consumerism. They possessed the necessary technical skills to a much greater extent than the immigrants from the Islamic countries. Their central values tended to be secular, universalistic and achievement-oriented. In contrast, the deeply rooted value-orientation of the Oriental immigrants—familism, personalism and traditionalism—were not conducive to effective functioning and advancement in a rapidly changing industrial society,[8] however praiseworthy on other grounds.

Another factor that must not be overlooked is that most of the groups arriving from the Islamic countries had become separated from their modern and intellectual elites.[9] Thus, they were lacking leaders to pave the way and guide them on the new road. A notable exception to this pattern were the Yemenites whose "absorption" was quite "successful." [10] (Nevertheless, they are now being pushed into the dichotomous ethnic classification together with other groups from the Islamic countries, under the "Oriental" label.

Along with the perception of success in absorbing immigrants from European countries and of the lack of such success with many groups from the Islamic countries evolved the dichotomous labels and characterizations of the two multicultural categories. As far as the labels are concerned, some are considered respectable (Ashkenazim versus Sephardim, immigrants from the Orient versus immigrants from Europe, etc.) and others derogatory, such as *frankim* and *shehorim* (blacks), used by the Europeans to designate the others, and *vus-vus*, used by Orientals for the Europeans.[11] The dichotomous characterization developed as European immigrants who made it in the system began to look down on the others as being responsible for the inferior conditions in which they found themselves. After all, went the rationalization, they all started from the same point. And the governing elite was largely oblivious to the phenomenon that was shaping up before their eyes, for their egalitarian ideology and rhetoric prevented them from perceiving the new reality.

The rise of negative stereotypes of Orientals has hardly been studied in Israel. It would be especially interesting to explore how the stereotypes originally attached to specific geocultural groups with the greatest problems of adjustment—Moroccans and Kurds—have been extended to the broad ethnic category of Orientals (including Yemenites). These stereotypes are sometimes completely erroneous, but more often consist of "inflexible exaggeration of actual tendencies or attributes." [12] They constitute the predisposition to respond to individuals considered to be Orientals in a different way. In the everyday unguarded conversation of European Israelis you hear frequent allusions to the supposedly undesirable physical or social traits of the Orientals. "You look like a frank in this dress," I heard a young university student say to her mother. "We would like you to live in this house. You know, let them be well, but we don't like frankim in our houses," said a respected builder, while discussing the sale of an apartment.

Then there is the frequent talk of the danger of "Levantinization" of the country. The elite and not-so-elite pride themselves on their Western culture and look down on the others, when in fact the culture of some of the people from the Oriental countries, as Segre pointed out, "was in many ways more refined than that of many European-born Israelis." [13] The dignity and honor of their traditional ways are outside the field of perception of most Europeans. We know that in modern times the most common justification for differential treatment of ethnic groups has been racism. In Israel the European Jews are increasingly rationalizing and justifying their behavior toward the Oriental Jews by invoking "culturalism," to coin a phrase, the idea of culturally inherited superiority and inferiority. It differs from racism, which invokes biologically inherited superiority and inferiority. Still, it is intriguing, and in itself merits investigation, that the very Jews who suffered so much in Europe and now live in Israel take such pride in European ways and values and look down on the non-European Jews, even when the latter display traditional Jewish ways and values.

Thus, hand in hand with the dichotomous characterization is the presence of discrimination, the differential treatment of individuals who are considered to be Orientals. As far back as 1962, Judith Shuval spoke of the "growing evidence of certain forms of scapegoating," but hastened to add that "only rarely have these assumed extreme forms of expression." She and other Israeli sociologists point to the absence of quotas or formal discrimination on jobs to emphasize how mild the pattern is. Other Israelis of European background tend to refer to the absence of formal discrimination by way of dismissing the charge of the existence of discrimination in general. Nevertheless, Shuval specified that prejudice and discrimination generally manifest themselves "on the level of exclusiveness, unwillingness to maintain social relationships with certain groups, stereotyped perception . . . verbal hostility." [14] Although objectively speaking these manifestations may not be extreme (as compared with discriminatory practices in many other societies), the people subjected to them experience them acutely, precisely because the perpetrators are Jews and Israelis. In the countries where they formerly lived they were victims of prejudice and discrimination because they were Jews; now in Israel they are singled out because they are Orientals. The latter, although milder in form, may often be just as hard or harder to endure.

ETHNIC CONSCIOUSNESS OF ORIENTAL JEWS

One of the empirical generalizations in sociology, based on considerable evidence, is that under certain conditions people who are socially classified together come to conceive of themselves as being of a kind. Such a process is now taking place in Israel, and there is a growing sense of ethnic identity and consciousness among the people who are classified and treated as Orientals. Although originally they regarded themselves as Jews from different lands—Kurdish, Moroccan, Persian, Algerian Jews, etc.—increasingly they display a sense of common identity derived from the recognition of their common situation.

This growing sense of common identity has its base in the prejudice and differential treatment, discussed above, to which Orientals are subjected. It is also closely related to the objective inequality between their situation and that of the Europeans. As was stated at the beginning, a system of ethnic stratification is crystallizing: a system of structured inequality in the things that count in that society,[15] closely pinned to ethnicity. Much material exists on the extent of this inequality, especially the economic: occupation, income and wealth. Recently Israeli political scientists and sociologists have been turning their attention to the inequality in power. The latter is of increasing significance because of the growing importance of political power as a criterion of evaluation and as an avenue of access to high economic position.[16] For want of space we shall not review the data on the extent of objective inequality. Suffice it to say that, whatever we use as an indicator of socioeconomic class, we find a consistent and high correlation between class and ethnicity. The Oriental Jews are heavily concentrated in the lower social strata, regardless of length of stay in Israel.

Let us now make explicit what is implicit in the term "structured." It indicates the following: not only is there inequality, but this inequality is in the process of being perpetuated from generation to generation. Note that when we examine Israel's inequality today we are no longer confined to two categories of immigrants whose adjustment was substantially different. We also encounter two categories of sabras—young people born in Israel—whose life chances and life styles are different: those of European and those of Oriental background. Need it be said that the life chances of Orientals are inferior and that their style of life is considered inferior?

There is a much smaller rate of intergenerational upward mobility among Orientals than among Europeans. One of the most important factors in the low rate of upward mobility among the Orientals has been their high birth rate. The consistent findings from innumerable studies in many societies indicate that the upwardly mobile from the lower strata tend to come from small families. And yet for obvious reasons of national defense, little is done in Israel to discourage large families among the Orientals.

The Orientals—even the young sabras among them—differ substantially from the Europeans in their perception of opportunities for advancement. A much larger portion of them view Israeli society as a closed society. A study of occupational choice, conducted among urban youth in the sixties, found that only 2 percent of those of European origin but 29 percent of those of Oriental origin thought that there were *no* possibilities for advancement in Israel.[17]

What must be at least mentioned here is the formation of what Gunnar Myrdal would call an underclass, a group marginal within society, consisting predominantly of Oriental Jews, both born abroad and in Israel. It is composed of unemployed and underemployed and their families, for whom opportunities are becoming more closed as they grow more plentiful for the rest of the nation. Symptomatic of the situation is their high rate of family disorganization and juvenile delinquency, as compared with the rest of the nation. All this ought to be placed in juxtaposition with a belief very prevalent in Israel during the large immigration from the Islamic countries: if the immigrants would not become fully integrated, certainly their children, born in Israel, would.

Crucial to the perpetuation of economic, power and prestige in-equality from generation to generation is inequality in education. Educational achievement is the main source of occupational advancement in a bureaucratized industrial society. In the words of Parsons, "Experience in the course of formal education is to be regarded as a series of apprenticeships for adult occupational roles." [18] The tremendous inequality in educational attainment between European and Oriental Jews in Israel is well documented. Perhaps it can be capsulized in the following figures: Orientals constitute 60 percent of the children entering primary grades, 25 percent of those in secondary schools and 10 percent of the university students. It is true that the absolute level of educational attainment of those born in Israel is substantially above that of their parents. However, the gap between the sabras whose parents were born in the Orient and those of European-born parents is greater than between young immigrants from these two geographic areas.[19]

Those Israelis who maintain that ethnic stratification is not emerging often point to the growing rate of intermarriage. According to the data available, marriage across the Oriental-European line grew from 9 percent in 1952 to 15 percent in 1962, and there are indications tht the rate has gone up since 1962. However, one must note that "Israel-born of European origin" citizens deviate from the pattern of increased intermarriage, and their "inclination to marry within the group has even strengthened." [20] What is even more crucial, those who argue that ethnic stratification will not crystallize in Israel fail to face up to the fact that ethnic inequality may be perpetuated through cooptation: a process whereby the more "successful" members of the subordinate group are incorporated into the dominant group. Thus, it is quite possible that in the future the "Oriental" stratum will become a numerical minority, as more successful members intermarry. The dominant group would thus be a mixed group while the subordinate group would be Oriental. If so, the pattern would be similar to that which has occurred throughout history. The closest example is that of Latin America. The upper stratum considers itself white, of Spanish descent, when it fact it has much Indian and Negroid mixture. Similarly, the non-Oriental dominant group in the Israeli society of the future could in fact have a substantial amount of Oriental mixture and yet consider itself Western and draw a sharp line between itself and the Oriental minority.

To return to the present, the objective factors of inequality are having a sociologically predictable effect on forging an ethnic identity among the Jews from the Oriental countries and their children. It must be recognized that their perception of their relative lack of things that count in Israel is especially heightened by the changing life style of the country. The simplicity in style of life, so characteristic of the pioneering days, is being rapidly replaced by a preoccupation and fascination with consumer goods. Such goods are being imbued with great symbolic value and are displayed conspicuously. In such a climate, the feelings of relative deprivation of the Orientals are heightened.

THE MEANING OF THE BLACK PANTHERS

The increasing ethnic identity of the Orientals finds expression in their general attitude toward the Pantherim Shehorim, which contrasts sharply with the attitude of the Europeans. Having resided in Israel during the time of the rise of the Black Panthers, I must say that I have never encountered an Oriental who thought that the Panthers' grievances were wrong or who did not justify their actions. The only objection of some with whom I spoke was to the choice of the name, Black Panthers, since they, like Israelis in general, tended to associate the name with anti-Semitism in America. Amos Elon, in his article on the Black Panthers of Israel, also mentioned that the Oriental Jews condone them.[21] And Peter Grose, the *New York Times* correspondent in Israel, similarly concluded that there is much sympathy for the Pantherim Shehorim among the Oriental Jews and even among the old Sephardic families. He quoted Eli Eliachar, the head of the Council of the Sephardic Community, as saying: "I am all for what these young people are doing—for too long we Oriental Jews have lived for promises that never materialized." [22] That my casual observations and those of the above journalists are probably correct finds support in the "Open Letter to the People in Israel," placed by the Council of the Sephardic Community in Israeli newspapers, in which they expressed outright support for the Pantherim Shehorim.[23]

Diametrically opposite was the reaction of the non-Oriental Jews to this phenomenon, which received wide coverage in the mass media. Nationally televised protest meetings of the Panthers brought dramatically to the consciousness of the nation the existence of the group. The overall response of the Europeans was that of surprise, even shock. Golda Meir expressed the feeling of many when she reportedly said at a meeting of the Moroccan Immigrants Association, "How can a Jew throw a Molotov cocktail at another Jew or at a Jewish building?" This was the time when the chairman, Shaul Ben-Simchon, a Moroccan Jew, referred to the Panthers as "nice boys" and was corrected by Golda Meir, who said, "Excuse me, they are not nice boys." [24]

And yet, why the surprise? Is this really the first time that Jews have been involved in class conflict and violence against Jews? Jewish radicals in Russia and Poland did not hesitate to use militant tactics against Jewish capitalists. And the present governing elite of Israel are the radicals of that time or have had sufficient contact with them to know the history. To understand this reaction, it is helpful to bring to mind the sociological theorem that dominant groups in general tend to identify their interests and values with those of society as a whole. An organization—like the Panthers—which disturbs the stability of the dominant group is then perceived by members of that group as endangering the stability or existence of the nation. Add to this the specific Israeli factor that was touched on earlier: the egalitarian ideology which for at least a decade after independence prevented even the acknowledgment of the existence of the ethnic problem. The presence and the activities of the Pantherim Shehorim brought the problem to the forefront. They also helped to bring about the recognition that, in contrast to previous beliefs, the problem is not withering away. That most of the Panthers were sabras was living proof that integration was not achieved ipso facto in the second generation. The conscience of some Europeans was stirred to the extent that they became aware of and were a bit troubled by the conditions of the Orientals. But many more European Israelis seem to blame the Orientals for not being satisfied when conditions in Israel are so superior to conditions in the countries from which they came. The dominant group tends to claim that the fault lies with the Orientals, for equal opportunities exist for all. Still, the general sentiment was that, for the sake of the country, something ought to be done to alleviate tensions before it becomes too late.[25]

Despite the sentiment there is no public consensus concerning what action ought to be taken. And it is highly improbable that Israeli society will launch in the near future a full mobilization of its resources to solve the ethnic problem (even within the possibilities remaining after national defense expenditures are met).

What is likely to occur is that more ameliorative steps will be taken. The overall pattern is apt to be similar to that which followed the outbursts of 1959. (That there were such ethnic demonstrations before is a fact not widely known outside of Israel.) The violent demonstration in July 1959 by immigrants from North Africa in the Wadi Salib section of Haifa set off similar occurrences in other places. As in the case of the Panthers today, there was an organization behind the earlier demonstrations, the *Likkud Olei Tsfon Africa*. Like the Panthers, the demonstrators consisted mostly of young people, but in contrast to the Panthers, most of whom are sabras, these were immigrants who had spent five to ten years in Israel and had served in the army. In the army, according to them, they felt no discrimination, whereas in civilian life they were discriminated against. People of European background, however, thought them ungrateful because their living conditions were far superior to those they left behind in their countries of origin. As in the case of the Panthers today, "comment of this sort only made them angrier as, in the meantime, they had acquired the values of Israeli society and felt themselves entitled to live accordingly."

Nevertheless, then as now the Israelis became convinced of the necessity of doing something. The riots gave impetus to several palliative measures, both economic and educational. Cooptation occurred: "The inclusion (often in 'safe places') of Orientals . . . on the election candidates' lists of many parties." [26] Perhaps the greatest changes were introduced in education; at least that was the assumption. Until the riots of 1959, the official educational policy resisted any departure from what was considered the principle of equality. Accordingly, "all children, irrespective of their sociocultural backgrounds and individual attributes, were to be subjected to identical treatment in a uniform kindergarten and elementary school." The Ministry of Education, despite the evidence of the alarmingly high rate of failure among children of Oriental parents, rejected the idea of special programs. But after the riots, the Ministry decided on a number of measures. According to Aharon Kleinberger, professor of comparative education at Hebrew University, these were administrative measures "designed to produce immediate effects by remedying the statistical appearance rather than the substance of the Oriental groups' educational disadvantage." [27] Worthy of note is that the children exposed to such programs are to this day labeled by the most progressive educators of Israel, including Professor Kleinberger, as "culturally deprived," or from a "culturally impoverished environment," terms reflecting the bias of the dominant Europeans.

The one program which proved to be quite effective is considered too costly to be translated into a mass program. I am referring to the boarding schools for gifted children from disadvantaged homes. An evaluative study of the first two cohorts of students showed that their dropout rates were lower and their rates of passes in the comprehensive matriculation examinations higher not only than those of other Oriental students of corresponding ability but even of the non-Oriental students in selective secondary schools.[28] As for the general increase in the proportion of Oriental adolescents in secondary schools, it is difficult to determine to what extent it is due to the special educational programs and to what extent to the rising prosperity and reduced unemployment which lessened the economic obstacles to secondary education.[29]

Without passing a blanket judgment on the results of the special programs as a whole, the following fact must nevertheless be stated boldly: the bitter taste of failure in school continues to be the common experience of Oriental Jewish children and youngsters. What I wrote elsewhere about schools in the Southwest serving Mexican-American children can be said verbatim about the schools in Israel serving Jewish children of Oriental background:

> Thus we have found that the schools have managed to instill the goals and values of success. But they have failed drastically in developing behavior conducive to advancement. The result is a rising appetite for socio-economic success without a corresponding development in the capacity to satisfy it. The negative consequences inherent in such a situation are well known.[30]

Despite the rise in the expectations of the Oriental population and the increase in their feelings of relative deprivation, we do not anticipate a major national effort to attack the problem in the near future. One of the main factors is that the ethnic consciousness of the Orientals has not yet reached the level of effective political organization. Even the Panthers themselves do not display a high political consciousness. This is symbolized in their demands vis-à-vis the army. Their main grievance was that the delinquency records of a substantial number of Oriental youths made them ineligible for army service.[31] (Compare this with the grievances of the Black Panthers and the Chicano militants in the United

States who demand exemption from army service!) The other demands of the Pantherim Shehorim are for free education from kindergarten through college, for an end to discrimination, for government subsidies for slum clearance, and for an end to "black ghettos," housing developments inhabited solely by Orientals.

Housing represents one of the most acute immediate issues, since Orientals are plagued by substandard and overcrowded facilities. Because of this, a resentment is building up against the Russian immigrants who receive "luxurious" apartments as compared with those inhabited by many Orientals. Again, we have here a dramatic case of relative deprivation. As Shoshana Arbeli-Almoslino, a member of the Knesset, expressed it: "How long can a father of eight living in two rooms look out of his window and see the new flats that they are building for immigrants and contain himself? The situation is explosive." [32] Nevertheless, even the Panthers emphasize that they are not against immigration or the concept of the ingathering of exiles; they only insist that it should not be done at the expense of the poor.

In their demands for better housing the Panthers often strike a responsive cord not only among the Orientals but among young Israelis in general. Young people of European descent also face a housing problem and they, too, tend to resent the fact that Russian and American immigrants are placed before them as far as housing is concerned. This has been expressed in various actions, such as that of some 30 students of the Hebrew University School of Social Work who guided 11 members of an Oriental family from their one-and-a-half room apartment in one of Jerusalem's slums —Katamon Het—to a newly built, empty apartment waiting for immigrants. The students forced open the lock and planted the family.[33]

Despite the sympathy of the young, the Panthers are not likely to grow into a mass movement, and the factors operating against such growth are also operating against the Orientals becoming highly politicized.[34] Foremost among them is the persistent danger of war, with Russian arms poised on the border. This constitutes a strong cementing force for the whole nation—one which overcomes ethnic divisions. And so does the people's army, a source of pride for all Israelis. The third major factor is the existence of an Arab minority in Israel against whom the frustrations and resentments of Oriental Jews are often turned. (Studies show that the Orientals—who culturally as well as in terms of origin are closer to the Arabs—are more prejudiced and hostile toward the

Arabs than the Europeans are. Another factor which is often assumed to be a very important cohesive force is the common religion. However, one must question its present strength.) Most Europeans are highly secularized and the Orientals are rapidly becoming secularized. And so the bond that derived from simply being a Jew has weakened considerably.

Thus, the Pantherim Shehorim are essentially a preview of things to come. And when they come, the Panthers will be seen historically as another manifestation in the process of the development of political consciousness among the Orientals (just as the earlier Likkud and the Wadi Salib riots). What I am suggesting is that the dominant group in Israel—like dominant groups everywhere—does not see the urgency of the problems of the subordinates. The distinctive Jewish values, deeply tied to religious sources, have receded. The concern for justice and righteousness in dealing with others is often perceived as a relic of bygone days. Socialist values have become stale, while acquisition and consumerism are becoming more dominant. In this atmosphere it is unlikely that fundamental change will be initiated by the governing elite. One may note that in Israel, despite the demographic and social distance between the ethnic strata, there are no organizations which are explicitly geared to promoting social contact and primary relations across ethnic lines (comparable to the Conference of Christians and Jews in the United States). Ask an Israeli about his friends across the "European-Oriental" line and you will find that he seldom has any.

Only the demands of the subordinate group, the Orientals, backed by their political organization, are likely to bring a fundamental change in the ethnic stratification structure that is jelling in Israel. In the process of formulating an ideological basis for their demands, the Orientals might rediscover and return to some Jewish values. As remote as it may seem now, the future renaissance of Jewish values in Israel might come through Orientals and immigrants from the Soviet Union, if the latter reach Israel in large enough numbers. Therefore, I see no reason for fear when such phenomena as Black Panthers appear in Israel; rather, there is reason for hope. However, in Israel there is fear that the time of relative peace, with its Black Panther manifestations, previews the civil disorders to come with real peace. As a *New York Times* correspondent observed during the Jewish New Year holiday, people in Israel were asking, in addition to the old question, "Will the year bring peace with the Arabs?" a new question: "Will there be domestic, social and economic peace?" As he expressed it, "Israelis acknowledge that it has been the year of quiet along the borders that has allowed the internal discord to be heard so loudly." [35] And Israelis seem very fearful of internal conflict. This fear shows through the writing of intellectuals, including historians and sociologists, who ought at least to consider that a certain amount of conflict might be necessary for change. To quote from Talmon, who is often considered to belong ideologically to the Left: "Israel has . . . been blessed with good fortune. There has been no serious, certainly no collective attempt on the part of Oriental Jews to organize themselves into a separate political party. Any such attempt would have been fraught with grave dangers from demagogues and rabble-rousers." [36]

Talmon seems to fear such organization. Another illustration of how the intellectuals, members of the dominant group, fear the political organization of Orientals is found in a recent sociological study. The author, who found some support for the hypothesis of a growing link between voting and ethnic membership, evaluates his finding thus: "Such a prognosis has frightening meanings for the future of Israeli society." [37]

But why fear the organization of Orientals? I am convinced that if the Orientals succeed in organizing themselves they will succeed not only in improving their situation but in realizing the ideal of a unified people. True, today they are relatively powerless in comparison to the dominant Europeans. However, much potential power is vested in them. First of all, they are numerically a majority (60 percent of the Jewish population) and their proportion in the Jewish population is growing, due to their much higher birth rate. Secondly, in fighting for equality they could hold up the principles of the egalitarian ideology to which the dominant group subscribes. And finally, the failure of the dominant group to respond positively to the demands of the organized Orientals would threaten the existence of the nation. The last is reflected in the statement of Eli Eliachar, head of the Council of the Sephardic Community, who is reported to have said: "If we ever get peace in the Middle East we will have civil war at home." [38] I do not agree with this statement. I am confident that should the existence of the nation be in danger, the people of Israel would prove once more to be, as General Rabin characterized them, "a people who rises above itself in time of crisis." [39] Thus, I think that real peace would not lead to civil war or an eventual split but could lead to structural integration through the destruction of ethnic stratification.

Israel's Pantherim Shehorim are the personification not only of the nation's deepest failure but also of its greatest challenge, next to that of fighting for survival in a sea of enemies. It is my conviction that in time of peace the challenge will not prove to be insuperable for an Israel that has again and again demonstrated its extraordinary quality of rising to challenges and emerging victorious despite tremendous odds. Integration is more likely to come about in time of peace, because peace would allow for a certain amount of conflict, a prerequisite for change, which the nation threatened by war cannot afford.

NOTES

1. R. A. Schermerhorn, *Comparative Ethnic Relations: A Framework for Theory and Research* (New York: Random House, 1970) p. 156.

2. For sociologists, an ethnic group is "a collectivity within a larger society having a real or putative common ancestry, memories of a shared historical past, and a cultural focus on one or more symbolic elements defined the epitome of their peoplehood," *Ibid.*, p. 12.

3. S. N. Eisenstadt, *Israeli Society* (New York: Basic Books, 1967) p. 50.

4. The phrase coined by the Coles was adopted and made more widely known by Milton M. Gordon. See: Stewart G. Cole and Mildred Wiese Cole, *Minorities and the American Promise* (New York: Harper and Brothers, 1954) Chapter 6 and Milton M. Gordon, *Assimilation in American Life* (New York: Oxford University Press, 1964) pp. 88-114.

5. Eisenstadt, *Israeli Society*, p. 51.

6. J. L. Talmon, *Israel Among the Nations* (London: Weidenfeld and Nicolson, 1970) p. 161.

7. *Ibid.*, p. 199.

8. Dov Weintraub, *Immigration and Social Change* (Israel: Israel University Press, 1971), pp. 257-8.

9. Aharon F. Kleinberger, *Society, Schools and Progress in Israel* (Oxford: Pergamon Press, 1969) p. 63.

10. Akiva Deutsch, "The Character of the Elite in a Yemenite Suburb," *Megamoth* 9(1958): 328-39 (in Hebrew).

11. As far as I know, no studies of the emergence of these labels exist. It would make an interesting study in sociolinguistics.

12. Robert K. Merton, *Social Theory and Social Structure* (Glencoe, Ill.: Free Press, 1949) p. 54.

13. V. D. Segre, *Israel—A Society in Transition* (London: Oxford University Press, 1971) p. 193.

14. Judith Shuval, "Emerging Patterns of Ethnic Strain," *Social Forces*, 40 (May 1962): 323-29.

15. Celia S. Heller, *Structured Social Inequality* (New York: Macmillan, 1969) pp. 2-5.

16. Eisenstadt, *Israeli Society.*

17. Moshe Lissak, *Social Mobility in Israeli Society* (Jerusalem: Israel Universities Press, 1969) p. 66.

18. Talcott Parsons, *The Social System,* (Glencoe, Ill.: The Free Press, 1951) p. 240.

19. Kleinberger, *Society, Schools and Progress,* p. 284.

20. Lissak, *Social Mobility,* pp. 45, 50.

21. Amos Elon, "The Black Panthers of Israel," *New York Times Magazine,* September 12, 1971.

22. Peter Grose, "Muted Class Strife in Israel," *New York Times,* May 24, 1971, p. 8, c. 3.

23. *Jerusalem Post,* March 26, 1971, p. 5.

24. Ibid., May 20, 1971, p. 8.

25. Moshe Ater, "The Black Panthers and the Economy," *Jerusalem Post,* May 27, 1971, p. 4.

26. Eisenstadt, *Israeli Society,* pp. 306-8.

27. Kleinberger, *Society, Schools and Progress,* pp. 296, 304.

28. M. Smilansky et al., *Gifted Pupils from Schools in Culturally Deprived Environments,* First Report (in Hebrew) (Jerusalem: Szold Institute, 1966).

29. Kleinberger, *Society, Schools and Progress,* p. 307.

30. Celia S. Heller, *New Converts to the American Dream?—Mobility Aspirations of Young Mexican Americans* (New Haven: College and University Press, 1971) pp. 251-2.

31. See, for example, the portrait of one of the leaders, twenty-eight year old Ruevan Abergil, who complained of having been kept out of the army, *New York Times,* May 24, 1971, p. 8.

32. *The Jerusalem Post,* January 26, 1971.

33. *The Jerusalem Post,* June 8, 1971, p. 9.

34. This prediction proved to be correct. The article was written in the fall of 1971 when the Black Panthers of Israel were at the height of their activity, and when some people, especially outside of Israel, thought that they represented a rising mass movement.

35. Peter Grose, "Internal Issues Cloud Israeli New Year Mood," *New York Times,* September 22, 1971.

36. Talmon, *Israel Among the Nations,* p. 162.

37. Lissak, *Social Mobility,* pp. 99-100.

38. Peter Grose, "Muted Class Strife is Erupting in Israel," p. 8, c. 3.

39. Yigal Allon, *The Making Of Israel's Army* (London: Valentine, Mitchell, 1970) p. 33.

20

Henry Toledano

TIME TO STIR
THE MELTING POT

In Israel today an ethnic group which constitutes less than 40 percent of the general population enjoys so much power and prestige that it is able to set itself up as the dominant political force, prescribe the social norms and constitute itself as the cultural model, to which everybody else must conform. Naturally and unfortunately through this process this minority manages—perhaps not willingly or deliberately—to imbue the majority group with a sense of inferiority, with devastating effect on that most cherished Sephardic concept of *kavod*, dignity and self-esteem.

Comparisons are often made between the Negro problem in America and the ethnic problem in Israel. This is obviously an unsuitable comparison because, first, the Sephardim are not black; second, whereas the Negroes in America are a minority, the Sephardim in Israel are the majority; they constitute 60 to 62 percent of the total population; finally, the Sephardim were neither sold or brought to Israel as slaves. They came of their own volition, motivated sometimes by ideals, sometimes by need.

In 1969, I visited Israel and went to see one of my dearest friends, an Ashkenazi woman. Our conversation ranged rather broadly and inevitably got to the ethnic and intercommunity problem. This lady made an acute observation, saying, "They say Israel is a melting pot. I see the pot. I see everything in the pot. But, by God, somebody better start doing some stirring."

333

Her observation was more telling than 100 tables of statistics. The policies of integration and absorption of immigrants have failed miserably. The best proof of that failure is the emergence of the Jewish Black Panthers. In answer I said, "If you look at the bottom of the pot, you will not find the usual 'Made in Japan,' but 'Made in Russia.' "

Israelis tend to blame the problems which beset Israeli society today on the backwardness of the Orientals. Undoubtedly there are objective factors contributing to this failure of absorption, such as the industrial and intellectual unpreparedness of some of the Jews who came from the Moslem lands for the highly industrial and technological Israeli society. And there is no doubt that *some* of these Jews from Eastern lands have had gaps in their education —I say education, not culture. However, some of the Egyptian, Iraqi, Moroccan and Algerian Jews had had a very fine French education, and no education can be more Western than that of the French. However, these objective factors and others, do not sufficiently explain the miserable failure of our immigration and absorption policies.

One simply cannot, for example, compare a Martin Buber to a Moroccan who comes from the caves; such a gap is unbridgeable. But you can compare parallel generations. To me, the relevant parallel is the generation of Jews who came to America from Eastern Europe at the turn of the century. These Jews—not the great intellectuals, the rabbis, but the average men—had some intellectual baggage. They knew a little Bible and some Gemara, and they could read the Yiddish paper. Were it not for the fact that Yiddish was recognized as a language, these people would not have passed the literacy test required for entering the United States. The Jew who comes from Morocco or Algeria to Israel finds himself in much the same situation. He has some Jewish learning and can read the local papers in Judeo-Arabic, perhaps. Otherwise, he is unprepared, industrially and intellectually. Yet, three or sometimes two generations after arrival, given the tremendous educational opportunities that were open to them, the East European Jews became the intellectual and cultural elite of the United States and attained material affluence as well.

Most students of the Israeli scene are becoming more and more convinced that at the root of the difficulty lie patterns of stratification and ranking of ethnic-affiliation groups which prevailed in Israel before 1948 and became even more pronounced, perhaps dangerously so, with the mass immigration of Jews from the Middle East and North Africa after 1948.

To be labeled a Yemenite, a Hungarian or a Tunisian is not merely to be subjected to an objective, descriptive statement. In Israel, there are social-status implications in such labels. Belonging to one group rather than to another has great social meaning. Within this prevailing ranking pattern, Israelis from Europe or from America are automatically ranked higher than those from the Islamic or Arab countries. Regardless of the personal merits of the individual or his educational preparedness, to come from Poland, Britain or Rumania is ipso facto to belong to a more prestigious group than do those who came from Egypt or Iraq.

The origins of this ranking, this stratification, are not too hard to trace. Before 1948, most of the leaders, the propounders of Zionist ideology, the immigrants of the first, second, third and fourth aliyah, were from Russia. Obviously, they shaped the new yishuv, the new society in Israel, according to their own ideology and background. The religious among them, for example, perceived everything pertaining to religious life in terms of the Eastern European pattern familiar to them.

After 1948, those same people found themselves in the seats of power. They controlled the machinery of government, foreign policy, job distribution, the allocation of the country's resources and the formulation of immigration policy. That, of course, tended to perpetuate the ranking system, which has been the basic premise upon which the exclusive East European power elite in Israel based its immigrant absorption policy. Integration was conceived of along the lines of this ranking system, to the disadvantage of the Sephardim or Orientals.

The term *misug galuyot*, which is the pet phrase in Israel for integration, literally means the merging or mixing of the exiles. But in mixing, elements of group A and elements of group B are brought together to produce C. C is neither A nor B; it is made up of the best elements A and B have to offer. In Israel, however, the mixing—misug galuyot—apparently means simply the Ashkenization of the Sephardim.

Integration is said to take place in Israel when a Tunisian Jew is drawn into a Hasidic dance, or when a Moroccan rabbinic student grows *peot* (sideburns) and learns to discuss the Talmud in fluent Yiddish.. This was the process before 1948, and this is the process today.

HENRY TOLEDANO

Let me illustrate my point by three quotations from three different dates: 1953, 1965 and as recently as 1971. The first two of
my three authors are Ashkenazim, so no bias of mine is operating
here. Raphael Patai is an astute student of the integration problem
in Israel. Speaking of this orientation of Israeli integration, he
says:

> The old fashioned and short sighted view which unfortunately
> is expressed only too often, both orally and in writing in
> Israel, holds that the Oriental Jews are in need of complete
> re-education; that their entire being and thinking must be
> reshaped in the East European Jewish image, and that when
> this cannot be achieved through suasion and example, the
> situation calls for legislative measures.[1]

Twelve years later, another student of Israeli social problems says
of this attempt on the part of the Ashkenazim to remodel the
Sephardim:

> The motives underlying this cultural crusade are readily ap-
> parent. Immigrants outnumber the European veterans and
> they therefore appear to threaten the cultural foundations so
> carefully hewed during the formative period. In fact, how-
> ever, the intent has not been merely to mix the immigrants
> —which after all implies some preservation of cultural ele-
> ments—but rather to transform them.[2]

Nissim Rejwan, a Sephardic journalist, has written on the implications of the rise of the Israeli Black Panthers. Speaking of the concept of misug galuyot, Israeli style, he says:

> *Misug galuyot* is rather a problematic term, overcharged with
> emotion, sociologically devoid of real content and culturally
> somewhat arbitrary as a concept. In actual practice moreover,
> it often seemed to denote little more than "remodeling the
> Oriental immigrant to bring him up to our level" and make
> him something that he is not. The result has been decultura-
> tion, marginalization, educational and cultural deprivation.[3]

The effect of this stratification along ethnic lines and the relegating
of over half of the population to the out-group status can be very
well imagined. It leads to resentment, discontent and disaffection

on the part of those belonging to the lower group. The Israeli Black Panthers are the leading example of this.

Rejwan defines the way misug galuyot is applied in Israel as individual assimilation, the absorption into the prevailing social and cultural structure of certain qualified members of the out-groups individually, one by one. This is tantamount to a rejection of the out-group cultures. It says, in effect, "You can be one of us only if, first you surrender your group affiliation, and second, if you become like us." This, Rejwan continues "is the surest way to marginalize members of the out-group; it has also been a tool for social inequality and discrimination, especially in the case of societies such as Israel where the rights and privileges of an individual rest largely on the status received by the group to which he belongs rather than on his purely individual attributes."

This pattern of stratification and ranking along ethnic lines, needless to say, has effected the actual social status, economic position and educational achievement of the Sephardim. This is quite apparent, from certain long-term trends in the social, economic, educational and political mobility of these immigrants during the 1960s.

There is no denying that the Sephardim have, economically, moved up somewhat. They earn more in terms of absolute pounds; their standard of living has improved—some of them have radios, refrigerators, TVs and so on. But there is another way of looking at the picture.

Twenty percent of the Israeli population live below a narrowly defined poverty line, in crowded, highly dense housing, in slums, many without jobs. Now poverty is nothing new. There is poverty in every country. What is really disturbing is the coincidence between the lack of achievement, poor housing, low-paying jobs and ethnicity.

For example, over 90 percent of this impoverished 20 percent are Orientals. Of those employed, the average income per family of those coming from Eastern Europe, or the West, in 1968-1969, was 1,116 Israeli pounds as against 797 Israeli pounds for those who hailed from Moslem lands. When one considers that the average Sephardic family has 4.7 people, while the Ashkenazic has only 2.9, the real gap is even greater. The real income of the Sephardic family is, in fact, no more than 44 percent of that of the Ashkenazic.

Secondly, workers from Asia and Africa constitute only 34 percent of the total work force in Israel; yet 53 percent of the construction workers, 41 percent of the industrial workers and 48 percent in service jobs come from their ranks. This means that they are heavily concentrated in unskilled and semiskilled jobs, low in prestige and low in payment.

On the other hand, they constitute only 16 percent of the total professional work force, only 19 percent of the white-collar workers, and only 1 to 2 percent of high government positions. This means they have very little chance of affecting their own destiny.

What is most interesting is that 40 percent of all government workers do not have a higher education. If the real criterion for holding government positions were education, one would expect, at least among these 40 percent without higher education, that the percentage of Sephardim would be greater. Yet even within this 40 percent, the percentage of Sephardim still wavers between 1 and 2, according to Dr. Sciaki, Deputy Minister of Education in Israel.

Other statistics, comparing income by occupation, show the following order: the highest earners are the European veterans, that is, those Europeans who came to Israel before 1948; next are European immigrants; then Jews from the Middle East, veterans who came before 1948; and finally, Oriental immigrants since 1948.

These statistics show that the income of Europeans has risen so fast, and so much faster than that of those from the Middle East, that it is even higher than that of those Orientals who have been in Israel since before 1948. Obviously, the only possible conclusion is that ethnic affiliation is more important than the length of time one has spent in Israel. Europeans as a group are more mobile than the Jews from the Middle East, regardless of how much time they have spent in Israel, regardless of whether they came before 1948 or since 1948.

Obviously, again, more than objective factors are at work— namely, subjective variables such as prejudice and discrimination. Chief among these prejudices is the belief of the dominant European elite that Jews from Moslem countries brought deprivation and discrimination and backwardness with them. This is so deeply ingrained a belief among the Ashkenazim in Israel that it is repeated time and again by public officers.

Of course, many immigrants had hoped that time would cure all ills. They thought that once a generation had passed things would be better. Eshkol thought so, and so did many others. However, the latest statistics show that the gap is widening rather than narrowing. It is true that people of Middle Eastern origin are earning more, but those of European origin are earning much more. This means that the recent Israeli prosperity is channeled toward the Ashkenazi. To quote a famous Biblical verse, *"Hetiva Adonai la-tovim"*; translated into good idiomatic English this means, "The rich get richer."

Many immigrants who came to Israel from Morocco and Egypt, where they had been shopkeepers, realized that Israel does not need tailors or shoemakers or carpenters, and were willing to settle for whatever life they got. But they were hoping that their children would do better, and pinned all their hopes on education. Most Israeli leaders themselves believe that education is the key to significant change.

There is no denying that much has been done in this direction. Sephardic children are given extra years in kindergarten; more high school scholarships are going to Sephardic children. The first two years of high school are free today in Israel. Yet recent statistics (see Dr. Sciaki's recent article in *Panim El Panim*) are shattering: of all children entering the first year of kindergarten, 63 percent are Sephardim, Orientals. At the end of the line, among the Ph.D. recipients, only 3 percent are Sephardim. Only 1 percent of the faculty of Israeli universities is Sephardic.

What is happening? First, there is the elementary school dropout problem, with only 42 percent of entering Sephardic children remaining to the end of the eighth grade. With the difficulties of paying for high school, only 28 percent graduate from *tichon* (twelfth grade), and only 9 to 12 percent even enter university. Of these, only 7 percent earn the B.A., 5 percent the M.A., and a bare 3 percent complete the Ph.D.

Economics is obviously the major villain, on every level. On the elementary level, a mother is sick; she begs the older girl to stay home to take care of the younger baby. That lasts for three or four days. By the time the girl goes back to school she is behind in her work, she is afraid of the teacher; she goes back home. Many drop out in this way.

Of course, housing conditions and the lack of proper nutrition also contribute to the dropout problem. On the high school level, he who earns less necessarily can spend less on education. I visited a friend in Israel who came from Meknes, where there is a very strong tradition of learning. Ninety percent of the Jews in Meknes finished the equivalent of French and Moroccan universities.

This gentleman worked as a clerk in the post office because he could not meet university requirements. He made all kinds of sacrifices, living in a shack somewhere, so that his daughter could finish high school. I asked him, "How about your boy?" He said, "How much can you cut? We have to eat, too. As soon as my daughter finishes high school I can switch funds to the boy." But he could not send both to high school at the same time.

There was a tradition of learning in my family too. My own sister had to work very hard in Israel, but she did manage to help her older son, who already had learned a lot in Morocco, to graduate. He's now teaching Talmud in Bar Ilan University. But five other brothers and sisters with the same potential did not finish high school; the family could not afford it, so they all work as clerks.

Economic factors operate even more restrictively on the university level. Those who finally overcome all these obstacles and do go on to the university are still faced with the problem of money. Before Dr. Sciaki became a Deputy Minister of Education, he was the dean of students in Tel Aviv University. Many times brilliants students came to him and said, "Dr. Sciaki, *anachnu nishbarim*: we are at the breaking point." He was often able to give them further funds to help keep them in school.

I will not discuss specific cases of discrimination—and there are such. I do not deny Golda Meir's contention that there is no official discrimination in Israel. There is none. But when I apply for a job for which I am otherwise qualified I don't apply to Golda Meir or to Abba Eban or to the Minister of Labor; I apply to a lower-echelon bureaucrat, the head of a factory who has his own prejudices, which he translates into discrimination. When a brilliant student applies for a scholarship, he doesn't apply to the Minister of Education, he applies to some bureaucrat in the office of the university. Cases of discrimination on these levels abound.

However, there is another factor, besides the economic one, which is important: the cultural factor. Alex Weingrod writes about the cultural factors which work against the Sephardim:

> The school curriculum is heavily slanted toward European tradition. The teachers are also predominantly European and this too gives advantages to European students. So long as Middle Eastern and North African students, children, are approached as if they are European, the students are unlikely to perform well. Similarly, approaching these children as if their cultural heritage were empty, will not lead to the desired results.

Yet this is exactly what happens in the Israeli schools, and this is not an insignificant cause of the high dropout rate.

There are all kinds of explanations for the education problem: lack of motivation on the part of Sephardic children; or intellectual inferiority; sometimes, they say, parents prefer to buy a refrigerator than to send the children to high school; or the Sephardim didn't bring their own leaders. All these answers are petty. Today, the Sorbonne and the University of Strasbourg, Montpellier Polytechnic are all teeming with bright Moroccan and Algerian students. Moroccan Jews have succeeded everywhere, in France, in Canada and in New York, commercially and academically. There's only one place where they can't get ahead and that is in Israel.

The argument that is often advanced is that the Iraqi Sephardic community did not have this trouble because the whole community came over, whereas in the case of Morocco, those who had the greatest capacity for learning and leadership went to France.

However, the argument is false: the Iraqis also suffer. An associate professor of neurology at the University of Cincinnati wrote to me and said, "I am an Iraqi Jew who immigrated to Israel in 1955 and stayed there until 1966, when I could not endure the discrimination any longer and I left the country. Now I am lecturing everywhere to tell the truth as it is."

Furthermore, not all leaders are born leaders. Children have the potential of becoming leaders—or Black Panthers. A survey has found that children who remained in Morocco or France and had the opportunity for real education did develop into leaders. Their peers, sometimes their own brothers, who went to Israel at the same age and from the same economic background, did not develop into leaders. It was not their fault; the element of opportunity was missing. No one is born a leader. We still have to fall back on the philosophic concept of the *tabula rasa*. You're born with nothing. Whatever you acquire is given you.

Another statistic is relevant here: In France, a Catholic country, there are reportedly about 15,000 North African Jews—not only Moroccans—on the various faculties of the universities and lycées. There isn't even that number of students in all the Israeli universities combined.

Finally, there is what one might call cultural discrimination or repression. Cultural dominance by the Ashkenazim manifests itself in many ways.

Kol Yisrael broadcasts official programs for every holiday. They will offer, for example, the story of Esther—the Megillah—*Al taharat hanusah haashkenazi,* in pure Ashkenazic style. Then they will say, "And now we will chant chapters according to melodies of the ethnic groups." Sixty percent of the population are "ethnic groups" and the other 40 percent are the norm—as if the Rumanians, the Hungarians and the Germans make up one homogeneous, Ashkenazi society.

I was traveling in 1968 from Tel Aviv to Jerusalem. It was around the month of Elul and they were broadcasting the Selihot services from the radio of the Israel army's official school of Hazanut. I was startled to hear the Ashkenazi *nusach.* I have nothing against it. I have lived long enough with Ashkenazim to like both, but it's not my ritual. I turned to my friend and I said, "I don't understand. The population of Israel is 60 percent Oriental and, given the large Sephardic family, I'm sure that the percentage in the army is even greater. How then do they dare sing *Tefilot* according to their own rituals?"

The taxi driver, who happened to be an Iraqi, turned to me and he said, "Mister, you're naive. You don't understand. This is not Sephardi, this is not Ashkenazi. This is the official Israeli *nusach*"—which shows how much the Sephardi is being brainwashed into believing that the Ashkenazi ritual is the proper, official version. And this attitude is often given expression in off-the-cuff remarks by Israeli leaders, such as the remark that Golda Meir made recently—six months ago or so—to a group of East European Jews: "Anyone who doesn't speak Yiddish is not a complete or perfect Jew."

This, of course, infuriated the Black Panthers, and they reacted in a very ugly way. Golda said, "I didn't meant that for every Jew. I meant it for the Ashkenazim." But a slip of the tongue can be very revealing.

Professor Talmon, a well known historian at the Hebrew University was recently reported to have said on television that he saw in Israel a direct continuation of the Eastern European tradition—this despite the fact that 60 percent of these Jews have never been in Eastern Europe, don't know Eastern European traditions and are totally unfamiliar with them.

Another vignette which I cherish concerns the Ashkenazi author, Agnon, the Nobel Prize winner in Hebrew literature. He is my favorite Hebrew writer—even above the Sephardic writers. His novel, *Shirah,* has just been published posthumously. It is a delightful book, a satire on scholarship. Agnon pokes fun at the scholars who spend all their time indexing cards, etc. He quotes a professor who said that were all Jewish life to become extinct, were all the Jews and all the libraries to be burned, except for the words of Sholem Aleichem, one would be able to reconstruct the history of the Jews from them, the works of Sholem Aleichem. And Agnon goes on to say, "How naive can our professors be? Don't they realize that outside the Pale of Settlement in Russia there were other Jewish communities who considered themselves Jews, who had developed their own Jewish institutions and their own valid Jewish way of life?"

This, then, was the reaction of a pure Ashkenazi writer. Unfortunately, this Ashkenazi ethnocentricity is even more pronounced in the Israeli curriculum, which is totally slanted toward East European culture in its approach, its content and its criteria for achievement.

I have a friend, a former Israeli of Moroccan origin, who is now in New York. He is an ex-Black Panther. He told me that he had gone through the whole education system in Israel. "I learned about Bialik, and Tchernichovsky, I studied Hebrew literature and Jewish history," he said. "I learned about every pogrom in Europe, about every movement and counter movement, Maskilim and fundamentalists, Hassidim and Mitnagdim, but not one word about my people, about my culture."

When I lectured on this subject at an American university, an Israeli student challenged me. "Don't you realize," he said, "that the very survival of Israel depends on its being a highly Western culture?" I replied, "My dear man, how is the survival of Israel threatened if a Moroccan student learns that there were Jews in Morocco?"

Ashkenazi ethnocentrism is very evident also in religious matters. What difference can there be between Ashkenazim and Sephardim in religious matters? There is a story about an American woman in Israel who boarded a bus. She sat down next to a Hassid, complete with *streimel* and *peyot*. The minute she sat down the man jumped up and sat somewhere else. The poor lady was terribly offended. She had never seen a Hassid in her life. She turned to the gentleman sitting next to her and asked, "Tell me, did I do anything offensive? Is there anything offensive about my perfume, my dress?" The man said, "Oh, lady, relax. He is a very pious Jew, and because of his religious convictions he will not sit next to a lady."

She was reassured. Five minutes later, a Sephardic rabbi boarded the same bus, and of all the empty places, picked the seat next to her. She said, "Rabbi, I am totally baffled. He is a rabbi, you are a rabbi; he has a beard, you have a beard; he has a cane, you have a cane; with differences of local color, you are so much alike; yet he ran away from me; you chose to sit next to me." The rabbi said, "Don't you see, lady, he is a Hassid, I am a Hacham" (literally, wise).

Certain attributes, certain ways of looking at things religiously, are taken for granted. Religious attitudes and modes of religious behavior which are often not at all germane to the Sephardic tradition, are taken as the norm. For example: I visited a friend in Israel in September. The school year had already begun and the temperature was very uncomfortable. His children came back from school and his daughter, nine years old, was in tears: The teacher had told her not to dare to come with short sleeves to religious school.

My friend was hurt and wanted to take her out of the religious school. "We don't need this kind of fanaticism," he said. We Sephardim also appreciate the concept of *zniut*, modesty, but not at nine years of age. We don't dream of burdening a nine-year-old child with the concept of sin. My father always used to say, "We Sephardim take religion—and God—with a grain of salt."

Another story dramatizes this relaxed attitude of the Sephardim. My father was a rabbi, a Rosh Yeshivah in Meknes. Most of his students today are *rabbanim* in Israel. One is a *dayan* in Haifa, one a rabbi in Gvar Yom. Once, in Morocco, there was a drought. When there is no rain in countries like Morocco, where all life depends on the crops, people get really panicky. What do they do? They pray; they fast. The Arabs have special prayers for rain, and we Jews do, too. We have all kinds of prayers for everything, not only for rain. We still have a manuscript at home of a special Yom Kippur Katan service for rain. Anyway, we prayed, we fasted, blew the shofar, and still there was no rain. Then, around Purim, a saintly rabbi by the name of Rabbi Chaim Dahant passed away.

Now, there is Talmudic tradition that when a saintly man dies he atones for the sins of his generation. The rabbinical leaders in Morocco took their cue from that tradition and gave this rabbi the full treatment. They had all the children of the Talmud Torah come out of school and recite *Tehillim* (Psalms) before the funeral; they blew the shofar, etc. Just to make sure God got the message, they wrote a note and buried it with Rabbi Chaim. Needless to say, it didn't rain. Yom Kippur, nine months later, my father was conducting the services in our synagogue. Suddenly, in the middle of Neilah, it began to rain. His sense of humor got the better of him and he stopped and said, "Ladies and gentlemen, I want you to know that Rabbi Chaim has just arrived."

Certain inflexible attitudes in *halachah* are imposed from above. Sephardic students who go to Ashkenazi yeshivot are taught intricate *pilpulistic* patterns of thought which are very strange to us. Certain religious modes of behavior, Hassidic or otherwise, which to a modern American would seem somewhat irrational, bizarre, not in the spirit of normative Judaism, are glorified in Buberian or Heschelian terms. But when similarly different patterns are found among Sephardim, they are labeled superstition.

Yigal Yadin recently had the boldness to see the problem for what it is. He was quoted in *Ma'ariv* (December 10, 1971) as saying that Israel must once and for all raise the banners of external security and internal reform together, for, he said, "The internal problems are so pressing that if they were to be neglected on the pretext that we have too much of a defense problem, those very internal problems would be so exacerbated they would threaten the very security of Israel." Yadin actually said in so many words that Israel has two fronts. On the one front, we have the best possible leadership—in the area of military and foreign policy we have geniuses. But, he said, on the internal front we have shlemiels. He suggested that the Prime Minister appoint a deputy prime minister to deal exclusively with these problems, with an adequate budget and properly trained assistants.

A number of steps can and must be taken if disaster is to be avoided: if Israel is not to grow a new crop of Black Panthers. If things are not taken care of, ten years from now today's Black Panthers will look like Uncle Toms. We have had bitter experiences. In 1959, there was a revolt at Wadi Salib. Instead of doing something about it the Israelis bought off the leaders. Mr. Ben Arosh was given a job and a house, and no one heard of Wadi Salib anymore. The problem was brushed aside, and ten years later we had the Black Panthers.

On the educational front, secondary school must be made free to all, but not obligatory. Those who do not want it, but want to learn a trade instead, should have that privilege. But it should be free. It should be accessible to those who want it—for those who want to pull themselves up by their bootstraps. Furthermore, families with a large number of children should be given some kind of financial assistance so that they may be able to take advantage of this free education, as is done in many countries.

There is also need for political reform which would give the Sephardim adequate representation so that they may have some kind of control over their destiny. True, Golda Meir and everybody else in the government has good will, but they have no control of the lower echelons. Every now and then they give us a ministry. Do you know what ministry they give the Sephardim? The post office. I don't know what use the post office is for the Sephardim. We don't even collect stamps. In welfare, education, labor, those which affect us more directly, we have no say whatsoever.

On the cultural level, too, official Israeli cultural presentations should reflect both Ashkenazi and Sephardi elements on an equal basis; there must be a true misug galuyot rather than the present Ashkenization of Sephardim. Ashkenazim in Israel must realize, once and for all, that over half of the population may and does, in fact, prefer its own version of Jewish life to that of the East European *shtetl*. I am not denigrating Ashkenazic Jewish life; it is good for Ashkenazim. But we Sephardim have lived in our respective lands for centuries, millennia; we have developed our own institutions, our own ways of celebrating holidays; our own approach to Talmudic learning; we cherish our ways, and we don't want to give them up for anything else.

The syllabi of Israeli schools should include information on the culture and the history of the Sephardim, their rabbis, their heros —spiritual and otherwise, their Jewish institutions, all that makes up their distinct culture. Exhibits of Oriental and Sephardic arts and crafts, public gatherings commemorating the achievements of historic Sephardic leaders, rabbinic as well as lay leaders—all these would help restore the cultural balance in Israel. At the same time, it would help restore the personal dignity and pride of Sephardim which have been so severely hurt.

When I first came to America I was very conscious of the difference between our prayers and the Ashkenazi prayers. The formulation is different. One prayer in particular always offended me. It reads, "May He who performed miracles for our fathers, redeem us . . . and may He gather our exiles from the four corners of the earth," and concludes with the phrase "*chaverim kol Yisrael*" —may all Israel be friends. You ask for the miracle of redemption, granted; for the ingathering of exiles, granted. But to pray for all Israel to be friends? *Aren't* we all friends? Lately, after 25 years of the Israel experience, I realize how profound that phrase is. Perhaps realization of the prayer for all Israel to be friends will require no less a miracle than that which made possible the in‑gathering of the exiles. My only hope is that we may see its realization in our own day.

NOTES

1. Raphael Patai, *Israel Between East and West* (Westport, Conn.: Green‑wood, 1953).

2. Alex Weingrod, *Israel: Group Relations in a New Society* (New York: Praeger, 1965).

3. Nissim Rejwan, "From Mixing to Participation," *The New Middle East,* May 1971.

21

Seymour Martin Lipset

THE ISRAELI DILEMMA

The phenomenon of the dominant minority in Israel should be viewed in the larger context of general systems of stratification of ethnic-national relationships. The existence of dominant culture or ethnic minorities is a historic characteristic which goes back to the formation of nations and cultures.

Stratified values and systems of hierarchical preference have existed on a world scale. Values have been absorbed from the most powerful and prestigious sector of the larger society. This is exhibited by the universal phenomenon of the integration or development of common cultures among peoples. The Roman Empire spread throughout much of Europe and produced the Romance languages which were forms of vulgar Latin. Latin had developed within a tiny group of people. As this group became powerful and conquered lesser groups, hundreds of millions of the defeated learned to speak some form of Latin. Arabic spread in the same way throughout North Africa and various parts of western Asia. Byzantium ruled an enormous area that was Hellenized.

The worst consequence of this process of ethnic, racial or class stratification is that people who are defined as inferior by the powerful accept the definition of their own inferiority.

Hierarchical values also press the dominant group (or dominant individuals) to preserve its position regardless of how committed individuals are to egalitarian values. Plato noted this in his discussions of the conditions necessary for a communist society. In *The Republic* he argued that to have real communism it would be necessary to get rid of the family totally and completely; to take children away from their parents soon after birth, because the family is the origin and the source of stratification and inequality. As long as the family persists, said Plato, there is going to be hereditary inequality, because endemic in the value relationships of people in a common family—whether it be a nuclear family or an extended one—is the desire to pass on to those for whom you feel affection and obligation the same position, the same value status you have yourself. Both Rousseau and Robert Owen reiterated this argument more than two millennia later. Sociological studies of education and class mobility, completed in Eastern Europe, the Soviet Union and Israel in the last half dozen years as well as in the United States have yielded highly similar results. They all indicate that family and neighborhood (social class) environment is far more important in affecting the capacity of youth to learn than anything done in school, including race or social class mixing.

These results have important implications for the Israeli system of ethnic stratification which Toledano has described in such accurate detail earlier in this book. Before turning to a consideration of Israeli education as a path of mobility or equalization, I would like to consider the political issues involved. There is tremendous variation in levels of effective power in Israel, and these variations are related to ethnic background. In spite of the fact that Israel is a political democracy—one man, one vote—efforts to create Sephardic parties which appeal to the political concerns of the deprived Sephardim to remedy the inequality they suffer have invariably failed badly in national elections. As a matter of fact, Sephardic parties have received only 1 or 2 percent of the vote. There has been no effective organization by the Sephardim around their political needs and political interests.

One of the reasons for this lack of political following is lack of political leadership. Clearly, political leaders do not require formal education. The Irish were able to make it in the United States largely through politics. The small group of college-educated or even the high-school-educated Irish were not the men who organized political machines. Rather, Irish leadership developed from a community of transplanted, uneducated peasants.

Comparable Sephardic leadership and protest is only beginning to develop now. In the United States, ethnic political group organization develops first in municipal politics around local issues. Israel seems to be following in the same direction.

True ethnic representation is made impossible by the Israeli electoral system of bloc nominations for the Knesset. In Israel, people cannot vote for an individual, whether Sephardic or Ashkenazi; they must vote for Mapam or Mapai or the Alignment or some other party group. The parties simply list their candidates in an order of preference. If a party gets 20 per cent of the vote, it is entitled to 20 per cent of the seats of the Knesset, which means that the first 25 members on its list are elected. Most of the people at the top of these lists are old-settler Ashkenazim. Consequently, the overwhelming majority of members of the Knesset are Ashkenazim. But nothing prevents the Sephardim from voting for a Sephardic party ticket.

Some of the more left-wing parties and protest groups have made unsuccessful attempts to get Sephardic support. In fact, the Israeli Arabs seem to cast more protest votes against the Israeli establishment (by opting for the communists or for Mapam) than do the Sephardim. Unlike the Arabs, the Sephardim tend by their behavior to accept the existing distribution of political privilege.

This political passivity cannot be blamed on lack of political ability. Rather, the behavior of the Sephardim is evidence of the fact that one of the consequences of economic and educational inferiority is the inability to organize on one's own behalf.

In Israel, the Sephardim must learn to organize for their own self-interest. They could easily secure 20 to 30 percent of the Knesset seats. Consider how much power the religious minority has in affecting government policy. They are only 15 percent of the electorate, but that 15 percent imposes its will on the majority. Special laws demanded by the Orthodox are passed, because that 15 percent is needed in order to have a coalition majority. Radical atheists vote for legislation they bitterly dislike, in order to get religious votes for economic bills.

If Sephardim had a bloc representing 25 percent of the Knesset, they would win many things from the government. In order to get this kind of representation, they would have to develop effective leadership, which is difficult. Statistics show that the great majority of the well-educated, well-to-do North African Jews went to France, Canada or other places; Israel received the poorer, less-educated ones. The better educated, well-to-do Turkish Jews never emigrated; the poorest ones went to Israel. In part, the poor Jews did so because they were more religious, but they also migrated because they saw economic hope and possibilities in Israel. Those North African Sephardim who had money or skills moved to

France and other wealthy countries, where they saw even greater opportunity than in Israel.

To mention these facts is not to deny the existence of discrimination, of prejudice, in Israel. There is much discrimination and there is much prejudice, but in part they are produced by the social situation. Negative group stereotypes, even though grossly exaggerated, even though grossly maligning the stereotyped group, are generally rooted in some sort of reality, some characteristic of the group. For example, groups which are poor, who live in slums, generally do have high crime rates as the blacks do in the United States, or as some of the North African groups do in Israel. And as a result, the average person in the society, who is relatively unsophisticated, judges or generalizes about these groups from his surface impression. He says, "These people are dirty, violent, poor; they are not as educated or hard-working as we are. There must be something wrong with them." That kind of reaction to the facts of social and economic inferiority occurs everywhere in the world. It is almost inevitable, and once it occurs, it becomes part of the mechanism which perpetuates inequality, because the feeling that you are superior, or that there is something wrong with the other group, makes you less sympathetic, less inclined to do something about the inequality.

The educational system plays a prime role in absorbing immigrants in the United States and Israel. In the United States at any time most people spoke English and were part of the dominant culture. The large majority were Protestants, primarily of the Methodist and Baptist denominations. Nevertheless, the United States had to absorb many millions of people coming from different cultures, religions, ethnic groups and races.

Basically, the major way which the United States has used to absorb immigrants and to upgrade the people at the bottom has been the school system. Education has been the American key to equality of opportunity, in contrast to the European method, which has put more emphasis on welfare, on lifting up the bottom. Americans always had the notion of opening the race to everybody through giving people equal educational opportunities.

Although as early as the 1840s Americans understood that having a common school requires lowering the level of the educational system, at least through high school, the Israelis still do not understand this. They have *gymnasia*, on the old German model, not common schools. The Israeli high school is incredibly difficult. An Israeli high school student has to take around 14 subjects. Every year he studies chemistry, physics, biology, math, English, Arabic or French, history, Jewish culture and more. He goes to school six days a week, and has four to five hours of homework every day. In this kind of system no child from an underprivileged background, no child who lacks a well-working, supportive family, can possibly do well, unless he is, by some miracle, super-motivated.

Unintentionally, therefore, the Israeli Ashkenazi have developed a school system that does not permit the Israeli underprivileged to succeed. The system thus discourages upward mobility by discouraging those from non-Euro-American high educational cultures.

Many Israelis, Ashkenazim and others—in the government, in the universities, in the Education Ministry—are aware of this. They are consciously concerned with the problem, and are trying to do something about it. But the problem lies in large part with the parents and the teachers. To suggest lowering the educational level of the Israeli high school threatens the status of an Israeli high school teacher, who is like the *lehrer* at a German *gymnasium* or the professor at a French *lycée*. Lowering the intellectual content challenges their status, their identity and their jobs. It is understandable that their unions resist.

The parents resist, too; that is, the parents who themselves are well educated, or moderately well educated, object to changes which appear to give their children a much worse education than earlier generations received. The middle-class parents resist lowering the level of the school—and they constitute a tremendous bloc. The present system also appeases the larger Jewish ethos which assumes that Jews should have the best education possible, that the great contribution of the Jews is as intellectuals, as scientists, as educated people. To propose that Israel should lower its educational level rather than raise it is unthinkable.

There is only one way to break this resistance, and that is a Sephardic political party. When a large group of Sephardim sit in the Knesset and shriek, "We're not going to vote for the budget; we're not going to vote for the government, until you change the school system," they will get action.

This kind of change requires the type of tactics which keep the Sabbath legislation on the books: it requires political punch, and there is none. Only when the Sephardic majority of Israel manifests itself politically are they going to get the privileged groups to give up their privileges. Karl Marx said, and I agree, that no class gives up its power voluntarily. Nobody gives important things away; they may give away a little bit, if they are very rich, but no one gives away the whole basis of his identity, ego, position. He sees these things in his children's education. That is what is involved. Equality in Israel, despite the nation's existing socialist, egalitarian philosophy, will take a long political struggle, comparable to the fight for black civil rights in the United States.

Israeli politicians are no better and no worse than American. They may even be a little bit better, but a little bit, even a lot better, wouldn't make a big difference, would not modify the social processes that make for sharp stratification and perpetuate inequality. These can be changed only by political power.

The effect of political nonparticipation on stratification can be seen in a society which prides itself, at least ideally, on being more egalitarian than the United States or Israel: the Soviet Union. But the Soviet Union does not permit political demonstration, mass movements or contested elections. The Soviets have a large poverty problem, and since the poor cannot apply political pressure, government planners assume that poverty levels will remain the same and construct their budgets accordingly. Further, as documented statistically by sociological surveys by Soviet scholars, inegalitarian patterns of stratification, both ethnic and class, are reinforced in the school system. According to official statistics, the Soviet universities have become less "equal" in recent years. That is, they have smaller percentages of worker and peasant children going to universities; the proportion from what they call the intelligentsia, the nonmanual workers' families, increases. The demand to get into universities grows much more rapidly than does the number of places available. And in an open, competitive system, the children from culturally and economically advantaged backgrounds win out.

Israeli sociological research yields the same findings as do the Soviet and American surveys concerning the continuation of inequality within the educational system. A sociologist, Tessa Blackstone, reviewing much of the literature on the educational experiments in Israel, points this out in the December 1971 issue of the *Jewish Journal of Sociology*. A great deal of American government money for research purposes was promised to Israel on the assumption that in a smaller, more controlled situation, it would be possible to test various proposals to improve the educational level of culturally deprived children. But the Israeli, Russian, and American studies all find that family values, achievement orientation and cultural deprivation are much more potent than anything done in school. Headstart failed in Israel, also, proving that the school cannot make up for the class system. The school cannot drastically change values and orientations which are class-delineated.

It is obvious, of course, that economic factors, not just cultural values, are involved. Not having room to study, cramped housing conditions, being forced to go to work at an early age, the environment of larger families as against smaller families—all constitute disadvantages. Sephardim have larger families than Ashkenazim. Whether this is good or bad from a moral point of view may be left to the rabbis to discuss. But sociological research is definitive in its results; the smaller the family a child comes from, the better he will do in school. In America, blacks object, and in Israel, Sephardim object to the idea of being told that they should have smaller families. They are free to make this choice, but it has clear consequences. There is, of course, need for government subsidies, for government support for children, so that, regardless of the advisability of having larger or smaller families, given children here and now already born, money will be put into improving their environment at a very, very early age, to make up for some of these inhibiting factors.

Some suggest that the army in Israel is an effective integrator and educator, and no doubt good things can be said about its efforts. Yet most of the studies evaluating the army's educational role do not suggest that it presents any great solution, though it does deal fairly well with problems of illiteracy.

One of the interesting things that has come out of some of the sociological studies on education in the army is the discovery that when Israelis with little or no prior education were sent to school immediately after induction, results were disastrous. The new conscripts resisted education; they even rioted. These were Israelis for whom school had been a negative, punitive experience. These conscripts had done badly in school; they had received low grades; they were considered dopes. Going into the army was to be their great opportunity—and to be sent back to school immediately was to be sent back to a painful environment.

The army, therefore, changed its policy. It let the illiterates and the undereducated become soldiers first. (Many of the skills needed for soldiering do not require much schooling.) The army let the soldiers earn their medals and ranks, and then in the latter part of their time in service, sent them to school; that is, after they had acquired dignity and status. And many youths who had done miserably before then did quite well. The fact that they had some success under their belt, some sense of achievement, offset the negative experience of having once been defined as stupid, as unteachable. But the army has too little time to really provide a substantial education.

But whatever the distribution of education, it remains true that in all existing societies there remain both unskilled work and work that requires a high degree of education; and that those employed in either type of job are differentially rewarded. The more common and less skilled the job, the lower the pay; the more skill, the more education the job requires, the better the pay.

Until we devise a workable system giving equal rewards regardless of social position (whether defined by intellectual ability, height, skin color or other factors), the whole rigmarole of stratification, punishment, self-hatred—all of the painful and morally disastrous aspects inherent in social hierarchy—are inevitable.

As Paul Samuelson, the Nobel laureate economist, has noted, it is possible to make a good case for inequality on economic grounds; it is very difficult to make it on moral grounds. Economists and others may argue that there must be differential rewards for skill and dedication, to motivate people to train and study and so on, but it is impossible to defend the proposition that somebody should be better rewarded just because of the accident of birth, for being born in a privileged or cultured family. There is no moral argument which can be made for a person getting a better job, a better education, better skills, better motivation, simply because of his family background.

The moral case for equality is undeniable; but so far no complex society has attempted to counter inequality, and therefore there are tremendous social and economic disparities in nations throughout the world. Clearly, it is possible to have an effectively functioning yet more egalitarian society than exists anywhere at the moment.

Although Israel is as committed to pressing for more equality as any nation on earth, its situation is complicated further by the related problems of continuing immigration and of the Arab proletariat. As a Zionist state, Israel seeks to bring in Jews from all over the world, which today means Jews from relatively affluent, well-educated communities—the United States, Western Europe, South America, and above all, the Soviet Union. The need to encourage immigration involves, in fact, a commitment to further inequality, since potential immigrants are, largely, advantaged people who in most cases have standards of living that are higher than those of all but a handful of the very wealthy Israelis. This excludes the Georgian Jews, but the bulk of Russian Jewish immigrants are well educated and in Russia occupied relatively good positions, as did almost all of the Jews who come from the United States and Latin America. Clearly, to encourage such immigration it is necessary to say to those interested: "We cannot give you the standard of living you're accustomed to, but we can give you a decent apartment, economic opportunity, a good chance for your children to go to college," and so on. That is, Israel must commit itself to placing the new immigrants close to the top of the social hierarchy.

In most countries which have admitted large numbers of immigrants, the newcomers almost invariably entered at the bottom. This certainly was the American experience. Unskilled people, relatively poorly educated people came in from Ireland, Italy, Russia and other places. The first generation came in and took the low-level jobs. The second generation, as reported in the census from 1880 on, had higher-level jobs; the third generation were equal to or even a little better off than the native born of native parents. In effect, each second native-born generation could move up because there always was a recent immigrant group at the bottom.

Currently, the blacks, the Puerto Ricans and the Mexican-Americans are playing this role. They have migrated into the lowest level of the urban system. The only way to have upward mobility is to have new people come in at the bottom.

The Swiss have learned this lesson. They run a magnificent bourgeois society. A million Italians do all the dirty work, but they have no rights, cannot vote, cannot join unions, get no social security and cannot bring their families in. There is a real danger that Israel will become another Switzerland, with West Bank and Gaza Arabs playing the role of the Italians. This possibility—a Jewish bourgeoisie and an Arab proletariat—was the nightmare of the Labor Zionists. It means recreating the situation of the Jews in the affluent Diaspora.

The beginning of such a system may be seen in Israel at five o'clock every day as 25,000 Arab workers line up at the bus stops to go back home to the West Bank. As workers employed by the Jews these Arabs truly have all the economic opportunity that the Israelis now boast about. But this situation is affecting the Israeli social structure. Later, if and when a peace is made, whether the

West Bank becomes independent or semi-independent, presumably some aspect of a common-market customs union will continue. This will mean that the West Bank Arabs, the Palestinian Arabs, will continue to be the proletariat of Israel, even though technically, they live outside the country.

There is a real danger that Israel may gradually slip into the South African-Swiss situation: a labor reserve which resides outside of the country but which does the dirty jobs. This, of course, would permit poor Jews, the Sephardim and others, to move up. In the long run, however, it is a horrible prospect for Israel as a nation and would mean the failure of the aspirations of Zionism. It is terribly tempting for the Israelis to accept Arab labor; even to boast about it, as they're doing now, since it is true that they are raising the standard of living of the Gaza Arabs and the West Bank Arabs. But it is also true that, like the Swiss, they are acquiring a proletariat without political rights.

The depressed situation of the Palestinian Arabs, the limited participation of Israeli Arabs in the cultural, economic and political activities of the state, and the military weaknesses displayed by the Arab states and their guerrillas, combine to reinforce the negative stereotypes of Arabs held by most Jewish Israelis. Opinion polls by local organizations, and by the Louis Harris survey conducted by *Newsweek* earlier this year, indicate clearly that the majority of the Jews regard the Arabs as an inferior people. As in other multi-ethnic societies, the long continuation, within one nation, of different peoples living at sharply varying levels of culture, education and skill, produces or sustains the phenomenon described as institutionalized racism in the United States. In effect, the varying components of the social system serve to prevent the depressed group from gaining access to the good things, while they give the dominant one an ideological defense for their birthright superiority. The Sephardim may improve their situation, but Israel, if it retains its Arab proletariat, will become a racist state like the worst of the gentile states.

There are other and morally preferable ways of solving the problem of the Sephardim. As I indicated earlier, progress lies in the organization of the Sephardim as a political force. They must recognize that they cannot ask the Ashkenazim to be good. No dominant minority in history has ever been good. The Ashkenazim must be pushed. From this perspective the Black Panthers may not be such a bad thing—at least not in name or concept. They may be the beginning of militant organization. Unfortunately, effective

Sephardic activism is held back by the fact that the North African Jewish leadership did not immigrate; only the less educated, less privileged part of the society came to Israel.

The struggle for equality in Israel is buttressed by the nation's fundamental values, much as it is in the United States. Gunnar Myrdal, the Swedish economist and sociologist, wrote a book in the 1940s on the American Negro problem called *The American Dilemma,* in which he made the point that the blacks had one great political asset—namely, that the whites believed in equality, or more accurately, that the whites believed they believed in equality. Myrdal argued that in spite of the horrible racial inequality in the United States, the average American white was committed to the values of the Declaration of Independence, of a democratic egalitarian society. And, given that fact, he maintains his mental equilibrium by believing that the blacks really are not doing so badly, that there is not so much inequality in America. Blacks, therefore, should protest, should demonstrate, to show the whites that they are badly off, that they feel oppressed. The whites, Myrdal predicted in 1944, would not crack down on the black protest but would yield, because their own value system dictated it.

I think the same ideological forces are at work in Israel. Most of the Ashkenazim are socialists. It is hard to say what this means —what "socialist" Israelis are. The fact is, however, that self-identified socialists are more likely to feel guilty about ethnic inequality than are conservatives. Most conservatives believe in the social value or necessity of inequality and hierarchy and therefore have no tendency to feel guilty about being privileged. An affluent socialist is less likely to react against lower-class protest. If in the next few years the Sephardim can organize, they should be able to make gains through the political process. This is the part of the system they have to use first—just as the Irish did, and as the blacks are doing, in America.

The other ethnic problem, that of the Arab proletariat, is much more difficult. Nobody with influence inside the Israeli polity is really seriously concerned about the growth of an Arab proletariat. A few intellectuals write articles; some radicals make speeches in the Knesset; but basically, having people who cannot vote to do all your dirty work is the easiest solution for the problem of inequality for any politician, whether left, right or center.

American Jews cannot help much, since their criticisms can be written off as coming from the outside. But anyone concerned with Israel's future must be aware of the need to face up to the consequences of an external Arab proletariat when considering the problems of peace, of the relations of Israel to the Arab world, and of the nature of Israeli society, of Israel's identity as a nation. In the long run, therefore, the "Israeli dilemma" is not the position of the Sephardim, but that of the Arabs—whether they are to be lowly workers or full partners.

SOCIAL AND
EDUCATIONAL
CHANGE

22

Moshe Lissak

PLURALISM

IN ISRAELI SOCIETY

Modern-day Israeli society, or more exactly the Jewish society in
Israel, cannot be defined as institutionally pluralistic. Absent are
such defining qualities as the simultaneous presence of opposed and
estranged institutional systems, whose points of encounter are
only on the instrumental level. Rather than being exclusive, the
economic, family and cultural frameworks are theoretically and
practically open.

Actually, the political framework before 1948, which included
the Arab and British population, was institutionally pluralistic;
moreover, there were clear symptoms of institutional pluralism
within the Jewish society itself, caused partially by the lack of
political sovereignty. A few prominent remnants of this institutional pluralism exist in Israel at the present day; for example, we
can view as symptoms of pluralism the attempts of different
frameworks, such as the moshav and the kibbutz movement or
Histadrut, to maintain a certain amount of judiciary independence.

Although Israeli society can no longer be said to be institutionally pluralistic, we can still view Israeli society as pluralistic from
the cultural and social points of view. The question is, What is
the character of this pluralism, its degree of crystallization, the

Reprinted with the permission of the Israel Program for Scientific Transla-
tions, Kiryat Moshe, Jerusalem, Israel.

degree of consensus about its organizing principles, its strength and its vulnerable points? In the following discussion, we will deal mainly with the social dimensions of this problem; however, it is worthwhile to make a brief mention of its cultural aspects. Undoubtedly, during the last decade and a half there have been various forms of imitation or adoption of the mores and behavior patterns of the established population; this is particularly noticeable in the young generation. It is obviously difficult to determine the scope and quality of these processes; however, in a careful statement, it might be said that while the "conformity" shown by new immigrants in the early fifties usually referred to a few formal roles and values and was only overt and external,[1] in the mid-sixties as a result of the activity of various socializing agencies such as the school and the army, the pattern changed its character.

Today's conformity is not only less imitative and adaptive, but there is in it a considerable amount of internalization;[2] this is particularly true for those Oriental immigrants who succeeded at the educational and occupational levels. There is in the new conformity a kind of synthesis between authentic cultural elements of some of the Oriental communities and dominant cultural elements in Israeli society. Together with these changes in the bases of conformity of the new immigrants regarding some central values, there has been a complete recess, on the part of the political and cultural elite, from the conformity model which compelled the immigrants to accept unselectively the cultural patterns of the oldtimers. It seems that the melting pot concept has also lost its power of attraction; at any rate its radiance has paled and its realization has been postponed for a few generations. In other words, there has been a de facto recognition of cultural pluralism; this fact per se will lengthen the vitality and validity of this pluralism and, paradoxically, will ensure, *mutatis mutandis*, the realization of the "melting pot" ideal; we say "mutatis mutandis," because this depends on the character of the developing cultural pluralism.

Pluralism can be positively defined as existing in a society when there are cross-cutting encounter points between the various social categories, the entrance to which is voluntary. From a negative point of view it can be seen when there are many cross-cutting conflicts. One of the necessary conditions for the development of these social attributes is a certain degree of institutional dispersion, in which the various groups differing in their ethnic origin and their length of residence are not concentrated in professional, educational, economic and ecological categories but that they are more or less proportionally distributed according to their weight in the total population.

The statistical data do not leave any room for doubt about the fact that institutional dispersion is still far from being a fact. This can be seen from the analysis of the changes in the mobility patterns at the professional, educational, economic and political levels. In order to illustrate this problem we have chosen three categories representing three levels (high, middle and lower middle) of occupation, education and income.[3] A summary of the findings follows:

Dispersion of length of residence and ethnic origin on the occupational level. The central facts on this topic can be seen in Table 1 and can be summarized as follows:

1. Among those occupied in the academic professions and in senior administrative posts, European born (and Israeli born of European origin) are a decisive majority. However, we already find in this category 12 percent of Oriental born and another unknown, but very small, percentage of Israeli born of Oriental origin. Our data explicitly shows that institutional dispersion is smaller when the focus of comparison is country of birth (and length of residence is held constant); the proof of this is that the gap between the overrepresentation of the oldtimers (and the Israeli born) amongst the professionals and between their weight in the total employed population is much smaller than the gap between the overrepresentation of European born (and Israeli born of Western origin) among the professionals and their representation in the total population of the country in this category. The same applies to the comparison of the representation of new immigrants in this category as compared to the representation of Asian-African born (see Table 4).

2. In the occupational category of businessmen, salesmen, etc., we again find both the European population and oldtimers are overrepresented; there is a recurrence, then, of the same phenomenon, by which social (ethnic) origin is a more difficult obstacle to the institutional dispersion of the immigration waves than length of residence.

3. The category of tradesmen, industrial and construction laborers, etc., is the only one in which we are approaching optimal institutional dispersion from an ethnic point of view. When we hold length of residence constant, the partial monopoly in this area is in the hands of those whose stay in the country has been shorter. The proportion of Israeli born

365

Table 1. DISTRIBUTION OF THE EMPLOYED JEWISH POPULATION,
ACCORDING TO CONTINENT OF BIRTH, LENGTH OF RESIDENCE
AND SPECIFIC OCCUPATIONAL CATEGORIES, 1965

	Old-timers	New Immigrants	Israel Born	Total
Total Number Employed:				
Asian-African Born	4.0%	28.7%	–	32.7%
European Born	22.5	27.2	–	49.7
Israel Born	–	–	17.5%	17.5
Total	26.5	55.9	17.5	99.9
Professionals and Executives:				
Asian-African Born	1.3	10.7	–	12.0
European Born	29.1	30.2	–	59.3
Israel Born	–	–	28.7	28.7
Total	30.4	40.9	28.7	100.0
Businessmen, Salesmen, etc.:				
Asian-African Born	6.4	20.7	–	27.1
European Born	29.1	35.3	–	64.4
Israel Born	–	–	8.5	8.5
Total	35.5	56.0	8.5	100.0
Tradesmen, Industrial and Construction Workers:				
Asian-African Born	4.6	40.8	–	44.4
European Born	15.6	26.1	–	41.7
Israel Born	–	–	12.6	12.6
Total	20.2	66.9	12.6	99.7[a]

a-In this case the total sum is not 100 percent because there are 0.3 percent of unclear cases.

in this category is lower than their proportion in the total employed population.[4] These data point to the fact that in spite of the considerable monopoly of the Western population in two central occupational categories, there are signs that cross-cutting encounter situations are being created, at least regarding quantitative proportions. Many Orientals face (at least theoretically) a decision—and this by itself is quite an achievement—of whether to join groups to which they are ethnically close or groups to which they are occupationally close. However, it must be remembered that despite the importance of criteria such as length of residence, ethnic origin and occupation, they are not the only considerations in decisions regarding the joining of primary frameworks, even when there are no other obstacles and joining is the result of a completely voluntary decision (the latter being quite an unlikely event).

Dispersion of length of residence and ethnic origin on the educational level. It is easy to find the causes for the small extent of institutional dispersion on the educational level (see Table 2).

1. There is an overconcentration of European-American born oldtimers and their Israeli-born children in the area of higher education (13 or more years of study). European-born new immigrants are represented in this category almost proportionally to their weight in the population. We found the highest disproportion among Asian-African born who immigrated after 1947.

2. Parallel disproportions, although to a smaller extent, can be found among the medium educated (nine to 10 years of study).

3. The disproportional representation of the Oriental communities on the one hand and of the new immigrants on the other, which was prominent in the last two educational categories, changes in the lowest category (one to four years of study) to overrepresentation. It must be mentioned that European-American-born new immigrants are equally responsible for the overrepresentation of new immigrants in this category, since their weight among those with one to four years of study is equal to that of the Asian-African-born new immigrants.

Dispersion of length of residence and ethnic origin on the economic sphere. The reasons for the unbalanced dispersion of ethnic origin and length of residence on the economic level are the same, to a great extent, as those explaining the disproportional distribu-

Table 2. DISTRIBUTION OF JEWISH POPULATION AGED 14 AND OVER
ACCORDING TO CONTINENT OF BIRTH, LENGTH OF RESIDENCE AND
YEARS OF STUDY, 1961

	Old-timers	New Immigrants	Israel Born	Total
Total Population Aged 14+:				
Asian-African Born	4.1%	29.6%		33.7%
European Born	21.1	28.1		49.2
Israel Born	–	–	17.0%	17.0
Total	25.2	57.7	17.0	99.9
13+ Years of Study				
Asian-African Born	1.6	8.6		10.2
European Born	34.0	30.0		64.0
Israel Born	–	–	26.0	26.0
Total	35.6	38.6	26.0	100.2
9-10 Years of Study				
Asian-African Born	2.5	19.7		22.2
European Born	26.3	28.1		54.4
Israel Born	–		23.4	23.4
Total	28.8	47.8	23.4	100.0
1-4 Years of Study				
Asian-African Born	4.9	40.6		45.5
European Born	8.6	41.4		50.0
Israel Born			4.4	4.4
Total	13.5	82.0	4.4	99.9

Adopted from publications of the *Population and Housing Census*, No. 15, Table 28.

tion of the occupational and educational levels (see Table 3). However, there are a few significant variations:

1. In the high-income categories there is a considerable monopoly of European-American-born oldtimers and their children. The proportion of European-American new immigrants is smaller than their proportion in the total population; the same applies, to a much greater extent, to Asian-African-born new immigrants and oldtimers.

2. In the second category there is somewhat less disproportion. The improvement concerns mainly European-American born who immigrated after 1947 and Asian-African-born oldtimers; Asian-African-born new immigrants are considerably backward in this category as well.

3. The definite majority of the Oriental oldtimers and new immigrants is, of course, in the lower occupational category (although not yet the lowest); however, European-American born are also represented in this category slightly above their weight in the total population.

These data make clear that the extent of the dispersion of ethnic origin and length of residence on the various levels that we have considered presents variations which are important to take into account (although the dispersion seems to be the same in all levels). Table 4 presents a comparative summary of these variations.

In the highest category [5] (which includes the highest level of the three mentioned status elements) we find that, ethnically, the most proportional representation occurred in the early sixties on the income level; after that on the occupational level; and at the end on the educational sphere. Regarding length of residence the situation is reversed; the most proportional representation (relatively) is found on the occupational sphere, after that on the educational sphere, while the income sphere is the area where the new immigrants are most highly frustrated. Israeli born enjoy superiority on all levels and especially on the occupational one. In the second category,[6] which includes the medium degree of the three status elements, Asian-African born are not represented proportionally to their weight in the population; the disproportion appears first on the educational level, and then on the income and occupational levels. Regarding length of residence, new immigrants (regardless of their ethnic origin) are adequately represented in the occupational level; this is not the case at the income, and even less so at the educational levels. It is interesting that Israeli born, who are overrepresented in the second educational level, are not adequately

Table 3. DISTRIBUTION OF FAMILIES OF JEWISH SALARIED WORKERS,
ACCORDING TO NET INCOME GROUPS AND ACCORDING TO
CONTINENT OF BIRTH AND IMMIGRATION PERIOD OF
HEAD OF FAMILY, 1963-1964

	Old-timers	New Immigrants	Israel Born	Total
All Salaried Families:				
Asian-African Born	4.4%	27.5%	–	31.9%
European Born	22.8	33.5	–	56.3
Israel Born	–	–	11.3	11.3
Total	27.2	61.0	11.3	99.5
Earning 800+ Israeli Pounds:				
Asian-African Born	2.5	9.9	–	12.4
European Born	39.6	30.2	–	69.8
Israel Born	–	–	17.3	17.3
Total	42.1	40.1	17.3	99.5
Earning 500-599 Israeli Pounds:				
Asian-African Born	5.0	20.0	–	25.0
European Born	26.8	38.9	–	65.7
Israel Born	–	–	9.8	9.8
Total	31.8	58.9	9.8	100.5
Earning 300-349 Israeli Pounds:				
Asian-African Born	5.3	45.3	–	50.6
European Born	7.6	35.9	–	43.5
Israel Born	–	–	5.6	5.6
Total	12.9	81.2	5.6	99.7

Table 4. POPULATION DISTRIBUTION ACCORDING TO ETHNIC ORIGIN, LENGTH OF RESIDENCE, OCCUPATION, EDUCATION AND INCOME

	Occupation	Education	Income
First category			
Asian-African Born	-20.7%	-23.5%	-18.5%
European-American Born	+ 9.6	+15.0	+13.6
Israel Born	+12.2	+ 9.2	+ 6.2
Oldtimers	+ 3.9	+10.4	+14.9
New Immigrants	-15.0	-18.9	-20.8
Second category			
Asian-African Born	- 5.6	-11.5	- 6.8
European-American Born	+14.7	+ 5.2	+ 9.5
Israel Born	- 9.0	+ 6.5	- 1.1
Oldtimers	+ 9.0	+ 3.6	+ 4.6
New Immigrants	+ 0.1	- 9.9	- 8.1
Third category			
Asian-African Born	+11.7	+11.8	+18.7
European-American Born	- 8.0	+ 0.8	-12.7
Israel Born	- 4.9	-12.5	- 5.7
Oldtimers	- 6.3	-11.7	-14.3
New Immigrants	+11.0	+24.3	+20.2

represented in the occupational level on this category. In the third category,[7] the acute backwardness of the Oriental immigrants is manifest in their overrepresentation at the economic level, less so at the educational and occupational ones. Regarding length of residence, the new immigrants' position is at its worst on the educational and income levels, and less so on the occupational one.

Summarizing, it appears that the achievements of certain groups from among the Asian-African born, in the process of their mobility until the mid-sixties, were better in the high and medium categories of the income level than they were in the occupational (except for the medium category) and educational levels. In other words, institutional dispersion from an ethnic point of view is more successful on the income level than on the occupational and educational levels. On the other hand, new immigrants (regardless of ethnic origin) succeed first and foremost on the occupational level; their achievements are small on the economic level and poorer still on the educational one. These relative gains attest to the fact that the central mobility patterns for the Oriental communities (oldtimers and new immigrants, and to a certain extent also for Western new immigrants) are mainly on the occupational and economic levels.[8] However, their achievements are still quite limited when compared to those of the Western oldtimers and their children, who were also mobile in this period, and in many cases their mobility took on a much quicker pace than that of the Oriental communities. It would be difficult to define the achievement of the Oriental communities as the attainment of serious bargaining positions or of assets exchangeable for other power positions. We might say, then, that above all, the main asset of this group is its quantitative weight, this factor being relevant mainly on the political level. Indeed, on the highest category of the three levels (occupation, education and income) there are on the average about 11 percent of Asian-African born and in the medium categories about 25 percent, and these are not negligible achievements; however, it would obviously be a mistake to assume that everyone belonging to the 11 percent in the high category (and the same applies to the 25 percent in the medium category) has parallel achievements in all the three status elements. On the contrary, many sources provide evidence of the fact that the status profiles of a considerable number of people in these categories are inconsistent, and their status components are "spread" over two or three levels of achievements. It is also worth mentioning that in the low educational category (one to four years of study) the absolute number of European-American born is higher than the number of Asian-African born, although proportional to their weight in the total population the latter carry a considerable overrepresentation in this category; the reason for the more or less equal weight of the two groups in this category is that a high percentage of the European new immigrants did not receive formal education, even at the elementary level, as a result of World War II. In the additional educational category of illiteracy, the situation again changes and the Asian-African born are the decisive majority—84 percent. We find, then, first signs of the existence of cross-cutting encounter situations which can serve as integration mechanisms, although there is no assurance that they will be used for this purpose or that this will be the trend of development in the future. Moreover, the decisive point in the understanding of the problem of integrating the new immigrants on the social and political level is not the existence of a sufficient number of favorable conditions in the quantitative aspects of institutional dispersion which might make social pluralism viable. The fact that we still face a simultaneous, though unequal, monopoly over the political and economic power and occupational prestige is the disturbing factor on the way to the consolidation and institutionalization of a pluralistic society which could effectively deal with the tensions typical of such a structure. In order to achieve such results, it is important not only that there be a relatively good dispersion of length of residence and ethnic origin on the medium levels of the occupational, educational and income scale; what counts is the extent to which there are homogeneous profiles regarding length of residence, ethnic origin, education, income and occupation on the highest, but more specially on the lowest levels. Moreover, the process of homogenization of status is still very intensive among European born, and at times it seems to overcome, on the short range, the process of institutional dispersion which moves at a slower pace and whose results can only be seen in the long range. This situation, in spite of its transience, and maybe precisely because of it, is extremely critical, because the relatively slow mobility of the Oriental community has caused a gap, greater than at any other time before, between the combination of income, education and occupation on the one hand, and political power and social prestige on the other. Moreover, this gap between the positive—in absolute terms—changes in the status elements and the negative—relatively and comparatively—changes is subjectively a potentially dangerous situation and an ideal breed-ing ground for the growth of predispositions towards aggressive acts.[9]

At any rate, there is no doubt that the legitimacy of the old rules governing the contact and the encounter between the differ-ent ethnic groups is being shattered, and in the process of its destruction the old bases of integration (the voluntary ones of the yishuv period and the bureaucratic power ones of the early fifties) are also being shaken. It is typical of the transition period that while the dominant side does not rush to redefine the balance of forces, the side that is being frustrated becomes increasingly impa-tient. Until a new constellation appears in the stratification system which is more permissive and flexible and less hierarchical and scaled than it is today, this transition period is a time in which there are real dangers to the proper functioning of the integrative mechanisms of the pluralistic society, which is full of potential antagonisms. Their failure can result either from the fact that these mechanisms are still very young or from their being inten-tionally or unintentionally hurt; moreover, the possibility of re-gression or freezing must not be excluded. Do we have any guar-antee that this breakthrough into the socioecological enclaves will continue until a (quite mysterious) optimum of partial overlappings is achieved and cross-cutting loyalties are developed? Key positions in these processes will certainly be fulfilled by the elites of the different communities, who will mold the collective symbols of identity and the degree of militancy or aggression of the bearers of this identity. The influence that this elite can exert is of course a function of its composition regarding length of residence, age and the achievements of its members, particularly their generally un-successful attempts to attain power positions in the Knesset, in the government bureaucracy and in the party centers.[10]

In view of the increasing identity between voting and class— ethnic consciousness—there is no escape from the conclusion that a significant part of these elites has taken the path of political— ethnic—class struggle, either in the framework of opposition parties or in independent ethnic lists. Those relatively mobile on the eco-nomic, educational and occupational levels are the ones who em-phasize the political aspect of the struggle; they are extremely dis-illusioned by the impossibility of translating their achievements into real political power on the one hand and diffuse prestige on the other, and feel, more than others, the relative oligarchization of the power elite of Israeli society. The burden of the struggle in the more narrow sphere of income, namely, the struggle to ensure minimal economic security, falls upon the shoulders of the non-mobile or, more exactly, upon those whose mobility results from fluctuations in the relative position of classes as a whole (or entire classes) and not from their personal achievements, which is a phenomenon very typical of immigration countries.[11] Either way, the changes in the stratification system of the Oriental communities have led to the growth of a movement which demands changes in the whole stratification structure, as a result of the intensification of the power orientation in the elite of the Oriental communities. This orientation, which had been extremely strengthened in the oldtimers' population as a result of the sudden influx of hundreds of thousands of potential voters into the political arena, has found new stepparents, who are even more extreme and fanatical than its forefathers. There is no doubt that the intensification of such an orientation might increase particularistic identifications, focus diffuse feelings of deprivation around specific problems and turn latent aggression into open hostility. This can, first of all, be expressed in independent political organizations such as the presentation of ethnic lists to the Knesset and the municipalities. Another level at which this development might be reflected is in increasing pressure to change the qualifications for the senior appointments in the administration, education and in the centers of political power. Symptoms of this trend can be found now and they might gain more ground with the increasing impatience to shorten the way to key positions. In the long run, demands of this kind will be completely unnecessary, since the quantity and quality of Oriental candidates for top positions in the administration and in politics will considerably increase, even according to the most pessimistic prognoses. However, patterns of selection based on rational-achieving criteria might be disturbed to the extent that clearly particularistic selection patterns will be institutionalized instead. The Jewish population as a whole has experienced the difficulties connected with the establishment of universalistic selection patterns, since different patterns had been in existence at the time of the yishuv. It seems that these processes, although their strength cannot be predicted, may be inevitable as long as the concentration of political power, social prestige and economic positions in the hands of one sector is faster than the process of partial and unbalanced mobility on the part of the sector aspiring to change. Such a situation, given the rigidity and lack of differentiation of the involved processes, will be unable to give life to the potential points of encounters.

The blurring of the pluralistic character of Mapai and of the other parties that are frequent partners in the governmental coalitions on the one hand, and the homogenization of the traditional opposition parties on the other, might have implications as to the character of the political activity in the state as a whole. There is an important link between a consensus-democratic regime in a pluralistic society and socially heterogeneous parties. A pluralistic and heterogeneous structure softens the dangerous confrontation between socially, ethnically and religiously homogeneous units. The pluralistic party digests and strains the pressures and demands; moreover, through its struggle with its heterogeneous electorate, the party achieves understanding and appreciation for its middle frameworks, which mediate between the party elite and the mass of members. A party of this kind cannot, and is not even interested, in preventing the creation of factions, pressure groups and voluntary organizations, either for ad hoc purposes or of a more definite character; even if it does not hasten to award formal recognition to such structures, neither does it try to organize all this complex system in a hierarchical way. A pluralistic party does not insist on clear definitions regarding the placing of the jurisdictions and the power centers, and its perspective is more egalitarian-horizontal than authoritarian-vertical. This approach is usually applied on the national level; pluralistic democratic parties will encourage the creation of voluntary bodies, and, what is more important, will be more restrained and lenient towards independent or semi-independent power centers. Homogeneous or bipolar parties do not digest easily the existence of independent power centers which act as middle links between the power elites and the population; they are not "trained" to deal with them because of the absence of such links within their parties.

In analyzing the trends in the integration of the Oriental communities in the political and stratification systems of Israel, one is tempted to make a slightly pessimistic and anxious prognosis for the next decade. However, this pessimism is definitely relative and conditional; we have pointed here to the slow formation of mechanisms which might, in the long run, contribute to a fuller integration of Israeli society. An intelligent view of the sources of the crisis, an understanding of the processes and an attempt to regulate them will prevent the regression of Israeli society from a stage of advancement towards social and cultural pluralism to a stage of institutional pluralism based on ethnic principles. The danger of such a deterioration is indeed small, and there are several factors in Israeli society which might soften such a development, although to consider them is not within the scope of this chapter. However, we must not ignore the implications which the next decade might have for the future character of Israeli society. It is not sufficient to raise the standard of education or to ensure economic security, without guaranteeing more practical integration in positions of power and prestige. How this should be done is a problem in itself. At any rate, ignoring this problem will increase the tension, encourage particularistic ideologies and, in the end, will bring about the appearance of a charismatic leader, who will lead his flock into a deeper struggle, the results of which cannot be foreseen.

NOTES

1. S. N. Eisenstadt, *The Absorption of Immigrants* (London, Routledge & Kegan Paul, 1954), pp. 213-214.

2. This generalization has to be read with reservations. Various studies have proved that the achievements are still small. See L. Adar and H. Adler, *Hahinukh leArakhim beVatey-Sefer liyladim Olim* [Education towards values in schools for immigrant children], (Jerusalem: School of Education, Hebrew University, and the Ministry of Education), 1965, pp. 109-110.

3. The three occupational levels are levels in the prestige scale of Israel: see M. Lissak, "Pattern of Change in Ideology and Class Structure in Israel," *Jewish Journal of Sociology* (June 1965), pp. 46-48. See also "Haribud hahevrati bayishuv uvamedina" (Social stratification in the Yishuv and the State), *Molad*, (November 1964) vol. 22, no. 195-196.

4. It must be pointed out that although institutional dispersion in this category is better than in other occupational categories, this generalization does not take into account that a considerable part of European born in this category are foremen, etc. and the Asian-African born are their subordinates.

5. This category includes professionals and executives on the occupational level, university graduates and with a net income of over 800 Israeli pounds a month (in 1963/1964).

6. This category includes businessmen and commercial agents on the occupational level, with 9-10 years of study, earning 500 to 600 Israeli pounds a month.

7. This category includes skilled laborers on the occupational level with 1 to 4 years of study, earning 300 to 350 Israeli pounds a month.

8. See also M. Lissak, "Zipiyot leMobiliut Hevratit uVehirat miqzoa beqerev Noar Ironi beIsrael" (Expectations of social mobility and occupational choice amongst urban youth in Israel), *BaHistadrut*, no. 4 (1965-66), pp. 2-40.

9. J. Galtung, "A Structural Theory of Aggression," *Journal of Peace Research*, vol. 1 (1964), pp. 97-99.

10. The average of Asian-African born Knesset members in the six Knessets is 7 percent (in the first Knesset 2.5 percent; in the sixth Knesset 12.5 percent). The percentage of members of Oriental communities within the senior ranks of the civil service is 28 percent. In the Zionist Executive, out of 80 members, there is not more than one member of the Oriental communities.

11. S. M. Miller, "Comparative Social Mobility," *Current Sociology*, vol. 60, no. 1 (1960), pp. 5-10.

23

Nancy Datan

YOUR DAUGHTERS SHALL PROPHESY: ANCIENT AND CONTEMPORARY PERSPECTIVES ON THE WOMEN OF ISRAEL

Israel, where feminists coexist uncomfortably with traditionalism and orthodoxy, contains a broad spectrum of dramatically contrasting life styles; and these contrasts, I believe, can provide some unique insights into the new meanings of "female" and "male" which are evolving out of today's movements for women's rights. As an American woman and a social scientist, I encountered a set of paradoxes when I immigrated to Israel and especially when I participated in a cross-cultural study of 1,200 women of five Israeli subcultures, ranging from modern European Jewish immigrants to traditional Arab Muslim villagers.[1]

Before I contrast ancient and contemporary role expectations for the women in Israel and describe the peculiar consequences my colleagues and I have discovered, I would like to highlight some contrasts between the worlds of American and Israeli women. In the United States, Shirley Chisholm's declaration of candidacy elicited the question, Is this country ready for a woman president? That question was not asked in Israel when Golda Meir stepped into the office of Prime Minister. Yet when one says "husband and wife" in Hebrew, one says *ba'al v'ishah*—owner and woman; and a standard congratulatory telegram to the parents of a newborn baby girl is "A firstborn daughter is a sign of many sons." In brief, then, in Israel one sees that a woman of ability can rise to the head of government—side by side with indications that, among certain sectors of the population, women are emphatically the second sex.

Recently there has been some critcism within Israel of the self-righteous smugness of Israeli women who have, by and large, disdained the American women's movement. Shulamit Aloni [2] claims that their disdain is increasingly unjustified. It is true that in Israel a framework of progressive legislation is already present; and Aloni notes almost in passing that in the professions and in the universities success is as open to women as to men, both because there is no discrimination by sex and because the recent history of the state includes the tradition of the dynamic, pioneering woman. Before I move to her criticisms, I want to point out that these are exactly the goals of the American Women's Liberation Movement; in these terms Israel can be described as a feminist's utopia.

Aloni, however, argues that the achievements of the early pioneers are steadily being eroded by a number of factors: the hardships of the early days, when the scarcity of manpower forced women into the fields and onto the frontiers, have given way to comparative affluence. Affluence has in turn permitted women to withdraw from the labor market, and simultaneously led to advertising oriented toward the woman as consumer in a life style of leisure. Aloni concludes that the women of Israel need to be responsive to the worldwide women's rebellion while it is still true that no rebellion is needed in Israel and while there is still time to achieve equality of status merely by exercising rights already written into the laws of the land.

While I support this position in most respects, I find the collapse of the Israeli feminist revolution—which is paralleled by a decline in American feminism from 1920 until quite recently—intriguing rather than dismaying. It suggests that equality of opportunity will not lead at once to the disappearance of sex-role differentiation, and it raises the possibility that there may be something of value in traditional sex roles.

Israel is the land which gave Western civilization its traditions of male dominance and female subordination. The traditional sex roles are expressed in Genesis as Adam and Eve are expelled from the Garden of Eden: Eve is told, "In sorrow thou shalt bring forth thy children; thy desire shall be to thy husband and he shall rule over thee," and Adam is told, "By the sweat of thy brow shalt thou eat bread." With the passing of time, men's sweat has been mitigated by modern industrial technology, and modern medicine has mitigated women's woe in childbirth; perhaps these alterations in traditional labor have caused the most recent disruption—the challenge to the husband's rule.

There are a number of facets of Orthodox Judaism which, according to most anthropological criteria,[3] are constraints on women, and indicate male dominance and female subordination: these include the traditional bride-price, menstrual separation, ritual periods of uncleanness following childbirth—and the fact that the period of uncleanness is twice as long for the birth of a daughter as for a son.

Judaic ritual was altered very little until the period of enlightenment in Europe. A movement to reform Orthodox Jewish religious practices grew up in Central Europe in the nineteenth century: women no longer sat to worship in the screened, secluded gallery, but sat together with men; the elaborate network of sexual and menstrual taboos was simplified and reduced, with more room for individual variation in ritual observance. These changes signified a rejection of the traditional subordinate status of women set out in Biblical codes.[4]

Simultaneously with the nineteenth-century European movement for religious reform in Judaism, the economic changes which accompanied increasing urbanization led to a strong movement for equality of women's rights, and women, in turn, began to achieve prominence in a number of areas. Although there was a high proportion of Jewish women in the movement for emancipation, no specific large-scale Jewish women's movement existed until the twentieth century.[5]

Israel's primary role models, of course, were the Russian-Jewish women who immigrated in the Second Aliyah, between 1905 and 1914, bringing with them a pioneering ideology, secular and egalitarian, which was perfectly suited to the circumstances of the land: dry, swamp or rocky, it was available for redemption only through the marshalling of all available human resources. Radical changes in sex roles occurred in the pioneering period; it is well known that child-bearing was made collective, so that women were free to share the duties of heavy labor and military defense. Men did not, however, take the primary responsibility for child-rearing by becoming child caretakers, so we might say in a sense that the kibbutzim, at least at first, masculinized everyone in the service of egalitarianism.

The pioneering farmwomen were joined by the subsequent wave of immigration from Central Europe in the 1930s; this second stream brought an alternate model of the emancipated woman, professional rather than farmer. A number of forces converged at this point in the history of Israel to support and further the emancipation of women from their traditional roles; and at the time of the founding of the state a number of fundamental laws were passed guaranteeing equal rights regardless of sex.

It should be pointed out, however, that coexisting with these pioneering women were groups of women who were quite traditional in various ways. There were devout, Orthodox Jews of Central Europe, who were as highly educated as their secular, pioneering counterparts, but continued to observe religious ritual. There were Jews from Near Eastern countries, where no comparable movement for religious reform had occurred, and where the movement for the emancipation of women (which had occurred in Europe 100 years before) was only beginning. Finally, there were traditional Arab Muslim villagers, whose life style has been compared by Raphael Patai [6] to that of the Biblical Hebrews.

Aaron Antonovsky, Benjamin Maoz and I carried out a study of 1,200 Israeli women from five ethnic groups which represent varying degrees of modernization. We studied modern, urban Europeans; transitional Turks, Persians and North Africans; and traditional Arab villagers. Our study did not include kibbutz women or significant numbers of devout but highly educated Europeans, or modern, urban Muslim or Christian Arabs, so many fascinating questions about various subtle facets of modernity and the revolution in women's roles in Israel were not tested in our research.

We were interested in a rather straightforward issue: what is the effect of the degree of modernity on a woman's success in adapting to the changes in middle age? We had some tentative hypotheses as we began our work. My male colleagues felt that the traditional woman would adapt more successfully: she had borne a large family; she could expect to rise to the status of matriarch, with authority over son's wives and greater personal freedom than before. Conversely and certainly not by chance, I was convinced that the modern woman would adapt more successfully: she had alternate roles and was not dependent on motherhood for self-esteem, so the departure of children from the home would pose no crisis. Support could be found for either viewpoint in the conflicting literature on the psychology of women.

It should be stressed that we all expected that the degree of modernity would bear a linear relationship to the measure of adaptation; we differed in the direction of our predictions. Some of our findings have been reported in detail elsewhere;[7] for the purposes of the present essay, I simply want to describe the fate of our predictions. On such measures as social role satisfaction, psychological well-being and response to menopause, we obtained a fairly clear answer to the question of the effect of the degree of modernity on the success of adaptation to middle age. It turned out that each theory was half right: the most successful adaptation was seen at the two poles of the traditionalism-modernity continuum—among the Arabs and the Europeans.

With the wisdom of hindsight, we all wondered why we could not have foreseen this pattern as the most likely. Clearly the Europeans and the Arabs, despite the dislocations of World War II and the Israeli wars of independence, Sinai and 1967, were living in relatively stable environments in terms of cultural continuity. It may be surmised that transitional women are subject to a particular stress because the cultural cues that they learned in childhood and young adulthood no longer serve them. The immigrant European entered a society where the dominant cultural values were those of enlightened European Jewry; the Arab woman, like the immigrant Near Eastern Jew, also witnessed the penetration of new life styles, but change came more gradually into the villages. The transitional women, born in countries where the transformation from folkways to modernization was taking place fairly rapidly, were then transplanted to a country where modernization was complete and their relatively traditional life styles were outmoded: their greater problems may have been due to the stress of meeting the demands of a modern environment with outmoded responses.

As we move from traditional through transitional to modern groups in this study, we see the emergence of the woman from a position of subordination and subservience to a more egalitarian status. In general, the process of modernization has been associated with increased psychological well-being.[8] Many factors are involved in this pattern: socioeconomic status rises with modernization; furthermore, even most of the traditional villagers have some exposure to the mass media, and therefore some awareness that the world is moving on while they are not, that material comforts are available but not to them—and that their children may move forward to achieve these comforts and in rejecting traditional folkways perhaps reject their parents as well. Yet in our study, the transition toward modernity, and the resulting emancipation and liberation, did not by themselves bring about increased psychological well-being: on the contrary, as I have remarked elsewhere,[9] the process of liberation appears costly and painful.

At one level of interpretation, I have suggested that modern and traditional women are alike in that each is adapted to her environment, and is equipped with the appropriate skills for manipulation. Magic and ritual evolved as tools for control, the primitive forerunners of a professional education: both groups of women, then, are educated for achievement, each in our own way. This is certainly an adequate explanation of our data, and indeed we do not have sufficient exploratory, descriptive data to permit any more elaborated explanations.

However, I have been intrigued by the similarity in successful adaptation seen at the two extremes of the traditionalism-modernity continuum in our study, and my exposure to the American women's liberation movement over the past year and a half in the United States has sensitized me still further to the puzzles of bisexuality. Accordingly, I have some speculations to offer about some aspects of maleness and femaleness which I have observed under the special conditions of dramatic contrast which obtain in Israel.

In addition to the legally prescribed favoritism shown to males, Israel is guilty of many practices which discriminate between men and women. The language itself discriminates: Hebrew is a highly inflected language and one cannot make a simple declaration such as "I work" without simultaneously declaring one's sex through the form of the verb. Just as in English, the generalized singular pronoun is "he," but worse than that, there is no common plural gender in Hebrew corresponding to the English "they" or "them," so that if there is a gathering in Israel of nuclear physicists, consisting of 200 hundred women and one man, the press will use the masculine plural to describe the crowd.

I would like to suggest, however, that discrimination between men and women is not inevitably discrimination against women. Only where sex is inextricably bound to status does it seem necessary to strive for the elimination of sex-based differentiation. I have previously noted that the kibbutzim, even at their most revolutionary, always assigned women to the children's houses, and I have heard American feminists criticize this practice as discriminatory. What is not obvious to an American audience is that the role of caretaker is very much prized, and so women seek to achieve it, rather than seek to be liberated from it. On a similar note, a Communist Chinese woman declared, "The education of children is directly related to the liberation of women," and I agree, but she went on to say, "Women used to worry about how to run a family and serve her husband, but now our great ambition is to make revolution." I don't think that is the liberating message in the excellent system of preschool education in China or in Israel. Rather, a nation which cares so intensely about the education of its children is raising the status of its women in a far more essential way than merely by "liberating" them from child care: it is affirming their irreplaceable importance as childbearers by sharing in the process of child rearing.

One of the paradoxes of the feminist revolution on the Israel kibbutzim was that women did aspire to the role of caretaker in the children's house. This is in no way inconsistent with the emphasis Judaism has always placed on the education of its children, but it is inconsistent with the apparent aim of the kibbutzim to achieve complete egalitarianism in sex roles. It suggests, in fact, that when the traditional role of housekeeper-mother does not entail secondary status, it exerts a powerful attraction even to pioneers and revolutionaries; and this in turn helps to explain the endurance of traditions which appear to discriminate against women without any obvious compensation.

Arguments against sex discrimination have by now become public currency. I don't dare argue in a public forum *for* sex discrimination of any sort, because the issue has become so polarized that I would find myself in the company of a number of ideological bedfellows whose views I do not share in any way. However, I have begun to feel that the continual, rather tense interplay between tradition and liberation in Israel serves a number of functions. First, tradition defines the status of women with absolute clarity. This has two consequences: for the traditional woman, a viable set of guidelines is provided for a role which, although it is secondary in status, is vital to family functioning.

The best illustration of the breadth of ritual expectations is in the verses *eshet hayil* (a woman of valor) whose price is above rubies. The woman of these verses is very different from the current stereotype of the traditional woman, for she not only sees to the household but conducts a thriving business in linen with the

Canaanites—in short, she is exercising a broad range of talents in a variety of roles both domestic and economic. To repeat: she is not "confined" to the household; more likely, her energies and abilities are stretched as far as they will go, inside and outside the home. This has been true of traditional women generally, and it is only when industrialization and urbanization remove most of the traditional woman's economic and domestic functions that we begin to see the stereotype emerge: a woman confined, whose energies are going to waste. However, Orthodox Judaism continues to provide vital roles for women with regard to religious ritual, and my observation—although I would like to see the question systematically tested by research—is that Orthodox Judaism provides sustenance for women as well as men.

However, some feminists are bound to remark that certain meanings in the very beautiful verses of *eshet hayil* emerge more clearly if it is altered slightly and we recite, "A man of valor, who can find? for his price is above rubies." There is no question at all in my mind that no man would want his price discussed—no matter how high it is fixed—for it immediately raises the question of who is doing the buying and selling.

This leads me to the second consequence of the clear traditional prescriptions on the status of women. While the traditional woman is obviously given a definite set of guidelines, paradoxically, I believe, the woman who is seeking a new self-definition is also aided by the clarity of tradition. In contrast to American women, who currently oppose not only legal inequities but also a set of diffuse, invisible constraints in the unspoken American role models, and are forced to extremes of protest in order to make these constraints visible at all, those who oppose the status of women in Judaism deal with specific instances where women and men do not have equality. I have begun to feel that the visibility of these constraints serves to liberate women from diffuse feelings of inferiority by defining the issues they wish to challenge.

I have said that the interplay between tradition and liberation in Israel serves to define the status of women in two ways: first, the traditional role of wife, mother and homemaker is a clear one, and even to an outsider much of the religious ritual assigned to women can be seen as the source of great potential satisfaction. Second, the clarity of definition also delineates areas of controversy on the status of women, and I have suggested that this may indirectly lead to a measure of psychological liberation for the feminist.

The final point of this chapter links both of the observations thus far expressed: first, that the Israeli revolution for equality of sex rights has lost much of its original impetus, and on the kibbutzim as well as elsewhere there has been a return, to some extent, to the traditional feminine role; second, that our research suggested that both traditional and modern women were better off than women in the middle stage, transitional between traditionalism and modernity. It seems apparent that these observations grow out of a common base, which is the viability of the traditional female role.

I have come to believe that feminists and revolutionaries have something to learn from tradition. I suspect that the history of feminism in Israel teaches us that a movement intended to erase sex-role differences is bound to fail, simply because in its strong opposition to sex-linked status inequities the movement ignores the appeal of tradition. I am not, then, predicting total failure for the feminist revolution: instead, I want to assert that female roles will forever involve tension between sex-typed roles and egalitarianism. The pull toward sex typing is rooted in male and female polarities, biological imperatives which urge us into a sexual dialectic, a part of which is to affirm our sexual differences.

I want to suggest, further, that signs of sex discrimination in Israel such as those that I have earlier described may have a latent function in addition to their manifest function of preserving tradition. These sexual labels of language, work and ritual—sexual stigmata, if you wish—also serve as sexual self-affirmation. For the feminist in Israel, then, tradition not only states issues to which she is opposed, but also defines her as female—sparing her, it may be, the need to take on a sex-typed role to maintain this definition.

I take as axiomatic that the assertion of femaleness and maleness is natural to us, and that the expression of one's sexuality is intrinsically good. But sex differences have been linked to status differences throughout human history, and so feminist movements of the past and present have generally had to strive to eliminate both. This has been true of the feminism of the pioneering generation in Israel and will be true also, I expect, of any women's liberation movement in Israel today. The unique good fortune of the women of Israel is the remarkable cultural pluralism in contemporary Israeli society, offering a spectrum of role models from the secular pioneer to the traditionalist. This cultural pluralism includes contradiction and conflict as well as opportunity, but I believe that some measure of contradiction is inherent in attempts to resolve sexual identity with equality, and this resolution may forever take the form of ongoing conflict between some form of sex-typing and some form of egalitarianism—with pluralism the most successful outcome.

NOTES

1. The study was directed by Aaron Antonovsky of the Israel Institute of Applied Social Research; Benjamin Maoz of the Beilinson Medical Center was project codirector. The study was supported by a grant from the U.S. National Institute of Mental Health.

2. Shulamit Aloni, "Israeli Women Need Women's Lib!" *Israel Magazine*, vol. 3 no. 4: 58-68.

3. Pauline Bart, "Depression in Middle-Aged Women: Some Socio-Cultural Factors" (Ph.D. diss., University of California at Los Angeles, 1967).

4. Rufus Learsi, *Israel: A History of the Jewish People* (New York: World, 1966).

5. Howard Morley Sacher, *The Course of Modern Jewish History* (New York: Dell, 1958).

6. Raphael Patai, *Sex and Family in the Bible and the Middle East* (New York: Doubleday, 1959).

7. Aaron Antonovsky, Benjamin Maoz, Nancy Dowty, and Henricus Wijsenbeek, "Twenty-Five Years Later: A Limited Study of the Sequellae of the Concentration Camp Experience." *Social Psychiatry* (Jerusalem: Academic Press, 1973).

Nancy Dowty, *Women's Attitudes towards the Climacterium in Five Israeli Sub-Cultures* (Ph.D. diss., University of Chicago, 1971).

Nancy Dowty, Benjamin Maoz, Aaron Antonovsky, and Henricus Wijsenbeek, "Climacterium in Three Cultural Contexts," *Tropical and Geographical Medicine*, 22 (1970): 77-86.

Benjamin Maoz, Nancy Dowty, Aaron Antonovsky, and Henricus Wijsenbeek, "Female Attitudes to Menopause," *Social Psychiatry*, 5 (1970): 1.

8. Daniel Lerner, *The Passing of Traditional Society: Modernizing the Middle East* (Glencoe, Ill.: The Free Press, 1958).

9. Nancy Dowty, "To Be a Woman in Israel," *School Review*, vol. 80, no. 2 (February 1972): 319-332.

24

Elad Pelled

EDUCATION:

THE SOCIAL CHALLENGE

Israel's most significant social experiment is itself. Created in May of 1948, it is entirely a nation of emigres transplanted from all corners of the world, all within the last 80 years. Israel is home today to people hailing from 102 different countries, speaking no less than 78 different languages and dialects. The large majority of this vastly heterogeneous population arrived in the country after its inception. Numbering three million, the entire population is settled on a land area roughly the size of New Jersey. It is evident that Israel is not a melting pot, for that theory clearly implies a relatively lengthy process of assimilation and integration into a solid mass. Rather, one can liken Israel to a pressure cooker where events take place with great rapidity and, given the mixture of ingredients, without any clear notions as to the characteristics and texture of the final product. One must also bear in mind that a pressure cooker is prone to explosion, unlike a pot, which is only likely to overflow.

It is in this context that I wish to address myself to the question of social experimentation in the country. Whatever experimentation exists can be likened to adding spices to the cooker—in the hope (but without the surety) that the recipe (or the society) will be improved.

Historically, Israel was founded by immigrants from East European countries, deeply imbedded in the liberal form and cultural

389

traditions of the West. This founding group remains the dominant power in the country in most spheres of life. The political institutions and machinery are Western oriented, the educational system is in its entirety a product of Western development, as is much of institutional and cultural life. Furthermore, due to sundry geopolitical considerations, the orientation of Israel is Western. It is neither an accident nor a result of political and economic expedience that Israel deems itself part of the developed Western world rather than the developing worlds of Asia and Africa.

Unlike most new and small nations, Israel succeeded, in the early years of its development, in avoiding the pitfalls of an inner-directed parochialism and a locally centered identity. Multidimensional relations with international Jewry, contact with international agencies in the intellectual and scientific fields, in arts and music, socialist alliances as well as a complex network of technical assistance programs in the developing world gave Israeli society an openness and orientation to world events. Though removed geographically from world centers and surrounded by a sea of hostile neighbors, Israel as a society developed a wide range of interests and relationships. Disturbing changes in this picture have been in evidence since the Six Day War. The current trend is in the opposite direction— towards increased isolationism. This withdrawal coincides with the maturing of a large generation of Israeli-born youth and a dramatic expansion in the numbers of Israelis of Middle Eastern origin. As a rule neither of these groups has shared the orientations and characteristics previously described.

Despite Israel's rapid growth and the changes in population characteristics, social change and innovation have been slow to occur. Indeed, the institutional structure of the country is remarkably stable. Zahal—the Israel Defense Forces—is, perhaps, the only institution that has both expanded rapidly and incorporated changes on a broad scale.

A few words about the country's demographic composition might well serve to clarify some of these points. While in 1948 only 15 percent of Israel's Jewish population hailed from Oriental countries, 48 percent did so in 1967, and by 1971 well over 50 percent of the population were of Oriental background. Barring dramatic changes in immigration patterns the overall percentage of Orientals in the population will reach 70 to 75 percent by the end of the century. This forecast is, of course, subject to radical change through alterations in immigration patterns such as those now inherent in the new and welcome immigration of Soviet Jews. The absorption and integration of this population has, in the past 20 years, been Israel's primary social challenge. It is largely in the context of Oriental versus Occidental that social experimentation in Israel need be discussed.

Although generalizations are dangerous one must be aware of the fact that Oriental origin denotes a certain cultural tradition that the majority of the newcomers brought with them to Israel. It is generally fair to characterize the average Oriental family as being large, bereft of financial resources, with the adults either ill or noneducated in Western terms and certainly unprepared for undertaking an active role in a modern, Western, industrial state.

The prevailing attitude in Israel today is that the Oriental segment of the population is not culturally deprived and, consequently, attempts to derive special educational programs are not aimed at what might be considered cultural rehabilitation. Indeed, it would be wrong, states this view, to deprive or detach this population from its cultural background—a background which is quite rich. Rather, the approach adopted appreciates the differences in the civilizations of the developing areas whence this population originated and the civilization evolved in the Western industrial state which Israel emulates. This philosophy underlies much of what might be considered social experimentation in the educational context.

One basic policy concept forms the operational underpinning of all activity in this sphere: Israel has adopted an overall policy of "national protectionism" in regard to its Oriental population. In essence this is interpreted to mean that state-initiated-and-run programs aimed at the advancement of the Oriental population receive top priority. Coupled with the intense belief that such programs are crucial to the continued existence of the state as conceived by its founders and leaders, this approach creates a framework within which a wide variety and large number of programs are conducted.

A second notion upon which educational programs are predicated states that compensatory activities must relate to the entire person and not only to a specific age group which, on the surface, might seem to be more appropriate. Furthermore, the individual is conceived of as a member of a family and all members of that family need be catered to. In consequence, compensatory programs encompass a broad range of activities beginning with early childhood and culminating in an active adult education network. Fully one out of every three Israelis is, in one fashion or another, enrolled in state-initiated or supported educational endeavors.

A brief description of the educational system might shed further light on the manifestation of these conceptions. A large network of nurseries enrolls a large majority of children between the ages of three to five. This complements day creches where two- to three-year-olds congregate; as yet only 30 percent of that age group are enrolled. One year of kindergarten—between the age of five and six—is free and compulsory for all children, Israel being one of only three countries that legally provide for this preprimary year. Nine years of primary and first-stage secondary education is also compulsory and free. This is followed by three years of secondary education divided into three distinct categories—academic, vocational and agricultural. Continuation rates between the compulsory cycle and the noncompulsory secondary stage are around 80 percent. Seven academic institutions of higher learning and a variety of professional postsecondary courses comprise Israel's tertiary education level. Adult education activities of different sorts ranging from a literacy campaign through popular universities and vocational retraining form the country's notion of continuing education.

Superimposed on this sketch are a number of compensatory and "second chance" experiments, most of which are primarily aimed at the Oriental population. These begin with the fact that nursery education is subsidized in developed areas to such an extent that it is free. It is also programmed and is conceptually developmentally oriented. Programs such as extended school days, tutoring in homework and grouping are prevalent in the primary cycle. Dropouts from the system—there are few—as well as recent immigrants who were not in the country during the years in which they would have attended primary schools are required by law to complete their primary education even after having reached the upper age limit (14). Secondary education, no longer free, is heavily subsidized through a program of graduated tuition so that children from needy families may attend despite economic constraints. A relative newcomer to compensatory education is a network of pre-academic schools attached to the universities. These are aimed at bringing nonqualified Orientals who completed secondary schools either poorly or incompletely, to meet university entrance requirements. At present nearly 2,000 youths are enrolled in these centers, greatly swelling the proportion of people of Oriental background entering universities. Graduates of these centers may also take advantage of tutorial services during their academic careers.

One aspect of Israeli secondary education is not widely known but highly significant. Twenty-five percent of all secondary school students are enrolled in boarding schools. This is by far the highest proportion of boarding education of any secondary school system. The raison d'etre of such a large number of live-away-from-home schools does not stem from an attempt to draw students away from their families or backgrounds but rather is a manifestation of the belief that learning conditions in situations where families are large and quarters narrow severely hinder the student's potential for success. Students, in fact, are most actively encouraged to return to their homes at frequent intervals and a conscious attempt is made to maintain contact with and involvement in the home. Most of these boarding institutions are publicly supported or subsidized.

The Hebrew language lacks a word for assimilation. It is, perhaps, for that reason the term "integration" is most often used to describe the theme of compensatory programs. It is the assimilation of a widely diverse population into a cohesive, viable modern society that we seek rather than the social integration of deprived elements within the population into a predetermined social pattern. Some degree of change in the civilization patterns of groups of Oriental origin as well as indications of upward mobility are, in consequence, utilized as yardsticks of attainment of the various efforts.

While it is true that there still exists a wide gap between the Oriental and Occidental population groups the following few statistics are ample evidence of the trends: a startling change in the possession and use of durable goods such as refrigerators, gas stoves and washing machines has occurred among the Oriental population. Refrigerator ownership rates have risen from 8 to 95 percent, gas stove possession from 14 to 90 percent and washing machines from 3 to 41 percent. Family size of "absorbed" Orientals has dropped from the high of 6.6 live births among families where parents had had no schooling to 4.4 among mothers with primary schooling. There is a marked increase in interethnic marriages. In the political realm there has, thus far, been only a slight increase in the numbers of members of Knesset of Oriental origin but a most dramatic increase in their participation in political roles at the local and municipal levels.

While these statistics and others like them indicate a trend in the desired direction they certainly do not mean that the current undertakings have succeeded. The educational system faces many dilemmas in the formulation of its protectionist policies. A near-canonical insistence on uniformity coupled with an academic orientation immediately raises the issue of compromise of standards. Can national protectionism be extended to the extent of lowering the standard? What standards form the minima beyond which there can be no further retreat? Thus far the overriding tendency has been to discourage any tampering whatsoever with accepted standards. The result has been a reluctance to allow experimentation in certain directions within secondary and higher education. To a degree this attitude has turned secondary and tertiary education institutions into highly selective ones where the proportion of students of Oriental origin has been low. In terms of upward mobility these institutions have been the bottlenecks of educational compensation programs. Although the tendency regarding standards remains as a rigid guideline, it is now clear that primary education has virtually exhausted its compensatory potentialities. To its credit might be chalked the achievement of having prevented a widening of the gap. In planning and operational terms this means that, in future years, the focal point of compensatory activities will have to shift to secondary and higher education. Israel is currently in the throes of searching for meaningful ways in which this focus can be sharpened, keeping in mind the dictum that the horizon cannot change.

Several problems arise in relation to the various compensatory programs that are being conducted. The first relates to the methods and approaches employed. There seems to exist little relevant experience, either in Israel or elsewhere, as to the optimum modes of dealing, in a pedagogical sense, with the type of population with which we are confronted. This, of course, creates a situation wherein the large part of the ongoing effort is essentially trial-and-error experimentation. However, we are not yet satisfied that we have developed the most meaningful and adequate approaches and are, consequently, constantly experimenting on all levels. Currently, emphasis is being placed upon compensatory programs for early childhood and postsecondary stages. Coinciding with all activities are the various attempts to train teachers and develop new approaches to the teaching of specific subjects. Two national centers, one for science teaching and the other for the teaching of the humanities are now in existence and actively engaged in the search for new curricular and methodological approaches. A specially appointed task force is engaged in an examination of early childhood education. All this is mentioned in order to indicate that there is a serious, ongoing effort to redefine targets and revise working approaches. This is also an indication of a general approach that refuses to accept that which has been developed and instituted as being the optimum.

A further problem arises in connection with the students involved in these programs. Throughout their scholastic careers, they are, in one way or another, coached fairly closely. Over a period of time the impression is that they develop a reliance upon external assistance such that their capabilities to function independently are somewhat compromised. Blatantly put, is Israel raising a generation of intellectual invalids or is it, as is intended, raising a new generation of competent, self-sufficient citizens?

A word must be said about Israel's approach to what is usually labeled nonformal education. From the beginning, as education developed during the Mandatory period, youth movements, extra-curricular activities and adult programs were considered essential elements of the educational system. These have been greatly expanded both quantitatively and qualitatively over the years and now form a very crucial part of the system. Conceptually, nonformal education is not considered in Israel to be a complement to formal frameworks, but, rather, an equal partner of similar status. All this stems from the predication that the aim of the educational system is not merely to satisfy the country's need for qualified personnel and its desire for an intellectually competent population, but from the more elemental target of peopling the country with active and positive citizens in all spheres of life. Israel's future is, of course, contingent upon the former aspects. It is also largely contingent upon the country's ability to create a unified population sharing the same aspirations and overall targets from the virtual Tower of Babel that formed its initial population base. In this sense the social experiment that is Israel is a unique one in the annals of mankind. It is a challenge that we take most seriously and to which we attempt to bring the most creative thinking available to us.

25

Walter Ackerman

"REFORMING"

ISRAELI EDUCATION

Among the most urgent of the many pressing problems with which
the new state of Israel was confronted at its creation in 1948 was
the demand for a government school system that would serve the
needs of the citizens of a sovereign state in the latter half of the
twentieth century. Both the traditional Jewish concern for education and the realities of statehood are reflected in the laws which
effected the transfer of authority in education from the agencies
of the Zionist movement and the quasi-governmental Va'ad Haleumi
of the Mandate period to the appropriate instrumentalities of the
new state.[1] The Compulsory Education Act of 1949 provided for
free and compulsory education for all children between the ages
of five and 13 and for adolescents between the ages of 14 and 17
who have not completed their elementary education. The nine
years of compulsory schooling required by the law encompass the
kindergarten, which the child enters at age five, and an eight-year
elementary school. Adolescents who have not completed elementary
school are compelled by law to attend special schools which offer
late afternoon and evening classes. Secondary education, though
neither free nor obligatory, was encouraged by an elaborate system
of tuition grants and a variety of other incentives.

The State Education Act of 1953 abolished the system of "trends"
—separate educational networks supported and maintained by
the various political parties of the Zionist movement—and estab-

lished a unified system of state education. The 1953 law provided for "state education": "education provided by the State on the basis of the curriculum, without attachment to a party or communal body or any other organization outside the government and under the supervision of the Minister [of Education and Culture] or a person authorized by him" and "religious state education": "state education with the distinction that its institutions are religious as to their way of life, curriculum, teachers and inspectors." A more orthodox sector of the population, fearful of government involvement in the education of its children, subsequently withdrew from the religious state education system and established a system of its own. This "independent education" system maintains officially recognized schools which, even though they are outside the state school system, are eligible for government subsidies so long as they subscribe to minimal curricular demands.[2]

The rationalization of the state educational system and the centralization of its conduct in the Ministry of Education and Culture, together with the commitment to free and compulsory education through the eighth grade of the elementary school, all served as background to the growth and development of education in Israel in the two decades that followed immediately upon the creation of the state. Successive waves of immigration during the fifties and sixties forced a rapid expansion of facilities and programs on every level and in every form of educational effort. Some idea of the increase of the educational enterprise in Israel during this period may be gained from Table 1.[3]

The commonplace problems which accompany rapid growth and development—the need to create programs for a wide variety of student aptitudes and abilities, the danger of lower standards of achievement which result from nonselective enrollment, the diminution of the status of the profession which stems from the necessity to train and qualify large numbers of teachers in a short time, the financial burdens of building and maintaining adequate physical plants, and the tension between local needs and a rigid centralized administration—were in this instance greatly exacerbated by the influx of a large number of school-age children from the underdeveloped Arab countries. By the middle of the sixties more than half of the youngsters entering the first grade of the country's elementary schools were the children of parents whose origins were in non-Western societies. The presence of so large a percentage of children whose cultural background, life experience and early childhood training were significantly different from that of the

398

Table 1. GROWTH AND EXPANSION
OF EDUCATION IN ISRAEL – 1948-1969

	1948-1949	1969-1970
No. of Pupils		
Jewish (All Levels)	129,688	715,249
Arab (All Levels)	11,129	110,537
Total (All Levels)	140,817	825,786
No. of Teaching Posts		
Jewish (All Levels)	6,283	42,324
Arab (All Levels)	186	2,890
Total (All Levels)	6,469	45,214
No. of Institutions		
Jewish Kindergartens	709	3,235
Jewish Elementary Schools	467	1,519
Jewish Post-primary Schools (All Levels)	98	544
Arab Schools (All Levels)	56	257
Total (All Levels: Jewish and Arab)	1,342	5,574

native-born or immigrant child of European and Western origin, for whom the standard curriculum was intended, created a major crisis in Israeli schools and cast a shadow over the future development of the country.

The fact that large numbers of children were unable to cope with the academic demands of the regular school program resulted in a variety of experimental approaches calculated to compensate for the cognitive deprivations of early childhood. Pupils designated as "culturally disadvantaged" were afforded the opportunity of added instruction within the framework of an extended school day; nursery and kindergarten programs for three- and four-year-olds sought to provide preparation for the regular preschool, which be-

gins with five-year-olds; patterns of remedial instruction were developed for pupils in grades two through five; school-wide homogeneous grouping for instruction in Hebrew language, mathematics
and English was instituted in the seventh and eighth grades; in addition, enrichment programs, special instructional materials and new
methods of language teaching were introduced throughout the
school system.

The net effect of these efforts, maintained during a period of
continued external threat to Israel's existence, was more a reflection
of good intent and high purpose than a solution to the problem.
While an increasing number of disadvantaged children were able
to manage successfully and to continue their studies on both the
secondary and collegiate levels, a disturbingly large percentage
remained incapable of mastering the skills and techniques required
for post-elementary education and economic self-sufficiency in a
technological society. An analysis of the results of the 1966 *Seker*,
an examination administered to all eighth grade students during the
last year of the elementary school which determines secondary
school placement, disclosed that while 75 percent of the students of
European and Western parentage achieved passing scores, two-
thirds of the children of the "Eastern" communities failed the examination. Depressingly similar statistics can be cited for every
index of school achievement—dropout and continuation rates, part-
time or full-time post-elementary studies, attendance at day and
evening high schools, enrollment in academic or vocational secondary schools, university registration. The slowly but steadily
growing number of children of non-Western origins who learned
to cope with the demands of school and subsequently moved on
to higher levels of training and education seemed only to highlight the problems of the larger numbers who lagged behind.

The constant search for new ways of dealing with the widening
educational gap which threatened to perpetuate the existence of a
"Second Israel" led to the appointment in 1965 of the Praver
committee, which was asked "to investigate the possibility of ex-
tending the Compulsory Education Act and providing free and
compulsory education through the ninth grade." The positive
recommendation of the committee regarding the feasibility and
desirability of at least nine years of schooling for all Israel's children was tied to three conditions:

1. A restructuring of the school system which would replace
   the eight-year elementary school and four-year high school
   pattern with a six-three-three arrangement.

2. The creation of new curricula for the proposed three-year "middle school" consisting of the seventh, eighth and ninth grades.
3. The development of new programs of teacher training geared to the requirements of the new curricula and the needs of the pre-adolescent pupil of the suggested "middle school."

The posture of the Praver committee was clear: the addition of a year of study would be of little avail in solving the problem of the disadvantaged child without a radical reorganization of structure, material and method in the country's schools.

The proposals of the Praver committee for the reform of education in Israel sparked an intense discussion that touched on every aspect of schooling and led ultimately to the appointment of a special parliamentary committee whose task it was to examine the structure of elementary and post-elementary schools within the context of a review of the problems and prospects of the entire school system. The late Zalman Aranne, then Minister of Education and Culture, outlined the mandate to the committee in telling terms. Its function, he stated, was to devise ways and means by which schools of all kinds and on all levels could become more responsive to the needs of the country, to propose solutions to the pressing problem of an increasing dropout rate, to suggest procedures to be adopted by the schools that would reflect the needs of a variegated population and bridge the gap between the various sectors of the community and, finally, to determine what was required to strengthen the "national and social" education of the younger generation.[4] The proposals which the parliamentary committee submitted to the Knesset were an endorsement of the recommendations of the Praver committee. Specifically the parliamentary committee proposed, among other things, that:

1. The existing structure of Israeli education be replaced by a six-three-three pattern of organization.
2. The three-year "middle school" (grades seven, eight and nine) and the three-year "upper school" (grades ten, eleven and twelve) be joined in six-year regional comprehensive schools.
3. All students who complete six years of elementary school be guaranteed admission to the "middle school" and that graduates of the "middle school" be automatically admitted to the upper school.
4. The scope of free and compulsory education be extended

to include the 14- to 15-year-old age group by 1972 and the 15- to 16-year-old age group by 1975.[5]

The debate which followed in the Knesset reflected the passions aroused in the country at large by the recommendations of the parliamentary committee and provides an accurate summary of the positions taken in the discussions which were conducted in every public forum for months afterward. Few issues in Israeli life of the past few years have engendered as much heat and interest as the proposed "Reforma." [6]

While there was general agreement concerning the upward extension of the Compulsory Education Act, few of the other recommendations of the parliamentary committee were without strong, and sometimes bitter, opposition. The supporters of the proposed reform saw in the new regional comprehensive school an opportunity for better equipped schools, more variegated programs of instruction and more inclusive pupil services. The elimination of the upper grades of the neighborhood elementary school held the promise, they claimed, of greater integration of the disparate elements of the student population. In addition, it was pointed out, the close contact of the middle school and the upper school would permit closer articulation of programs and help reduce the dropout rate on the high school level. The inadequacies of a terminal eight-year elementary school in an age of increasing technological development and information explosion pointed to the desirability of a special school unit geared to the specific needs of the pre-adolescent.

The opponents of the "Reforma," while acknowledging the shortcomings of the existing elementary schools, doubted that a change in the structure of school organization would be of much effect. The time, effort and money required for the building of new school plants, the development of new curricula and the training of teachers could more effectively and efficiently be spent on improving the already-established elementary school. A constant theme of the opposition was that the problems of the schools were rooted in the content of the course of study and not in organizational structure. Those opposing the reform further pointed out that the removal of the disadvantaged youngster from the neighborhood school would decrease rather than increase the prospect of integration; the need to change schools at age 12 and the contact with children of different backgrounds could only threaten the security and self-confidence of the underprivileged child whose place in school was tenuous at best. Far from reducing the dropout rate, went the argument, the new middle school and the dislocation it would require would only increase the number of those who left school before the completion of a secondary school program.

The most stubborn and continued opposition came from within the ranks and leadership of the teachers union, whose membership is drawn largely from among elementary school personnel. The validity of the entire concept of the middle school was questioned at the same time as the virtues of the neighborhood elementary school were enumerated. The elimination of the upper two grades of the elementary school meant the emasculation of that institution: the few remaining male teachers would be absorbed in the middle school; the older pupils who contributed to the spirit of the lower school and performed many vital services for their younger fellows would be gone; and the development of new methods, materials and services so desperately needed in the lower grades would be diverted to the middle school. Officials and supporters of religious state education bemoaned the elimination of the daily prayer service that would follow on the departure of 12- and 13-year-old boys from the precincts of the elementary school and expressed the fear that the proposed six-year comprehensive regional school would divert sizeable numbers of students from the high school *yeshivot*.

The most telling arguments were made by those who felt that compensatory education is best begun in the early years of a child's life and that intervention during the junior high school years comes too late to be productive. Their position was that the nursery school, the kindergarten and the primary grades should serve as the major locus of massive inputs of effort, experimentation and funds. This position was joined by those who feared that the "streaming" of pupils which was part of the proposal for the development of the comprehensive high school would only further widen the gap that separated the different population groups of the country. The experience of the "11+ exam" in England, coupled with the egalitarian philosophy of a significant segment of the people, conditioned the view that a pupil's record in the middle school was too fragile and tenuous a bit of evidence on which to base his educational future and his life prospects. This tone of absolute opposition was somewhat tempered by those who doubted the validity of the proposals but were willing to be convinced; they suggested that a carefully controlled experiment in a limited number of selected locations should precede a final commitment to a sweeping reform of the educational structure.

Several central themes emerge from among the welter of argument and counterargument summarized above. There is, first of all, a worried sense of "something gone wrong." The evidence of social and economic stratification which was the root cause of the move for educational reform seems to have forced a shocked recognition that the egalitarian society which was so much a part of the ideology of socialist Zionism and the experience of the early days of the yishuv was perhaps slipping over the border of no return. The mood of urgency engendered by the fear of a dream irrevocably lost prompted appeals to the ideals and visions of an earlier day and evoked a reiteration of the belief in the perfectability of many and the attainability of a just society. The focal point of the debate, the nation's schools, reflected a deeply held commitment to the idea of education and an almost naive reliance on the power of schooling for the solution of society's ills. The unanimous agreement on the need for remedial action very often foundered, however, on the specific means to be adopted. More than one party to the debate, confessing ignorance of the technical problems involved and looking for guidance, complained of the conflicting and often contradictory evidence brought from the social and behavioral sciences. Their quandary was not unlike that expressed in this country in recent discussions of education for disadvantaged minority children:

> What I have not learned is what we should do about these problems. I had hoped to find research to support or to conclusively oppose my belief that quality integrated education is the most promising approach. But I have found very little conclusive evidence. For every study, statistical or theoretical, that contains a proposed solution or recommendation, there is always another, equally well documented, challenging the assumption or conclusions of the first. No one seems to agree with anyone else's approach. But more distressing: no one seems to know what works. As a result I must confess, I stand with my colleagues confused and often disheartened.[7]

The government's approval of the recommendations of the parliamentary committee and the passage of the bill by the Knesset authorizing the proposed changes in the structure of Israel's schools were in no small measure due to the persistent and persuasive efforts of Zalman Aranne. An unusually sensitive and literate man, Aranne made the cause of the disadvantaged child the major motif of his tenure as Minister of Education. The "Reforma" is a monument to his single-minded passion for equality of educational opportunity and represents a personal triumph over the objections and hesitations of the many who were not as willing as he to mortgage the future of the country's educational system to one bold move.

The plan for the implementation of the "Reforma" as prepared by the Ministry of Education involved three separate yet related elements—physical plant, curricula and teacher training. The six-year regional comprehensive middle school and upper school was to be housed in new buildings specifically designed and equipped for this type of school. The introduction of the new plan in any locality was contingent upon the availability of the proper plant. A newly organized department of curriculum development of the Ministry of Education and Culture was charged with the responsibility of preparing the program of study and instruction for the new school unit. The first results of curriculum reorganization reflect the influence of recent trends in American curriculum theory and practice which emphasize cognitive development and learning by inquiry and discovery. The total program of curriculum development projects the introduction of new subjects of study on every level, the reorganization of existing subject matter to reflect the new knowledge, and the introduction of some material at an earlier level than had been the case heretofore. The actual preparation of materials for teacher and pupil use was delegated to working committees consisting of teams of curriculum specialists, subject matter experts, psychologists and classroom teachers. The thrust in teacher training was toward the "academization" of personnel in the middle school. Experienced seventh and eighth grade teachers who were chosen for assignments in the middle school were required to participate in in-service training courses designed primarily to bring them abreast of scholarly developments in the various areas of study. At the same time the country's teacher-training schools, which till then were independent of the universities and trained only nursery, kindergarten and elementary school teachers, were to add a year to the traditional two-year course of study, with the purpose of raising the level of subject matter competence of their graduates who were preparing to teach in the middle school. Finally, the universities which had concerned themselves with preparing teachers for high schools only were asked to develop programs for prospective teachers in the middle school.

The organization of the program in the middle school reflected the major purpose of the reform—the integration of students of different economic, ethnic and social backgrounds. Heterogeneous grouping is the rule in most of the areas of the program of studies for the seventh grade. During that first year students are grouped homogeneously in only three subject areas—Hebrew language, mathematics and English. In the eighth grade a greater degree of differentiation is introduced at the same time as a common core of studies is required of all students. The second year of the middle school marks the introduction of vocational education. By the ninth grade the "common subjects" represent 25 percent of the school curriculum. At this point a student's record and counselling services determine his placement in one of three tracks:

1. Studies leading to continuation in an academic high school or a four-year agricultural or vocational high school and the matriculation examination which is a prerequisite to university entrance.
2. Studies leading to the completion of an academic high school and the winning of a diploma or entrance to a three-year vocational school.
3. Studies for the weak student who will not be able to meet the demands of secondary school and for whom the ninth grade may be terminal.

The new program first took effect in the fall of 1968. Eight middle-school units were established in six localities for the 1968-1969 school year. Thirteen hundred students from 30 different elementary schools were organized in 41 classes taught by 144 teachers. Of that number of teachers, 62 were experienced in the upper grades of the elementary school and had obligated themselves to continued study as a condition of employment in the new unit; 48 were high school teachers who had volunteered to transfer to the middle school; and 34 were recent university graduates who had opted for work in the novel setting of the new program. The following year, 1969-1970, saw the expansion of the program to 36 units, of which four were in Arab communities, which embraced 8,865 pupils in 284 classes. The school year 1970-1971 brought the addition of 30 more middle-school units, which placed some 20 percent of all seventh grade students within the framework of the reform. The projections of the Ministry of Education indicate that by the start of the school year 1973-1974, 145 middle-school units will have been established and approximately 50 percent of all seventh grade students in the country will be enrolled in that type of school.[8]

The rate of expansion of the reform is obviously conditioned by a variety of factors. Budgetary problems, a shortage of teachers, the lack of adequate facilities and other limiting influences have slowed down the pace of reorganization and forced a reassessment of the time required to complete the task. Latest estimates indicate that not until the school year 1984-1985 will all of the children of that level be in the first year of regional comprehensive post-elementary school. There is no small measure of poignancy in the posture of Yigal Allon, Aranne's successor as Minister of Education and Culture, in the face of criticism of the slowness of progress. Commenting on the shortage of buildings which impeded the full development of the new plan, he noted, "We were unable to predict that so many construction workers and building materials would have to be diverted to the construction of air-raid shelters . . . that we would be required to expend so much effort and funds on fortifications or that so many new immigrants would be arriving and so create a need for housing (which further diverted construction from school buildings)." [9]

It is obviously too soon to know the effects of the "Reforma" or to judge whether or not the investments of time, effort and funds will produce the hoped-for results. The initial stages of the program's introduction encountered difficulties not uncommon to any plan of institutional change. After much debate, the teachers union promised cooperation; some parents preferred established high schools for their children and were unwilling to be part of a yet-to-be-proven experiment; the usual bureaucratic bungling did not help convince the doubters; many complained that a desire to speed up the pace of reform very often led to poor planning or no planning at all; and the wisdom of hindsight, citing evidence from the American experience in compensatory education, called into question the heavy emphasis on academic achievement and cognitive development which characterize the new curricula. None of this, however, can obscure the excitement created by the idea of reform and the hopes awakened by the knowledge that the government was prepared to grapple seriously with a problem of overriding importance.

NOTES

1. Summary descriptions of Jewish education in pre-state Palestine may be found in: Joseph S. Bentwich, *Education in Israel* (Philadelphia: Jewish Publication Society of America, 1965); Randolph L. Braham, *Israel: A Mod-*

ern Education System (Washington, D.C.: Department of Health, Education and Welfare, 1966).

2. For material concerning the legal basis of Israeli education see: Ruth Stanner, *The Legal Basis of Education in Israel* (Jerusalem: Ministry of Education and Culture, 1963).

3. *Sh'naton Statisti L'Yisroel,* vol. 21 (Jerusalem: Halishka Hamerkazit L'Statistika, 1970) pp. 543-45.

4. *Divrei Ha'Knesset,* May 18, 1966, p. 1456 ff.

5. The complete report of the committee may be found in *Divrei Ha'-Knesset,* July 29–July 31, 1968, pp. 3037-41.

6. The discussion which follows is based on *Divrei Ha'Knesset,* July 23, 1968, pp. 2810-33; July 29, 1968, pp. 2915-27; March 12, 1969, pp. 1906-26; March 19, 1969, pp. 2071-74; June 9, 1969, pp. 2915-34; June 15, 1970, pp. 2081-105; February 15, 1971, pp. 1355-95; February 22, 1971, pp. 1500-8.

7. U.S. Senator Walter Mondale in an address before the American Education Research Association, New York City, February 1971.

8. Department of Development, Ministry of Education and Culture, no title, no date.

9. *Divrei Ha'Knesset,* February 22, 1971, p. 1504.

26

Rustum Bastuni

THE ARAB ISRAELIS

To understand the position of Israel's Arabs we must discard the myth that holds that these people are emotionally and culturally tied to the vast Arab nation of the Middle East and which claims that the problem of the Arabs in Israel is therefore part of the overall problem in the Middle East. That is not true. The problem of the Arabs in Israel is purely an Israeli question.

The Arabs in Israel, of whom I am one, are citizens of the state of Israel: they participate in practically every activity inside the state of Israel; they are judged by Israeli courts; they have almost all the privileges any other citizen has in Israel. They must not be examined through the prism of the Arab-Israeli conflict.

For Israel's Arabs the political ideologies of the Middle East—both Zionism and Pan-Arabism—are essentially irrelevant. The Arabs in Israel are not directly affected by the Pan-Arabist philosophy or by the Zionist movement. The problems of Arab integration in Israel are social and economic and have very little to do with ideological questions. Of course the Zionist ideology affects the Jewish population in Israel and influences the extent to which Israeli Jews want to allow the Arabs in Israel to be integrated into the whole complex of life in Israel; but this is a Jewish, not an Arab problem. If we exclude consideration of these elements—Pan-Arabism on the one hand, and Zionism on the other—a clearer picture of the Arabs in Israel emerges. No analogy can be drawn between the Oriental Jews in Israel and the Arabs. The integration of the Sephardic Jew into Israeli society is essentially a question of means, of techniques.

The Oxford Dictionary defines integration as "the making up of a whole by adding together or combining the separate parts of an element." This means for our purposes making a whole out of separate parts or elements of a society. These separate elements retain their culture, their nature, their attitudes, their own way of life; but together they constitute one whole. This definition applies to the Arabs, but does not apply to Jews in Israel. The Jew in Israel, whatever culture he comes from, tends to leave that culture, his previous behavior, his previous way of living, and is assimilated into a new culture. The problem is not the integration of the Jew in Israel, but the assimilation of the disparate parts of the Jewish Diaspora to Israel.

The Arabs are not going to be assimilated into Israeli society, but the Jews are. The Sephardic Jews are resisting this assimilation to some extent, but in a few generations this resistance will have vanished. The Arabs in Israel want to integrate as a unit, as a whole, as an element in the state of Israel. This has nothing to do with Zionism. Zionism and the state of Israel are two distinct phenomena.

While the Oriental Jew faces the problem of assimilation, the Arab in Israel faces the problem of integration. It is erroneous to assume that Israel is a monocultural, homogeneous society. Today there are about 390,000 Arabs in Israel, about 11 percent of the population; they have their own culture and their own way of life. Israel must learn to accept the idea that it is not one culture, one people and one nation: there is no such state anywhere in the world.

In order to understand the situation of the Arabs in Israel, we must examine the situation in Palestine before 1947. At that time there were two structures, two peoples, two cultures side by side in Palestine. From 1929, when the first disturbances took place between the Palestinian Arabs and the Jews, until the establishment of the state of Israel in 1948, the two never integrated. They had no common ventures, either economic or social. The first suggestions for the partition of Palestine were made in 1936, when the Royal Commission visited Palestine. The members viewed the problem and said that the only way to solve it was to divide Palestine. Why?

Because something had gone wrong. Something had gone wrong in the Arab outlook towards the problem of Palestine; something had gone wrong with some of the Jewish leaders, who envisioned a Jewish state in Palestine; and something had gone wrong with the Mandate government ruling Palestine at the time.

Even before the Balfour Declaration the Zionist movement had decided to establish a homeland for the Jewish people throughout the Diaspora. Relations between the Jews coming to Palestine and the Palestinian natives living in Palestine at the time were secondary. From a historical point of view, this is easily understood. Because the Jews were oppressed, they wanted to come to Palestine; during the whole period from the first aliyah to the establishment of the state of Israel, the Jews were preoccupied with their own problems in building a homeland.

In those early days, the relationship between such an effort and the fate of the native population of Palestine was not seriously explored by the Jewish leaders. For their part, the Arabs resented the people who were coming to what they believed to be their home, occupying it and building in it their own national entity.

Under these circumstances, there could never be any real rapprochement between the two communities. There were simply two ghettos, a Jewish ghetto and a Palestinian ghetto. There were people of good will from both sides, but they had little influence. There remained two separate societies, side by side. To talk about a binational state or a non-Jewish state is to falsify history; such a state has no roots in the reality of history of the Middle East in the last century.

It was no surprise to me when the state of Israel was established. I was living in Palestine, studying at the Haifa Technical Institute, and I was well acquainted with the structure of the Jewish community. The state was actually there; all that was needed was to declare it. But the Palestinian Arabs, on the other hand, were not prepared to run their own state in 1948, when the Partition Plan was proposed in the United Nations. The Jewish yishuv at that time had its own democratic identity, its own educational system, institutions such as the Jewish Agency and so on. The Arabs lived in complete chaos. The tragedy of the Palestinians was that the 1948 war reduced the population of Palestinian Arabs from 1,320,000 in the whole of Palestine to only 156,000 in the area in which the state of Israel was established.

Those Arabs who remained after the establishment of the state found that what little structure had existed was gone. Haifa, where I then lived, had had a population of more than 100,000 Arabs, and within two or three days only 200 or 300 of us remained in the whole city. Similar depletions occurred in other parts of the country. Undoubtedly this exodus colors the Israeli-Arab situation today, and one cannot predict when its effect will stop.

The Arabs who remained in Israel after the state was established

411

felt very insecure, and did not know what their future was to be or how to behave vis-à-vis a more dynamic and more progressive society. They were remnants of a people who were only beginning to develop modern institutions prior to 1948.

The years after the establishment of the state were rather interesting. First, the government appointed a Minister of Minorities to deal with the Israeli Arabs. They assumed that the Arabs had problems different from those of other people in Israel. There was the question of future relations with all Middle Eastern Arabs, which they linked with the problem of peace and war in the Middle East. So to deal with the Arabs, there had to be a Ministry of Minorities. Every government office had its own Arab Department.

Second, some Jewish leaders, after the establishment of the state, actually contemplated the idea of an exchange of populations, i.e., to exchange the Arabs in Israel for the Jews in the Arab countries. The idea was a product of honest good will. They thought that the Arabs would not feel at home in a Jewish state, therefore why not try to convince the other Arab countries to take the remaining Arabs out of Israel and bring Jews in from Iraq, Morocco, and so forth?

The third action that helped define the character of the Arab-Jewish relations in Israel in the first years was the establishment of the military administration, based on the emergency laws inherited from the British Mandate. In most of Israel after 1948 the Arabs were governed by this military administration. Its functions were not—and are not—only military. It was responsible for all services rendered to the Arab villages.

These early policies or actions, then, helped determine the special character of Israeli Arabs. People assumed that the Arabs in Israel were exactly like the Arabs outside. When peace came in the Middle East, all "Arab" problems would be resolved. Until then, they were to live in a way set apart from other Israelis.

These early policies have proved to be completely wrong-headed. There are certain key ideas which may clarify proper dealings with and a proper vision of the Arab situation in Israel.

The first problem confronting the Arabs in Israel is that of education, a prime necessity in building a community. The Arabs have made great progress in education since the establishment of the state because the law of compulsory education applies to everybody in Israel, regardless of nationality or race. Every child must go to school, or his parents face penalties, even imprisonment. This creates problems among the Arabs because Arab girls' fathers don't like them to go on to the higher grades. But the girls must go to school, and thus the educational level of all Israel's Arabs rises.

It is important, though, that there are two systems of education, one the Israeli system and the other Arab. The Arab boy goes to a school which teaches a certain curriculum. It includes the *bagrut* (matriculation) examination, but it stresses Arab culture. The Jewish boy—who has a choice among several types of education—goes to a school where the main language is Hebrew and the stress is on Jewish culture, history and literature.

It must be understood that any child can go to any school. There is no segregation in the educational system such as has been legally sanctioned in some states in the United States. But since there are two systems of education, two curricula, the Arab child generally prefers to go to an Arab school and the Jewish child to a Jewish school.

In essence this means that the Israelis are creating two societies, one based on one set of values, one on another. The late Abba Houshi, Mayor of Haifa, was first to sponsor the idea of Arab-Jewish schools, and since the municipalities run the schools, he was able to open a school in which Arab and Jewish boys sit together and learn together, from both Arab and Jewish teachers. They teach in two languages, and the school has been a success. The Haifa municipality has been trying another venture, which also has been successful. It sponsors a youth center in which Arab and Jewish youth work together and pursue cultural activities together. There were many doubts about the project, but once started it became a success. After all, when a Jewish boy and an Arab boy sit together and learn together and listen to lectures and play music together, they forget their respective nationalities. If Israelis want to integrate the Arabs into Israeli society, the first thing that must change is the educational system.

A Jewish child should know Arabic: it is a necessity for him. Most Arab youth know Hebrew very well because their lives are with Jews. In a school where Arab and Jewish boys study together they learn all the scientific and technical subjects together, in two languages with two kinds of teachers. To learn Arab or Jewish literature, religion and culture, the class can be divided. Education remains one of the main barriers to the real integration of the Arabs in Israel.

The whole system of education must be revised to encourage a new spirit in coming generations. One can speak separately about

Judaism, about Islam, about Arabism—but when one speaks about the state and politics and the forging of a society in its own environment, the state of Israel prevails, because all inhabitants are Israelis —Arabs, Jews and other peoples. This is the main reason that there is still division in Israel.

The second main obstacle to true integration of the Arabs is the laws regarding military defense. The Arabs do not serve in the Israeli army (although the Druses are accepted as volunteers) because the basic concept of national defense is Jewish. It is said that although the Arab is a citizen of the state of Israel, "We don't know if he would make a good soldier." In reality, it has proved otherwise.

In 1967, when I was living in Haifa, the situation was dangerous. War was raging and we could not know what the outcome would be, nor what casualties there might be in Haifa. We formed a committee to deal with such problems that we thought might arise. Young Arabs came to this committee asking us, "Why don't you recruit us? We can fight." I looked quizzically at them and asked, "Why do you want to fight?" They said, "We want to fight not because we love Jews. This is not a matter of love or hate, but we feel that we are in danger, our homes are in danger. If someone attacks us, we want to be able to fight back." That an Arab cannot fight another Arab is a myth. One cannot build military theory on myths. Arabs have been fighting and slaughtering Arabs since the beginnings of Islam.

To help forge a strong Israeli society, Arabs must serve in the army. The Druzes, who were in the ranks in 1967, fought in the Golan Heights, although the Druzes who live in Israel have very close relatives in Syria. They didn't say, "We don't have to fight." The Druzes enlisted and they fought for their *own* country and their *own* society. Israel is an Israeli-Arab country too, and Israeli Arabs must serve in the army. Whether or not they like it is another story. Most of the Jewish inductees aren't so glad to be in the army either.

Military or defense thinking pervades most official dealings with Israeli Arabs. People say the Arab is a potential fifth columnist in Israel. At crucial times the loyalty of the Arab is in question; no one questions the loyalty of Israel's Jews. But there are Jews who are not loyal to the state of Israel. It is a fact that most espionage cases in Israel have involved Jews and not Arabs. In the United States nobody questions one's loyalty simply because he is a Jew. Why then question the loyalty of the Arabs to Israel? If an Arab chooses, of his own free will, to live in Israel, it means that he chooses to be loyal to Israel.

There is another basic problem confronting the Arabs in Israel. Since 1948 there has been a metamorphosis in Arab society. The old tribal society—feudal, patriarchal, primitive—does not exist any more. The government of Israel launched a five-year plan to provide basic services to the Arab villages. More than 70 percent of the Arab population in Israel was provided with water, electricity, power, public housing, municipal councils, schools, school buildings and so on. It was a great step forward in helping the Arab population to integrate into a more dynamic society.

A study of the development of the Arab village from the days of the Mandate until recently, including plans of the villages, as they were initially, as they were in 1948 and as they are today, shows that they have undergone vast changes. There are villages which have expanded to three times their original area, where there is a lot of building and where local industry is developing. All of the villages are linked to the electric network of the country. There is little similarity between Arab villages in Israel and Arab villages in the Arab countries today. Whatever Nasser may have thought about land reform, we know that nothing was done between 1952 and today either in Egypt or in Syria and the other Arab countries.

The provision of basic services has improved the quality of life in Israeli Arab villages, and it has also had other important impacts on Arab society. It has been transformed from a basically agricultural society into something else. Before 1948, more than 70 percent of the Arab population lived in villages and through agriculture; only a very small minority of city dwellers earned their living in ways other than agriculture. Now it is the other way around: agriculture is practiced by a very small minority of the Israeli Arabs.

This kind of transformation from an agricultural society has had a tremendous effect on the Arabs in Israel. The basic patriarchal family, the tribal family, does not exist any longer. The head of the family does not have the influence he once had: its economic basis has vanished. Relations between man and wife in the Arab family have also changed since 1948, and the life of young people too, has undergone basic changes.

At one time I was commissioned by the Minister of Housing to advise on housing for Israel's Arabs. I journeyed through the Beersheba area, discussing housing preferences with many people. An old sheikh wanted two houses because he had two wives, and he wanted them to be complete with balconies. His son urged me not to listen so much to the old man. "We want to have a shikun" (a housing development), he said, "a bathroom with all facilities. I want to live right in Beersheba."

This is the Arab generation gap in Israel today. I was once assigned to build a shikun in Um el Fahem, a town in Galilee. I made a study of native Arab life and saw how the head of the house had a diwan in which to entertain his guests. I combined the traditional and the modern, and came up with a plan which looked good to me. About 80 such units were built.

Some time later I visited Um el Fahem, and I was shocked— shocked because I had planned the *diwan* to be somewhat separated from the rest of the house, to give the head of the family the traditional privacy for receiving his guests. One family head had punched a door to the street and opened the diwan as a shop. He wanted to sell things; he no longer needed the diwan to receive guests.

We must be careful not to exaggerate the hold of tradition; if we have dynamism in our society we must look forward. The Arabs in Israel have gone far in this sense. I don't yet know their precise direction: much of the labor force in Israel has moved from agriculture to services. More than half of the building trade is composed of Arab workers. Such workers are the first group to suffer when there is any dislocation in the economy. Moreover, no Arabs own industries or big concerns; there are only a few Arabs in government offices. Should there be any serious economic problems in Israeli society the fate of the Arabs would be highly uncertain.

We must consider, finally, the reality of Arab-Israeli relations since the Six Day War. The war had a great impact upon the Arabs in Israel, and upon Jewish attitudes towards Israeli Arabs. I was shocked when I saw the plight of the Palestinian Arabs in the occupied areas. Half of them were refugees, having lived in refugee camps for the past 23 years—sponsored originally by their Arab brothers in Arab countries. I could not communicate with those who are considered my own people, the Palestinian people, even those of my own generation.

The link that bound Israeli Arabs to the Palestinian Arabs has been lost over the years. Their way of thinking, their mentality, their emotions, the propaganda they have been fed for 23 years has made of them people altogether different from the Israeli Arabs.

How, then, ought one to deal with Israeli Arabs? Should we see them as ex-Palestinians, or as Israelis?

The Six Day War made it clear that the Arabs in Israel are part of Israel, and not part of any other state. They can maintain their contacts, relations, their outlook, their mentality, but they must not be equated with the Arabs of the occupied areas; they must be seen as part of the society in which they live. Then, too, the Six Day War clarified the feelings of Arabs in Israel. It is no secret that some of the Israeli Arabs—young and old—questioned the fate of Israel in the event of another war. It was thought possible that Israel might be conquered by the Arabs; the Arabs were considered strong. The shock came when the fate of the battle was decided in three hours, with the strike of the Israeli Air Force. It was a shock for the Jewish population, and for us the shock was even greater. Today, except for a few negative elements, the Arabs in Israel believe that Israel is here to stay, at least for a generation or two. And this belief affects their whole attitude towards the state in which they live.

Prior to the Six Day War there were Israeli Arabs who believed that the Palestinians were living in paradise in Arab countries. We have seen the refugee camps; we have seen the villages, and today if we were to poll the Palestinians as to where they would choose to live, it is likely that more than 90 percent would choose Israel itself, rather than a purely Arab city such as Amman.

On the other hand, there have also been some negative reactions among Jews in Israel in the aftermath of the war. Yochanan Peres of the Tel Aviv University did a study on ethnic relations in Israel. He questioned several test groups and compared the answers from before and after the war. He compared prejudice against the Arabs in Israel among Oriental and European Jewish respondents after the 1967 War. One question was: Would it be better if there were fewer Arabs in Israel? Ninety-one percent of European Jews said yes, and 93 percent of the Orientals said yes, they would be happier if there were fewer Arabs. Another question was: Does every Arab hate Jews? Seventy-six percent of the Europeans and 83 percent of the Orientals thought they did. Would you rent a room to an Arab? Eighty percent of the Europeans answered in the negative and 91 percent of the Orientals. Would you agree to have an Arab as a neighbor? Fifty-three percent of the Europeans said No, and 78 percent of the Orientals.

These are very disturbing statistics, but I don't believe that they can be fully trusted. Negative feeling did rise after 1967, but I believe this to be a phase which will pass with the years. But the negative feeling does exist today, and the question is what to do now.

The future of the Arabs in Israel must be resolved by Israel itself. We must divorce the situation of the Arabs in Israel from that of the Arabs outside Israel. But the main issue affecting the Arabs in Israel is the question of the separation of church and state. This is a major issue—not for Arabs only, but for Israel itself. Israel is a modern state, and to confuse religious laws and conceptions with state policy is very dangerous. It is high time we separate the issues.

Once we see ourselves, all of us—Arabs, Jews, Moslems, Christians—as Israelis, half the problems of the Arabs in Israel will be solved.

27

E. O. Schild

ON THE MEANING

OF MILITARY SERVICE

IN ISRAEL

The Western stereotypes of "military" and "army" may not be very applicable to present-day Western militaries, but they are certainly disastrously misleading when applied to Israeli society. Yet an understanding of the real meaning of the military is central to an understanding of many important aspects of Israeli life. Service in the Israel Defense Forces (IDF) is, apart from elementary school, the one universal experience of Israeli youth—more accurately, of Israeli young men. Women may claim exemption for religious reasons, and less than 50 percent are actually drafted. Few observers would say that this experience is not in general a positive one. For example, there is an obvious difference between the majority of students, who come to the university after their compulsory service, and those who are granted academic deferments and postpone their real service until after the completion of their studies. While the former encounter difficulties in their readjustment to the

I am happy to acknowledge my great debt to Colonel (Res.) Mordechai Bar-on, past chief educational officer of the IDF. In the present essay I am drawing heavily on his insight and knowledge, both in personal conversation and in his booklet, *Education Processes in the Israel Defense Forces.*

role of student after three years in the army, their greater maturity and responsibility make them clearly preferable students.

Any full scale description of the social climate of the IDF is seriously hampered, however, by the scarcity of publishable data. Hard data are usually classified, and soft data are—soft. This essay is, then, frankly impressionistic, but I do claim a fairly intimate acquaintance with several branches of the IDF; and at the very least there is no evidence to contradict and much to support the following.

However, two qualifications are important—both as qualifications, and because they make an important point concerning the nature of the IDF. One is that different units may differ greatly in their social climate. Not only is the Navy a very different phenomenon from, say, the Armored Corps, but two armored brigades may have very different styles. (Thus, one armored brigade—call it the n'th brigade—was once known for its unique emphasis on discipline, so that a popular crack was the question to a soldier: "Do you serve in the n'th brigade—or do you serve in the IDF?".) This is in part a consequence of the considerable autonomy given individual units. While this autonomy is rooted in combat practice and considerations of combat effectiveness, it carries over to routine and social characteristics. A description of features of *the* social climate of the IDF thus becomes by necessity a Weberian analysis of an "ideal type."

While the first qualification concerns differences between units, the second concerns differences across points in time. In many respects the IDF is a highly flexible organization, both in its adaptability to external changes and in its openness to experimentation. Because roles are rotated frequently there is a high turnover in senior positions; this turnover, coupled with the autonomy mentioned above, makes for frequent changes in climate within given units and, with respect to turnover in the very top positions, changes in entire branches. Since 1970, however, the IDF has grown in size and has experienced a steep rise in technological sophistication. The effects of these changes on the fundamentals of the social climate remain to be seen.

RELATIONS TO THE CIVILIAN CONTEXT

In a famous essay,[1] Goffman has discussed the characteristics of "total institutions," establishments which encompass all activities—sleep, play, work—of an individual who belongs to the establishment. Several of these characteristics are found in all armies, including the IDF; this is so because armies are concerned with what is "the key fact of total institutions," that is, "the handling of many human needs by the bureaucratic organization of whole blocks of people."[2] Several of these characteristics will serve as pivots for the organization of the following observations, not because it is remarkable that life in the IDF differs from life in the analytically pure total institution, as, of course, it does, but because the extent and the form of the differences tend to highlight the basic social characteristics of the IDF.

The IDF exhibits extraordinary differences from the model total institution because one of the central dimensions of the theoretical total institution is the barrier between it and the outside world. Such barriers happen to be less characteristic of the IDF than of most other armies. Since its inception, the IDF has been built on a small nucleus of professional soldiers (primarily in senior positions and positions demanding technical expertise) and an overwhelming majority of civilians, serving as draftees or reservists. (At the completion of regular service the soldier is transferred to the reserve, and as a reservist the Israeli civilian is called up for 30 to 45 days of service annually.) The crucial point is not in the proportion of draftees to professional soldiers, but in the universality of the draft (which covers almost all men and about half of the women) and in the regular reserve duty. Thus the distinction between "civilian" and "military" as two different sectors of the population becomes diluted. Instead, there is a distinction between two spheres of activity for the same person.

Even the draftee experiences frequent shifts between his civilian and his military context. One important factor is the small size of Israel. Until 1967 the great majority of draftees were stationed close enough to home so that they could visit family and civilian friends on free weekends or even evenings after duty. This is longer true for soldiers serving in the Sinai and other areas held since the Six Day War. An interesting sidelight on the climate in the IDF is that this situation is considered a serious problem, and that arrange-

ments for its alleviation are given high priority (geographical rotation of units, regular air transportation of individual soldiers and
other devices). Moreover, initial steps have recently been taken to
facilitate contact between the soldier and his family from the
opposite direction: at any time parents may visit children who
are in basic training, and may spend time with the soldier whenever
he is not engaged in actual duty.

But it is not only the soldier-civilian who remains linked to both
contexts. The professional soldier is not segregated from the civilian
sector. This is immediately obvious in the social networks of the
senior officers, most of whom maintain social relationships and personal friendships with civilians who are not professionally linked
to the military establishment.

But more basic is the career pattern institutionalized in the IDF.
In 1954 Dayan, then Chief of Staff, introduced the principle of a
"second career" for professional officers: officers, whatever their
rank, should retire at an early age from the military and start a
new career in civilian life. This principle has been maintained in
the IDF, although it is true the age of retirement has crept upward. If the original notion was to have the top positions filled
by people in their thirties, the present-day incumbents tend to be
in their forties. But it still holds that even the most successful and
senior officers (including the chiefs of staff, who retire after three
or four years of service in this role) leave the army at a time when
they still have several decades of productive life ahead of them.

The explicit rationale for this norm was intraorganizational and
was intended to ensure the youth and presumed attendant flexibility
and openness to innovations of the senior officers; similarly, the
rapid turnover of personnel should prevent freezing of doctrines
and procedures. It may also have broader implications: in a country
which is continuously under the threat of war, the military by
necessity gains considerable prominence and power. Thus, in spite
of a basic ideology of this subordination of the army to civilian
authority (an ideology which has been a matter of course in the
IDF), there is a real risk that a powerful "generals' clique" might
someday emerge. The principle of "up *and* out," and the conse-
quent short life span of generals as generals, is probably a very
healthy preventive measure.

However, in the present context the importance of a second
career is inculcated into the officer while he still is in the army.
As he advances in the military hierarchy and gets more and more
of a voice in shaping the nature of the army, this very process is

accompanied by the growing knowledge that his military profession is temporary, and that ultimately his occupational future lies in a civilian profession. Whatever the process of anticipatory socialization involved, the outcome is an increased permeability of the borderline between civilian and military life.

All of this does not imply that there are no important differences between the IDF and civilian organizations. The IDF is first and foremost an organization with military functions, with all of the structural and cultural implications of such functions. The question is not one of similarity, but of linkages rather than segregation. The IDF is strongly integrated into the general society, not only on a global, analytical level, but in terms of the daily experiences of soldiers and civilians.

COMMAND RELATIONS

"In total institutions" writes Goffman, "there is a basic split between a large managed group, conveniently called inmates, and a small supervisory staff. . . . Social mobility between the two strata is grossly restricted; social distance is typically great and often formally prescribed." [3]

Earlier I discussed the differentiation between the military and civilian life; here I shall turn to differentiation within the military, specifically between commanders (officers, squad leaders) and men.

There is no need to elaborate the differences, ritual and pragmatic, between the status of a commander and the status of a private. From principles of discipline to the existence of separate officers' mess, sufficient evidence is available concerning the "basic split" mentioned above. However, there are a number of factors which militate against the maintenance of "great social distance" between soldiers and their immediate superiors. A major one is the pattern of mobility. In many total institutions the absence of channels by means of which inmates may become staff serves to maintain the social distance between the two strata. In the IDF the same sociological principle has the opposite effect: only inmates can become staff; that is, all staff are recent inmates—which clearly operates against drastic social distance.

The program for becoming an officer in the IDF involves going through all steps: basic training, service as a private (or slightly higher rank), NCO school, service as an NCO, officer's school. In practice, the process is frequently abbreviated (e.g., the candidate goes directly from the completion of NCO school to officer's school), but it holds without fail that the entire staff is recruited from among ordinary draftees. Moreover, the entire process takes place during the soldier's regular compulsory service (although, if the candidate arrives at officer's school at a late stage in his service, he may be required to extend his stay in order to serve at least one year as an officer after completion of school). Thus junior command positions at squad and platoon level are occupied by regular draftees.

This has some important implications. First, the age difference between a soldier and his commander is likely to be no more than a year (and as promotion in the junior ranks is rather rapid in the IDF, the age difference between the soldier and commanders somewhat further removed is not likely to be impressive, either). This proximity in age and similarity in basic societal status—both being draftees and both serving prior to the establishment of "real" careers—will tend to discourage attempts at establishing great social distance. Second, because of the pattern of mobility, the commander faces many men who are potentially his future peers. In fact, because the junior commanders are draftees, and because most of them leave the army upon completion of their compulsory service, there is a rapid turnover in these positions—and consequently the prospects of mobility for the private are realistic indeed.[4]

Thus, while at any given moment staff is staff, and inmates are inmates, the future distinction is not nearly as clear. Now it is clear that not all soldiers have equal chances for mobility. Soldiers from the most disadvantaged social and deficient educational backgrounds are not, and are not seen as, the future peers of the commanders. But the point is not the extent of relations between the commander and any specific soldier. Rather, the important concern is that the structure of mobility militates against a great formal or informal social distance; and this is what shapes the general social climate within which all commanders and all soldiers function.

To the structural factor an ideological one is added. The IDF was shaped by, and is still dominated by, officers who come from collective and cooperative settlements, or at least from socialist youth movements. From time to time heated controversies have broken out concerning the importance, or lack of importance, of hierarchical differences and symbols of formal discipline and authority. But whatever the shifts in doctrine and practice in this respect, the pervasive undertone has always been one of an egalitarian ideology. This is clearly seen by the fact that in past controversies the burden of proof was laid upon—and accepted by—those who argued in favor of more hierarchical practices.

The restrictions on social distance are thus reinforced by a consensual assumption: that strategies increasing the distance need specific, instrumental legitimation; strategies decreasing the distance are intrinsically legitimate.

An ideological point of particular interest concerns the participation of the commander in the activities of his men. The IDF prides itself in its doctrine of "follow me": in combat a commander is in front of his men, calling "follow me," rather than in back, calling "forward." Actually, there seems to be nothing unique about the IDF in this respect, as far as commanders in the lower echelons are concerned. Several nations (most recently the U.S. marines in Vietnam) report identical practices up to the level of company commander. However, the IDF may have a special point in regard to senior commanders: these, even at brigade level and higher, have been known to participate in face-to-face combat. A few years ago a brigade commander, acting as platoon leader, was killed in an encounter with an Arab guerrilla squad. Several voices were raised in public, calling for senior officers to be forbidden participation in such skirmishes. However, the Chief of Staff and the Minister of Defense reaffirmed the basic IDF doctrine, according to which such participation is accorded great value.

However, the truly interesting point does not concern combat practice, but the ideology in respect to noncombat activities. To a considerable extent the "follow me" doctrine carries over to tasks in routine conditions. In many armies when a jeep gets stuck in the mud, it is perfectly proper for the lieutenant to tell the sergeant to get it out; for the sergeant to instruct the corporal; and for the corporal to do the pulling with the men. I once mentioned this possibility in a class at the university (of course practically all of the students had been in the IDF) and the class spontaneously burst out in laughter. As one of the students commented, "That's a funny way to get things done." The norm in the IDF would call for the personal participation of the lieutenant. I am not concerned with the frequency with which the norm actually is honored or violated in the IDF or in any other army; in the present context it suffices that the norm clearly exists.

The generalization of the norm of "follow me" then interacts with the underlying egalitarian ideology, and the specific structural conditions of mobility, to produce a situation in which the obvious and important differentiation between commanders and men co-exists with no less important bonds of cooperation and sharing.

ORGANIZATION AND DISORDER

Among the major features of total institutions Goffman lists: "all phases of the day's activities are tightly scheduled, with one activity leading at a prearranged time into the next, the whole sequence of activities being imposed from above by a system of explicit formal rulings and a body of officials. Finally, the various enforced activities are brought together into a single rational plan. . . ." [5]

This sounds like an apt description of an efficient bureaucracy; and, if we are to trust some Western journalists who have presented the Israeli armed forces as a marvelously smooth and frictionless fighting machine, it is a valid description of the IDF, as well. However, as any Israeli observer can confirm, this is far from the truth. Confusion, disorder and misplanning are as characteristic of the peacetime IDF as of any other army. I shall argue that these are not just regrettable weaknesses of structure or personnel, but are in one sense intrinsic to the climate of the IDF.

The IDF certainly does not denigrate planning. As a past Chief of Operations stated, "We have plans for anything—including how to conquer the North Pole." But at the same time combat doctrine assigns a limited role to prior planning. (As a popular saying in the IDF goes: "Definition of a plan—a basis for changes.") A concise statement of the doctrine is found in the briefing given by General Tal, commander of one of the divisions fighting in Sinai in 1967, to his subordinates:

> Now, when the plan is clear to all of us, and when the moves drawn on the map are known, I want to say a few more words. In the battle *nothing will take place as it is drawn in this blueprint*. In reality the lines and the axes will be entirely different, but this should not disturb anybody, because battle never develops according to the arrows on the map. One thing must happen exactly according to the blueprint—the principle and the concept which lie behind this drawing. [Emphasis in the original].[6]

426

Organizations may approach future problems in two ways. The first is to take preventive measures; the second, to be able to create solutions once troubles have occurred. The IDF doctrine seems to assume that no planning or organization can prevent snags and confusion on the battlefield; optimal strategy is then to recognize the inevitability of this disorder, and to adapt structure and train personnel to handle the anticipated disorder.

It is the task of the student of warfare to evaluate the strategy implications of this orientation, and indeed to evaluate its similarity or difference to doctrine in other armies. My interest is in the fact that the orientation towards *solving* problems, rather than *preventing* them, is carried over to the routine functioning of the IDF.

Of course, smooth functioning, thorough planning and efficient scheduling are highly valued in the IDF—and presumably are found in the higher levels of organization and strategic planning. But in terms of the social climate prevalent in lower and middle echelons, there is considerable resistance to the red tape, dogmatism and bureaucracy implied in such scheduling.[7] "Don't worry—everything will be OK" is an almost standard response (to the despair of superiors) to attempts at detailed scheduling of future activities. Nobody is really surprised, nor overly condemnatory, when snags occur and disorder reigns—these are taken as facts of life—but if the person in charge does not succeed in straightening things out, disapproval is general. A soldier's resourcefulness is a highly valued trait, far more important than orderliness or following instructions in detail. "Clinging to the goal" (i.e., persevering regardless of difficulties until the goal is reached) is a stock phrase and a supreme value in the IDF; I have never heard tributes paid to "sticking to the plan."

Again, I am not evaluating the costs and benefits of this approach with a managerial orientation. But its implications for the experience of the soldier are obvious. Rather than facing the detailed scheduling that is characteristic of the ideal type of total institution, he is in a situation with many degrees of freedom, and where deviation (albeit within limits) is not only accepted, but even, under the labels of "initiative" and "innovation," approved.

E. O. SCHILD

COMBAT AND ROUTINE

In the two preceding sections I have emphasized the carryover of combat practices to routine life. That is, in evaluating and structuring standards for routine activities, combat principles are emphasized. An important illustration is the very conceptualization of the role of "officer."

In the U.S. army, for example, the image of an officer beyond junior rank is fundamentally the image of a manager. (And indeed his tasks may be very similar to those of a manager in a major civilian organization.) In the IDF the basic image is much closer to that of a combat leader. All officer-candidates in the IDF go through basic Infantry Officer's School, even if they belong to a very different branch of the army. This contributes to the solidarity and common culture of the officer corps, but a major function is the one related to my present argument: the infantry officer represents the peak of "combatness," he is in immediate contact with both his men and the enemy, separated by relatively little technology; he interacts primarily with soldiers rather than with equipment.

Thus the candidate's image of an officer is that of a combat leader. As a norm this is reinforced by the special events mentioned above, when senior officers personally participate in combat, and by the more general practice according to which senior officers are physically close to the scene of combat. Thus, both during the years of retaliation raids in 1954-1956 and during the war of attrition in 1968-1970, it was common for a unit returning to the lines after a raid in enemy territory to be received and informally debriefed by the Chief of Staff.

The officer, whatever his actual job, is thus defined (as an image, if not a description of reality) as a combat leader. It goes without saying that combat activities also have the highest prestige, induced by the fact that they also are given the highest priority. If a civilian, employed by the IDF in his professional capacity (say, as a psychologist), also is an officer in the reserves, he will typically, during his annual call-up, be sent to his combat unit. Economically it would probably be more profitable for the IDF to keep him in his professional job at the reservist's low pay, rather than conceding his professional services for the 45 days during which he is a platoon leader. But the norm of priority to combat is the dominant

428

one. And the result is the penetration of combat standards into the sphere of routine activities.

The intimate linkage between combat and other activities is also symbolized in organizational structure. To take two illustrations of activities which are far removed from the battlefield: the same branch which is charged with providing supplementary education for culturally disadvantaged draftees and running periodic seminars for officers on topics of general cultural interest is also charged with formulating and communicating doctrines of military leadership. Similarly, the officer who is in charge of the public relations of the IDF is *ipso facto* in charge of field security.

The linkage between and generalization of combat standards to routine conditions has a strong impact on the social climate. All armies report drastic differences between styles of interaction, social relations, norms and other factors in combat and behind the lines. Obviously these differences, rooted in the different adaptive requirements of the battlefield and the barracks, exist in the IDF as well. But they are less vivid. Many of the peculiarities of the social climate of the IDF are based on this generalization from combat, and this means that the noncombat climate in IDF routine life will have points of similarity to the combat climate in other armies.

IDENTITY AND SELF-IMAGE

These, then, are some of the major features of the social climate into which the newly drafted soldier enters, and within which he matures.

"In our society," states Goffman, total institutions "are the forcing houses for changing persons; each is a natural experiment on what can be done to the self." [8] And Goffman vividly describes the various processes by which the self is "mortified," and the unique identity of the inmate curtailed, in order to make him manageable—a standard element to be conveniently manipulated and scheduled by the staff.

Undoubtedly the IDF experience changes the person. Moreover, in part this change is in the direction indicated by Goffman. A most visible indication, in the IDF as in all armies, is the replacement of civilian clothes—freely chosen and one of the ways by which the individual can express his identity—by the uniform.

(Note the very word *uniform*: "uniform in character and uni-
formly distributed." [9]) His private actions are regulated, and potential expressions of individuality by posture, action and speech
are restricted. The possibilities for privacy are constrained. All
of these are essential elements in the suppression of individuality.

In the IDF, too, you may hear the famous slogan, "You have
to break the civilian in order to make the soldier" (and if official
doctrine denounces this approach, it is not strange to those actually
engaged in the training of recruits). Basic training is no more
pleasurable in the IDF than in most armies, not only in terms of
physical discomfort, but primarily in the assigned identity as lowest
man on the totem pole and in the psychological adjustments demanded in establishing a new self.

But this part of the change, the submerging of the individual
self and the uniformization of identity, is strongly modified by the
social climate described previously. The strong linkages to the
civilian world mean that the soldier can maintain an anchorpoint
for his identity in the role relations and the social arrangements of
his past and future. The nature of the relations between commander and men implies that while the status of the soldier is a
clearly inferior one, he may still claim a respectable identity. And
finally, the almost institutionalized gaps in the scheduling of his
activities, frequent opportunities for exploiting some measure of
disorder, and the social rewards for resourcefulness—all these provide potentials for self-expression.

It may well be that the presence of women (in many, though not
all, army bases) also makes a contribution to the maintenance of
individuality. The encounter between 18 to 20-year-old men and
women is not devoid of erotic tension, even when they are in
uniform. And the competition for the favors of the opposite sex
calls for the pursuer to emphasize his or her individuality, the
valuable characteristics possessed uniquely by the individual which
make him or her a more desirable partner than others.

Within the general framework calling for the uniformization of
identity, there are, thus, strong forces promoting the maintenance
of a unique self-image; thus the "mortification of self" is very
much alleviated. But this does not at all imply that the self-images
of the draftees remain stable; on the contrary, as in all transitions
from one social context to another, the service is a fertile period
for changes in self-image.

A vivid example of changes in self-image can be seen in one of
the IDF's experiments in compensatory education. For many years

the IDF has maintained special courses for soldiers who have not completed eight years of primary school. This intensive course in elementary school subjects was offered to the soldier in his *last* three months of service, during which he was released from regular duty, but during 1963 and 1964 the course was advanced to the *first* three months of service on the assumption that a higher educational level would make any individual able to function better in the Army.

However the experiment was a failure. Not only did the participants not learn much, if anything, but severe disciplinary problems arose. Although the curriculum was identical to the one offered at the end of the service, and although the teachers had the same qualifications, a massive resistance to learning was encountered.

The difference in response between these soldiers and those who took the course at the end of their service was much larger than can possibly be explained by difference in age at the time of the course. What, then, was the cause of this extraordinary phenomenon? Let us look at the self-image changes that IDF soldiers undergo during their service. The soldier who is a candidate for this program enters the Army after a career as a failure: failure in school and failure to obtain rewarding work after dropping out. He has been thoroughly persuaded of his identity as a failure, both in general and in the educational framework in particular. No wonder, then, that he responds negatively when the Army puts him back into the kind of school situation where he knows that he cannot succeed.

At the end of the service the picture is quite different for most of these soldiers; they have for the first time in their lives experienced a measure of success in a socially prestigious activity. The very status of "soldier" is in many respects a satisfactory one; any traveller on Israeli highways can observe the greater ease with which soldiers can obtain a ride, as compared to civilian hitchhikers. But also within the Army the soldier from the disadvantaged background has considerable opportunities for success. Many obtain promotion, at least to PFC; and even those who are not promoted experience, during the later part of their service, the status accorded to the "senior," experienced soldier who knows the ropes. In the IDF old and new soldiers are typically mixed within small units, thus affording ample opportunity for the older ones to bask in the appreciation of the greenhorn.

Moreover, many of these soldiers pass through courses in elementary military skills—and do so successfully. I have the general impression that instruction in the IDF is more successful with the soldier-student from a disadvantaged background than in the civilian system; one reason may be the accountability of the military instructor, whose own career depends on the success of his students.

Thus, when looking at himself at the end of his service, the soldier sees a new image: he has "made it" for the first time in his life. And he has made it within a climate which reinforced initiative and resourcefulness, and where he experienced more closeness (in the sense of lower social distance) to superiors than in school or civilian employment. At the same time the linkage to civilian life makes it possible for him to generalize this new self to the anticipated future outside the military. Now he is ready for the challenge of schooling.

This change in self-image may in the long run be the most important meaning of military service for the disadvantaged soldier—and as far as nonmilitary implications are concerned, for Israeli society in general.

NOTES

1. Erving Goffman, "On the Characteristics of Total Institutions," in *Asylums*. Here cited from the British edition (Harmondsworth, Middlesex: Penguin Books, 1968).

2. Ibid., p. 18.

3. Ibid., pp. 18-19.

4. For an elaboration of this point, see Mordechai Bar-On, *Education in the Israel Defense Forces* (Tel Aviv: Israel Defense Forces, 1966), pp. 28-29.

5. Ibid., p. 17.

6. Facsimile of Tal's briefing is found in Mordechai Bar-On, ed. *Six Days: Israel Defense Forces* (Tel Aviv: Ministry of Defense, 1968), p. 38.

7. An interesting description of such resistance when the Armored Corps structured and formalized procedures, is found in Shabtai Tevet, *The Tanks of Tammuz* (London: Weidenfeld and Nicolson, 1969). It is intriguing that the initiator of this formalization and tightening was the same General Tal who is quoted above. He distinguished clearly between adaptation to the inevitable confusion of the battlefield, and the generation of such confusion in normal conditions.

8. Goffman, *Asylums*, p. 22.

9. Ibid., p. 28.

CONTRIBUTORS

Walter Ackerman
Vice President, University of Judaism, Los Angeles

Myron J. Aronoff
Assistant Professor of Political Science, Tel-Aviv University, Tel-Aviv

Shlomo Avineri
Professor of Political Science, Hebrew University, Jerusalem

Rustum Bastuni
Architect and town planner.

Yoram Ben-Porath
Professor of Economics, Hebrew University, Jerusalem

Bruno Bettelheim
Distinguished Service Professor and Professor of Psychology
and Psychiatry, University of Chicago, Chicago

Mordecai S. Chertoff
Executive Director, American Histadrut Cultural Exchange Institute,
New York

Michael Curtis
Professor of Political Science, Rutgers University, New Brunswick,
New Jersey

CONTRIBUTORS

Nancy Datan
Associate, Israel Institute of Applied Social Research

Milton Derber
Professor of Labor and Industrial Relations, University of Illinois, Urbana

Daniel J. Elazar
Professor of Political Science, Temple University, Philadelphia

Zvi Gitelman
Assistant Professor of Political Science, University of Michigan, Ann Arbor

Fred M. Gottheil
Professor of Economics, University of Illinois, Urbana

Celia S. Heller
Professor of Sociology, Hunter College and The Graduate Center of the City University of New York

Suzanne Keller
Professor of Sociology, Princeton University, Princeton, New Jersey

Ralph M. Kramer
Professor at the School of Social Welfare, University of California, Berkeley

Uri Leviatan
Associate, Center for Social Research at the Kibbutz, Givat Haviva, Israel

Seymour Martin Lipset
Professor of Government and Sociology, Harvard University, Cambridge, Massachusetts

Moshe Lissak
Professor of Sociology, Hebrew University, Jerusalem

J. Joseph Loewenberg
School of Business Administration, Temple University, Philadelphia

Judah Matras
Professor of Sociology, Hebrew University, Jerusalem

Howard Pack
Associate Professor of Economics, Swarthmore College, Pennsylvania

Raphael Patai
Professor of Social Sciences, Fairleigh Dickinson University, New Jersey

CONTRIBUTORS

Elad Pelled
Director General, Ministry of Education and Culture, Israel

Oded Remba
Professor of Economics, Staten Island Community College, City University of New York

Menahem Rosner
Director, Center for Social Research on the Kibbutz, Givat Haviva, Israel

E. O. Schild
Professor of Sociology, Hebrew University, Jerusalem

Henry Toledano
Assistant Professor of Hebrew and Arabic, City College of New York

INDEX

Acre Steel Works, 272
Academic Workers Union, 261
Achdut Haavoda, 32, 104, 276
Afro-Asian Institute, 274
Agricultural Center, the, of Histadrut, 294
See also, Histadrut
Agnon, 342
Agudat Yisrael, 76, 86
Aharoni, Hannah, 285
Akademaiim, 70-1
Akzin, Benjamin, 72
Aleichem, Sholem, 343
Alignment party, the, 351
Aliyah, Aliyot, 87, 315
See also, Ashkenazi; Sephardic; Oriental Jews
Aloni, Shulamit, 380
Alliance Israelite Universelle, 284
Allon, Yigal, 285, 292, 407
Altalena, 304
American Council for the Behavioral Sciences, the, 163
Amidar, 39, 49-55, 58, 61
Antonovsky, Aaron, 382

Arabs, 24, 176; education, 413-4; countries, 246; incomes of, 239; in Gaza, 358; in Israel, 87, 409, 417; local councils, 24; in Palestine, 358, 417; in Palestine and Israel, 237; region, the, 247; sector, the, 176; villages, 18, 415; West Bank, 358; workers, 79, 244, 357
Arab Department of the Prime Minister's Office, 239
Arab-Jewish Schools, 413
Aranne, Zalman, 401, 404
Arbeli-Almoslino, Shoshana, 328
Ascoli, Max, 15
Ashkenazi, Ashkenazim Jews, 21-2, 86, 201, 287, 294, 307, 334; attitude to Arabs, 418; cultural dominance of, 341-4, 346; historic centers, 308-9; incomes, 210; ideology, 359; in the Knesset, 351; in kibbutzim, 108; school system, 353
Avodah Kehilatit, 49

437

INDEX

Bagrut, 413
Balfour Declaration, the, 411
Baltic States, immigrants from the, 68-9, 75, 79, 90
Balvashvili, *see* Yedidiah, Yitzhak
Bank of Israel, the, 295
Bar Ilan University, 340
Bar-Lev, Chaim, 74
Becker, Aharon, 260, 265-6, 269
Bedouin, 24
Beigin, Menachem, 89, 284
Ben Aharon, Yitzhak, 212, 302
Ben-Gurion, 108, 285
Ben-Simchon, Shaul, 325
Ben Zvi, Itzhak, 285
Bessarabia-Bukovina, immigrants from, 69
Black Panthers, 184, 188, 199, 281-2, 292, 299, 302, 310, 313, 324-7, 329, 331, 334, 336-7, 341-3, 345, 358
British Mandate, 5, 16-18, 29, 238, 240, 283, 316-7, 395, 397, 412
Buber, Martin, 334
Butrashvili, Rabbi Yehuda, 86
Byelorussia, immigrants from, 68

Center for Social Research, 163
Central Bureau of Statistics, 79; census, 241
Chisholm, Shirley, 380
Cohen, Eric, 9, 12, 28, 33
Cohen, Yeruham, 285
Communist Party (MAKI), 73
Compulsory Education Act, the, 397, 400, 402
Council of the Sephardic Community, 324, 330

Dahant, Rabbi Chaim, 344-5
Damari, Saadia, 285
Damari, Shoshana, 285
Dayan, Moshe, 74, 89, 292, 422
deGaulle, Charles, 288
Developing countries, the, 161, 167, 176
Development towns, 7; Arad, 7, 80; Ashdod, 5, 7, 85, 276; Ashkelon, 5, 7, 85; Beer Sheba, 5, 7, 8, 13, 48, 80, 289, 290; Beit Sha'an, 7, 299; Carmiel, 7; Dimona, 7, 13, 80, 85, 299; Eilat, 7, 49; Hazor, 7; Kiryat Hayovel, 299; Kiryat Gat, 7-8, 13, 30, 80; Neve Sharett, 83; Kiryat Malahi, 7-8, 85; Kiryat Menachem, 299; Kiryat Shemona, 7, 48; Kiryat Yedidim, 122; Lachish area, 30; Maalot, 7; Migdal Haemek, 7-8; Mizpeh Ramon, 7, 31; Nazareth Elit, 31; Netivot, 7; Ofakim, 7; Or-Yehuda, 60; Sederot, 7; Shfar'am, 241; Yeruham, 7
diwan, 416
Druzes, 414-5; local councils, 24
Dziewonski, K., 241

Eban, Abba, 340
Economic and Social Research Institute, the, 200
Egged, 59
Eisenstadt, S. N., 317
Eliachar, Eli, 284, 324, 330
Eliav, Arie, 292-3

Fatah, 282
Fellaheen, 245